Contending Voices

Contending Voices

Biographical Explorations of the American Past

VOLUME II:
SINCE 1865

SECOND EDITION

John Hollitz

Community College of Southern Nevada

Houghton Mifflin   Boston   New York

Publisher: Charles Hartford
Sponsoring Editor: Sally Constable
Development Editor: Jeffrey Greene
Editorial Assistant: Uzma S. Burney
Senior Project Editor: Aileen Mason
Editorial Assistant: Katherine Leahey
Senior Art and Design Coordinator: Jill Haber Atkins
Composition Buyer: Chuck Dutton
Associate Strategic Buyer: Brian Pieragostini
Marketing Manager: Katherine Bates

Cover image: Margaret Chase Smith and Senator Joseph McCarthy at a Congressional Hearing, Margaret Chase Smith Library, Skohegan, Maine.

Photo Credits: p. 2 (left) Library of Congress, (right) © Bettmann/CORBIS; p. 23 (left) © Bettmann/CORBIS, (right) Collection of The New York Historical Society; p. 45 (left) Courtesy of Hargrett Rare Book and Manuscript Library, University of Georgia Libraries, (right) Henry W. Grady papers, Manuscript, Archives, and Rare Book Library, Emory University; p. 65 (left) The Schlesinger Library, Radcliffe Institute, Harvard University, (right) Courtesy MIT Museum; p. 87 (left) Rare Book and Manuscript Library, Columbia University, (right) Library of Congress; p. 98 Reprinted in James R. Mock and Cedric Larson, *Words That Won the War: The Story of the Committee on Public Information, 1917–1919* (Princeton, N.J.: Princeton University Press, 1939).

Photo credits continue on page 315.

Printed in the U.S.A.

Library of Congress Catalog Number: 2006922776

Instructor's exam copy
ISBN-13: 978-0-618-73178-7
ISBN-10: 0-618-73178-4

For orders, use student text ISBNs:
ISBN-13: 978-0-618-66088-9
ISBN-10: 0-618-66088-7

1 2 3 4 5 6 7 8 9-MP-10 09 08 07 06

Contents
VOLUME II

4

Sex, Anarchism, and Domestic Science in Progressive America:
Emma Goldman and Ellen Richards   **64**

5

Progressives at War:
Randolph Bourne and George Creel   **86**

6

Science, Religion, and "Culture Wars" in the 1920s:
William Jennings Bryan and Clarence Darrow   **106**

7

Politics and the Big Screen in the Great Depression:
Upton Sinclair and Louis B. Mayer **129**

8

Racism and Relocation During World War II:
Harry Ueno and Dillon Myer **148**

9

Confrontation and Compromise in the Cold War:
James Byrnes and Henry A. Wallace **167**

10

Politics and Principle in the Second Red Scare:
Joseph McCarthy and Margaret Chase Smith   188

11

From Black Protest to Black Power:
Roy Wilkins and Fannie Lou Hamer   **211**

12

The Battles of Vietnam:
Robert McNamara and Jan Barry   **231**

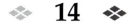 **13**

From Mystique to Militance:
Betty Friedan and Gloria Steinem **253**

14

Individualism and the Environment in the 1980s:
Edward Abbey and James Watt **273**

15

Conservatism and the Limits of Consumer Capitalism:
Irving Kristol and Ralph Nader **292**

Preface

The encouraging reception from students and instructors to the first edition of *Contending Voices: Biographical Explorations of the American Past* has led me to create a second edition. As before, this book uses paired biographies to bring alive the debates and disagreements that have shaped American history. It is based on the assumption that students find history more engaging when they realize that it is full of conflict. Through biography, individual men and women emerge from the tangle of events, dates, and facts that often make history so challenging for students.

Following the organization of most survey texts, each chapter examines two individuals who stood on different sides of an important issue. Their stories, combined with a small set of primary sources in each chapter, show students how individuals—from pre-English settlement of the New World to the presidential election of 2000—influenced their times and were influenced by them. At the same time, the book's biographical approach naturally incorporates political, social, economic, cultural, religious, and diplomatic histories while underscoring the diversity of those who shaped the past. This biographical approach highlights competing perspectives, prompting students to think about issues from multiple viewpoints. The biographical essays that introduce the sources were written with these pedagogical goals in mind.

Although students will encounter familiar names in these pages, many of the thirty individuals in each of *Contending Voices'* two volumes rarely appear in survey texts. All of them, however, addressed significant events and issues of their times. In Volume I, sixteenth-century *conquistador* Hernán Cortés and Dominican priest Bartolomé de Las Casas contest the fate of Native Americans. In the seventeenth century, the pitched battles between governor William Berkeley and rebel Nathaniel Bacon reveal forces shaping early Virginia. Other chapters illuminate the Great Awakening, the American Revolution, and the ratification of the Constitution. Later, the life-and-death conflict between William Henry Harrison and Tecumseh reflects the larger struggle between whites and Indians sparked by westward expansion in the early nineteenth century. In the same period, chapters pairing union organizer Sarah Bagley with industrialist Nathan Appleton and Governor Juan Bautista Alvarado of Mexican California with merchant Thomas Larkin focus on the rise of the factory system and Manifest Destiny. At mid-century, George Fitzhugh and Hinton Rowan Helper debate slavery's impact on the South and reveal deep fears at the heart of a growing sectional conflict. Still later, anti-war Democrat Clement Vallandigham and radical Republican Benjamin Wade demonstrate the limits of dissent during the Civil War, while black Congressman Robert Smalls and white Senator Carl Schurz underscore the limits of Reconstruction.

New biographies in Volume I include abolitionists William Lloyd Garrison and Frederick Douglass who highlight the disagreements among abolitionists over the best way to end slavery; Catharine Beecher and Elizabeth Cady Stanton who face off over the proper place of women in antebellum society; and David Atchison and Sara Robinson who battle over the fate of "bleeding Kansas."

Volume II offers a similar diversity of individuals and topics. The new biographies in Volume II feature William Jennings Bryan and Clarence Darrow who square off in the "culture wars" of the 1920s as they battle over teaching evolution in the public schools; Margaret Chase Smith's declaration of conscience in the face of Joseph McCarthy's anti-communism hysteria; and anti-Vietnam war activist Jan Barry taking on war architect Robert McNamara.

In the late nineteenth century, tycoon Jay Gould and union leader Terence Powderly engaged in a bloody conflict between capital and labor. In the early twentieth century, the radically different views of home economics pioneer Ellen Richards and anarchist Emma Goldman illuminate both progressive reform and the changing role of women in American society. Anti-war critic Randolph Bourne and war propagandist George Creel further illuminate aspects of progressive reform as well as the new power of advertising and the effects of World War I on American society. Japanese-American internee Harry Ueno and internment director Dillon Myer illustrate the experience of Japanese relocation during World War II. Later battles are brought to life in chapters pairing civil rights activist Fannie Lou Hamer with black leader Roy Wilkins; women's rights champion Betty Friedan with feminist Gloria Steinem; and Interior Secretary James Watt with novelist Edward Abbey. They illustrate the challenges confronting the civil rights, women's, and environmental movements and the conflicts dividing them. Finally, the "godfather of neoconservatism," Irving Kristol, and consumer activist Ralph Nader advance competing visions about the regulation of business—views that helped shape policy in the late twentieth century and continue to guide political discussion today.

While permitting easy access to often unfamiliar topics, *Contending Voices* is also designed to build students' critical thinking skills. Each chapter begins with a brief essay providing an introduction to the lives and ideas of the two individuals who held conflicting views on an important issue. The essay does not offer a complete accounting of subjects' lives—an impossible task—but focuses instead on aspects that illuminate the chapter's main topic. Each essay begins with a short vignette designed to capture the reader's attention and includes a running glossary, which defines terms that may be unfamiliar to many survey students. A set of four to seven primary sources illustrating and amplifying the chapter's central themes follows each essay. These sources demonstrate the variety of sources historians use to understand the past and reflect another premise behind this book—that the best way for students to learn history is to explore it themselves. Their explorations are assisted by a brief set of Questions to Consider following the primary sources. In addition, references to each primary source appear in the essays, helping to integrate the primary and secondary material. A brief introduction to each primary source also aids student analysis. Finally, a brief Further Reading section contains both biographical and general works that will help interested students explore each chapter topic further.

Many people made valuable contributions to these volumes. At the Community College of Southern Nevada (CCSN), Charles Okeke offered welcome encouragement, administrative assistants Venus Ramirez and Cindy Ray provided technical assistance, and Lisa Lipton read a portion of the manuscript. As usual, CCSN Interlibrary Loan librarian Marion Martin cheerfully and efficiently tracked down needed material. I am also grateful for a sabbatical leave granted by CCSN. It proved crucial to the timely completion of the manuscript. At the University of Nevada, Las Vegas Wiener-Rogers Law Library, librarians Tom Boone, Paula Doty, and Jennifer Gross went out of their way to locate material. At Houghton Mifflin, Jeffrey Greene oversaw the revision process. Jan Fitter brought a deft hand to the manuscript. Her numerous suggestions and insights improved these volumes in countless ways, and I am deeply indebted to her. Teresa Huang and Aileen Mason carefully guided the manuscript through the production phase, while Bruce Carson worked diligently to secure appropriate images. Jay Boggis copyedited the manuscript and Stella Gelboin proofread it. Both did so with keen eyes.

Numerous colleagues around the country reviewed these chapters and offered many useful ideas, suggestions, and criticisms. These volumes benefited greatly from their efforts. They included Ginette Aley, Indiana State University; Jacqueline A. Akins, Community College of Philadelphia; Michael A. Colomaio, Alfred State College; Christine K. Erickson, Indiana University—Purdue University, Fort Wayne; Robert C. Galgano, University of Richmond; Kenton Gatyas, Morton College; Kenneth Hermann, Kent State University; Michael P. Morris, Dalton State College; Zachary M. Schrag, George Mason University; and Elisabeth Evans Wray, University of Richmond.

As always, my biggest debt is to Patty. Once again, dedicating this book to her only begins to make things even.

—J.H.

CHAPTER 1

Race and Redemption in the Reconstructed South: Robert Smalls and Carl Schurz

In the predawn hours of May 13, 1862, the small Confederate ship *Planter* made its way out of Charleston Harbor. As it steamed toward the ships blockading the South Carolina port, Union lookouts strained their eyes, then prepared to sound the alarm to open fire on the small vessel. Suddenly, one lookout spotted a white flag flying on the boat, and the Union ships held their fire. As the *Planter* came alongside, Union naval officers were shocked. No whites were on board. Instead, they saw only black men, women, and children, who were dancing, singing, and shouting for joy. When a Union officer boarded, a well-dressed black man stepped forward to address him. "Good morning, sir! I've brought you some of the old United States guns, sir!" Indeed he had. An armed Confederate vessel, the *Planter* contained a cargo of unmounted cannon and sixteen slaves who had captured the boat and escaped to freedom. The man who had organized the capture was the ship's pilot, a twenty-three-year-old slave named Robert Smalls.

About three months later in Virginia, a thirty-three-year-old German immigrant named Carl Schurz met Confederate forces at the Second Battle of Bull Run. In the First Battle of Bull Run a year earlier, Union forces had been routed. The second battle ended the same way. Brigadier General Schurz, however, performed with distinction. After the battle, he was promoted to major general and given command of a division composed mostly of German Americans. The next year, Schurz and his troops made a gallant stand on Cemetery Ridge at the Battle of Gettysburg. Still later, he saw action against Confederate forces in Tennessee.

By the time the Civil War was over, Robert Smalls and Carl Schurz had served the Union well. That was not all they had in common, though. Both men were committed Republicans. Both would go into politics after the war and serve in Congress—Smalls as a representative from South Carolina and Schurz as a senator from Missouri. Both men also would support their party's efforts to reconstruct the South and guarantee political equality to the freedmen. But before the period known as Reconstruction was over, they had split over what to do with the South and the freedmen. One would hold fast to his hopes for the former slaves; the other would retreat from his commitment to them. Smalls

1

❖ *Robert Smalls*   ❖ *Carl Schurz*

and Schurz were only two of the millions of Americans who contributed in one way or another to the Union victory in the Civil War. Like so many of their countrymen, they did not necessarily agree about the meaning of that victory. For that reason, the stories of these two Union veterans may help us understand why Reconstruction turned out as it did.

"The Smartest *Cullud* Man"

Robert Smalls had something in common with Carl Schurz and with the leader of his own Republican Party, Abraham Lincoln. Like Lincoln, Smalls had arisen from utter obscurity. He was born in 1839 in Beaufort, South Carolina, to a slave woman who worked as a domestic servant. His father was an unknown white man, although many believed that he was John McKee, his mother's master. John McKee died when Robert was six, and his son Henry sent Smalls to live with relatives in Charleston when he was twelve. He lived in the home of his master's sister-in-law, working as a waiter, a lamplighter, and a stevedore. Smalls was "hired out," meaning that he worked for wages. He kept some of his pay for himself and sent the rest to his master. This situation gave the young slave relative autonomy. He may even have had enough freedom to pursue an education during his years in the city. Smalls apparently taught himself to read and possibly attended for a few months a school run by one of Charleston's many black societies. Formed in violation of the South Carolina law that prohibited more than four slaves from assembling at one time, such societies often provided education and other services to the African-American community.

In 1858, Smalls married Hannah Jones, a hotel maid who was also a slave. He was nineteen; she was thirty-one. Smalls said he married Hannah because he wanted "to have a wife to prevent me from running around—to have somebody to do for me and to keep me." Slaves, of course, were not allowed to marry legally, but Smalls made a deal with his master. He would pay McKee fifteen dollars a month so that he could marry Hannah. Smalls made a similar deal with Hannah's master, paying him five dollars a month. This allowed the two slaves to keep enough money to support themselves and even have children. Smalls later agreed to purchase his wife and daughter for eight hundred dollars. When he fled the city in 1862, he had seven hundred dollars, having never paid any of the agreed-upon amount to his wife's owner. How he accumulated this sum and managed to keep his household running is difficult to imagine. His own wages as a deck hand in 1861 amounted to only sixteen dollars a month, and Hannah probably made no more than ten dollars a month as a maid, assuming that she continued to work after their marriage.

Somehow the little family managed to make it, probably due to Smalls's abilities as a trader. His position as a deck hand on the *Planter* allowed him even greater autonomy than his job on the docks. Traveling on the river and coastal steamer, Smalls was able to make regular visits to friends and associates in a wider area. He traded goods within the slave community and probably with whites as well. As a sailor, Smalls acquired valuable skills. He learned to handle the ship and eventually became a wheelman. (Actually, he was a pilot, a title white Southerners refused to give blacks.) When the Civil War offered him the opportunity to escape bondage, his skills, education, and position served him well. Smalls carefully planned the escape of his family and friends. One night when the ship's three white officers were on shore, he pulled off his plan in dramatic fashion.

The theft of the *Planter* brought not only freedom but also an economic windfall. The northern press jumped on the story of Smalls's heroic action. *Harper's Weekly*, for instance, ran a picture of Smalls and an article on the "plucky Africans." One New York newspaper commented that few events during the Civil War "produced a heartier chuckle of satisfaction" than the theft of the *Planter*. The "fellow" behind the feat, it observed, "is no Small man." Given such favorable reaction, Smalls and his fellow hijackers were awarded a bounty by Congress for liberating the *Planter*. As leader of the party, Smalls got the largest share, fifteen hundred dollars. He continued to work as a pilot on the *Planter*, which was now operating as a troop transport for the Union. The ship shuttled men and supplies between the Sea Islands* off South Carolina and mainland areas occupied by Union forces. In addition, he piloted other ships, including some engaged in unsuccessful attacks on Charleston.

At the same time, Smalls worked to improve the condition of fellow blacks. In Union-occupied Beaufort, he engaged in fundraising to assist freedmen with education and employment. He also traveled to New York during the war to raise awareness of the condition of the growing ranks of free blacks in the

*Sea Islands: Low-lying islands off the coast of South Carolina and Georgia. Occupied early in the war by Union forces, the islands were home to a large number of blacks who worked on the rice plantations there.

South. He had been sent north by freedmen in Beaufort County who were eager to help themselves rather than wait for charity or government assistance. Such efforts were widespread throughout the postwar South, but African Americans in Beaufort County became organized—and politicized—several years before those in most other areas. A highly concentrated black population, early occupation by Union forces, and a large number of black soldiers and white teachers and missionaries contributed to their efforts. Already in 1864, blacks in the area had expressed their political preferences by organizing a delegation to the Republican convention in Baltimore. Although the delegates could not secure official representation at the convention, they made it clear that they were ready to "fight for the Union [and] die for it" and that they also wanted the right to "vote for it."

Unfortunately, that right was not immediately forthcoming, even when the Civil War ended. When Andrew Johnson became president after Lincoln's assassination in April 1865, he promoted a Reconstruction plan that excluded blacks from politics. Committed to white rule in the South, Johnson wanted a policy that would bring the rebellious states back into the Union without a fundamental restructuring of southern society. Under his Reconstruction plan, white Southerners—often former Confederates—quickly reorganized state governments. By early 1866, southern state legislatures elected under the president's plan had passed Black Codes. These laws severely limited the rights of African Americans to own property, assemble, move about freely, and vote. Often they prevented interracial marriage and upheld labor contracts that favored white landowners. The Black Codes in South Carolina legalized harsh labor practices regarding blacks and placed severe restrictions on freedmen. At a convention in late 1865, South Carolina blacks protested the new laws. In an address to the state's whites, the convention demanded that blacks "be governed by the same laws that control other men." **[See Source 1.]**

For several years after the war, Smalls was more concerned with improving his own position than with getting involved in politics. Even before the war ended, he returned to Beaufort and opened a store. He did well enough to purchase his former master's house by paying the back taxes on it. In 1867, he purchased an eight-room building at a government tax sale and deeded it "to the Colored children" of Beaufort as a school. These actions are a measure of his status in the community. One observer, capturing the dialect of Sea Island blacks, noted that Smalls was "regarded by all the other negroes as immensely rich, and decidedly 'the smartest *cullud* man in Souf Car'lina.'" Widely known, well-off, obviously intelligent, and self-possessed, Smalls was a natural leader in his community. His emergence as a prominent black politician during Reconstruction was almost inevitable.

"Their Minds Were Fully Made Up"

When Carl Schurz was born in Prussia (now Germany) in 1829, few would have predicted that he would have an impact on a former slave like Robert Smalls. Certainly, his early circumstances were far removed from Smalls's oppressive world. Schurz's father was a teacher and businessman with minor connections to the local nobility. Carl was educated at schools in the nearby city of Cologne, then went on to the University of Bonn. He entered the university in the fall of

1847, just in time to become embroiled in the Revolutions of 1848, uprisings against the monarchies and oppressive regimes that controlled much of Europe. Some of the rebels hoped to create nations based on republican principles and free-market economies; others advocated socialism. Along with other revolutionaries, Schurz wrote articles, organized workers, and made rousing speeches in support of revolution. After a failed attempt to capture an arsenal, he barely escaped arrest. Forced to hide in attics and crawl through sewers, he fled to France. Later, he returned to Germany, bribed a prison guard, and assisted one of his jailed professors in a dramatic escape. By the time he made his way to England, he was a famous man. For the next few years, he made his living as a journalist and teacher in England and France. In 1852, he married the daughter of a wealthy Hamburg cane merchant and moved to the United States, where he hoped to write a history of his adopted country that would appeal to both Americans and Europeans.

Schurz and his wife settled in Philadelphia, where he wrote and lectured. His wife's inheritance also gave him the freedom to travel. As he journeyed across the northern United States, he had an opportunity to learn about his new country. He also found a more suitable home in the upper Midwest, where many other Germans had migrated in the early nineteenth century. In 1856, Schurz and a growing family moved to Watertown, Wisconsin, where he went into real estate, dabbled in other businesses, bought a farm, and continued to write. His real calling, however, was politics. Before long, he joined the Republican Party, largely because of his opposition to the expansion of slavery. As a young revolutionary fighting European despotism, Schurz was a fervent opponent of an institution that violated the principles of political equality. Although many Republicans were staunchly anti-immigrant, Schurz believed that the new party offered possibilities for the German immigrant community to gain political power. Energetic, charismatic, famous, and bilingual, Schurz was the perfect leader to build Republican strength in an important ethnic community. He could use his background to counter the appeal the Democrats had for many German Americans and then forge them into a powerful Republican bloc.

In the following years, Schurz worked tirelessly for the Republican Party. He attempted unsuccessfully to become Wisconsin's lieutenant governor and even its governor. In 1860, he led the Wisconsin delegation at the Republican National Convention and quickly threw his support to Abraham Lincoln. After Lincoln won the Republican nomination, the party elected Schurz to the Republican National Committee in hopes that he would be able to secure the German-American vote. Schurz helped deliver enough German-American votes to be awarded a post as minister to Spain in 1861. Watching the war from Europe, he decided that emancipating the slaves might be the only way to keep the European powers out of the war. Thus he lent his voice to the cause of the Radical Republicans,* who urged Lincoln to free the slaves and transform the conflict from a war for the Union into one for freedom.

Radical Republicans: Those Republicans who wanted the abolition of slavery, an extension of citizenship to former slaves, and punishment of Confederate leaders. After the war, the Radicals believed that Reconstruction could not be achieved without a restructuring of southern society.

It was a natural position for Schurz. As a revolutionary, he had fought tyranny and oppression in Europe. He had joined the Republican Party because of the Democrats' support of slavery. Now his belief in liberty and equality led him to give up his diplomatic post and return to the United States to fight. He was commissioned as a brigadier general just in time to see action at the Second Battle of Bull Run in August 1862. Rewarded for his performance with a command over a largely German-American division, Schurz saw action in many major campaigns, including Chancellorsville, Gettysburg, and Chattanooga. He frequently squabbled with his commanders, though, and was later removed from action at the front. In fact, Schurz was constantly politicking. In the fall of 1864, he campaigned for Lincoln's reelection, and at the end of the war, he looked forward to helping Lincoln carry out his Reconstruction policy. After Lincoln's assassination, Schurz hoped for a close relationship with Andrew Johnson. When the new president's Reconstruction plan resulted in new southern state governments committed to white supremacy, Schurz joined with other Republicans intent on bringing about radical changes in southern society and politics. Led by politicians such as Benjamin Wade of Ohio (see Chapter 14) and Thaddeus Stevens of Pennsylvania, the Radical Republicans called for legislation that would enfranchise the freedmen, distribute to them land confiscated from former Confederates, and establish legal and social equality for blacks.

Schurz played a critical role in helping the Radicals seize control of Reconstruction policy. As white southerners began to organize new governments by the summer of 1865, Schurz took an inspection tour of the South. He reported that Johnson's policies allowed former Confederates to keep their hold on power and that the new governments were passing Black Codes severely limiting the freedom of blacks. Although the Thirteenth Amendment had abolished slavery in 1865, a new labor system had arisen that made African Americans slaves in all but name. Moreover, white supremacists were using violence to keep down those who opposed the new governments. Schurz's report presented ample evidence of the attitudes of many white southerners toward blacks. The slightest resistance on the part of freedmen to white control was merely proof in whites' minds that blacks were unfit for freedom. One Georgia planter came to that conclusion because "one of his negroes had . . . impudently refused to submit to a whipping." Schurz came away from his contact with white southerners convinced that in most cases "their minds were fully made up" about the failure of the South's new free labor system. **[See Source 2.]**

"This . . . Untutored Multitude"

Published later in 1865, Schurz's report fed the growing alarm of many northerners about the new southern state governments. It also helped rally the Radical Republicans to action. In 1866, the Fourteenth Amendment was passed in Congress and submitted to the states for ratification. The amendment extended citizenship to African Americans, barred former Confederates from holding office, and penalized states that did not allow blacks to vote by reducing their representation in Congress. All but one of the former Confederate states rejected the amendment (although it was ratified in 1868). The governor of South Carolina expressed the sentiment of many southern whites when he declared that blacks were "steeped in ignorance, crime, and vice" and should not be allowed to vote. This resistance to the wishes of Congress further angered many northerners, who now believed that Johnson and the southern politicians were overturning the Union's victory in the war. In late 1866, therefore, Republicans made big gains in the congressional elections, and the Radicals in Congress seized the initiative. Early the next year, they passed the first of the Reconstruction Acts,* which overturned the governments established under Johnson's plan and imposed military rule on most of the former Confederate states. Under the watchful eye of the military, the freedmen would be registered to vote, new state constitutions drafted, and new elections held. Across the South, Republicans were swept into power.

In South Carolina, the overturning of the Johnson government finally gave the freedmen a chance to exercise the citizenship rights they had long desired. After helping to form the Beaufort Republican Club, Robert Smalls received its nomination as a delegate to the state's constitutional convention. Meeting early in 1868, the convention brought together 124 delegates, 78 of whom were black. Although one South Carolina newspaper charged that the black delegates were "misguided as to their true welfare," South Carolina's new constitution was revolutionary for the South and reflected the concerns of the state's black majority. It called, for instance, for state assistance to help people in "their homeless and landless condition." It declared that "no person shall be deprived of the right of suffrage for non-payment of the poll tax."* It abolished segregation. The delegates also recognized that the maintenance of a government "faithful to the interests and liberties of the people" depended "in great measure on the intelligence of the people themselves." Thus, following a resolution offered by Smalls, the constitution provided for free elementary schooling for all children.

Submitted to South Carolina's now largely black electorate, the new constitution was overwhelmingly approved. Shortly after that, new elections brought Republicans to power. Smalls won a seat in the lower house of the legislature— the only one in the reconstructed South made up of a majority of black legislators. In fact, the majority of the state's legislators were ex-slaves. Smalls and the other freedmen often deferred to whites and the better-educated freeborn blacks, but Smalls continued to fight for issues that affected his black constituents. He served on a commission "to establish and maintain a system of free common schools" and sponsored a bill to enforce the Civil Rights Act of 1866, which granted the same civil rights to all persons born in the United States. He also served on a panel that investigated the intimidation, even murder, of Republican voters in the state during the 1868 election.

Smalls devoted much of his energy in the legislature to mundane issues that benefited his constituents in Beaufort County. He championed the construction of roads, railroads, government buildings, and docks in his district. He

---

Reconstruction Acts: Passed in 1867 and 1868, the Reconstruction Acts divided the former Confederate states into five military districts, subjected them to martial law, and gave military commanders the power to register voters and oversee elections.

Poll tax: A tax established in many southern states as a requirement for voting in order to discourage blacks from casting ballots.

mobilized voters with brass bands and torchlight parades, and he knew how to arouse them with passionate rhetoric. He called on black voters to "bury the democratic party so deep that there will not be seen even a bubble coming from the spot where the burial took place," and he vowed to "pour hot shot into the ranks of traitors." At the same time, his financial support of the widow and family of his former master built up the goodwill of many whites in the county. All these efforts paid off, as Smalls built a political machine* based largely on the loyalty of his constituents. As one observer put it, "The men, women and children seem to regard him with a feeling akin to worship." Although Smalls was not highly educated, another noted, he was "a thoroughly representative man among the people" and had "their unlimited confidence." That confidence was evident in 1870, when he handily won election to the upper house of the state legislature. Smalls sat in the state senate for four years and then in 1874 won election to the U.S. House of Representatives. Mobilizing his Beaufort County machine, he swamped his opponent by a margin of more than four to one.

Taking his seat in Congress in 1875, Smalls continued to mind the needs of his South Carolina constituents—white and black. In 1876, for example, Smalls fought a minor battle over federal control of the Citadel, the military school in Charleston that had been seized by the national government during the war. The takeover of the school had upset many white South Carolinians, and Smalls demanded that the secretary of war at least pay rent to the city of Charleston for use of the grounds. As in the state legislature, however, much of his energy was devoted to the passage of bills concerning such mundane matters as appropriating funds for the maintenance of harbors. Although such work was not glamorous, Smalls recognized its importance for his district's well-being. At the same time, he had not lost his commitment to Reconstruction. In 1876, he fought against a bill calling for the reduction of the army in South Carolina. Such a move, he knew, would make it easier for white vigilante groups to terrorize black voters in an effort to overthrow Republican control of the state. In one particularly gruesome incident that summer in Hamburg (now North Augusta), South Carolina, a mob of about a thousand armed whites surrounded a black militia unit and murdered a number of the militiamen after they surrendered. As one newspaper put it, they "were shot down like rabbits." Shortly after, Smalls unsuccessfully attempted to amend the force-reduction bill, arguing that no military forces should be withdrawn from South Carolina "so long as the militia of that State . . . are assaulted, disarmed, and taken prisoners, and then massacred in cold blood by lawless bands of men." **[See Source 3.]**

Eight years after formally entering politics, Smalls was at the height of his power. Yet the Hamburg incident and others like it did not bode well for Smalls or Reconstruction. The bastion of anti-Reconstruction whites, the Democratic Party, had made a remarkable comeback by 1876. In fact, when Smalls first took his seat in Congress that year, the Democrats had a majority in the House of Representatives for the first time in eighteen years. About two-thirds of the Democrats in the House were southerners, and eighty of them were veterans

---

Political machine: A type of political organization that often dominated city and state politics in the late nineteenth century. The bosses who ran these machines often built up support by dispensing favors to constituents.

of the Confederate military. Calling themselves Redeemers,* these southern Democrats launched a violent assault against Republican rule. As white terrorist organizations such as the Ku Klux Klan and the Red Shirts used violence and even murder to intimidate Republican voters, the Democrats began to regain political control in one state after another.

South Carolina was a particularly fertile field for the growth of vigilante groups. By 1876, whites in South Carolina had organized about three hundred rifle clubs, with twenty-four in mostly black Beaufort County alone. Often organized by former Confederate officers, these clubs were nothing more than armed bands of nightriders. At the same time, South Carolina Democrats launched a vocal propaganda campaign against the alleged corruption and mismanagement of the Republican-controlled state government. As with the Reconstruction governments in other states, South Carolina's legislature had made large expenditures to help rebuild the war-torn South. Increased spending on a shrunken, war-ravaged tax base made these Republican regimes inviting targets. So did the presence in them of northerners, who were derisively called carpetbaggers.* The Redeemers railed against the wasteful excesses of "carpetbag" governments that had spent once responsible states to the brink of bankruptcy. Most of all, though, the Redeemers played on the deeply held racism of the white southerners. "Ignorant" blacks, they charged, had been taken advantage of by grasping "Yankees," and the result was a disgraceful riot of incompetence and theft. With its black-majority legislature, South Carolina was especially vulnerable to this charge. *New York Tribune* reporter James Pike wrote an influential book titled *The Prostrate State: South Carolina Under Negro Government,* in which he referred to the actions of the legislature as a "shocking burlesque upon legislative proceedings" and to the black legislators themselves as an "uncouth and untutored multitude." **[See Source 4.]**

The next year, the Democrats were victorious in the three southern states not already "redeemed," including South Carolina. The deadlocked presidential election in late 1876 gave the Redeemers their opening. The Democratic candidate, Samuel J. Tilden, won the popular vote, but twenty electoral votes in the Deep South were in dispute. When a special commission appointed by Congress met to resolve the issue, it awarded all twenty electoral votes—and the presidency—to the Republican candidate, Rutherford B. Hayes. The Democrats lost the presidency by one electoral vote, but they had gained something, too. Although the Republicans retained control of the presidency, the Democrats got federal troops withdrawn from the remaining Republican states in the South. Without the protection provided by these forces, the Republican governments

---

Redeemers: Conservative white Democrats who vowed to save, or redeem, the South from Republican rule.

Carpetbaggers: The label applied by white southerners to northerners in the South during Reconstruction. The term was used to suggest that these "Yankees" carried their worldly goods in their carpetbags (suitcases) and therefore had no roots in the community. Because some of the northerners were involved in Reconstruction politics, the label also implied that they were corrupt—that is, out to enrich themselves at the public's expense.

were doomed. With the so-called Compromise of 1877,* conservative Democratic rule was restored across the South. Reconstruction was over.

Smalls was one of the Redeemers' victims. After the Democrats won control of the South Carolina government in 1877, they set out to prove the corruption of the prior Republican regimes. In his second term in Congress, Smalls was a prime target of their investigations. While serving in the state senate, he had chaired the Printing Committee, which oversaw the government's printing contracts. Now the Democrats accused him of accepting a bribe in connection with those contracts. Smalls said that he was innocent, but he was convicted by a jury and sentenced to three years in prison "with hard labor." He appealed the verdict before the state supreme court and lost, but the Democratic governor pardoned him when the Republicans promised to drop their investigation into Democratic election fraud. In reality, Smalls probably had overstepped the bounds of legality, but the evidence was scanty, others also were involved, and his crime paled in comparison to those committed by other politicians of the day. It was obvious that Smalls had been a political target and that the Democrats wanted control of his congressional district.

The Democrats had not seen the last of Smalls, however. In 1878, he ran for reelection to Congress. As they had done throughout the South, the Democrats influenced the election by frightening voters away from the polls. Smalls lost, but he was undeterred. Two years later, he ran for Congress again. Despite all their advantages, the Democrats realized that it would be a close race. To counter Smalls's popularity among black voters, the Democrats stuffed the ballot boxes. The fraud was so obvious that Smalls was awarded the victory when he challenged the results. By the time he took his seat, however, his term was almost over. To ensure their victory when Smalls ran again in 1882, the Democrats in control of the state legislature redrew the boundaries of his congressional district so that he was unable even to win the Republican primary. Denied the nomination, he would regain his seat in 1884 when the Republican winner died in office and a party convention selected him to finish out the term. Later that year, he was reelected. The Democrats were still determined to have his seat, however, and in 1886 they once again resorted to violence, tossing out Republican ballots and forcing black voters away from the polls to defeat Smalls for good.

"Ignorance and Inexperience"

In the 1870s, Carl Schurz was far removed from the maneuvering in South Carolina that ultimately cost Smalls his office. In a way, though, Schurz also had something to do with Smalls's demise. After all, the fate of the Reconstruction governments was not determined solely by events in the South. The shifting attitudes of many prominent northern Republicans also played a big part, and few of them underwent a more dramatic change of heart regarding Reconstruction than the former German revolutionary.

Compromise of 1877: The political deal struck between Republicans and Democrats to break the deadlocked presidential election of 1876. It allowed federal troops to be removed from the South in exchange for the election of the Republican presidential candidate.

In 1869, Schurz had ridden the Radical Republican cause right to the U.S. Senate. After the war, he had moved to St. Louis and helped rally the city's large German-American community for the Republicans in the 1868 presidential election. The next year, he was rewarded by the Missouri legislature with election to the Senate. With the election of Ulysses S. Grant as president in 1868, the Republicans now controlled the presidency, the Congress, and the reconstructed states of the South. From his new position, Schurz fully intended to support stern measures for former Confederates, as well as the Republican governments already established under congressional Reconstruction. Political practices in his own party began to disturb him, though. Schurz was disgusted by the use of patronage—the dispensing of government jobs as political rewards. The Civil War had greatly expanded the federal bureaucracy, and as it continued to grow after the war, both Republicans and Democrats used the spoils of office to their advantage. One of the powers of a political machine, such as the one Robert Smalls had built in South Carolina, was to give government jobs to supporters. A Republican machine in Missouri had secured Schurz's own election to the Senate. Increasingly, though, he was appalled by corruption in the Grant administration, and by the early 1870s he was leading the calls for civil service reform.*

Schurz's concerns about honesty in government made him especially vulnerable to the Redeemers' arguments about the Republican regimes in the South. In truth, these governments were no more corrupt than those that had preceded them or those that followed. Nonetheless, Schurz and many other northerners swallowed the argument that ignorant blacks in league with wily carpetbaggers were responsible for shocking corruption. His first public disagreements with the Radical Republicans arose over the readmission of Georgia to the Union in 1870. After the state was readmitted, Democrats in Georgia passed laws excluding blacks from the government. Republicans in Congress responded by insisting that Georgia ratify the Fifteenth Amendment,* which guaranteed freedmen the right to vote. Convinced that the South had been punished long enough, Schurz warned against continued federal interference in the states. Soon Schurz opposed every Radical bill, even the Ku Klux Klan Acts,* which were designed to curb the power of that terrorist, antiblack organization.

Schurz's new stance shocked many of his Republican friends: The Radical was now on the side of the Redeemers! Yet Schurz's shift was not as dramatic as it seemed. His radicalism was rooted in the idea of the political equality of free citizens. When placed against Old World monarchies and aristocracies, that

---

Civil service reform: Changes that would result in the awarding of government jobs on the basis of merit rather than as political rewards, as under the so-called spoils system.

Fifteenth Amendment: Ratified in 1870, this constitutional amendment prohibited states from denying the right to vote on the basis of "race, color, or previous condition of servitude." Thus, unlike the Fourteenth Amendment, it did not give states the option of denying voting rights to blacks.

Ku Klux Klan Acts: Passed in Congress in 1870 and 1871, these acts resulted from overwhelming evidence of widespread white terrorism against blacks. They gave the president new powers to put down such violence, including the detention of whites.

belief seemed revolutionary indeed. Yet in the post–Civil War period, the emphasis on political equality also could lead to support for Reconstruction policies that stopped well short of a revolution in southern society. In fact, like most Republicans, Schurz believed that securing political equality for freedmen was the central goal of Reconstruction. Like most Americans, however, he associated political freedom with free enterprise and the protection of private property. Thus sweeping government action such as property redistribution to address the dire economic condition of the freedmen violated the economic rights of free citizens. With emancipation and ratification of the Fourteenth Amendment, blacks now stood with whites as free citizens. Just like whites, they were able to advance themselves in a free-market economy as far as their talents and abilities would take them. Unfortunately, it would not take much evidence to convince many northern whites that the condition of blacks reflected their abilities. And, in their minds, those alleged abilities seemed to justify the Redeemers' position. Thus it was relatively easy for Schurz to come to the conclusion that Republican Reconstruction had allowed "ignorance and inexperience" to have too much influence on "public affairs." **[See Source 5.]**

Schurz would pay a price for his pro-Redeemer views. In fact, his support of the restoration of former Confederates' voting rights helped Democrats regain control of Missouri's legislature, which then denied him reelection to the Senate in 1875. Yet he would not be denied political office. The next year, Schurz rallied the German-American vote for the Republican presidential candidate, Rutherford B. Hayes. Ironically, the proponent of civil service reform would enjoy the spoils of victory when Hayes appointed him secretary of the interior. By then, of course, Reconstruction was over, and Schurz, like other Americans, turned his attention to other matters. One of them was the "Indian problem" in the American West. Schurz's view of Native Americans was similar to his view of freedmen. Like many other white Americans, he saw them as another "ignorant and inexperienced" people. That widespread view was reflected in a federal policy that forced Indians onto reservations in the late nineteenth century—a policy that Schurz helped enforce.

At the same time, the Democratic Redeemers began to strip the freedmen of their political rights and erect a rigid system of legal racial segregation. Left impoverished, most African Americans were tied to small plots of land belonging to others. By the end of the nineteenth century, their dire circumstances once again caught the attention of Schurz, who had become close friends with Booker T. Washington, the foremost black leader at the turn of the century. Washington had helped found the Tuskegee Institute in Alabama, a vocational school for blacks. Throughout his career, Washington preached a self-help gospel that naturally appealed to Schurz. Blacks, Schurz continued to believe until his death in 1906, simply had to pull themselves up by their bootstraps to achieve equality. Perhaps Robert Smalls could have convinced Schurz otherwise. Appointed a collector of customs for the port of Beaufort when the Republicans won the presidency in 1888, he served in that position on and off until 1913, one of the few black officeholders in the South. Until the day he died in 1915, however, he was convinced that Reconstruction had been a failure.

PRIMARY SOURCES

SOURCE 1:   Zion Presbyterian Church, *"Memorial to the Senate and House of Representatives"* (1865)

The freed people of the South were at the heart of Reconstruction. In this document, African Americans from Zion Presbyterian Church in Charleston, South Carolina, present a list of demands to the U.S. Congress. What do these demands reveal about the people's desires?

Gentlemen:

We, the colored people of the State of South Carolina, in Convention assembled, respectfully present for your attention some prominent facts in relation to our present condition, and make a modest yet earnest appeal to your considerate judgment.

We, your memorialists, with profound gratitude to almighty God, recognize the great boon of freedom conferred upon us by the instrumentality of our late President, Abraham Lincoln, and the armies of the United States.

"The Fixed decree, which not all Heaven can move,
    Thou, Fate, fulfill it; and, ye Powers, approve."

We also recognize with liveliest gratitude the vast services of the Freedmen's Bureau together with the efforts of the good and wise throughout the land to raise up an oppressed and deeply injured people in the scale of civilized being, during the throbbings of a mighty revolution which must affect the future destiny of the world.

Conscious of the difficulties that surround our position, we would ask for no rights or privileges but such as rest upon the strong basis of justice and expediency, in view of the best interests of our entire country.

We ask first, that the strong arm of law and order be placed alike over the entire people of this State; that life and property be secured, and the laborer free to sell his labor as the merchant his goods.

We ask that a fair and impartial instruction be given to the pledges of the government to us concerning the land question.

We ask that the three great agents of civilized society—the school, the pulpit, the press—be as secure in South Carolina as in Massachusetts or Vermont.

We ask that equal suffrage be conferred upon us, in common with the white men of this State.

This we ask, because "all free governments derive their just powers from the consent of the governed"; and we are largely in the majority in this State,

SOURCE: Reprinted in James S. Allen, *Reconstruction: The Battle for Democracy, 1865–1876* (New York: International Publishers, 1937), appendix, pp. 228–229; originally from South Carolina African Americans' Petition, November 24, 1865.

bearing for a long period the burden of onerous taxation, without a just representation. We ask for equal suffrage as a protection for the hostility evoked by our known faithfulness to our country and flag under all circumstances.

We ask that colored men shall not in every instance be tried by white men; and that neither by custom nor enactment shall we be excluded from the jury box.

We ask that, inasmuch as the Constitution of the United States explicitly declares that the right to keep and bear arms shall not be infringed and the Constitution is the Supreme law of the land—that the late efforts of the Legislature of this State to pass an act to deprive us of arms be forbidden, as a plain violation of the Constitution, and unjust to many of us in the highest degree, who have been soldiers, and purchased our muskets from the United States Government when mustered out of service.

We protest against any code of black laws the Legislature of this State may enact, and pray to be governed by the same laws that control other men. The right to assemble in peaceful convention, to discuss the political questions of the day; the right to enter upon all the avenues of agriculture, commerce, trade; to amass wealth by thrift and industry; the right to develop our whole being by all the appliances that belong to civilized society, cannot be questioned by any class of intelligent legislators.

We solemnly affirm and desire to live orderly and peacefully with all the people of this State; and commending this memorial to your considerate judgment.

Thus we ever pray.

Charleston, S.C. November 24, 1865
Zion Presbyterian Church.

Source 2:   Carl Schurz, *Report on the Condition of the South*   (1865)

In 1865, Carl Schurz toured the South to investigate the conditions there. His report to Congress was published and became a powerful tool for the Radical Republicans. In this excerpt, Schurz describes the opinions of whites in the South regarding African Americans. What does this report reveal about the attitudes of conquered white southerners?

That the result of the free labor experiment made under circumstances so extremely unfavorable should at once be a perfect success, no reasonable person would expect. Nevertheless, a large majority of the southern men with whom I came into contact announced their opinions with so positive an assurance as to produce the impression that their minds were fully made up. In at least nineteen cases of twenty the reply I received to my inquiry about their views on the new system was uniformly this: "You cannot make the negro work without

Source: Carl Schurz, *Report on the Condition of the South* (1865; reprint, New York: Arno Press, 1969), pp. 16–17.

physical compulsion." I heard this hundreds of times, heard it wherever I went, heard it in nearly the same words from so many different persons, that at last I came to the conclusion that this is the prevailing sentiment among the southern people. There are exceptions to this rule, but, as far as my information extends, far from enough to affect the rule. In the accompanying documents you will find an abundance of proof in support of this statement. There is hardly a paper relative to the negro question annexed to this report which does not, in some direct or indirect way, corroborate it. Unfortunately the disorders necessarily growing out of the transition state continually furnished food for argument. I found but few people who were willing to make due allowance for the adverse influence of exceptional circumstances. By a large majority of those I came in contact with, and they mostly belonged, to the more intelligent class, every irregularity that occurred was directly charged against the system of free labor. If negroes walked away from the plantations, it was conclusive proof of the incorrigible instability of the negro, and the impracticability of free negro labor. If some individual negroes violated the terms of their contract, it proved unanswerably that no negro had, or ever would have, a just conception of the binding force of a contract, and that this system of free negro labor was bound to be a failure. If some negroes shirked, or did not perform their task with sufficient alacrity, it was produced as irrefutable evidence to show that physical compulsion was actually indispensable to make the negro work. If negroes, idlers or refugees crawling about the towns, applied to the authorities for subsistence, it was quoted as incontestably establishing the point that the negro was too improvident to take care of himself, and must necessarily be consigned to the care of a master. I heard a Georgia planter argue most seriously that one of his negroes had shown himself certainly unfit for freedom because he impudently refused to submit to a whipping. I frequently went into an argument with those putting forth such general assertions, quoting instances in which negro laborers were working faithfully, and to the entire satisfaction of their employers, as the employers themselves had informed me. In a majority of cases the reply was that we northern people did not understand the negro, but that they (the southerners) did; that as to the particular instances I quoted I was probably mistaken; that I had not closely investigated the cases, or had been deceived by my informants; that they *knew* the negro would not work without compulsion, and that nobody could make them believe he would. Arguments like these naturally finished such discussions. It frequently struck me that persons who conversed about every other subject calmly and sensibly would lose their temper as soon as the negro question was touched.

Source 3: *Representative Robert Smalls Protests the Withdrawal of Federal Troops*   (1876)

In the face of rising vigilante action against blacks in South Carolina, Robert Smalls introduced an amendment to a bill in Congress that would have reduced federal military forces in the state. What does Smalls's testimony reveal about the threat to Republican rule in the state?

I offer the amendment which I send to the desk. The clerk read as follows:

Add to the first section the following:

Provided, That no troops for the purposes named in this section shall be drawn from the State of South Carolina so long as the militia of that State peaceably assembled are assaulted, disarmed, and taken prisoners, and then massacred in cold blood by lawless bands of men invading that State from the State of Georgia.

I hope the House will adopt that proviso as an amendment to the bill. As I have only five minutes I send to the desk a letter published in one of the newspapers here from an eye-witness of the massacre at Hamburgh [*sic*], and I ask the Clerk to read it.

The Clerk read as follows:

The origin of the difficulty, as I learn from the best and most reliable authority, is as follows: On the Fourth of July the colored people of the town were engaged in celebrating the day, and part of the celebration consisted in the parade of the colored militia company. After marching through the principal streets of the town, the company came to a halt across one of the roads leading out of the town. While resting there two white men drove up in a buggy, and with curses ordered the company to break ranks and let them pass through. The captain of the company replied that there was plenty of room on either side of the company, and they could pass that way. The white men continued cursing and refused to turn out. So the captain of the militia, to avoid difficulty, ordered his men to break ranks and permit the buggy to pass through. . . .

Late in the afternoon General M. C. Butler, one of the most malignant of the unreconstructed rebels, rode into the town, accompanied by a score of well-armed white men, and stated to the leading colored men that he came for the purpose of prosecuting the case on the part of the two white men, and he demanded that the militia company should give up their arms and also surrender their officers. This demand the militia was ready to comply with for the purpose of avoiding a difficulty if General Butler would guarantee them entire safety from molestation by the crowd of white desperadoes. This Butler refused to do, and persisted in his demand for the surrender of the guns and officers, and threatened that if the surrender was not immediately made he would take the guns and officers by force of arms. This threat aroused the militia company to a realizing sense of their impending danger, and they at once repaired to a large brick building, some two hundred yards from the river, used by them as an

Source: *Congressional Record*, 44th Cong., 1st sess., 1876, 5, pt. 5: 4641–42.

armory, and there took refuge. They numbered in all about forty men and had a very small quantity of ammunition. During this time, while the militia were taking refuge in their armory the white desperadoes were coming into the town in large numbers, not only from the adjacent county of Edgefield, but also from the city of Augusta, Georgia, until they numbered over fifteen hundred well-armed and ruffianly men, who were under the immediate command and direction of the ex-rebel chief, M. C. Butler. After the entire force had arrived, the building where the militia had taken refuge was entirely surrounded and a brisk fire opened upon it. This fire was kept up for some two hours, when, finding that the militia could not be dislodged by small arms, a messenger was sent to Augusta for artillery. During all this time not a shot had been fired by the militiamen. The artillery arrived and was posted on the bank of the river and opened fire on the building with grape and canister.

[An attempt to interrupt reading fails.]

The militia now realized that it was necessary to evacuate the armory at once. They proceeded to do so, getting out of a back window into a cornfield. They were soon discovered by the ruffians, and a rush was made for them. Fortunately, by hiding and hard fighting, a portion of the command escaped, but twenty-one were captured by the bushwhackers and taken immediately to a place near the railroad station.

Here a quasi-drumhead court-martial* was organized by the blood-hunters, and the last scene of the horrible drama began. It must now be remembered that not one of the twenty-one colored men had a pistol or gun about them. The moment they were captured their arms were taken from them, and they were absolutely defenseless. The orderly sergeant of the militia company was ordered to call the roll, and the first name called out to be shot in cold blood was Allan T. Attaway, the first lieutenant of the company, and holding the position of county commissioner of Aiken County, in which county Hamburgh is situated. He pleaded for his life, as only one in his position could plead, but his pleading were met with curses and blows, and he was taken from the sight of his comrades and a file of twelve men fired upon him. He was penetrated by four balls, one entering his brain, and the other three the lower portion of his body. He was instantly killed and after he was dead the brutes in human shape struck him over the head with their guns and stabbed him in the face with their bayonets. Three other men were treated in the same brutal manner. The fifth man when taken out made a dash for his life, and luckily escaped with only a slight wound in his leg.

In another portion of the town the chief of police, a colored man named James Cook, was taken from his house and while begging for his life brutally murdered. Not satisfied with this, the inhuman fiends beat him over the head with their muskets and cut out his tongue.

Another colored man, one of the marshals of the town, surrendered and was immediately shot through the body and mortally wounded. He has since died. . . .

Drumhead court-martial: A court-martial held in the field for the purpose of trying offenses during military operations.

Are the southern colored citizens to be protected or are they to be left at the mercy of such ruffians as massacred the poor men of Hamburgh? Murdered Attaway was a man of considerable prominence in the republican party of the county. He was a law-abiding citizen, held a responsible office, and was well thought of by very many people. The other murdered men were good citizens and have never been known to infringe the law. The whole affair was a well and secretly planned scheme to destroy all the leading republicans of the county of Aiken living in Hamburgh. M. C. Butler, who lost a leg while fighting in the ranks of the rebels, and who is to-day the bitterest of Ku-Klux democrats, was the instigator of the whole affair and the blood-thirsty leader of the massacre. He boasted in Hamburgh during the fight that that was only the beginning; that the end should not be until after the elections in November. Such a man should be dealt with without pity or without hesitation. The United States Government is not powerless, and surely she will not be silent in an emergency like this, the parallel of which pen cannot describe. In this centennial year will she stand idly by and see her soil stained with the blood of defenseless citizens, and witness the bitter tears of women and children falling upon the murdered bodies of their loved ones? God forbid that such an attitude will be assumed toward the colored people of the South by the "best Government the world ever saw." Something must be done, and that quickly, or South Carolina will shed tears of blood and her limbs be shackled by democratic chains.

What I have written in this letter are facts which I vouch for entirely, and are not distorted in any degree. It's a "plain, unvarnished" narration of painful and horrible truths.

SOURCE 4:   James Pike, *The Prostrate State*   (1874)

In 1873, New York Tribune *correspondent James Pike traveled to South Carolina to report on conditions under the state's Republican government. Many whites in the North seized on his articles and book,* The Prostrate State: South Carolina Under Negro Government, *as evidence that Reconstruction was a failure. What is Pike's view of the South Carolina legislature in this excerpt from* The Prostrate State? *Why do you think many white northerners were so ready to accept it?*

We will enter the House of Representatives. Here sit one hundred and twenty-four members. Of these, twenty-three are white men, representing the remains of the old civilization. These are good-looking, substantial citizens. They are men of weight and standing in the communities they represent. They are all from the hill country. The frosts of sixty and seventy winters whiten the heads of some among them. There they sit, grim and silent. They feel themselves to be but loose stones, thrown in to partially obstruct a current they are powerless to resist. They say little and do little as the days go by. . . .

SOURCE: James S. Pike, *The Prostrate State: South Carolina Under Negro Government* (New York: D. Appleton and Company, 1874), pp. 12–13, 14, 19–20.

This dense negro crowd they confront do the debating, the squabbling, the law-making, and create all the clamor and disorder of the body. These twenty-three white men are but the observers, the enforced auditors of the dull and clumsy imitation of a deliberative body, whose appearance in their present capacity is at once a wonder and a shame to modern civilization. . . .

Their struggles to get the floor, their bellowings and physical contortions, baffle description. The Speaker's hammer plays a perpetual tattoo all to no purpose. The talking and the interruptions from all quarters go on with the utmost license. Every one esteems himself as good as his neighbor, and puts in his oar, apparently as often for love of riot and confusion as for any thing else. It is easy to imagine what are his ideas of propriety and dignity among a crowd of his own color, and these are illustrated without reserve. The Speaker orders a member whom he has discovered to be particularly unruly to take his seat. The member obeys, and with the same motion that he sits down, throws his feet on to his desk, hiding himself from the Speaker by the soles of his boots. In an instant he appears again on the floor. After a few experiences of this sort, the Speaker threatens, in a laugh, to call "the gemman" to order. This is considered a capital joke, and a guffaw follows. The laugh goes round, and then the peanuts are cracked and munched faster than ever; one hand being employed in fortifying the inner man with this nutriment of universal use, while the other enforces the views of the orator. This laughing propensity of the sable crowd is a great cause of disorder. They laugh as hens cackle—one begins and all follow.

SOURCE 5:   Carl Schurz, *Speech in the Senate* (1872)

By the early 1870s, Carl Schurz had reversed his stand on Reconstruction. In this excerpt from a speech in the U.S. Senate on January 30, 1872, how does Schurz attack the Republican governments in the South?

But the stubborn fact remains that they [Southern black voters and office-holders] were ignorant and inexperienced; that the public business was an unknown world to them, and that in spite of the best intentions they were easily misled, not infrequently by the most reckless rascality which had found a way to their confidence. Thus their political rights and privileges were undoubtedly well calculated, and even necessary, to protect their rights as free laborers and citizens; but they were not well calculated to secure a successful administration of other public interests.

I do not blame the colored people for it; still less do I say that for this reason their political rights and privileges should have been denied them. Nay, sir, I deemed it necessary then, and I now reaffirm that opinion, that they should possess those rights and privileges for the permanent establishment of the

SOURCE: Reprinted in Frederic Bancroft, ed., *Speeches, Correspondence and Political Papers of Carl Schurz* (New York: G. P. Putnam's Sons, 1913), II, pp. 326–328; originally from Carl Schurz speech in Senate, January 30, 1872.

logical and legitimate results of the war and the protection of their new position in society. But, while never losing sight of this necessity, I do say that the inevitable consequence of the admission of so large an uneducated and inexperienced class to political power, as to the probable mismanagement of the material interests of the social body, should at least have been mitigated by a counterbalancing policy. When ignorance and inexperience were admitted to so large an influence upon public affairs, intelligence ought no longer to so large an extent have been excluded. In other words, when universal suffrage was granted to secure the equal rights of all, universal amnesty ought to have been granted to make all the resources of political intelligence and experience available for the promotion of the welfare of all.

But what did we do? To the uneducated and inexperienced classes—uneducated and inexperienced, I repeat, entirely without their fault—we opened the road to power; and, at the same time, we condemned a large proportion of the intelligence of those States, of the property-holding, the industrial, the professional, the tax-paying interest, to a worse than passive attitude. We made it, as it were, easy for rascals who had gone South in quest of profitable adventure to gain the control of masses so easily misled, by permitting them to appear as the exponents and representatives of the National power and of our policy; and at the same time we branded a large number of men of intelligence, and many of them of personal integrity, whose material interests were so largely involved in honest government, and many of whom would have cooperated in managing the public business with care and foresight—we branded them, I say, as outcasts, telling them that they ought not to be suffered to exercise any influence upon the management of the public business, and that it would be unwarrantable presumption in them to attempt it.

I ask you, sir, could such things fail to contribute to the results we read today in the political corruption and demoralization, and in the financial ruin of some of the Southern States? These results are now before us. The mistaken policy may have been pardonable when these consequences were still a matter of conjecture and speculation; but what excuse have we now for continuing it when those results are clear before our eyes, beyond the reach of contradiction?

QUESTIONS TO CONSIDER

1. What does the career of Robert Smalls reveal about the goals of blacks at the end of the Civil War? What role did Carl Schurz play in the achievement of those goals during Reconstruction? What role did he play in undermining them?

2. What do the essay and sources in this chapter reveal about some of the factors influencing the ultimate outcome of Reconstruction? What would have been required to change the outcome?

3. Some historians argue that the Reconstruction governments in the South were overturned because the Republicans paid too much attention to securing political rights for the freedmen and not enough attention to their economic security. On the basis of the material in this chapter, do you agree with that assessment?

4. Based on the essay and sources in this chapter, what attitudes do you think were to blame for the way Reconstruction turned out? To what extent do Smalls and Schurz each represent these attitudes?

FOR FURTHER READING

Eric Foner, *Reconstruction: America's Unfinished Revolution, 1863–1877* (New York: Harper & Row, 1988), offers a recent synthesis of the Reconstruction era. Foner argues that Reconstruction provided opportunities for reform that were not taken and correctly places African Americans at the center of the story.

Edward A. Miller Jr., *Gullah Statesman: Robert Smalls from Slavery to Congress, 1839–1915* (Columbia: University of South Carolina Press, 1995), is a useful biography of the African-American leader.

Kenneth M. Stampp, *The Era of Reconstruction, 1865–1877* (New York: Random House, 1965), views Reconstruction as a positive and successful policy.

Hans L. Trefousse, *Carl Schurz: A Biography* (New York: Fordham University Press, 1998), emphasizes the importance of ethnic politics in Schurz's political career.

Craftsmen and Buccaneers in an Industrial Age: Terence Powderly and Jay Gould

Terence Powderly could not believe his eyes or ears. Before him sat the hated Jay Gould, the greedy railroad magnate who put profits before all else. This was the "Wizard of Wall Street," who had made a fortune at the expense of unwary investors. This was the man who supposedly had said he could hire half the working class to kill the other half. The frail, soft-spoken man sitting in front of Powderly did not seem to live up to his reputation. Only Gould's piercing eyes offered any hint of his notorious past. And now Powderly, the charismatic union leader, could not believe the words coming from Gould's mouth.

Powderly had been shocked enough by Gould's invitation to a Sunday meeting in March 1886 at the capitalist's New York mansion. The purpose, Powderly assumed, was to continue their negotiations concerning the strike by Powderly's union—the Knights of Labor—against Gould's railroads. For a businessman even to agree to discuss terms with labor was rare enough. To invite the workers' representative to his own home was extraordinary. Now, in his ornately decorated Gilded Age parlor, Gould stunned Powderly again. The quiet little man announced that he would arbitrate all differences between labor and management and rehire striking employees. With soaring spirits, Powderly accepted the terms and agreed to end his union's strike. Right here by Gould's fireplace, Powderly believed, workers had just won a great victory.

After the meeting, Powderly ordered his men back to work. Yet the leader of the nation's most powerful union had been fooled. The master businessman had carefully worded his terms. Without actually admitting that he had lied, Gould rescinded the agreement. Telegrams contravening the order to arbitrate— sent over Gould-controlled telegraph wires—instantly reached various officials who ran the magnate's sprawling railroad empire. In fact, Powderly had fallen completely for his clever plot to destroy the Knights of Labor. When Powderly heard what had happened, he fired off orders for the strike to continue. It was too late, though. The well-organized action against the Gould properties quickly dissolved into violence. Disillusioned with Powderly's leadership, the rank and file began to lose confidence in him. Before long, hate mail began piling up at his door. Gould had outsmarted his opponent and won the day. In the end, the

Terence Powderly   Jay Gould

dramatic meeting between Gould and Powderly stood as a fitting symbol not of labor's victory, but of the challenges it faced as it confronted the concentrated power of capital in the late nineteenth century.

"When I Want a Monkey . . . I'll Send for You"

By the time Jay Gould and Terence Powderly met in 1886, Gould's public reputation had already been sealed. To journalists, labor leaders, and social reformers, he was a speculator who took over businesses built by others, looted them, and then moved on. As newspaper publisher Joseph Pulitzer put it, he was "one of the most sinister figures that has ever flitted bat-like across the vision of the American people." In short, he was the archetypical "robber baron," a reference to the legendary European nobles of the Middle Ages who had pillaged the countryside. The term would dog him until he died. Gould understood that capitalism was ruthless. He knew that he was never as powerful as his opponents assumed. He also knew that he had constructed efficient and profitable companies and that he would do whatever it took to increase his profits. Of one thing he was absolutely certain: His enemies knew little about his life. In fact, they were even mistaken about his background. Inspired by their own anti-Semitism, they believed that he was the perfect example of the grasping, deceitful Jewish financier. In truth, he was actually a descendant of old Protestant stock.

Gould was born in 1836 in Roxbury, New York. His father was a farmer and storekeeper and often on the edge of financial ruin. The small, frail Jay quickly demonstrated a powerful intellect and driving ambition, walking many miles from his home to the academy where he studied. He worked in his father's store by day and studied surveying by night. By age sixteen, he was a skilled surveyor and operated his own business. Soon he attracted the attention of Zadock

Pratt, a well-respected tanner who wanted to expand his operation and offered Gould the chance to work with him in opening a new tannery in eastern Pennsylvania. From Pratt he learned the details of tanning and management. Pratt, however, began to distrust Gould's bookkeeping. When an accounting investigation proved his suspicions wrong, Pratt nonetheless forged ahead with plans to oust his junior partner by demanding that Gould either sell out to him or purchase the business. Pratt never suspected that the young man would be able to raise the capital to buy him out. Gould responded by putting together a partnership of his own and taking over the tannery.

Gould's new partner, Charles Leupp, suffered from mental illness. As his condition declined, the pair argued frequently. In 1859, three years after taking over the tannery with Gould, Leupp committed suicide. Later critics would claim that Gould had driven his partner to kill himself, a vicious distortion of the truth. Meanwhile, Gould's new partners began arming employees in an attempt to take control of the tannery and warehouses. The real battle, however, was fought in the courts. In a case that dragged on for years, Gould was finally forced out. Yet he had learned a valuable lesson about the cutthroat nature of business. It was perfect preparation for his next venture: the pursuit of profit on Wall Street.

By the time Gould turned to stock speculation, Wall Street was coming into its own. Founded in 1792, the New York Stock Exchange provided a specialized market for the trading of securities. In effect, it offered a way for enterprises requiring capital to secure it from individuals who had funds they were willing to invest. The middlemen who performed this vital function in a growing commercial capitalist economy were brokers. Initially, they traded mostly bank stocks or government bonds. After the War of 1812, they also traded canal stocks. By the middle of the nineteenth century, however, the stock market had been transformed. During the Civil War, the government was forced to raise millions of dollars through the sale of bonds. In the coming years, a railroad-building frenzy further spurred the stock market's growth. More than other enterprises, railroads required enormous capital. As the companies in this industry raised funds by floating stocks and bonds, Wall Street boomed.

For an ambitious young man prepared to live by his wits and already bruised by the hard knocks of business, the stock market was a natural attraction. Virtually unregulated, it was a hive of unscrupulous operators who preyed on a gullible and unsuspecting public. One of their favorite devices was the "pool," formed when a group of speculators came togther to bid up the price of a stock with heavy buying. As outsiders began to buy, unaware of the true reason for the stock's rise, the pool unloaded its shares at a profit, usually just before the price collapsed. Even better was a "short squeeze." The big losers here were investors who sold a stock short*—that is, who borrowed shares,

---

Sold a stock short: Short selling, a practice that still occurs in financial markets, involves the sale of borrowed securities. Short sellers hope to "cover" their position by buying shares back at lower prices and, in effect, returning the shares to the lender. The difference between the sale price and purchase price represents the short seller's profit. Of course, if the price of the stock rises, short sellers lose money because they have to purchase the shares back at a higher price.

sold them, and pocketed the proceeds. As the pool operators bid up the price of a stock, panicked short sellers rushed into the market to buy back the shares they owed to their lenders. Often, though, they found few shares available for purchase because the pool operators had artificially dried up the supply. Scurrying to cover their positions as the price rose ever higher, they were caught in a "squeeze." As the desperate short sellers often bid the shares up to astronomical levels, the pools were then only too happy to sell their stocks to them. The pool operators profited handsomely, and the shorts were often wiped out.

Wall Street was the perfect home for the wily and self-aggrandizing Gould. Moving to New York during the Civil War, he built on acquaintanceships from the leather business and forged a partnership in a small trading firm. Then, with his contested holdings in the tannery as capital, he took the plunge. He was an adept trader and quickly absorbed the nuances of high finance. While learning the ropes of the stock market, Gould fell in love with the daughter of a respected grocery merchant. Helen Day Miller was a small, unassuming, conservative woman. Gould was struck by her modesty and kindness, and the two married in 1863. He would remain devoted to Helen and their six children throughout his life. His other passions were books and flowers. He accumulated a large library and built an enormous greenhouse at his home, where he grew flowers and learned everything he could about them.

Shortly after the Civil War, Gould teamed up with a dry goods merchant named Jim Fisk. "Jubilee Jim" had made a tidy fortune selling provisions to the Union army during the war. Like Gould, he set his sights on Wall Street after the war. Their partnership would last until Fisk was killed in 1872 by the jealous lover of his former mistress.

In 1867, the two partners joined Daniel Drew, a cattle drover turned steamboat operator and stock market speculator. Drew's reputation as a sharp dealer was sealed by the rumor that he had routinely fed his cattle salt while driving them to market. At the last minute, he had allowed them to slake their thirst by drinking water, which artificially added to their weight at auction. The practice gave rise to the term "watered stock," a reference to securities that actually had far less value than the issuing corporations let on. By 1854, Drew was treasurer of the Erie Railroad, a position he used to line his pockets. In 1867, he teamed up with Gould and Fisk. Gould had already bought stock in the firm and captured a seat on the board of directors. Together, the three men took control of the line, and in short order Gould became its president.

In 1867 railroad tycoon Cornelius Vanderbilt made a move to buy the Erie Railroad. The result was the Erie War, a monumental battle for control of the company that lasted until 1868. The Erie provided a crucial link between the Hudson River and the Great Lakes and competed with the New York Central, an amalgam of railroads that also linked New York City with the interior. After gaining control of the New York Central in 1867, Vanderbilt took on Gould and his partners by purchasing 100,000 shares of Erie stock. He soon discovered, however, that Gould and Fisk had set up a printing press in the company basement to churn out stock certificates, making it impossible for Vanderbilt to gain voting control. The partners' efforts to fend off Vanderbilt were ultimately successful, thanks in part to Gould's bribing New York state legislators. A little later, Gould and Fisk double-crossed Drew in a clever short squeeze that cost Drew millions of dollars and left him broke. By then, however, the Erie was nearly bankrupt as well. Together, Gould, Fisk, and Drew inflated the value of the Erie's stock from $24 million to $78 million by issuing new shares to the public without increasing the real value of the rail property. In 1872, when irate company directors realized the full extent of his manipulation, Gould was forced out as president of the line. Now worth millions, he was ready to move on.

In fact, the restless Gould had already made one of the boldest moves of his career. In 1869, he had borrowed heavily to take over the Wabash Railroad, a small western line that depended heavily on farmers' shipments to make money. The volume of such shipments depended in turn on a high price for grain. And the price of grain, for complicated reasons that Gould understood perfectly, depended on the price of gold: the higher the price of one, the higher the price of the other. For Gould, the connections were as clear as falling dominoes. If he could raise the price of gold, grain prices—and the Wabash's profits—would rise, and so would his chances of paying back his debt. To spike gold prices, however, he also needed the cooperation of President Ulysses S. Grant, who might be persuaded to restrict the Treasury Department's sale of gold. After wining and dining Grant and bringing the president's brother-in-law into the scheme, Gould started to buy. In effect, he aimed to create a huge short squeeze in gold. At one point, Gould and his syndicate had purchased $40 million in gold contracts, and prices soared. Meanwhile, desperate short sellers scrambled for funds to cover their positions in gold by selling stocks. That set off a crisis that Gould had not foreseen: a panic on Wall Street. On "Black Friday"—September 24, 1869—the stock market crashed in a flurry of selling. Grant quickly ordered the Treasury Department to sell enough gold to break gold prices and shore up the stock market. By the time the panic had subsided, Gould's attempted corner was smashed and his reputation ruined.

He was just getting started, though. In fact, after Gould was ousted from the Erie, stock speculation became his forte. Over the next couple of years, he made a series of swift strikes buying and selling—and sometimes even shorting—stock, mostly of railroads. One move, a successful corner in Chicago & Northwestern railroad stock, netted him a small fortune. Afterward, one of his victims, a livid short seller named Henry Smith, confronted Gould. "I will live to see the day," he fumed, "when you have to earn a living by going around this street with a hand organ and a monkey." Gould was unmoved. "Maybe you will, Henry," he replied softly. "And when I want a monkey, Henry, I'll send for you."

Such maneuvers proved profitable, but what Gould really wanted was a railroad empire. He had his opportunity in 1873, when the failure of a prominent banking house sparked a financial panic and severe depression. The railroads, often the victims of mismanagement and scandal, were especially hard hit. None was harder hit than the Union Pacific, a major western rail system near bankruptcy. The next year, Gould shocked Wall Street by swooping down on the stricken company and taking it over. Over the next six years, he mastered the intricacies of the railroad from top to bottom. To the amazement of many observers, the stock speculator eliminated inefficiencies and got the Union Pacific back on its feet. Yet this holding was no more permanent than the Erie. Temperamentally unsuited to holding a property patiently until it paid dividends, he always wanted more action and a bigger return. So when the federal government insisted that the Union Pacific owed it millions of dollars in loans issued to build the line years earlier, Gould moved on. Unable to reach an agreement about the debt, he sold his stock in the company in 1878.

With the proceeds from the Union Pacific, Gould built a massive railroad empire from scratch. Defying conventional wisdom that a rail system had to be anchored on a transcontinental trunk line, Gould began buying small, seemingly insignificant railroads and forged a southwestern transportation empire. The foundation of his system was the Missouri Pacific, which ran between St. Louis and Kansas City. He also owned or controlled the Kansas Pacific, the Denver & Rio Grande, the Iron Mountain and Southern, the Wabash, and the Texas & Pacific. Gould strategically acquired each one because it would help bring more traffic to another road, had the potential for more development, or would deny access to a certain area to his competitors. Observers were amazed at the speed and efficiency with which he built his system. They were further impressed when he extended his holdings in the Midwest, North, and East. By 1880, Gould controlled more than eight thousand miles of track—more than anyone else in the world. Yet the railroads were only a part of his vast transportation and communications empire. He soon gained control of the Western Union Telegraph Company and an important elevated rail system in New York City. It seemed that the great "robber baron" had actually built something worthwhile—a sound and efficient business empire.

To protect these interests, Gould poured thousands of dollars into the coffers of politicians. He feared that the government would pass legislation to control freight rates or the sale of land along his lines' routes. Such measures would limit profits, making it more difficult to pay back the large debts incurred in acquiring and upgrading those lines. In the midst of his whirlwind empire building, however, he ran into a threat of another sort. By the 1880s, Gould faced a growing conflict with his workers. Their demands for higher wages would also make it more difficult for him to maximize profits. Yet Gould was determined that they, too, would not stand in his way.

"Grand Master Workman"

Like Jay Gould, Terence Powderly was a scrawny boy whose looks belied his toughness. Born in Carbondale, Pennsylvania, in 1849, the eleventh of twelve children of Irish immigrants, young Terence gave up his formal education at thirteen to go to work as a switch operator for a small Pennsylvania railroad. He was soon promoted to brakeman and then served an apprenticeship in the company's locomotive shop under a master machinist. Amid the pounding noise of the shop, the young apprentice learned a trade and absorbed the pride that the artisan class had in its skills. He would soon discover, however, that many employers did not value their employees' work.

In the growing industrial economy after the Civil War, the spread of machine production was fast eroding the position of the skilled artisan class. Increasingly, skilled craftworkers were simply employees who were paid for their time. Often, too, they were merely appendages of machines. Mass production divided the labor process into small tasks, requiring workers to perform the same actions over and over. Thus a worker in a shoe factory might be required only to nail the heels to the soles of shoes. One company's standards called for twenty-four hundred pairs of shoes to be completed each day. Moreover, as industrialization spread, the workday—often ten hours or more—was divided into shifts. Each shift included workers who were interchangeable. That way, each employee could perform the same tasks in the same way, producing at the same level. As one machinist put it in the 1870s, mechanization was "fast rendering trades useless." Wage levels reflected the machine's assault on skill levels. Wages, many workers found, were too low to make ends meet.

Powderly got his introduction to the emerging industrial order when his company laid him off a few months after he became a regular machinist. He remained unemployed for nearly a year before finally finding a position in Scranton, Pennsylvania, with the Delaware, Lackawanna and Western Railroad. Meanwhile, Powderly observed the violent strikes in the coal mines that eventually resulted in the hanging of several members of the Molly Maguires,* a militant labor group blamed for the unrest. The strikes had an impact on Powderly, and by the time he joined the Machinists' and Blacksmiths' Union in 1871 and was elected president of the local two years later, he was convinced that strikes were dangerous. Throughout his career, Powderly would prefer peaceful negotiation and persuasion to agitation and violence.

Even that approach met with limited success, though. In the late nineteenth century, the owners of companies typically regarded unions as interfering with the natural laws of supply and demand that ruled the business world and set wages. Employees, they believed, needed to negotiate with employers on an individual, rather than a collective, basis, as they always had. Workers found little sympathy for their pleas for better wages and shorter hours. Hard times made matters worse. As business declined and companies went under, increased competition for jobs sent union activity spiraling downward. During the depression that followed the Panic of 1873, Powderly was blacklisted for his union activities. Forced to become a wandering tradesman, he traveled from place to place seeking whatever employment he could find. All the while, he continued to work for the Machinists' and Blacksmiths' Union.

At the same time, Powderly was attracted to a budding movement to create a national labor organization. Before the Civil War, labor unions represented workers in various locales. After the war, some craft unions representing the same skill joined together to form national trade organizations. In 1866, these trade organizations joined with others to form the National Labor Union (NLU), a nationwide union representing numerous crafts. Powderly was quickly drawn into the NLU. Unable to maintain unity among various workers, however, the union dissolved in 1873.

Through the NLU, Powderly came under the influence of labor reformer Ira Steward. A champion of the eight-hour workday, Steward believed that increasing wages and shortening the workday would allow laborers to escape the factory jobs that turned them into commodities. It also would permit them to become self-employed. Every worker could be a "capitalist" either by owning his own business or as a member of a cooperative. Owned by their members,

---

Molly Maguires: A secret organization of miners with roots in Ireland that promoted labor violence in Pennsylvania mines starting in the 1860s. By the mid-1870s, two dozen members had been convicted in connection with the violence and ten had been executed.

cooperatives would allow workers to be property owners in the face of industrialization, the rising power of corporations, and the spread of skill-eroding machine production. In short, Steward's aspirations for workers were for them to become middle-class property owners. This was an appealing idea, especially to artisans who spent years learning their trades. And it conformed perfectly to widespread assumptions about opportunity and upward social mobility in the nineteenth century. In the pre–Civil War economy of farms and small shops, ambitious workers often had not been permanent wage earners. Rather, they eventually joined the employer or propertied class by rising naturally from apprentices to journeymen to craftsmen. As master craftsmen, they would own their own shops and employ upwardly mobile apprentices and journeymen of their own. In an expanding industrial economy in which the factory was rapidly expanding the class of permanent wage earners, Steward and other labor reformers assumed that many workers could continue to join the propertied class.

Powderly, like Steward, emphasized the goal of economic independence for workers and moderate political and social reforms to achieve it. He took up the call for social reforms such as graduated property taxes,* women's rights, temperance, and cooperatives. These reforms had less to do with changing the workplace than with changing the larger society, and Powderly soon came to believe that the only solution to labor's problems was political power. After his union activity made him Scranton's foremost labor leader, he naturally turned to politics. In 1878, he easily won election as the city's mayor. In office, he pursued a course of moderate reform that included the establishment of a board of health, tax reform, expanded fire and police departments, and a public works program that paved streets and built sewers. Powderly's program appealed to many workers, and he won reelection twice. Like other workers, however, he eventually realized that politics alone would not solve the mounting problems of low wages, long hours, and the erosion of skills posed by machines.

In the face of these threats, many workers were already turning to secret organizations for help. One of them was the Noble and Holy Order of the Knights of Labor. Founded in Philadelphia in 1869 by a tailor named Uriah S. Stephens, it quickly began to appeal to a wide spectrum of wage earners. The order's secrecy offered protection to members, while its fraternal rituals instilled loyalty and a sense of community. Stephens and many of his followers also shared a widespread assumption dating back to pre–Civil War artisans that workers were independent producers, much like farmers. Their labor added value to commodities by transforming them from raw materials to finished products. In this view, society was divided into two great classes: the wealth producers and those who lived off them. Unlike Karl Marx,* who saw private property itself as the problem facing workers, the Knights defined "non-producers" as the

---

Graduated property taxes: Taxes structured so that people with substantial property holdings pay taxes at a higher rate than those with less property.

Karl Marx: The German-born economic philosopher who argued that human labor rather than capital added economic value to goods. Marx concluded that because capitalists unfairly claimed a portion of this value, private property and capitalism itself should be abolished.

enemy. It was a compelling notion in the expanding commercial and industrial economy of the nineteenth century. Many people found themselves increasingly dependent on distant markets that they only vaguely understood. It was easy for them to see far-off bankers, brokers, and others who manipulated those markets for their own benefit as "non-producers." Thus Stephens, too, was an advocate of workers' cooperatives. In the long run, they were the only way to free the "wealth producers" from "wage slavery."

Like many skilled craftsmen, Powderly shared this "producer" ideology, and in 1876 he became a member of the Knights. The following year, the charismatic and articulate Powderly helped found a local in Scranton, and in 1879 he replaced Stephens as "grand master workman." As a devout Catholic, he was troubled by the church's rejection of the order's secrecy and rituals. Thus he quickly moved to transform the secret society into a public union. He also opened it up to a wide membership. In an age when most unions excluded blacks, the Knights welcomed them, and by 1886 the Knights claimed nearly sixty thousand African-American members. Powderly compromised on the race issue when it was clear that white members of the union would not accept integrated locals. Grasping the reality of entrenched racism, he accepted segregated locals, which would allow African Americans to participate in the union. Yet he refused to back down at the national level, and the Knights included black members in national and regional organizations. Powderly also insisted that the nobility of work entitled all workers to certain rights, no matter what their sex. He expanded the union's definition of work to include domestic servants and even housewives. Powderly's stand for women's rights was unparalleled. Most unions of the day were exclusively male and often fought against women working outside the home in order to protect men's jobs from further competition. He recognized, though, that the inclusion of women helped build a sense of community by uniting families in labor activities.

All the while, the Knights continued to reflect a "producer" ideology. The union excluded from membership only "non-producers"—lawyers, gamblers, bankers, and liquor sellers—and its rhetoric emphasized the nobility and independence of labor. Alarmed by the accumulation and concentration of wealth in the hands of the few, it decried the exploitation of the "toiling masses." Instead of revolution, the Knights offered a program of moderate reform and individual self-improvement. It promoted temperance and urged workers to make morality and hard work, rather than money, the standards for success. It demanded that the government preserve public land for homesteading by settlers rather than give it to railroads in massive land grants. It called for legislation to require corporations to pay their employees weekly. It supported the eight-hour workday. **[See Source 1.]** Higher wages and fewer hours, however, were merely short-run solutions to workers' problems. Above all, Powderly emphasized, the Knights needed to work for the reform of society through cooperatives. As he put it in 1880, they "will eventually make every man his own master." **[See Source 2.]** To many workers facing uncertain futures in the new industrial order, it was an appealing prospect, and by 1885 the union claimed 100,000 members. Powderly had emerged as the voice of the American worker and the leader of the nation's largest and most powerful union. Behind him was what he called an "Army of the Discontented." Shortly, he would lead it into its biggest fight.

"I Play No Game of Bluff"

By the 1880s, millions of workers toiled for long hours and low wages on railroads and in factories, mines, and mills. In that decade and the next, many of those workers would be involved in violent and bloody strikes. Labor unrest struck dozens of industries, but railroads—the nation's first big business—were the first and biggest target. In 1877, a major railroad strike involving thousands of workers resulted in the deaths of nearly one hundred people and the shutdown of two-thirds of the nation's rail system. Operating in the nation's largest industry, railroad companies were the first to employ large work forces. Jay Gould's lines were no exception. By the beginning of the decade, his Texas & Pacific alone employed some nine thousand workers. Busy building a railroad empire in the 1880s, Gould shared the typical attitudes of business tycoons toward them. "My idea," he told a Senate committee, "is that if capital and labor are let alone they will regulate each other." In another way, though, Gould was unique. In the 1880s, he was the biggest target of Terence Powderly's powerful union.

The battle between Gould and Powderly started in 1885, when Gould slashed wages on his Wabash line. Gould was in the midst of another financial restructuring that would allow him to expand his holdings. At the same time, the nation's economy had turned down again. When the financier took advantage of the slump and cut wages, the Knights of Labor responded with a strike against the Wabash. Gould countered by locking out the Wabash workers. The Knights then threatened to launch a strike against all of Gould's southwestern railroads. By shutting down nearly twenty thousand miles of rail, the action would have had a crippling impact similar to the railroad strike of 1877. Realizing the danger, Gould agreed to meet with Powderly and the governors of Missouri and Kansas, who offered to mediate the crisis. The result was shocking: Gould capitulated. Rather than face a strike, he backed down and reinstated locked-out employees. Workers across the country rejoiced over "Brother Powderly's" great victory. In less than a year, about 600,000 more workers flocked to join the Knights of Labor.

Gould's defeat was only temporary. The sly market operator had learned long before when to hold a position and when to fold. He knew that his financial situation was too precarious in 1885, so he backed down. But he did not give up. Rather, he continued to fire members of the Knights on another line, the Texas & Pacific. The Knights demanded that the line return the discharged men to work and pay unskilled workers at least $1.50 a day or face a strike. Powderly knew that the Knights of Labor was nearly broke and could not afford to pay strike benefits if a major walkout occurred. He also knew that every major strike since the Civil War had ultimately failed. Though praised for his stunning victory over Gould, Powderly opposed further action against Gould's lines. The union's local leadership, however, overrode Powderly's objections and ordered another strike after Gould rejected the Knights' demands. Now Powderly had to go along with an action that he did not want and was sure the union could not win. Claiming to speak for "500,000 organized men," Powderly declared, "I play no game of bluff or chance." That was not true, of course, but it worked. Before long, Gould called for the dramatic meeting in his home in March 1886 and apparently capitulated once again. The rail baron agreed to arbitration and to rehire fired workers, except those who had destroyed company property. Powderly responded by ordering the strike to end, and the Knights began to celebrate another great victory.

Gould's plans, however, were executed to perfection. When he rescinded his order to reinstate workers, the frantic Powderly had little choice but to reverse his order and continue the strike. By then, Powderly had lost control of the situation, and the strike quickly disintegrated into widespread violence and chaos. Enraged Knights stormed depots and roundhouses* and destroyed property worth hundreds of thousands of dollars. The violence threw Gould and Powderly into a desperate and heated correspondence. "I began life in a lowly way," Gould reminded the Knights' leader, "and by industry, temperance, and attention to my own business have been successful." Now he faced the choice of destruction by the Knights of Labor or loss of his "manhood." **[See Source 3.]**

Such communication did little good. Already Knights of Labor locals had stepped up their assault on Gould. **[See Source 4.]** Mobilized against him, the strikers were in no mood for compromises. As the entire Southwest slipped into commercial paralysis, a frightened public turned against the strikers. Emboldened, Gould dug in his heels and refused all attempts at arbitration. Rivals in the Knights seized the opportunity to attack Powderly, placing the blame squarely on his shoulders. They claimed that his resistance to strikes had undermined their efforts from the beginning. In early May, the Knights capitulated to Gould, calling off the strike. Then, immediately, Powderly and his union suffered another blow. The day after the Knights ended their strike against the Texas & Pacific, a Knights of Labor protest against a lockout at the McCormick reaper works in Chicago spun out of control. When police arrived to disperse a crowd at nearby Haymarket Square, a bomb exploded, killing seven policemen. Although the bomb throwers were never positively identified, the Haymarket Riot brought the trial and conviction of eight anarchists. Now the Knights were associated in many Americans' minds with murder and violence.

Just a few months after his great victory over Gould, Powderly's union collapsed as hundreds of thousands of disillusioned members fled the Knights. By the early 1890s, local and regional Knights of Labor organizations carried out strikes and violent attacks in open defiance of Powderly's orders. In 1893, he was forced to resign, and the following year, he was expelled from the order. By then, the union's ranks had fallen to fewer than 100,000 members, and within a few years, the union had virtually disappeared. Laboring for abysmal wages under wretched conditions, workers wanted concrete gains, not Powderly's sweeping reforms. Compared to a vast restructuring of the economy through cooperatives, the short-term goals of better wages, hours, and working conditions seemed far more important to most workers. Achieving the Knights' reform goals through politics, of course, would have required the organization of the entire labor force. The romantic Powderly never understood how unlikely that was. Indeed, his later career reflected how removed Powderly became from the concerns of most workers. After his ouster, he returned to politics, studied law, and became an attorney. Later, he took up the cause of high tariffs because

---

Roundhouses: Circular buildings for housing and switching locomotives.

he believed that protection from foreign imports benefited workers. He even joined the protariff and probusiness Republican Party. In fact, before he died in 1924, he received numerous appointments to federal positions, mostly at the hands of Republican presidents.

Meanwhile, another labor organization had replaced the Knights as the dominant union in the United States. The American Federation of Labor (AF of L), founded in 1886, limited membership to skilled craftsmen and promoted strikes and boycotts. It rejected Powderly's producerism, his belief that workers could join the owner class, and his romantic vision of a cooperative commonwealth. Instead, it accepted the idea of workers as permanent wage earners. In place of political and social reforms, AF of L president Samuel Gompers demanded goals such as higher wages, shorter hours, and the right to organize, and he endorsed strikes to achieve those goals. Gompers rejected Powderly's policy of "one big union." Thus the AF of L discriminated against women and African Americans. By 1900 Gompers's union had nearly a million members and stood as the major force for workers in their continuing struggle against capitalists.

Gould, meanwhile, had delivered the Knights of Labor a blow from which it would never recover. After he broke the Texas & Pacific strike, his badly beaten workers would submit to poor wages and working conditions for years. He also had shown other corporate owners the way to deal with labor. As the labor wars continued into the next decade and beyond, corporations emulated his iron-fisted approach by hiring strikebreakers, enlisting Pinkerton detectives,* black-listing union employees, and insisting on ironclad (anti-union) oaths. All the while, Gould continued to build his empire. Long a believer in rate wars to eliminate competitors, he reversed course after his Texas & Pacific victory and promoted price stability. He realized that the rapid expansion of the railroad industry was behind it and that now the industry needed improved efficiency and better service. To bolster his bargaining position, he even retook control of the Union Pacific and three other systems in the fall of 1890. It was his last bold maneuver. By then, his health was broken. Diagnosed with tuberculosis, a secret he kept even from his family, he spent entire nights without sleeping. As he walked for hours outside his home, he plotted his next moves and coughed up blood from his wasting lungs. Continuing to oversee every detail of his sprawling empire, he literally worked himself to death.

When Gould died in 1892, his holdings were left entirely to his family. He hoped that his sons would carry out his plans. But the empire he had worked so hard to construct would not endure. Mismanagement brought inefficiency and poor service to the railroads, and gradually the Gould empire broke up. Rather than an enduring business empire, Gould's legacy was his image as the foremost robber baron of the age. Ironically, although the romantic Powderly labored so hard to organize American workers, the practical-minded Gould may actually have done more to achieve that goal. His attitude toward labor and the bare-knuckle tactics he pioneered to defeat the Knights of Labor helped make unions inevitable. **[See Source 5.]** In the end, the union movement that Gould tried so hard to smash may have been his greatest monument.

Pinkerton detectives: Agents employed by the Pinkerton Detective Agency, a private security and investigation firm founded in 1850 by a former Chicago policeman named Allan Pinkerton.

P R I M A R Y   S O U R C E S

SOURCE 1:   Terence Powderly, *Preamble to the Constitution of the Knights of Labor* (1878)

The Knights of Labor was formed as a secret society in 1869, but Terence Powderly turned the organization into an open trade union. In 1878, he helped write a new constitution for the Knights. This excerpt is the preamble to that constitution. What issues does it address? How do the Knights propose to improve the condition of workers?

The recent alarming development and aggression of aggregated wealth which, unless checked, will invariably lead to the pauperization and hopeless degradation of the toiling masses, render it imperative, if we desire to enjoy the blessings of life, that a check should be placed upon its power and upon unjust accumulation, and a system adopted which will secure to the laborer the fruits of his toil, and as this much-desired object can only be accomplished by the thorough unification of labor, and the united efforts of those who obey the divine injunction that "In the sweat of thy brow shalt thou eat bread," we have formed the [Knights of Labor] with a view of securing the organization and direction, by co-operative effort, of the power of the industrial classes, and we submit to the world the object sought to be accomplished by our organization, calling upon all who believe in securing "the greatest good to the greatest number" to aid and assist us:

I. To bring within the folds of organization every department of productive industry, making knowledge a standpoint for action, and industrial and moral worth, not wealth, the true standard of individual and national greatness.

II. To secure to the toilers a proper share of the wealth that they create, more of the leisure that rightfully belongs to them, more societary advantages, more of the benefits, privileges, and emoluments of the world, in a word, all those rights and privileges necessary to make them capable of enjoying, appreciating, defending, and perpetuating the blessings of good government.

III. To arrive at the true condition of the producing masses in their educational, moral, and financial condition, by demanding from the various governments the establishment of bureaus of Labor Statistics.

IV. The establishment of co-operative institutions, productive and distributive.

V. The reserving of the public lands, the heritage of the people, for the actual settler—not another acre for railroads or speculators.

VI. The abrogation of all laws that do not bear equally upon capital and labor, the removal of unjust technicalities, delays, and discrimina-

SOURCE: From Terence V. Powderly, *Thirty Years of Labor* (Philadelphia, 1890), pp. 128–130.

tions, in the administration of justice and the adopting of measures providing for the health and safety of those engaged in mining, manufacturing, or building pursuits.

VII. The enactment of laws to compel chartered corporations to pay their employees weekly, in full, for labor performed during the preceding week, in the lawful money of the country.

VIII. The enactment of laws giving mechanics and laborers a first lien on their work for their full wages.

IX. The abolishment of the contract system of national, state, and municipal work.

X. The substitution of arbitration for strikes, whenever and wherever employers and employes are willing to meet on equitable grounds.

XI. The prohibition of the employment of children in workshops, mines, and factories before attaining their fourteenth year.

XII. To abolish the system of letting out by contract the labor of convicts in our prisons and reformatory institutions.

XIII. To secure for both sexes equal pay for equal work.

XIV. The reduction of the hours of labor to eight per day so that the laborers may have more time for social enjoyment and intellectual improvement, and be enabled to reap the advantages conferred by the labor saving machinery which their brains have created.

XV. To prevail upon governments to establish a purely national circulating medium based upon the faith and resources of the nation, and issued directly to the people, without the intervention of any system of banking corporations, which money shall be a legal tender in payment of all debts, public or private.

Source 2:   *Terence Powderly Calls for Cooperatives*   (1880)

In his first annual address to the General Assembly of the Knights of Labor, Terence Powderly discussed the long-range goals of the Knights, including the reform of the "present order of things" through worker-controlled cooperatives. Why were Powderly and many craftworkers drawn to the idea of transforming society in this way? Was it realistic?

The wage system, at its inception, was but an experiment, and for a time doubts were entertained as to its adoption; but the avaricious eye of the Shylock of labor saw in it a weapon with which he could control the toiler, and today that system has so firm a hold upon us that every attempt at shaking off the fetters, by resorting to a strike, only makes it easier for the master to say to his slave, *You must work for lower wages.*

We must teach our members, then, that the remedy for the redress of the wrongs we complain of does not lie in the suicidal strike; but in thorough,

Source: Terence V. Powderly, *The Path I Trod: The Autobiography of Terence V. Powderly* (1940; reprint, New York: AMS Press, 1968), pp. 269, 270.

effective organization. Without organization we cannot accomplish any-thing; through it we hope to forever banish that curse of modern civilization—wage slavery.

But how? Surely not by forming an association and remaining a member; not by getting every other worthy man to become a member and remain one; not by paying the dues required of us as they fall due. These are all important factors in the method by which we hope to regain our independence, and are vi-tally important; they are the elements necessary to complete organization.

Organization once perfected, what must we do? I answer, study the best means of putting your organization to some practicable use by embarking in a system of

COÖPERATION

which will eventually make every man his own master—every man his own employer; a system which will give the laborer a fair proportion of the products of his toil. It is to coöperation, then, as the lever of labor's emancipation, that the eyes of the workingmen and women of the world should be directed, upon coöperation their hopes should be centered, and to it do I now direct your at-tention. I am deeply sensible of the importance, of the magnitude, of the under-taking in which I invite you to engage. I know that it is human nature to grow cold, apathetic, and finally indifferent when engaged in that which requires deep study and persistent effort, unattended by excitement; men are apt to believe that physical force is the better way of redressing grievances, being the shorter remedy; but even that requires patience and fortitude as well as strength. . . . The laboring man needs education in this great social question, and the best minds of the Order must give their precious thought to this system. There is no good reason why labor cannot, through coöperation, own and oper-ate mines, factories, and railroads.

<hr>

SOURCE 3:   *Correspondence of Jay Gould and Terence Powderly* (1886)

In addition to their face-to-face meetings during the strike of 1886, Jay Gould and Terence Powderly exchanged letters. In excerpts from some of these letters, the two men argue over the results of their dramatic March meeting in which Gould seemed to capitulate to the Knights of Labor. What do these letters reveal about each man? What is the argu-ment of each?

April 11, 1886
[To] Jay Gould, Esq., President Missouri Pacific Railroad
Dear Sir—The events of the past forty-eight hours must have demonstrated to you the absolute necessity of bringing this terrible struggle in the southwest to

SOURCE: *Correspondence Between Jay Gould, T. V. Powderly, and Others in Regard to the Strike of Employ-ees of the Company* (1886; reprint, New York: Institute of Social Economics, 1902), pp. 6–20.

a speedy termination. You have the power, the authority and the means to bring the strike to an end. I have done everything in my power to end the strife. . . . In that conference with you on Sunday, March 28, I understood you to mean that arbitration [to end the strike] would be agreed to. . . .

You can settle this strike. Its longer continuance rests with you and you alone. Every act of violence, every drop of blood that may be shed from this time forth must be laid at your door. The Knights of Labor were not founded to promote or shield wrongdoing, and to-day the Order of the Knights of Labor stands between your property and ruin.

We are willing to absolve the men along your railways from their allegiance to our order. We leave that to themselves. We will not allow any claims which the order may have on them to stand between them and their restoration to their former positions. The Order of the Knights of Labor asks of no man to re-main a member if it is not to his interest to do so. You may deal with them as cit-izens if you will. We will surrender our right to claim these men as members if they wish, but we will not surrender our right to see this affair thoroughly in-vestigated. You have said that the Order of the Knights of Labor was a conspir-acy, a secret menace, etc. I am willing, as the chief officer, to lay everything connected with our order bare to the world, if you will; on the other hand, lay open to the public the means and methods whereby you have piled up the wealth which you control, and allow the tribunal of public opinion to pass in judgment on the two and say which is the conspiracy. Do you accept the challenge? . . .

There are people who say that this struggle is the beginning of the war be-tween capital and labor. The statement is false. This certainly means war; but it is a war between legitimate capital, honest enterprise and honest labor on the one hand, and illegitimate wealth on the other hand. This is a war in which we court the fullest investigation of our acts. Do you dare to do the same? . . .

I do not write this letter to you either in the spirit of anger or revenge. For you personally I have no dislike. I believe that if allowed to follow your own impulses in this matter you would have had the strike ended ere this. Those who advise you do not mingle with the people, they do not care for the people. You have been warned that your life is in danger. Pay no attention to such talk; no man who has the interest of his country at heart would harm a hair of your head. But the system which reaches out on all sides gathering in the millions of dollars of treasure and keeping them out of the legitimate channels of trade and commerce must die, and the men whose money is invested in the enterprises which stock-gambling has throttled must make common cause with those who have been denied the right to earn enough to provide the merest necessaries of life for home and family. When I say to you that we will meet you in the courts, I do not speak rashly or ill-advisedly. I have taken counsel from the best legal minds of the United States. We are prepared to face you before the courts and now await your action in the matter. This is no threat. I play no game of bluff or chance. I speak for 500,000 organized men who are ready to pay out the last farthing in order that justice may prevail. You have it in your power to make friends of these men by acting the part of the man, by taking this matter in your own hands. Will you do so, and end this strike in the interest of humanity and our common country? It is your duty to brush aside every obstacle, assert your authority and take this matter in your hands, settle every grievance, restore every man to his place, except those who have been engaged in the destruction of property or who have broken the laws. Will you do this? You can then make rules and agreements with your men which will forever preclude the possibility of another such disastrous conflict as this one has proved itself to be.

I remain yours very truly,
T. V. Powderly, G.M.W.K. of L.

April 14, 1886
T. V. Powderly, Esq., G.M.W.K. of L.
Dear Sir, . . . I have received your letter to me dated . . . April 11, 1886. . . .

In answer to these personal threats, I beg to say that I am yet a free American citizen. I am past forty-nine years of age, was born at Roxbury, Delaware County, in this State. I began life in a lowly way, and by industry, temperance, and attention to my own business have been successful, perhaps beyond the measure of my deserts. If, as you say, I am now to be destroyed by the Knights of Labor unless I will sink my manhood, so be it. Fortunately, I have retained my early habits of industry. My friends, neighbors, and business associates know me well, and I am quite content to leave my personal record in their hands. If any of them have aught to complain of, I will be only too glad to submit to any arbitration. If such parties or any of them wish to appoint the Knights of Labor or you as their attorney, such appointment is quite agreeable to me, but until such an election is made it will naturally occur to you that any interference on your part in my personal affairs is, to say the least, quite gratuitous. Since I was nineteen years of age I have been in the habit of employing in my various enterprises large numbers of persons, probably at times as high as 50,000, distributing three or four million dollars per month to different pay rolls. It would seem a little strange that during all these years the difficulty with the Knights of Labor should be my first. Any attempt to connect me personally with the late strike on the Southwestern roads, or any responsibility therefore, is equally gratuitous, as you well know. It is true I am the President of the Missouri Pacific, but when this strike occurred I was far away on the ocean and beyond the reach of telegrams. I went away relying on your promise made to me last August that there should be no strike on that road, and that if any difficulties should arise you would come frankly to me with them.

In the face of all this you notify me that unless by 5 o'clock I personally consent to something, precisely what I do not see, then personal consequences of a sort vaguely expressed, but not hard to understand, will at the hand of your order be visited upon me. Let me again remind you that it is an American citizen whom you and your order thus propose to destroy. The contest is not between your order and me, but between your order and the laws of the land. Your order has already defied those laws in preventing by violence this company from operating its road. . . .

Already for weeks your order, in your attack upon this company, has not hesitated to disable it by violence from rendering its duty to the public and from giving work and paying wages to men at least three times your own number, who, working as they were by your side, were at least deserving of your sympathy. . . . [Y]ou now turn upon me and propose that the wrongs you have hitherto inflicted on the public shall now culminate in an attack upon an individual.

In this, as I have said, the real issue is between you and the law of the land. It may be, before you are through, those laws will efficiently advise you that even I, as an individual citizen, am not beyond their care.

Very respectfully,
Jay Gould.

SOURCE 4: *Knights of Labor Attack on Jay Gould* (1886)

During the strike against Jay Gould's railroads in 1886, Knights of Labor locals issued their own statements about the union's action. What does this statement issued by three locals reveal about the workers' grievances? Do you think Terence Powderly would have approved of its contents?

ADDRESS OF THE KNIGHTS.
APPEALING TO BROTHER WORKERS AND BITTERLY DENOUNCING GOULD.

SAINT LOUIS, MO., *April 6,* 1886.

The joint executive board of assemblies 101, 93, and 17, Knights of Labor, this afternoon issued the following address:

"To the workingmen of the world:

"FRIENDS AND BROTHERS: Hear us, for we plead for our rights. Men of equity, look upon us, for we struggle against giants of wrong.

"Mad with the frenzy of pride and self-adulation, begotten as it is of the success of outrage and infamy, there stands before us a giant of aggregated and incorporated wealth, every dollar of which is built upon blood, injustice, and outrage. That giant of corporate wealth has centralized its power in and is impersonated in the eager fiend who gloats as he grinds the life out of his fellowmen, and grimaces and dances as they writhe upon his instruments of torture.

"Oh, ye workingmen of America, who love your liberty and your native land; ye great creators of wealth, who stand as the foundation of all national good, look upon your brothers to-day!

"THE ENEMY.

"Gould the giant fiend, Gould the money monarch, is dancing, as he claims, over the grave of our order, over the ruin of our homes and the blight of our lives. Before him the world has smiled in beauty, but his wake is a graveyard of hopes, the cyclone's path of devastation and death.

SOURCE: House, *Report of the Investigation of Labor Troubles in Missouri, Arkansas, Kansas, Texas, and Illinois,* 49th Cong., 2d sess., 1887, H. Doc. 4174, 419.

"Our strong arms have grown weary in building the tower of strength, and yet he bids us build on or die. Our young lives have grown gray too soon beneath the strain of unrequited, constant toil. Our loved ones at home are hollow-cheeked and pale with long and weary waiting for better days to come. Nay, more tha[n] this, the graveyards are hiding his victims from our longing eyes.

"Brother workmen, this monster fiend has compelled many of us to toil in cold and rain for 5 and 50 cents a day. Others have been compelled to yield their time to him for seventeen and thirty-six weary hours for the pittance of nine hours' pay. Others who have dared to assert their manhood and rebel against his tyranny are black-listed and boycotted all over the land.

"He has made solemn compacts with the highest authority in our order and then has basely refused to fulfill his pledge.

"He lives under and enjoys all the benefits of a republican form of government and yet advocates and perpetuates the most debasing form of white slavery. He robs the rich and poor, the high and low, with ruthless hand, and then appeals to corrupt and purchased courts to help him take our little homes away. He breaks our limbs and maims our bodies and then demands that we shall release him from every claim for damage or be black-listed forever.

"He goes to our grocers and persuades them not to give us credit because we refuse to be ground in his human mill. He turns upon us a horde of lawless thugs, who shoot among our wives and children with deadly intent, and then he howls for Government help when he gets his pay in coin alike.

"GOULD MUST BE OVERTHROWN.

"Fellow workmen, Gould must be [o]verthrown. His giant power must be broken, or you and I must be slaves forever. The Knights of Labor alone have dared to be a David to this Golia[t]h. The battle is not for to-day—the battle is not for to-morrow—but for the trooping generations in the coming ages of the world, for our children and our children's children. 'Tis the great question of the age—shall we, in the coming ages, be a nation of freemen or a nation of slaves?"

SOURCE 5:   *Jay Gould Testifies Before Congress*   (1886)

Shortly after the Knights of Labor action against the Gould railroad lines, the House of Representatives held hearings about the strike. One of the witnesses called to testify was Jay Gould. In these excerpts from his testimony, committee members ask him to explain his views about the strike, the settlement of labor troubles through arbitration, and the relationship between business practices and labor unrest. What do Gould's answers reveal about his attitudes toward his employees? What does this testimony reveal about the cause of the strike?

SOURCE: House, *Report of the Investigation of Labor Troubles in Missouri, Arkansas, Kansas, Texas, and Illinois,* 49th Cong., 2d sess., 1887, H. Doc. 4174, 31, 59, 60, 62–63.

The WITNESS [Gould]. . . . In the strike which took place in March—let me explain to the committee what that was, and what the effect would have been if it had been simply a strike. We had at the date of the strike, on the 6th of March, 14,317 men. I will give you the figures—14,315 employés. The Knights of Labor, the strikers, numbered 3,717; but they were not the men who were necessary to the operation of the road. They were the men in the machine shops, men along the track, men who performed the lower duties on the railroad. So that if this 3,700 men had struck and left the premises and the offices and the law and order of the community had gone on, we would not have missed a train. Our business would have gone right along, as we had all our train forces; but following this strike, following the leaving of our employ, what did they do? They exercised more than the right of eminent domain. They seized our property without paying for it. They seized our terminus. They took Saint Louis, they took Sedalia, they took Atchison, they took Kansas City, they took Parsons, they took Fort Worth, they took Little Rock, they took Texarkana, the terminal point of the road, they took forcible possession, and said no man shall run a train over that road. That is what they said. Now what did Mr. Hoxie* do when he found that state of things. He said "These men have taken possession of our road; we have got no earnings now," and he was forced to write an address to all the men, suspending the pay-roll—the only thing he could do. He suspended his pay-roll, and thus 10,000 men who were loyal to the company, who could run our trains every day, were thrown out of employment. . . .

Q. In your testimony . . . you seem to favor the principle of arbitration in the settlement of troubles between employer and employé. Would you be kind enough to give us the result of your experience and observation in regard to such principle?—A. Well, I think that arbitration is getting to be a very easy and popular way of settling difficulties between individuals, between corporations, and between corporations and their individual employés. I have always been in favor of it, and as long ago as last August, when I had my interview with Mr. Powderly, I expressed myself in the strongest terms in favor of it; and I have never changed my position. I regard the employés of a railroad company upon a different footing to the employés of a manufacturing company or any other business; and the reason I do so is this: A railroad corporation acts in two senses: first, as a private organization with ownership of it; secondly, as a public corporation with a contract with the State by which it has contract duties to perform; and these duties are to be performed not by the rails and the engines alone but by the entire organization, and they clothe themselves with these public duties from the president to the lowest employé that takes part in the railroad; they clothe themselves with those public duties which pertain to the operation of the road as an entirety. Just as the railroad itself has the right to take eminent domain, the property of the railroad is held for the public. It was created to carry their coal and their merchandise and supplies and produce to market; and they have rights which are paramount and superior to any other rights. I have always claimed, and it has always been my view, that all employés, from the president down, that are necessary to operate that road as an entirety, clothe themselves with public duties to that extent, each in his respective sphere. So that I regard the labor needed in the operation of a railroad on a different footing from mere private manufactories. . . .

*Mr. Hoxie: H. M. Hoxie, a manager for the Missouri Pacific Railway Company.

Q. Your idea, it seems to me, is, that this right of the public in the manner of the discharge of these duties is because of the peculiar nature of the service; because of the interest that the public have in railroads.—A. Yes, sir; because of public duties. The people have a right to have a railroad operated.

Q. And have an interest in the manner in which the officers discharge their duties. Now, any legislation which defines their duties and at the same time provides for arbitration between the railways and their employés, would be practical protection of the public rights, would it not?—A. But it would be arbitration after men have struck and seized your property and put your life in peril. This arbitration should come before, and should give the power to keep them at their duty. . . .

The CHAIRMAN. I will direct your attention and the attention of the committee to the combination of crafts, trades, and professions. Have you got any information as to the first combination that was made with the railroads running from the East to the West, what was called "pooling," when the directors of five lines of railroads would get together and regulate the price of the products of the West? Did not that commence before the men commenced to combine?

The WITNESS. Well, perhaps you had better get that from the men who manage those roads.

The CHAIRMAN. I expect to do so; but I want to know if the railroad companies can combine in that way and fix the price of the products of the earth thousands of miles from the point of delivery to the market; I want to know if the example has not been set by them to some extent, provided they do it. And you answer it properly. And I would further ask you another question, and we can get your suggestion, and it being a public question it would not be improper that we should understand whether railroads pay and what the difference is in the present capital of the railroads, their bonds and their stocks, and the actual cost of construction; but we can get at that in another way. I mean to say that the first combination, I think, Mr. Gould, was made by the managers of railroads before combinations were made by the men.

The WITNESS. You don't understand that I object to labor organizations? I am in favor of them. . . .

Q. What is your knowledge, from the information you gather officially, as to the real cause of the strike?—A. I think the cause of it was some of the leaders wanted to make big men of themselves, and their living off workingmen. They only get consequence when they stir up strife.

Q. There were statements made in testimony here, based upon reports to the witness who made the statement, that along the line of the Iron Mountain road the employés were taxed; those who were paid a dollar a day, 25 cents a month, and those who were paid $2 a day, 50 cents a month, and so on upward, for what was known as the hospital fund, and that when one of them got sick instead of being taken to the hospital he would be discharged.—A. I only know that we have a hospital service. That is an organization for the benefit of the men, and I supposed that the company contributes a portion of the expense and the men a portion, and that it is devoted to them when there is anything the matter with them. I don't know anything about the details of it.

Q. But the point that was made by the witness is that when one of the employés became sick he would be discharged.—A. I know nothing of that kind, and of course if the hospital transaction is not satisfactory to the men, we would only be too glad to get out of it. It is a fund for the benefit of the employés.

Q. Then there was another statement made here, to the effect that the railroad would sell a homestead to the employés on the installment plan, and about the time the last installment fell due the employé would be discharged and thereby be prevented from making the final payment, and the property would revert by foreclosure to the railroad company.—A. That is ridiculous.

Q. No such thing occurred? Are you in a position to say positively that it does not?—A. I know it is not so. . . .

QUESTIONS TO CONSIDER

1. Some historians argue that Jay Gould's image as a robber baron is a distortion. Do you agree? How would you describe his methods?

2. How would you characterize the approach of Terence Powderly and the Knights of Labor to the problems facing workers in the late nineteenth century? What experiences, factors, or ideas most influenced his views about the proper solution to those problems? Were they realistic?

3. What do the sources in this chapter reveal about the conditions confronting labor in the late nineteenth century? Do you see a connection between the financial practices of men like Gould and workers' conditions?

4. Why did the Knights of Labor fail? Do you think Gould or Powderly had more to do with its demise? Why?

5. Do you think Gould or Powderly had the greater impact on changing the conditions of labor in the long run? Why?

FOR FURTHER READING

Maury Klein, *The Life and Legend of Jay Gould* (Baltimore: Johns Hopkins University Press, 1986), is the best biography of Gould and offers a revisionist view of the railroad tycoon that challenges the robber baron interpretation.

Walter Licht, *Industrializing America: The Nineteenth Century* (Baltimore: Johns Hopkins University Press, 1995), provides a brief survey of the economic transformation of America during the nineteenth century and its relationship to other changes in society.

Craig Phelan, *Grand Master Workman: Terence Powderly and the Knights of Labor* (Westport, Conn.: Greenwood Press, 2000), is a recent and well-researched biography of Powderly.

Kim Voss, *The Making of American Exceptionalism: The Knights of Labor and Class Formation in the Nineteenth Century* (Ithaca, N.Y.: Cornell University Press, 1993), details the opposition of business to workers' efforts to organize in the late nineteenth century.

Farmers and the "New South": Tom Watson and Henry Grady

The audience at the Georgia State Fair in Macon grew silent as Tom Watson took the podium. Normally, state fairs were an occasion for farmers to show off the fruits of their labor and enjoy themselves. Nobody had to tell this crowd in November 1888, however, that all was not well on the farm. Ground down by years of low prices and high debt, farmers across Georgia and the rest of the South were sunk in despair. Now, like converts at a camp revival, they had come to hear Watson denounce the evil responsible for their plight. One of the most fiery orators ever to arise from Georgia's red clay soil, he would not let them down.

Watson was convinced that the devil was far away in the North. Northern capital—bankers, industrialists, and railroad tycoons—dominated the government and promoted policies designed to enrich them at the expense of the common white people of the South. Worse, those greedy interests had help from southerners, men who had betrayed their own region and people. And none, Watson believed, was guiltier than Henry Grady, the editor of the *Atlanta Constitution*. Grady was the loudest voice calling for the South to put its rural, agricultural past behind. As the editor of Georgia's most influential newspaper, he trumpeted the vision of a "New South," one allied with northern capital to stimulate business and industrialization. Grady was certain that the South's future should be filled with factories, mills, railroads, mines, and cities. Watson was just as certain that Grady was a traitor who had sold out the South to the capitalists of the North.

Looking out over his large state fair crowd, Watson quickly got down to business. After paying the usual homage to the "sacrifices of our martyrs" in the Civil War, he took aim at his main target. Grady, he declared, had earned his "place in history by the side of Benedict Arnold." This "big city editor" had betrayed the South's farmers by ignoring the problems they faced. "In Grady's farm life," Watson charged, "there are no poor cows. They are all fat! Their bells twinkle musically in clover scented meadows." In reality, he went on, "we find the poor bridled cow—with wolves on her back." Only by banding together, Watson concluded, could farmers fight the predators that men like Grady had unleashed on them.

Tom Watson   Henry Grady

The Macon crowd loved the speech, but Watson had no illusions about the task ahead. Here, as elsewhere across the state, he preached to the converted. Watson knew that he had the farmers on his side. Yet he was well aware that Grady was a formidable foe. The Atlanta editor was a silver-tongued orator whose speeches could bring grown men to tears. He also had the most powerful newspaper in the state behind him, and he had rich northern allies. Watson knew, however, that this battle had to be waged. At stake, he believed, was the future of the South and its common people.

"Strip . . . the Poor to Pamper the Rich"

Thomas E. Watson was perfectly suited to express the grievances of poor white southern farmers. Born in 1856 in a log home in Georgia, he grew up the son of a struggling farmer. Watson's grandfather owned forty-five slaves and more than thirteen hundred acres of land, making him a member of the Georgia up-country planter elite. But by the end of the Civil War, all of that was gone. Wealthy planters now found themselves struggling to put food on the table. Watson's father, a twice-wounded Confederate veteran, attempted unsuccessfully to grow cotton without slave labor on his own father's land. In 1868, he was forced to sell out and move his family to a small farm near Thomson, Georgia. Coming of age amid his family's distress, Watson knew firsthand the impact of the Civil War on southern agriculture and the crushing burden of debt and declining prices.

Despite the family's distress, young Tom managed to get an education. He attended local schools, and his mother introduced him to history and biography. He was an avid reader and demonstrated an early interest in rhetoric. In fact, by the time he entered Mercer University at age fifteen, his biggest ambition was to master the art of oratory. Doing so, he believed, would help him become a great man. He joined the debating society. In scrapbooks and a diary, he began writing down quotations and even whole texts to be used for speeches. He also developed his own style as a speaker. In particular, he practiced the art of what he called the "public democratical speech"—that is, presenting himself as one who understood his audience.

Unfortunately, the family's failing finances forced him to give up his attempt to earn a college degree. In 1874, after his sophomore year, he returned to Thomson. Unable to find work and without money, he was forced to sell his book collection at auction. "As each volume was cried off," he said later, "a great gulp rose in my throat." The family abandoned the farm and moved to Augusta. The future, Watson confided to his diary, "seemed robed in gloom," and he considered heading to Texas. At the last minute, though, he decided to study law under a judge in Augusta. Two years later, he moved to rural Screven County to start his law practice. There, in the backwoods, he was in his element. The area was dominated by simple farming folk, and the young lawyer often found himself "eating at their tables [and] sitting at their firesides." An accomplished fiddler, he played at barbecues and schoolhouse dances. "I gained a knowledge of these people which no books could give me—these plain, country people—and I love them," he said later. Their lack of financial means, however, did not help his legal practice, and he had to supplement his income with a teaching job. Within a year, he moved back to his hometown of Thomson penniless.

There Watson gradually built up a successful law practice. Acting as a defense counsel, he argued his cases before juries made up mostly of farmers. His ability to make "democratical" speeches came in handy. Soon his income would allow him to marry Georgia Durham, the daughter of a local physician. "I have a steady and lucrative practice in four counties," Watson said in 1881. Six years later, he had carved out one of the most lucrative legal practices in the state, rarely losing a case.

Even with an income in excess of ten thousand dollars, however, he could not ignore the plight of the people around him. As his reputation spread, Watson began to speak out publicly about the decline of the southern farm. It was a subject that he knew well. In fact, Watson had only to look to his own destitute father to be reminded of the farmer's desperate condition. Shortly after moving back to Thomson, Watson had visited his family, then living in a shack in nearby Jefferson County. He found his father sunk in a "hopeless stupor." Determined to help him out, Watson eventually purchased a seven-hundred-acre farm that had belonged to his grandfather and settled the family on it.

Watson knew from his clients that his father was not alone. In fact, by the early 1880s, southern agriculture had still not recovered from the Civil War. After the war, many plantations had been broken up into small farms that were often worked by tenants who were too poor to own the land. Lacking cash, they frequently gave the landowner a share of their crops as rent. As this system of sharecropping spread throughout the South, tenants were often unable to make ends meet and were forced to borrow money for provisions. This also was true of many poor farmers who owned their land. Whether "croppers" or landowners, farmers often found themselves in debt to local merchants, who frequently obtained loans from middlemen, known as commission merchants. These commission merchants in turn borrowed funds from banks. Local merchants often financed the purchases of farmers at an annual interest rate that averaged 60 percent. Until their debts were paid, the farmers were forced to continue to buy marked-up merchandise from the merchants. This meant that a farmer needing to buy a bag of seeds costing 20 cents would be sold the item on credit. The price would be boosted to 28 cents because it was advanced. By the time the farmer paid for the item plus interest, it would cost him around 42 cents—more than double the original retail price.

Making matters worse, farmers were forced to use their farms or their share of their crops as collateral to secure their loans. In effect, a lien was placed on their property, and the lien holder, or lender, was able to tell the farmer what crops to plant. Most often, that meant cotton, a nonperishable, readily marketable cash crop. Unfortunately, as more and more farmers planted cotton, the supply grew faster than the demand, and prices fell steadily. From 1866 to 1880, cotton prices plunged from 43 cents a pound to 12 cents. Before the end of the century, they would drop even further. Meanwhile, as lien holders demanded that indebted farmers and croppers plant cotton season after season, their nutrient-depleted land produced ever-smaller yields. Caught in a vicious cycle of ruinous interest, low prices, and declining yields, thousands of southern farmers faced forfeiture and eviction in the 1870s and 1880s.

As farmers sought an explanation for their plight, they increasingly focused on the North. Not only did their debts seemed to emanate from far-off northern bankers, but everywhere they looked, northern capital seemed to have a stranglehold on them. Since the end of the war, northern investors had poured huge amounts of capital into the South in industries such as railroads, iron and steel, textiles, mining, and coal, often with the encouragement of the Reconstruction governments. Like the American West, the South seemed to many northern businessmen and financiers a frontier ripe for exploitation. In many cases, this influx of capital yielded dramatic economic results. In the 1880s, railroad mileage in the South more than doubled—a growth rate much higher than the national rate. In the last quarter of the nineteenth century, southern pig iron production increased at more than twice the national rate. Yet northern bankers and industrialists controlled all southern industries except tobacco processing. Moreover, most of these industries were based on crude (rather than finished) processing of raw materials extracted from southern mines, forests, and farms. As a result, they employed large numbers of low-skill, low-wage workers. Under such conditions, it was easy for southerners to accuse northern capitalists of extracting profits from the South.

Indeed, in many ways the South was a captive economy, a colony of northeastern "interests." The steel industry is a good example. The U.S. Steel Corporation priced the output from its Birmingham, Alabama, mills on the basis of more expensive Pittsburgh steel. Then the company added the additional cost of shipping it from Pittsburgh, even though it was not made there. Therefore, Southern steel consumers were forced to pay higher prices for their cheaper steel. At the same time, many industrialists had secured protection from cheaper foreign competition with high tariffs. In effect, these import taxes allowed domestic manufacturers to raise prices, making their goods more expensive to consumers while increasing their profits. Southerners, who controlled little of the capital, reaped little of the benefit of the tariff. And southern farmers—still the overwhelming majority of the region's population—paid more for many of the goods purchased off the farm. As the financial condition of farmers worsened in the 1880s, many of them concluded that northern financial interests had shackled them as well.

Speaking to gatherings in rural Georgia, Watson began to express their economic concerns. Like the juries that he swayed so well, these audiences were composed of voters, and he knew how to appeal to them. He lashed out at the "vulture-like" commission merchants and lamented the "showers of gold" that entered the "pockets of men who never ran the cotton fields." By 1882, such language helped Watson win a seat in the Georgia legislature. There he fought unsuccessfully for impoverished tenant farmers and against the state's convict labor system. He also waged a losing battle to have taxes imposed on railroad property in the state. Finding "no happiness" in the legislature, Watson returned to his law practice after two years, but he did not leave the public stage. He continued to speak out against those who would "strip . . . the poor to pamper the rich"—railroads, banks, and other interests that he believed oppressed and impoverished Georgia's farmers. As he began to take aim at the men in the state who had sided with these "wolves," it was not long before Henry Grady came into his sights.

"Vast Hives of Industry"

Watson's background made him a natural spokesman for the South's downtrodden farmers. Henry Grady's upbringing also suited him perfectly to be the champion of its rising postwar business class. Born in Athens, Georgia, in 1850, Grady was the son of a prosperous merchant. He attended a private school run by the daughter of the University of Georgia's president. In 1861, he entered the University of Georgia, located in his hometown. His education was interrupted by the Civil War. Nonetheless, he continued to live in comfortable circumstances even after his father, a Unionist Democrat, lost his life serving in the Confederate army. While in college, Grady discovered a love for debate and oratory and threw himself into public speaking. Blessed with an exceptional memory, he was able to recite almost exactly an entire page after reading it just once. After graduating in 1868, he went to the University of Virginia as a graduate student with the idea of a career in politics. His immediate ambition, though, was to win the school's contest to be commencement speaker. After spending most of his spare time preparing for it, he lost the competition by three votes. Devastated, he decided to leave the university after his first year. He then decided to pursue a career in journalism.

Grady quickly succeeded in his chosen profession. In 1869, he became editor of a small newspaper in Rome, Georgia. He also married his childhood sweetheart, with whom he would have two children. Meanwhile, he submitted columns and articles to the Atlanta newspapers. In 1872, Grady became editor and part owner of the *Atlanta Daily Herald,* which eventually lost an expensive circulation war with the rival *Atlanta Constitution.* When the *Herald* folded in 1876, Grady became an Atlanta correspondent for the *New York Herald,* a successful freelance writer, and a contributor to the *Constitution*. By the late 1870s, he had also become interested in railroads and the economic development of the post-Reconstruction South. Atlanta had been founded before the Civil War as a rail center, and Grady was convinced that the rails held the key to the South's material progress.

In 1879, Grady covered the merger of several southern rail lines that promised to link Atlanta with other major rail centers. As a result, he made friends with Victor Newcomb of the Louisville & Nashville Railroad. Impressed by Grady and his reporting, Newcomb invited the journalist to travel with him by rail through thirteen states on a trip that ended on Wall Street. There Grady fell under the spell of the stock market and enthusiastically reported on the fortunes arising from "the Street." On the New York Stock Exchange, he declared, the "frenzy" of brokers and operators "kindles the blood of the looker-on as a battle would." In New York, Newcomb introduced Grady to Wall Street operator Cyrus W. Field, who agreed to lend the reporter twenty thousand dollars to purchase a one-quarter stake in the *Atlanta Constitution* and assist him with stock speculation to help pay back the loan. When the deal was consummated in 1880, Grady became managing editor of the paper.

Grady's engaging writing style and charming personality brought him more influential friends. By the early 1880s, he had become a backer of three powerful Georgia politicians: Joseph Brown, Alfred Colquitt, and John Gordon. Between 1872 and 1890, these men held seats as U.S. senator or governor of the state, trading these positions back and forth so often that they became known as Georgia's Democratic triumvirate. The trio also had been involved in overturning Republican Reconstruction and were associated with the industrial development of the South. They had profited handsomely from it. Brown was a backwoods plowboy who became president of several railroads and coal companies, part owner of an ironworks, and a multimillionaire. Colquitt, an industrial promoter, was associated with Gordon, a major railroad promoter, who resigned from the U.S. Senate in 1880 to work for Victor Newcomb's Louisville & Nashville Railroad. To the triumvirate, the promotion of the South's and their own prosperity was one and the same. As Brown told the Georgia legislature in 1880, his goal was "to build up the manufacturing interest of the country." By the early 1880s, Grady had become a vocal supporter of the triumvirate and the premier voice of southern boosterism.

From the pages of the *Constitution*, Grady issued a steady drumbeat for the economic development of the South through the investment of northern capital. He was especially fervent on behalf of Atlanta, which he envisioned as the capital city of the New South. He backed the International Cotton Exposition of 1881 and the Piedmont Exposition of 1887, conventions that promoted the city to capitalists. He even helped create Atlanta's first baseball team and served as the president of the Southern Baseball League. A baseball team, Grady believed, was a way not only to boost civic pride but also to unite with northerners. Yet he realized that an alliance with Yankee capitalists would require more than expositions and baseball teams. It would require an end to the lingering sectional antagonism between the North and South.

That was especially true after the election of 1884. With the victory of the Democratic candidate, Grover Cleveland, Republicans lost the presidency for the first time since the Civil War. After the election, many Republicans were convinced that the presidency could be regained only by winning back some Democratic states in the South. That, of course, could be achieved only if blacks were allowed to vote in large numbers. Many blacks had not yet been legally stripped of the right to vote under Democratic rule in the South, but large numbers were kept away from the polls by other means, including violence. When northerners called for federal supervision of southern elections, southern Democrats voiced their opposition. The so-called force bill controversy put new focus on racial violence in the South. It also raised suspicions among northern Republican businessmen about the South's ruling Democrats. And that, Grady feared, made northern investors leery about committing their capital to the South.

In the late 1880s, Grady went on the offensive to solve this problem. To save his dream of a new industrialized South, northerners and southerners had to be reconciled. And to do that, the South's race problem had to be confronted head-on. To allay lingering northern fears and stave off a force bill, white southerners had to demonstrate that they were the African Americans' "best friends." The alternative was to appease northern Republicans—and northern capital— by developing a two-party system in the solidly Democratic South and allowing large-scale black voting. Down that road, Grady believed, lay disaster. A two-party South would only divide white voters, bringing the return of Republican rule. That would put the balance of power in the hands of blacks—"an ignorant and dangerous class," according to Grady. Clearly, the South had to remain united behind white supremacy and Democratic rule. At the same time, however, it needed to burnish its image.

In 1886, Grady received an invitation to speak to the New England Society of New York, whose members included some of the most important industrialists and financiers in the nation. A number of them had investments in the South and were concerned about the sudden resurgence of sectional animosity. Using only a few notes scribbled on the back of a menu, he spoke to the more than three hundred guests, including financier J. P. Morgan, railroad tycoon Russell Sage, Standard Oil's Henry M. Flagler, and even General William T. Sherman, whose Union army had marched through Atlanta in 1864 and burned it to the ground. Grady's topic, "The New South," was evident from his opening lines. "There was a South of slavery and secession—that South is dead," he declared. "There is a South of union and freedom—that South, thank God, is living, breathing, growing every hour." After paying homage to Abraham Lincoln, he proceeded to paint an image of this New South. Southerners, he declared, had "planted the schoolhouse on the hilltop and made it free to black and white. We have sowed towns and cities in place of theories, and put business above politics." Rejecting the Old South and slavery, southerners had "fallen in love with work." And, Grady told the illustrious audience, southerners were working to solve the race issue with "honor and equity." **[See Source 1.]**

Grady's audience loved the speech, and New York's newspapers were aglow with praise the next day. Grady returned to Atlanta in triumph. When he arrived at the train station on Christmas Eve, he was greeted by a throng of a thousand or more people. Newspapers in the North and South began to call for Grady's nomination as President Cleveland's running mate in 1888. "This is, apparently, the first recorded instance," noted one paper, "in which an after-dinner oration . . . has been said to herald the way to the White House." Although the vice-presidential nomination never materialized, Grady's reputation as the chief spokesman for the New South was sealed. Meanwhile, he realized that his work had just begun and that he needed to direct his message to another key audience: white southerners.

In 1888, Grady delivered at the Texas State Fair in Dallas an address that had an impact comparable to his New York address two years earlier. Titled "The South and Its Problems," the election year speech urged southerners to embrace racial harmony. Racial equality, he declared, would be disastrous for the South. It would lead only to "assimilation" and the "debasement" of the white race. The "clear and unmistakable domination of the white race," he insisted, must be "maintained forever." That could not be achieved, however, through violence, which would alienate northerners and retard the development of the South. Racial "discord," he declared, "means ruin." Instead, the South needed to foster racial cooperation. And that would be easy, Grady believed, in the new, urban, industrial South. Given blacks' natural "inferiority," they could continue to work in agriculture. The "race that threatens our ruin," he observed, could "work our salvation as it fills our fields with the best peasantry the world has ever seen." Whites would then be free to work in the South's cities, which would become "vast hives of industry." The Dallas speech was read widely throughout the South, and enthusiastic crowds greeted Grady in Austin, San Antonio, Houston, Galveston, and New Orleans as he headed home to Atlanta.

"Made to Hate Each Other"

Grady held out a vision of a distant industrial paradise. To many farmers, though, it was nothing more than a mirage. In fact, by the late 1880s, an increasingly organized farmers' revolt was spreading across much of the nation. The expansion of agriculture in the West, foreign competition, and increasing mechanization had created a glut of goods and lower prices affecting farmers from Dixie to the Dakotas. Like their southern counterparts, northern farmers had to pay back bankers who charged high interest rates and were quick to foreclose on land offered as collateral. Meanwhile, a bushel of wheat that sold for $1.45 in 1866 brought only 80 cents in the mid-1880s. To deal with these horrible conditions, farmers in the Midwest and plains states formed the Northern Farmers' Alliance early in the decade. At the same time, their southern counterparts formed the Southern Farmers' Alliance, which claimed 3 million members, while the National Colored Farmers' Alliance boasted another 1.2 million members.

Grady realized that the alliances represented a threat as dangerous to the South as racial violence. With calls for public ownership of the railroads, a graduated income tax, reduced tariffs, and the coinage of silver,* the alliances had

---

Coinage of silver: Many farmers advocated expanding the gold-based money supply by coining silver. Expanding the amount of money in circulation with silver-backed money, they believed, would result in inflation, which would lift crop prices and make it easier for indebted farmers to pay their creditors.

attracted millions of poor farmers into organizations that could easily divide the white South. Confronting this growing agrarian anger, Grady took up the future of small white farmers. He also called for a balance between industry and agriculture. Yet he never offered specific solutions to farmers' grinding problems of debt and depressed prices. Instead, he merely blamed Republicans for the problems plaguing southern farmers and urged his audiences to remain politically united. [**See Source 2.**]

Tom Watson was not impressed. The more Watson listened to Grady's boosterism, the more suspicious he got. All the clamor about a "New South" seemed like nothing more than a cover for corporate exploitation. Speaking out around the state, Watson began to attack the very interests that Grady promoted. Bankers and industrialists stripped farmers of their dignity and their property. Southerners lived under a system that put the tenant farmer "in chains and stripes" because he "leaves his rent unpaid." At the same time, however, its "railroad kings" went unpunished. Capitalism's "consolidated empire" encouraged "the strong to oppress the weak." Instead of accepting the mirage of a New South, he called upon his audiences to stand "against tariff robbery, class legislation—the greed and growth of monopoly." Before any "big city editor" handed out advice, he declared, he should go to the rural areas and see firsthand the deplorable state of the farmer. "Mr. Grady in his great Dallas speech," he went on, "thinks that 'plenty rides on the Springing harvests!' It rides on Grady's springing imagination." The Atlanta editor's New South was "inspired clap-trap." [**See Source 3.**]

By the late 1890s, Watson was ready to reenter politics. As farmers' conditions steadily worsened, he caught a rising wave of agrarian anger. Running for Congress in 1890, he quickly endorsed the Farmers' Alliance program. "My interest," he declared, "is the same as theirs." His opponent in the Democratic primary, the president of a Georgia gas and streetcar company, did not have a chance. After handily winning the primary, Watson went on to crush his Republican opponent in the general election. By then, disgruntled alliance members and others had formed the Populist Party, which adopted the alliance program. Convinced that Grady, the Georgia triumvirate, and northern capital had hijacked the Democratic Party, Watson switched to the Populist Party, also called the People's Party, shortly after the election.

In Congress, Watson supported the Populist program, which called for the nationalization of railroads and telegraphs, the free coinage of silver, and a graduated income tax. [**See Source 4.**] He also worked to attract wage earners to the party. He supported a bill to investigate the bloody strike* by workers against the Carnegie steel company in Homestead, Pennsylvania. And he championed the Populists' demand for the passage of a law mandating an eight-hour workday. When railroad tycoon Jay Gould toured Georgia in 1891, Watson had a field day. "If the devil himself were to come to this town in a palace car," Watson said, "and proposed to haul the balance of the state to his

---

Bloody strike: In 1892, iron workers at the Carnegie company's Homestead, Pennsylvania, steel plant went on strike. When the company brought in three hundred Pinkerton detectives to protect strikebreakers, a gun battle broke out. Nine strikers and seven Pinkertons were killed.

infernal kingdom, and to allow Atlanta capitalists the profits on the transactions, they would cry, 'Hurrah for the devil. He's going to build up Atlanta!'" Such positions helped attract the support of some northern workers. Chief among them was Knights of Labor leader Terence Powderly, whose union had been crippled in a losing struggle against Gould. (See Chapter 2.) By 1892, the desperate union head was naturally attracted to the Populists' war against the very "interests" that the Knights had unsuccessfully opposed.

As the only Populist from the South in Congress, Watson also took the lead in formulating the party's policy toward blacks. He realized that poor black and white farmers had been polarized by the issue of race. Both groups were suffering from the same conditions and oppressed by the same forces, and "made to hate each other." Now the time had come to unite them on the common ground of class. **[See Source 5.]**

It was the fulfillment of Grady's worst nightmare. Agrarian unrest, Grady realized, could easily divide the South along class lines and end white unity behind the Democratic Party. The "agricultural and commercial interests," Grady said in 1889, "will find themselves in hopeless opposition." The result, he told twenty thousand alliance members at the Piedmont Exposition the same year, would be an end to the "clear and unmistakable domination of the white race." To Grady, the idea of a biracial political coalition was appalling. In late 1889, he addressed the Boston Merchants Association on the topic "The Race Problem in the South." Speaking to a crowd of prominent politicians and business leaders, including Andrew Carnegie, he again laid out his vision of a prosperous, industrialized New South and called on northerners to trust white southerners to deal with blacks fairly. The "love we feel for that race," he declared, "you cannot measure or comprehend." According to one Boston newspaper the next day, the speech had left two-thirds of the audience "in tears." The assembled guests did not know that Grady was ill with pneumonia. Although another huge crowd had turned out to greet his arrival back in Atlanta, by the time he arrived he was delirious and barely able to walk. Six days later, he died at the age of thirty-nine.

From the grave, Grady would get his revenge on Watson. Georgia's business class, of course, wanted to stamp out the growing Populist Party revolt. Thus when Watson ran for reelection in 1892, the state's Democratic press lined up against him, and the Democrats in the legislature redrew the boundaries to make his reelection more difficult. According to the *New York Tribune*, northern railroad and insurance companies funneled at least forty thousand dollars into Democratic coffers to defeat this "sworn enemy of capital." Watson's enemies also used election fraud to guarantee his defeat: His Democratic opponent received more than twice the number of votes legally possible in some districts. As if all that were not enough, the Democrats also resorted to violence. "They have intimidated the voter, assaulted the voter, murdered the voter," Watson wrote after the election. Even Georgia's governor allegedly declared that Watson "ought to be killed and that it ought to have been done long ago." To protect himself, the Populist surrounded himself with a bodyguard of armed men and carried a gun.

The Democrats' biggest weapon, though, was race. Like Grady, they well understood that the Populists threatened to end white supremacy in the South by dividing whites politically. As one Georgia newspaper put it, that was "the over-shadowing issue" of the campaign. They also knew that Watson had given them a potent weapon: white racial fears. Thus Watson's enemies accused the Populists of betraying their section and their race. Hecklers interrupted his campaign's inte-grated barbecues and threatened violence. Some of his black supporters were even murdered. The Democrats' tactics worked, and Watson was ousted from office.

Ironically, at the very moment of his defeat, Watson's day had finally ar-rived. By 1892, Populist fever was spreading rapidly across the South to the Great Plains and beyond. In that year, the party fielded its first presidential ticket. Then in 1893, the nation slid into the worst depression it had ever expe-rienced. With farm prices even lower than before and perhaps as many as 20 percent of the labor force out of work, the Populist message began to fall on many more receptive ears. Though out of office, Watson continued his attacks on the "interests" from the stump and in the pages of his weekly *People's Party Paper*. Politicians who did the bidding of industrialists came in for the worst re-buke. These men, Watson declared sarcastically, "agitat[e] the bowels of their compassion in behalf of the orphans who own the corporations." Such stinging rhetoric set Watson apart. Few Populists, including Kansans Mary Lease and Je-remiah "Sockless Jerry" Simpson and Minnesotan Ignatius Donnelly, were more able to rouse agrarian anger. And in the 1890s, that rising anger would shake the American political system to its foundations.

By the mid-1890s, the two major parties could no longer ignore the growing appeal of the Populists. Democrats were especially fearful that the agrarian in-surgency would undermine their party's traditional southern and rural sup-port. Therefore, in 1896 they nominated William Jennings Bryan of Nebraska as their presidential candidate. By speaking the language of hard-pressed farmers and advocating the coinage of silver, Bryan stole much of the Populists' thun-der. He also put the party in a bind. The Populists had to decide whether to "fuse" with the Democrats by nominating Bryan as their presidential candidate or nominate their own candidate. To Watson, Populists who endorsed fusion had placed too much emphasis on the silver issue at the expense of others. Bryan was not a true Populist, and the party needed to stick to its principles. En-dorsing the Democrat, he said, would be to "return as the hog did to its wal-low." But the fusionists believed that such a move represented the best hope for the Populists to get at least part of their program enacted.

It was a bitter battle, but the fusionists finally won the day. When Watson reluctantly went along to save the party, he was rewarded with a spot on the ticket as Bryan's Populist Party running mate. In effect, the Populists had staked their future on the success of the Bryan campaign. It was a risky bet. To attract voters in rural and small-town America, the Democrats had embraced part of the Populist agenda. At the same time, though, Bryan was unable to attract many urban, working-class voters. When the campaign was over, the probusiness Republican candidate, William McKinley, had triumphed and the Populists' gamble had failed. After the election, the Populist Party rapidly fell apart. Fu-sion and the return of prosperity at the end of the decade delivered blows from which it would not recover.

Watson was humiliated by his about-face on the issue of fusion. After the election, he withdrew from politics, convinced that he had been destroyed by a conspiracy of northern industrialists. Later he returned to the Democratic Party, and in the early 1900s became involved in Georgia politics. In 1906, an anticorporation lawyer named Hoke Smith ran for governor against a more conservative candidate. Watson threw his support to Smith in the Democratic primary even though Smith was in favor of the elimination of blacks from politics in Georgia. With his dream of a biracial Populist crusade shattered, Watson adjusted to the new political reality and embraced race hatred to rally white voters. In stinging editorials, he denounced blacks as "ungrateful" and declared that "Civilization" owed them "nothing." One disappointed northern admirer told Watson that his new position put him in "the same category with the men you censure"—that is, one "merely out for his own advantage." Watson was unmoved by such criticism.

In fact, after Smith won the election, Watson embraced racial politics with a vengeance. Now one of the most bigoted politicians in the South, he found numerous enemies to keep whites united. With violent rhetoric, he denounced socialists, communists, Catholics, blacks, and Jews. In 1915, he attacked a Jewish man named Leo Frank, who was unjustly accused of murder. The "next Jew who does what Frank did," Watson declared, "is going to get exactly the same thing that we give to Negro rapists." Such pronouncements helped lead to the lynching of Frank. Even so, in 1920, Watson won a seat in the U.S. Senate. "Never before," one writer observed after Watson's election, "has so conspicuous, so violent, so flaming an apostle of every variety of race hatred been invested with the power and dignity of the Senatorial toga." When Watson died two years later, the most lavish tribute at his funeral was an eight-foot-high cross of roses sent by the Ku Klux Klan.

Watson's career perfectly reflected the bitter racial settlement of the post-Populist South. Indeed, long before he died, the collapse of agrarian radicalism had sealed the political fate of blacks in the region. Frightened by the specter of poor white and black farmers uniting behind candidates such as Watson, southern Democrats played the "race card" to full effect. In the face of the growing biracial Populist threat, Democrats abandoned any pretense of Grady's New South racial moderation. Thus the same vicious racial charges and assaults that were leveled against Watson in 1892 were heard widely through the South by the mid-1890s. At the same time, the lynching of blacks skyrocketed. In this environment of heightened race hatred, the southern states moved to strip blacks of their voting rights. Across the South, literacy tests, poll taxes, and other devices had effectively disfranchised black voters by the early twentieth century.

If he had been alive, Henry Grady would not have been encouraged by the fate of either Watson or his beloved South. True, the Populist threat to the solidly white, Democratic South had been put down. From now on, the South would be divided by race rather than class. Indeed, the same year that Bryan went down to defeat, the Supreme Court upheld in *Plessy* v. *Ferguson** the constitutionality

---

Plessy v. *Ferguson:* The 1896 Supreme Court case in which the Court declared that as long as the public facilities provided for both races were equal, they could be separate. This "separate but equal" doctrine provided the legal foundation for the segregation of the races in public places until the 1950s.

of legal racial segregation. The South's solution to the "race problem"—a racial caste system ensuring white supremacy—had the blessings of the nation. But in many ways, Grady's New South dream had turned into a nightmare. The South had remained "solid" in its support of the Democratic Party, but not in the manner that he had envisioned. By the end of the century, as Watson so well demonstrated, white southerners had enforced their supremacy by sinking into a hate-filled morass of race baiting and lynching. And for all of Grady's banquet-room speeches, the South remained a largely agricultural economic backwater. Southern industry and southern cities continued to grow, but they would lag far behind the North's for decades to come. Likewise, much of the profit from southern industry continued to fall into the pockets of northerners. As a new century began, the South continued to be a place where the "strong" oppressed the "weak"—just as the Populist Watson had predicted.

PRIMARY SOURCES

Source 1:   Henry Grady, *"The New South"*   (1886)

Henry Grady's address "The New South," delivered in New York in 1886, is his most famous speech regarding his vision for the future of the region. According to this excerpt, what is new about the South?

We have established thrift in city and country. We have fallen in love with work. We have restored comfort to homes from which culture and elegance never departed. We have let economy take root and spread among us as rank as the crabgrass which sprung from Sherman's cavalry camps. . . . Above all we know that we have achieved in these "piping times of peace" a fuller independence for the South than that which our fathers sought to win in the forum by their eloquence or compel in the field by their swords.

It is a rare privilege, sir, to have had part, however humble, in this work. Never was nobler duty confided to human hands than the uplifting and up-building of the prostrate and bleeding South—misguided, perhaps, but beautiful in her suffering, and honest, brave and generous always. In the record of her social, industrial and political illustration we await with confidence the verdict of the world.

But what of the negro? Have we solved the problem he presents or progressed in honor and equity toward solution? Let the record speak to the point. No section shows a more prosperous laboring population than the negroes of the South, none in fuller sympathy with the employing and land-owning class. He shares our school fund, has the fullest protection of our laws and the friendship

Source: Reprinted in Ferald J. Bryan, *Henry Grady or Tom Watson: The Rhetorical Struggle for the New South, 1880–1890* (Macon, Ga.: Mercer University Press, 1994), pp. 103–104, 105; originally from *Atlanta Constitution*, December 22, 1886.

of our people. Self interest, as well as honor, demand that he should have this. Our future, our very existence depend upon our working out this problem in full and exact justice. We understand that when Lincoln signed the emancipation proclamation, your victory was assured, for he then committed you to the cause of human liberty, against which the arms of man cannot prevail—while those of our statesmen who trusted to make slavery the corner-stone of the Confederacy doomed us to defeat as far as they could, committing us to a cause that reason could not defend or the sword maintain in sight of advancing civilization.

. . . The relations of the southern people with the negro are close and cordial. We remember with what fidelity for four years he guarded our defenseless women and children, whose husbands and fathers were fighting against his freedom. To his eternal credit be it said that whenever he struck a blow for his own liberty he fought in open battle and when at last he raised his black and humble hands that the shackles might be struck off, those hands were innocent of wrong against his helpless charges, and worthy to be taken in loving grasp by every man who honors loyalty and devotion. Ruffians have maltreated him, rascals have misled him, philanthropists established a bank for him but the South, with the North, protests against injustice to this simple and sincere people. To liberty and enfranchisement is as far as law can carry the negro. The rest must be left to conscience and common sense. It must be left to those among whom his lot is cast, with whom he is indissolubly connected, and whose prosperity depends upon their possessing his intelligent sympathy and confidence. Faith has been kept with him, in spite of calumnious assertions to the contrary by those who assume to speak for us or by frank opponents. Faith will be kept with him in the future, if the South holds her reason and integrity. . . .

The old South rested everything on slavery and agriculture, unconscious that these could neither give nor maintain healthy growth. The new South presents a perfect democracy, the oligarchs leading in the popular movement—a social system compact and closely knitted, less splendid on the surface, but stronger at the core—a hundred farms for every plantation, fifty homes for every palace—and a diversified industry that meets the complex need of this complex age.

SOURCE 2:   Henry Grady, *"The Farmer and the Cities"*
(1889)

The rise of the Southern Farmers' Alliance in the 1880s was a disturbing development to Henry Grady because it threatened to disrupt the unity of the white South. What is his analysis of the problems facing farmers and what are his solutions to them?

SOURCE: Reprinted in Ferald J. Bryan, *Henry Grady or Tom Watson? The Rhetorical Struggle for the New South, 1880–1890* (Macon, Ga.: Mercer University Press, 1994), pp. 111, 118–119, 123–124; originally from *Atlanta Constitution,* July 26, 1889.

Now, here we are confronted with the most thorough and widespread agricultural movement of this or any other day. It is the duty alike of farmers and those who stand in other ranks, to get together and consult as to what is the real status and what is the patriotic duty. Not in sullenness, but in frankness. Not as opponents, but as friends—not as enemies, but as brothers begotten of a common mother, banded in common allegiance, and marching to a common destiny. It will not do to say that this organization will pass away, for if the discontent on which it is based survives it, it had better have lived and forced its wrongs to final issue. There is no room for divided hearts in this State, or in this Republic. If we shall restore Georgia to her former greatness and prosperity—if we shall solve the problems that beset the South in honor and safety—if we shall save this Republic from the dangers that threaten it—it will require the earnest and united effort of every patriotic citizen, be he farmer, or merchant, or lawyer, or manufacturer. Let us consider then the situation, and decide what is the duty that lies before us.

. . . [W]hen an outraged people turn to government for help what do they find? Their government in the hands of a party[1] that is in sympathy with their oppressors—that was returned to power with votes purchased with their money—and whose confessed leaders declared that trusts are largely private concerns with which the government had naught to do. Not only is the dominant party the apologist of the plutocrats and the beneficiary of their crimes, but it is based on that principle of centralization through which they came into life and on which alone they can exist. It holds that sovereignty should be taken from the States and lodged with the nation—that political powers and privileges should be wrested from the people and guarded at the capital. It distrusts the people, and even now demands that your ballot-boxes shall be hedged about by its bayonets. It declares that a strong government is better than a free government, and that national authority, backed by national armies and treasury, is a better guarantee of peace and prosperity and liberty and enlightenment diffused among the people. To defend this policy, that cannot be maintained by argument or sustained by the love or confidence of the people, it rallies under its flag the mercenaries of the Republic, the syndicate, the trust, the monopolist, and the plutocrat, and strengthening them by grant and protection, rejoices as they grow richer and the people grow poorer. . . .

Now, my friends, I am no farmer. I have not sought to teach you the details of your work, for I know little of them. I have not commended your splendid local advantages, for that I shall do elsewhere. I have not discussed the differences between the farmer and other classes, for I believe in essential things there is no difference between them, and that minor differences should be sacrificed to the greater interest that depends on a united people. I seek not to divide our people, but to unite them. I should despise myself if I pandered to the prejudice of either class to win the applause of the other.

But I have noted these great movements that destroy the equilibrium and threaten the prosperity of my country, and standing above passion and prejudice or demagoguery I invoke every true citizen, fighting from his hearthstone

---

1. The Republican Party.

outward, with the prattle of his children on his ear, and the hand of his wife and mother closely clasped, to determine here to make his home sustaining and independent, and to pledge eternal hostility to the forces that threaten our liberties, and the party that stands behind it.

SOURCE 3: *Tom Watson on "Silver-Tongued Orators"* (1889)

Tom Watson responded to Henry Grady's addresses with speeches of his own. What does this source reveal about the basis of Watson's appeal to many voters?

We are told in the splendid phraseology of silver-tongued orators from the city that our country is absolutely smothered under the plenteous flow of milk and honey of another Canaan. The city of Atlanta [is] especially noted for that kind of tom-foolery. Listening to the inspired clap-trap of some of its Politicians & Editors one would suppose that throughout the South there was no discomfort in the Present & no apprehension for the future.

Men who do not know the difference between a may pop* and a rabbit hunt find a poem in every boll of cotton, a romance in every ear of corn. . . . And yet our newspapers are absolutely crowded with advertisements of sheriffs' sales, and in the county of Richmond alone I noticed from the *Chronicle* that there were some two hundred [farms] for sale on the first Tuesday of November. . . . There is no romance in having landed property excluded from the banks, and in having twenty-five per cent upon our money; no romance in being fleeced by a fifty per cent tariff; no romance in seeing other classes and other properties exempted from taxation, and realizing fabulous dividends upon their investments, when the lands are taxed to their uttermost dollar and farming has paid no dividend since the war.

SOURCE 4: *People's Party Platform* (1892)

The Populist, or People's, Party platform of 1892 lays out a program for reform in the United States. What do the Populists want? How are they trying to reach out to workers?

May pop: A vine of the southeastern United States or the fruit of that vine.

SOURCE 3: Reprinted in C. Vann Woodward, *Tom Watson: Agrarian Rebel* (New York: Oxford University Press, 1963), p. 133; originally from The Watson Papers, University of North Carolina, Chapel Hill.

SOURCE 4: *The World Almanac 1893* (New York Press Pub. Co.: 1893), pp. 83–85.

While our sympathies as a party of reform are naturally upon the side of every proposition which will tend to make men intelligent, virtuous, and temperate, we nevertheless regard these questions, important as they are, as secondary to the great issues now pressing for solution, and upon which not only our individual prosperity but the very existence of free institutions depend; and we ask all men to first help us determine whether we are to have a republic to administer before we differ as to the conditions upon which it is to be administered, believing that the forces of reform this day organized will never cease to move forward until every wrong is remedied and equal rights and equal privileges securely established for all the men and women of this country. We declare, therefore—

First—that the union of the labor forces of the United States this day consummated shall be permanent and perpetual; may its spirit enter into all hearts for the salvation of the Republic and the uplifting of mankind.

Second—Wealth belongs to him who creates it, and every dollar taken from industry without an equivalent is robbery. "If any will not work neither shall he eat." The interests of rural and civil labor are the same; their enemies are identical.

Third—We believe that the time has come when the railroad corporations will either own the people or the people must own the railroads; and should the government enter upon the work of owning and managing any and all railroads, we should favor an amendment to the constitution by which all persons engaged in the government service shall be placed under a civil service regulation of the most rigid character. . . .

We demand free and unlimited coinage of silver and gold at the present legal ratio of 16 to 1.

We demand that the amount of the circulating medium be speedily increased to not less than $50 per capita. We demand a graduated income tax. . . .

We demand that postal savings banks be established by the government for the safe deposit of the earnings of the people and to facilitate exchange.

Transportation being a means of exchange and a public necessity, the government should own and operate the railroads in the interest of the people.

The telegraph and telephone, like the post office system, being a necessity for the transmission of news, should be owned and operated by the government in the interest of the people.

The land, including all the natural sources of wealth, is the heritage of the people, and should not be monopolized for speculative purposes, and alien ownership of land should be prohibited. All land now held by railroads and other corporations in excess of their actual needs, and all lands now owned by aliens should be reclaimed by the government and held for actual settlers only. . . .

Whereas, other questions have been presented for our consideration, we hereby submit the following, not as a part of the platform of the people's party, but as resolutions expressive of the sentiment of this convention. . . .

Resolved, That we condemn the fallacy of protecting American labor under the present system, which opens our ports to the pauper and criminal classes of the world and crowds out our wage earners; and we denounce the present ineffective laws against contract labor, and demand the further restriction of undesirable emigration.

. . . Resolved, That we cordially sympathize with the efforts of organized workingmen to shorten the hours of labor, and demand a rigid enforcement of existing eight-hour law on government work, and ask that a penalty clause be added to the said law. . . .

Resolved, That we oppose any subsidy or national aid to any private corporation for any purpose.

SOURCE 5:   Tom Watson, *The Negro Question in the South* (1892)

Tom Watson helped create the Populist Party as an alternative to Henry Grady's New South vision. In this speech, he lays out his strategy for the new party and addresses the issue of race. What does Watson believe will end the racial problems of the South?

Having given this subject much anxious thought, my opinion is that the future happiness of the two races will never be assured until the political motives which drive them asunder, into two distinct and hostile factions, can be removed. There must be a new policy inaugurated, whose purpose is to allay the passions and prejudices of race conflict, and which makes its appeal to the sober sense and honest judgment of the citizen regardless of his color. . . .

The white people of the South will never support the Republican Party. This much is certain. The black people of the South will never support the Democratic Party. This is equally certain.

Hence, at the very beginning, we are met by the necessity of new political alliances. As long as the whites remain solidly Democratic, the blacks will remain solidly Republican.

As long as there was no choice, except as between the Democrats and the Republicans, the situation of the two races was bound to be one of antagonism. The Republican Party represented everything which was hateful to the whites; the Democratic Party, everything which was hateful to the blacks.

Therefore a new party was absolutely necessary. It has come, and it is doing its work with marvelous rapidity.

Why does a Southern Democrat leave his party and come to ours?

Because his industrial condition is pitiably bad; because he struggles against a system of laws which have almost filled him with despair; because he is told that he is without clothing because he produces too much cotton, and without food because corn is too plentiful; because he sees everybody growing rich off the products of labor except the laborer; because the millionaires who manage the Democratic Party have contemptuously ignored his plea for a redress of grievances and have nothing to say to him beyond the cheerful advice to "work harder and live closer."

SOURCE: Thomas E. Watson, "The Negro Question in the South," *Arena*, October 1892, pp. 544–546, 547, 548.

Why has this man joined the PEOPLE'S PARTY? Because the same grievances have been presented to the Republicans by the farmer of the West, and the millionaires who control that party have replied to the petition with the soothing counsel that the Republican farmer of the West should "work more and talk less." . . .

The key to the new political movement called the People's Party has been that the Democratic farmer was as ready to leave the Democratic ranks as the Republican farmer was to leave the Republican ranks. . . .

The very same principle governs the race question in the South. The two races can never act together permanently, harmoniously, beneficially, till each race demonstrates to the other a readiness to leave old party affiliations and to form new ones, based upon the profound conviction that, in acting together, both races are seeking new laws which will benefit both. On no other basis under heaven can the "Negro Question" be solved. . . .

The People's Party will settle the race question. First by enacting the Australian ballot system.* Second, by offering to white and black a rallying point which is free from the odium of former discords and strifes. Third, by presenting a platform immensely beneficial to both races and injurious to neither. Fourth, by making it to the *interest* of both races to act together for the success of the platform. Fifth, by making it to the *interest* of the colored man to have the same patriotic zeal for the welfare of the South that the whites possess. . . .

The white tenant lives adjoining the colored tenant. Their houses are almost equally destitute of comforts. Their living is confined to bare necessities. They are equally burdened with heavy taxes. They pay the same high rent for gullied and impoverished land. . . .

Now the People's Party says to these two men, "You are kept apart that you may be separately fleeced of your earnings. You are made to hate each other because upon that hatred is rested the keystone of the arch of financial despotism which enslaves you both. You are deceived and blinded that you may not see how this race antagonism perpetuates a monetary system which beggars both."

This is so obviously true it is no wonder both these unhappy laborers stop to listen. No wonder they begin to realize that no change of law can benefit the white tenant which does not benefit the black one likewise; that no system which now does injustice to one of them can fail to injure both. Their every material interest is identical. The moment this becomes a conviction, mere selfishness, the mere desire to better their conditions, escape onerous taxes, avoid usurious charges, lighten their rents, or change their precarious tenements into smiling, happy homes, will drive these two men together, just as their mutually inflamed prejudices now drive them apart.

---

*Australian ballot system: A ballot that ensures secrecy in voting. It was an issue for the Populists because without it, white southerners could easily intimidate black voters.

Questions to Consider

1. Based on the essay and sources in this chapter, how would you compare Tom Watson's and Henry Grady's visions for the late-nineteenth-century South? How did Grady define the New South? What were Watson's main goals?

2. What major factors or influences in the lives of Watson and Grady shaped their views? What were their primary fears? What do those fears reveal about the divisions within southern society in the late nineteenth century?

3. What role did race play in shaping the plans of Watson and Grady? What impact did their battle have on African Americans?

4. Was Watson's or Grady's vision for the South more realistic? What were the main obstacles to the fulfillment of each man's vision?

For Further Reading

Ferald J. Bryan, *Henry Grady or Tom Watson?: The Rhetorical Struggle for the New South, 1880–1890* (Macon, Ga.: Mercer University Press, 1994), is a useful study of the debate between these two southern visionaries and includes the full text of some of their important speeches.

Harold E. Davis, *Henry Grady's New South: Atlanta, a Brave and Beautiful City* (Tuscaloosa: University of Alabama Press, 1990), emphasizes the importance of Atlanta in Grady's thinking.

Lawrence Goodwyn, *Democratic Promise: The Populist Movement in America* (New York: American Philological Society, 1976), interprets late-nineteenth-century agrarian radicalism as a democratic reform movement.

Stephen Hahn, *The Roots of Southern Populism: Yeomen Farmers and the Transformation of the Georgia Upcountry, 1850–1890* (New York: Oxford University Press, 1983), provides an interpretation of the populist movement in Watson and Grady's home state.

C. Vann Woodward, *Tom Watson: Agrarian Rebel* (1938; reprint, New York: Oxford University Press, 1963), is the classic biography of Watson.

Sex, Anarchism, and Domestic Science in Progressive America: Emma Goldman and Ellen Richards

As Emma Goldman lay in bed, she made her decision. Goldman and her lover were down to their last couple of dollars. They needed money immediately, and she knew there was one quick way to raise it. She would become a prostitute. The decision to sell her body was not easy, but there seemed to be no other choice. So Goldman took to the streets of New York to join the other solicitors. As it happened, her career as a streetwalker was very short. Her first and only client told her that she had chosen the wrong line of work. Speechless, Goldman watched the man get up before she had a chance to return the ten dollars he had given her for services never rendered. Goldman must have thought about that experience often as she spoke out about marriage in the early twentieth century. In fact, for this vocal anarchist, marriage and prostitution were one and the same. The social and economic inequality of women made the institution of marriage the equivalent of the "oldest profession." The only difference was whether a woman sold herself to one man or to many. In either case, she declared, women were "looked upon as a mere sex commodity." To achieve true equality and freedom, therefore, women needed to be liberated from this oppressive social institution.

Ellen Richards could not have agreed—and disagreed—more. Marriage, Richards believed, was a unique economic arrangement that had a harmful impact on women. Yet that was the extent of her agreement with Goldman on the matter of matrimony. The leading force behind the growing field of home economics, Richards also believed that women could be a powerful force for social improvement simply by performing their domestic duties better. Indeed, she said, the great opportunity for women lay in embracing their unique place within marriage. Women certainly did not need to compete with men as equals. They did not even need to have the right to vote. Rather, by applying scientific principles to household management, they would professionalize their domestic duties and thus exercise enormous power both in and out of the home.

By the early twentieth century, important economic and social changes were reshaping the lives of many women. During the period of progressive reform between the turn of the century and World War I, Goldman and Richards

❖❖ *Emma Goldman*   ❖❖ *Ellen Richards*

illustrated the impact of these changes. Both reflected the Progressive era's optimism about the potential of women for assuming new roles in American society. Like many progressives, Richards saw greater efficiency and education as keys to social improvement. Like many radicals, Goldman put her faith in a dramatic restructuring of social institutions. One worked for small improvements, the other for the wholesale destruction of the existing order. Both challenged important gender barriers and would become well known as a result. In the end, though, their visions for women could not have been more different.

"A Dangerous Person"

Ellen Richards believed in education and efficiency. As an adult, she worked tirelessly to stop waste and save time, resources, and energy. She was driven by a belief that social betterment would occur by performing even the most mundane chores with greater intelligence and efficiency. Perhaps this assumption stemmed in part from her rural New England upbringing. Born Ellen Swallow in 1842, she grew up on a boulder-strewn Massachusetts farm whose stubborn soil only reluctantly yielded a modest living. For her parents, sixth-generation New Englanders, waste and extravagance were unthinkable. Her stern and reserved father was sparing even in his approval of his only child—the object of the couple's devotion.

Ellen's upbringing also reflected the Swallows' Yankee respect for education. Ellen's parents were teachers, and they sacrificed to provide her with a good education. In fact, they even moved to a nearby town so that Ellen could attend school there. Their emphasis on learning had an obvious impact on her. She did so well in school that instructors asked her to tutor other students. After graduation, she went to work as a teacher. One of the only careers open to women, it was also an appropriate choice. As she put it later, she loved to "make the little ideas shoot." Without realizing it, she had found her life's work in educating others.

In fact, Swallow fell into a depression when her mother's declining health cut her teaching experience short. Her father needed her help in the general store he had opened, so for two years she nursed her mother, kept her father's books, and hired herself out to families to cook, clean, and tutor. All the while, she skimped and saved. "I lived for more than two years in purgatory," she said later. She endured long periods of lethargy and was eventually diagnosed with neurasthenia, a condition that late-nineteenth-century physicians frequently reported among their female patients. Characterized by weakness, irritability, anxiety, and various pains, it was believed to result from the physical weakness of women. Too much mental activity, many physicians thought, drew blood from the female nervous system and reproductive organs. Widespread reports of neurasthenia among educated, upper-middle-class women reinforced a common assumption that higher education could damage a woman's health. In fact, most of these disorders were probably psychosomatic, resulting primarily from a sense of confinement. The social reformer and settlement house founder Jane Addams, for instance, was a neurasthenic invalid until she left her family and threw herself into life outside the home. Swallow's experience was similar. During her own confinement, she constantly complained of feeling tired or sick. But when her "purgatory" ended, so did all of her symptoms.

In 1868, at age twenty-five, Swallow enrolled at Vassar College in upstate New York. There she joined a small but rapidly growing group of women who sought higher education. Established in 1861, Vassar was the nation's first academically oriented, well-funded college for women. In the coming years, it would be followed by others such as Wellesley, Smith, Bryn Mawr, and Radcliffe—all modeled on the elite, all-male Ivy League colleges. These female institutions and a growing number of coeducational state universities reflected the increasing acceptance of higher education for women in the late nineteenth century. In part, this was the result of the growing feminization of teaching. It was also due to the abdication of higher education by many males who believed that such schooling was unnecessary for a career in the masculine world of business. At the same time, female higher education remained controversial. Many critics continued to fear that it would make women unsuitable for marriage by imparting too much learning, destroying their health, and even driving them to insanity.

There was no need to worry about Swallow's health. Admitted to Vassar as a junior, she thrived. She threw herself wholeheartedly into her courses, especially her true love—chemistry. Granted a bachelor's degree in 1870, Swallow tried to find work as a chemical analyst, but without success. "I have tried several doors . . . but they won't open," she wrote a friend. The frustrated Swallow faced the same question that many other female college graduates encountered: what to do after college. Excluded from the professions and business, college-educated women found no accepted role other than teaching.

Swallow solved that problem by going back to college. Determined to pursue chemistry as her "life study," she became the first woman to enter the Massachusetts Institute of Technology (MIT). When she enrolled at the end of 1870, she was not entirely welcome. MIT waived her tuition, but only because administrators did not wish to show a female student on the school's rolls. Quickly adapting to life in this male bastion, Swallow was careful to "roil no waters." She learned never to be too assertive or competitive and kept herself deliberately plain in appearance. At the same time, she excelled. In 1873, she became the first woman to receive a degree from the institution. The same year, Vassar awarded her a master's degree. Although she was determined to earn a Ph.D. in chemistry from MIT, officials there, fearful of the "disastrous effect on the young men," prevented her from enrolling in the program. As one of her professors recalled long after, "She was treated for some time as a dangerous person."

When administrators agreed to let Swallow work as a lab assistant, she decided to remain despite the discrimination she had encountered. One reason was her growing relationship with Robert Richards, a mining and metallurgy professor at MIT. After the two were married in 1875, Ellen continued her work in chemistry at the school. The following year, she established a women's chemistry laboratory at MIT. By the time the school began the equal admission of women seven years later, Ellen Richards had become an instructor of sanitary chemistry. Committed to the education of women, she served in the coming years as the unofficial "dean of women," founded a campus women's club, and helped female students find financial assistance. In 1882, she also helped create the Association of Collegiate Alumnae (later called the American Association of University Women), which worked to make higher education more widely available to women. At the same time, however, she was increasingly frustrated in her own career. Though a nationwide leader in the field of water treatment, she received only one small promotion. "I might have made a name and fame for myself," she complained to a friend in 1889. "I have helped five men to positions they would not have held without me."

Richards's frustration was compounded by her firm conviction that women needed to understand science and be able to apply it to their own lives. In the practical application of science, she saw enormous possibilities for social improvement. Women could be trained to use mathematical skills in the purchasing of food and household items and in preparing nutritional meals with proper calories and nutrients. They could use chemistry to understand the ingredients in food and cleaners and to see the importance of sanitation. The result would be greater efficiency, better food, and cleaner houses. Stymied in her career, Richards sought a wider audience with missionary zeal. She began to deliver lectures on the practical application of chemistry in the "household economy." She published books with titles such as *The Chemistry of Cooking and Cleaning* (1882) and *Food Materials and Their Adulterations* (1885). She even set up a model kitchen to demonstrate her ideas for proper nutrition and scientific household management.

Before long, Richards found herself at the forefront of a growing movement to transform housework into a specialized field of study—a "domestic science." By the beginning of the twentieth century, a host of textbooks, as well as popular publications such as the *Ladies' Home Journal* and *Good Housekeeping*, were calling for a more scientific approach to housekeeping. At the same time, many high schools and colleges began offering domestic science courses or established housekeeping "experiment stations" to test new techniques of housework and new "scientific" approaches to spending. The energetic Richards had much to do with the growing vogue of home economics. She was one of the founders of the Lake Placid conferences, held from 1899 to 1908, where "domestic scientists" met to discuss and define their field of study. She also helped found the American Home Economics Association in 1908 and was elected the organization's first president.

Richards's work was not the sole reason for the growing popularity of "domestic science" at the turn of the twentieth century. Rather, the home economics movement reflected the concerns and assumptions of progressive reformers and was boosted by them. Progressives battled a host of social, political, and economic ills, from political corruption and the concentrated power of big business to inadequate or dangerous living and working conditions. Through moderate change, they believed, the worst abuses of an urban, industrial society could be eliminated. Imbued with a belief in the power of the environment to shape people, they sought to apply modern scientific and management techniques to reshape institutions. They also shared the new industrial society's faith in greater efficiency as a means of improvement. Thus they frequently turned to the guidance of "trained experts" who would uplift society by replacing traditional practices with "rational" or scientific standards and procedures. In many ways, the domestic science movement represented the extension of progressive reform into middle-class households.

Important changes in those households further reinforced the appeal of "scientific" housekeeping. By the turn of the century, industrialization had made it possible for women to buy an array of household items formerly made in the home. Technological advances such as indoor plumbing, furnaces, gas stoves, refrigerators, and electricity for lamps, washing machines, and other household appliances had dramatically changed the homemaker's life. As Richards put it in 1908, "The flow of industry has passed and left idle the loom in the attic, the sap kettle in the shed." Invaded by factory goods and new technology, the middle-class home became a center of consumption.

Women were most dramatically affected by the removal of production from the home. Lightened household chores made it easier for many women to seek work outside the home. Between 1880 and 1910, the number of female office workers increased from roughly 8,000 to nearly 600,000. In the same years, urbanization led to lower birthrates. One-quarter of the women who married between 1880 and 1910 had only one or two children. These changes stimulated new expectations regarding marriage. Declining birthrates were an indication, for instance, that women exercised greater control over sexual relations within marriage. Moreover, in the last decade of the nineteenth century, the divorce rate rose three times as fast as the rate of population increase, with most of the demands for divorce coming from women.

These trends combined to make the family and women's proper roles frequent topics of discussion by academics, journalists, and politicians. Some argued that women should be further liberated from housekeeping duties. Feminist Charlotte Perkins Gilman, for instance, proposed new living arrangements for women, including cooperative kitchens and homes without kitchens to free women to pursue careers outside the home. Yet many people believed that women were largely responsible for the problems of rising divorce rates and falling birthrates. According to traditionalists such as Theodore Roosevelt, women, by abandoning their proper roles in the home, threatened not only the family but also the "Anglo-Saxon race." The popular press was filled with alarms about "race suicide," a term that reflected fears about the overwhelming of native American stock by rapidly multiplying immigrants.

Many academic and popular commentators also linked the disturbing trends of rising divorce rates and falling birthrates to women's new role as consumer. Faced with the need to purchase a host of goods, they concluded, many women were lured to jobs outside the home in search of higher incomes. One University of Pennsylvania sociologist concluded in 1911 that "domestic institutions" were under a "burdensome strain" because of the modern need to "purchase many things formerly produced within the family itself." The conclusion was obvious: Rising material wants had caused a "growing crisis in home life." Thus, to save the family and the "race," women needed to do more than stay in the home. They needed special training as homemakers and especially as spenders.

By professionalizing housekeeping, the home economics movement promised to provide that training. As a growing number of women entered the workplace, the movement provided a powerful rationale for women to remain in their homes at their own profession. At a time of rising expectations on the part of women, it elevated women's role within the home by turning housewives into "efficient" household "managers." By converting the household into a business, home economics also promised to give women more power in the home. Because the modern household, like the factory, required a rational division of labor, women could think of their domestic duties as equal to their husbands' jobs outside the home. Women would oversee consumption, while men were responsible for production. Thus the woman was to be "the comptroller of consumption," "a good purchasing agent," or "a director of consumption." In short, domestic science dignified housework by turning the housewife into a "business partner" of the husband.

Few preachers of the domestic science gospel reflected its Progressive-era assumptions better than Ellen Richards. Like many other progressives, she was convinced that the social environment could be improved through the application of scientific principles. In fact, she gave the idea a new name: euthenics. Unlike eugenics, the movement to improve the human species by controlling heredity, euthenics was the "science of controllable environment." **[See Source 1.]** And nowhere was such control more imperative, Richards believed, than in the area of spending. Because consumers had "no real standard of value," she declared, their choices had to be "widely directed" by trained experts. Rather than being guided by advertisers, material wants could be socially guided to avoid the "temptations to buy needless articles." Such wise spending would promote domestic harmony by reducing the need for a second income. Keeping women in the home and placing it under rational or scientific management would thus solve numerous Progressive-era social ills. **[See Source 2.]** Elevated as trained "scientists," housewives could escape their husbands' domination. Reflecting the heightened expectations of women at the turn of the century, Richards and her movement suggested that housewives could achieve independence not by leaving the home but by staying in it. Women did not even need to participate directly in politics by winning the right to vote. As Richards put it, home economics demonstrated "that woman has a personality that is not in her husband's control."

"Free Love and Bombs"

Emma Goldman wanted nothing to do with the calls of Ellen Richards and other home economists for elevating women within marriage. Nor did she accept the demands of feminists such as Charlotte Perkins Gilman, who envisioned the liberation of women from domestic chores through new living arrangements. Goldman believed there was only one solution to the inequality that women confronted in the early twentieth century: freeing them from marriage itself. Only through emotional or psychological liberation would women ever be equal. And to achieve that, they first had to be sexually liberated. In an age that embraced moderate reform through greater efficiency and the application of scientific principles, few Americans offered a more radical prescription for changing women's roles than Goldman.

If Emma Goldman was no conventional thinker, perhaps it was because she had always been in many ways an outsider. Born in 1869 in Lithuania to Jewish parents, she grew up in czarist Russia, where Jews were marginalized and persecuted by an authoritarian regime. The Goldmans' economic status was no more secure. Emma's parents kept an inn and a small shop, but they were always in danger of losing their tenuous hold on the middle class due to financial setbacks. Even inside her family, there was no security. Emma's father had dreamed of having a son and never forgave Emma for being a girl. In an "atmosphere charged with antagonism and harshness," she grew so rebellious that not even her father's whip could control her. When she was seven, her parents sent her to live with an aunt and uncle, who proved even more abusive than her father. Later, she learned to rebel against the domineering teachers in her public school. In St. Petersburg, where the family moved when Emma was twelve, life was little more secure. When her father's business failed, Emma was forced to work in a garment factory. About the same time, she had her first sexual encounter when a young hotel clerk raped her. After this experience, she confessed later, she "always felt between two fires in the presence of men. Their lure remained strong, but it was always mingled with violent revulsion."

The repression in her family and the growing persecution of Jews in Russia led Goldman to flee both. In 1885, at age sixteen, she was on a boat bound for the United States. There she joined her older sister, who was married and already living in Rochester, New York. Emma found work in a factory at four dollars a week and quickly met and fell in love with a coworker, another young Jewish immigrant. Just as quickly, though, she discovered that her marriage, like her adopted land, was no paradise. Already drawn to political radicalism in Russia, she began to follow the trial of the eight anarchists accused of the Haymarket Square bombing* in Chicago, which had left seven police officers dead.

Haymarket Square bombing: The bombing of police officers at a labor demonstration in Chicago's Haymarket Square in 1886. The protest had been called by anarchists in response to the earlier killing of several strikers by police at the McCormick harvester works.

Convinced that the accused men were innocent, Goldman was totally engrossed by the trial, the men's convictions, and the execution of four of them. She also discovered an anarchist publication that followed the trial closely. It immediately struck a responsive chord in her. Tired of working in the factory, unhappy in her marriage, and longing for more, Goldman fled Rochester for New York City in 1889. There she joined an anarchist group and threw herself wholeheartedly into the movement.

For Goldman, by now disdainful of all forms of repression, it was a perfect fit. Anarchists denounced all forms of authority as they held up the ideal of absolute equality and individual freedom. In the anarchist vision, a society without government, private property, or any sort of repression would one day emerge. These beliefs made anarchists the most extreme political group of the late nineteenth and early twentieth centuries. Unlike many socialists,* anarchists rejected reforms such as the eight-hour workday and other social legislation as piecemeal. They also rejected the strategy of many socialists to work within the political system, which they believed was part of the problem. At the same time, they disagreed with Marxists,* who believed in the establishment of a working-class dictatorship as a way to achieve a stateless, classless, communist utopia. Anarchists believed that a society completely free of state authority could be achieved without such a period of dictatorship. They were divided, however, on the means. Some anarchists were peaceful and emphasized the formation of small, individualist communities where self-government was the only law. Others believed that the stateless utopia could not be born without violence, which led them to commit bombings, sabotage, and assassinations.

Goldman herself turned to violence when she helped plan an assassination with another Russian Jewish immigrant, named Alexander Berkman. She first met Berkman in a café where they attended anarchist meetings. Divorced now, Goldman was immediately attracted to Berkman, and the two became lovers. With two other young women, they formed a small commune in an apartment in New York. Meanwhile, Berkman preached what he called "propaganda by deed." With the help of Goldman and several others, he planned to put the idea into action by assassinating Henry Clay Frick, the manager of Andrew Carnegie's* steel mills, who had recently ordered three hundred Pinkerton detectives to help break up a strike by thousands of ironworkers at Homestead, Pennsylvania. The result had been a gun battle that had left seven Pinkertons and nine strikers dead. To raise money for Berkman's plot, Goldman took to the streets to sell her body. As it turned out, Berkman's attempt to kill Frick was no more

---

Socialists: Adherents of the belief that the productive assets of a society should be owned either all or in part by the state. Unlike communists, most early-twentieth-century socialists believed in achieving a socialist state through peaceful means and often endorsed more moderate reforms to address the social and economic ills of a capitalist society.

Marxists: Followers of the German-born economic philosopher Karl Marx, who looked forward to the abolition of capitalism and private property.

Andrew Carnegie: The owner of the Carnegie Steel Company, who amassed an immense fortune in the late nineteenth century, paid his workers meager wages, and preached the right of labor unions to organize while he was supporting union-busting tactics.

successful than Goldman's attempt at prostitution. Although Berkman shot and stabbed Frick, the Carnegie lieutenant survived, and his would-be assassin was tried, convicted, and put in prison in 1892. Goldman was never implicated in the plot, even though she had assisted in it.

After the failed murder attempt, Goldman gave up on violence as a political method. She continued to promote what she called "direct action" but explained that this meant nonviolent agitation. In the depression year of 1893, she emerged as a leader of demonstrations for the poor and hungry. With more than three million people unemployed nationwide, she urged a crowd at a New York City hunger demonstration to "go and get" bread. Three days later, at a similar demonstration, she urged the unemployed to take food if they needed it. About a week later, the authorities arrested Goldman and charged her with inciting a riot. Tried and convicted, she was sentenced to a year in prison. Upon her release, she continued to preach the anarchist gospel in speeches, demonstrations, and writings.

By the turn of the century, Goldman's activism had made her one of the best-known—and most notorious—anarchists in the nation. In 1901, when an anarchist assassinated President William McKinley, she was arrested for inspiring the assassin. Though freed for lack of evidence, she was in many quarters a hated woman. Her radical political and social ideas, spread in her monthly magazine *Mother Earth* and in speeches around the country, shocked Americans. "She was considered a monster," recalled a friend later, "an exponent of free love and bombs."

That assessment was only half right. Although she had given up on bombs, Goldman did preach free love. "If the world is ever to give birth to true companionship and oneness," she declared, "not marriage, but love will be the parent." At the same time, she practiced what she preached. While working to secure Berkman's release from prison, she entered into a long affair with another anarchist, named Edward Brady, who was also working to free Berkman. When Brady wanted her to become a wife and mother, however, she adamantly refused. Later, during a long-term relationship with a physician named Ben Reitman, she refused similar entreaties. Marriage, she insisted, was "primarily an economic arrangement" that stripped women of their rights and their humanity and perpetuated women's role as a "sex commodity." For each woman, the price of this arrangement was "her name, her privacy, her self-respect, her very life." Women had to throw off the bonds of tradition and seek new ways of relating to men and one another. Marriage, she insisted, kept women in a state of oppression and sexual exploitation. **[See Source 3.]**

Calling for a complete overturning of gender relations, Goldman dismissed the importance of winning the vote for women. In fact, concentrating on suffrage, she argued, only impeded fundamental social and economic changes. In a capitalist society, politics was inevitably dominated by powerful economic interests. The solution to the "woman problem" was not in access to the voting booth, which at best could change only "external realities." The only way women could ever be liberated, she insisted, was by overthrowing "internal tyrants." "True emancipation," she wrote, "begins neither at the polls nor in court. It begins in a woman's soul." Thus women had to free themselves "from the fear of public opinion and public condemnation." Only such psychological liberation would ultimately set women free. **[See Source 4.]**

"The All Powerful Ballot"

Goldman's position on woman suffrage, like Ellen Richards's, set her apart from the growing number of women committed to achieving voting rights. Led by reformers such as Jane Addams, longtime suffragists such as Elizabeth Cady Stanton and Susan B. Anthony, and younger suffrage leaders such as Carrie Chapman Catt, the largely middle-class woman suffrage movement had come of age by the turn of the century. Membership in the most prominent suffrage organization, the National American Woman Suffrage Association, jumped from thirteen thousand in 1893 to roughly seventy-five thousand in 1910. By then, the movement had been boosted by the rising expectations of many women and by the rise of progressive reform. Many progressives believed that social problems could be solved through the ballot box. The "people," properly educated and armed with the vote, could wrest control of the government from the "special interests" and then clean up politics and society. Thus Catt and other suffragists cleverly played on the nineteenth-century assumption that women were the guardians of moral virtue. Giving women the vote, they argued, would actually help end corruption. Women would serve as the "house-keepers" of politics: Armed with the vote, they would help clean up politics and promote progressive causes such as pure water, better sanitation, safe food, and law enforcement.

Goldman disagreed. It made no difference, she argued, whether women voted. Women were not morally superior to men, nor could a thoroughly corrupt political system ever be cleansed. To assume that a woman "would succeed in purifying something which is not susceptible of purification," she declared, "is to credit her with supernatural powers." In fact, far more important than a woman's right to enter the voting booth, she believed, was the right to determine when she would become pregnant. The decision to have a baby went to the very root of women's emancipation. Sex, she argued, should be for pleasure as well as for procreation. Thus birth control methods should be freely available to women. Only then could they prevent the unwanted pregnancies that often sentenced them to lives of toil and tyranny at the hands of husbands who monopolized them.

By 1914, Goldman had become a vocal supporter of the movement to legalize birth control led by Margaret Sanger. A nurse who worked in New York City's immigrant neighborhoods, Sanger had witnessed the deaths of numerous women who underwent back-alley abortions. In the early twentieth century, she took up the cause of contraception as a way to save lives and help poor women alleviate the financial hardship of having too many children. Goldman championed birth control for those reasons and to make women into more than "mere object[s]." **[See Source 5.]** After Sanger was arrested in 1914 for violating the Comstock Act—the 1873 statute that made it illegal to mail "obscene" material, including information on abortion and contraception—Goldman began to disseminate birth control information in public. In 1916, she was charged with violating a New York law that made it a crime to distribute "any recipe, drug, or medicine for the prevention of conception" and was sentenced to fifteen days in jail.

News of Goldman's arrest sparked increased interest in the birth control movement throughout the country. Before long, though, Goldman moved on to other, more "vital" issues. When the United States entered World War I in 1917, she turned her attention to antiwar and antidraft protests. That year, she was sent to prison for her opposition to the draft. Released in 1919 during the Red Scare,* she was deported, along with hundreds of others, to Russia. She spent the next two decades in exile, increasingly alienated from other anarchists and radicals. Only with her burial in Chicago after her death in 1940 did she return permanently to her adopted land.

The year after Goldman was deported, women nationwide finally won the right to vote with the ratification of the Nineteenth Amendment. Yet by the time Goldman was laid to rest two decades later, she may very well have felt vindicated regarding woman suffrage. Despite women's entrance into the voting booth, they still faced the daunting power of social conventions that Goldman had attacked so fiercely. They also remained in subordinate roles within the public and private realms. Although many progressives took up the call for the woman's vote, most of them defended traditional social mores and thus viewed as scandalous the movement for sex education and the right to use contraceptives. In fact, that right would not be firmly established until 1965, when the Supreme Court sanctioned the use of contraceptives by married persons in *Griswold* v. *Connecticut*. Equal pay, equal treatment under the law, sexual freedom, and freedom from gender roles shaped by social expectations would remain distant goals long after World War I choked off progressive reform.

In many ways, Ellen Richards and Emma Goldman illustrate the constraints on women in the Progressive era that worked against further changes in their status. The two women's careers were radically different, but both reflect the hazards that women faced in challenging traditional gender roles.

The practical-minded Richards believed that women could be more independent by learning to be efficient housekeepers. By becoming educated consumers, women could resist social conventions, become better spenders, and thus solve important social problems without ever leaving the home. At the same time, Richards did not believe that domestic science would necessarily tie women to the home. Instead, it could actually help lead them to careers in social work and other fields. In fact, she put so much faith in the elevating power of domestic science that she dismissed the potential of politics for the improvement of women's lives. As she put it, "I am not a Radical or a believer in the all powerful ballot for women." Yet Richards did not appreciate how easily domestic science could be subverted to other ends. She hoped that it would make women "rational" spenders but underestimated the power of advertisers to encourage the opposite. She declared that she did not "scorn womanly duties" but rather claimed it a "privilege to clean up." She did not see that by defining women's roles as primarily domestic, home economics could also reinforce traditional gender roles. [**See Source 6.**] In fact, Richards's own career demonstrates the limits imposed by those roles. By the time she died in 1911, she was recognized as the "mother of home economics," but she was never given the opportunity to teach a college home economics course. Instead, she spent the bulk

---

Red Scare: A wave of antiradical hysteria that began in 1919 and lasted for about six months. It was sparked by growing postwar labor unrest, several well-publicized bombings, and fears about the spread of radicalism after the Russian Revolution in 1917.

of her career teaching chemistry to young men destined to become chemists and sanitary engineers.

Unlike Richards, Goldman did not focus on small, "practical" changes. Rather, she stressed the total revamping of the economic, social, and emotional relations between men and women. In fact, Goldman's belief that the most important changes in women's lives were outside politics would inspire many feminists later in the twentieth century. As her career amply demonstrates, though, the call for radical changes in gender relations in the early twentieth century held its own dangers. Unable to focus for long on one injustice, Goldman was never able to work out a practical plan to achieve her utopia or to see any value in the mundane work of politics. Sweeping economic, social, and psychological changes, she believed, were far more important than political rights, even the right to vote. Thus she found it easy to combine an impolitic assault on conventional sexual morality with a radical condemnation of American society. She did so, however, at a time when even distributing birth control information was scandalous and illegal. In the end, she literally closed off her opportunities to work within American society to change the status of women.

Ironically, the most immediate influence of Richards and Goldman on the status of women was an unintended one. Although both sought to elevate women in their own ways, neither believed that winning political power had anything to do with it. Yet Richards's movement to professionalize homemaking reinforced the argument of many suffragists that politics was nothing more than housekeeping on a larger scale. With their faith in efficiency, many progressives could readily embrace the ideal that domestic "scientists" were uniquely qualified to uplift society in the broader arena of politics. Meanwhile, Goldman, by so dramatically condemning conventional morality, made suffragists' demands seem reasonable by comparison. Thus, in a backhanded way, both Richards and Goldman could claim some credit for the most tangible gain won by women in the early twentieth century.

PRIMARY SOURCES

SOURCE 1:   Ellen Richards, *Euthenics*   (1910)

Ellen Richards was the mother of the brief Progressive-era fad called euthenics, which she defined as the "science of controllable environment." It was based on the belief that science could improve the role of women within the home by making their work more efficient. In this excerpt from her book Euthenics, *Richards discusses the role of "household engineering" in the improvement of the social environment. How does her analysis reflect progressive assumptions? What role does she envision for women in society?*

SOURCE: Ellen Richards, *Euthenics: The Science of Controllable Environment* (1910; reprint, New York: Arno Press, 1977), pp. 146–147, 150–153, 158.

As an economic factor, the influence of the housewife is of the greatest moment. . . . The city and suburban dweller is a buyer, not a producer. In suburban and city life the housekeeper has more temptations to buy needless articles, food out of season, to go often to the shops, especially on bargain days. She thinks her taste is educated, when it is only aroused to notice what others like. She is led to strive after effects without knowing how to attain them. It has been estimated by advertising experts that ninety per cent of the purchases of the community are determined by women, not always according to their judgment, but by a suppression of it. Woman is made to think that she must buy certain lines of goods. . . .

Society is only just beginning to realize that it has at its command today for its own regeneration a great unused force in its army of housewives, teachers, mothers, conscious of power but uncertain how to use it. Perhaps the most progressive movement of the times is one led by women who see clearly that cleanness is above charity, that moral support must be given to those who know but do not dare to do right, and that knowledge must be brought to the ignorant. . . .

The keeping of the house, the laundry work, the cleaning, the cooking, the daily oversight, must have for its conscious end the welfare of the family. It cannot be done without labor, but the labor in this as in any process may be lightened by thought and by machinery.

Knowledge of labor-saving appliances is today everywhere demanded of the successful establishment EXCEPT of the family home. Is it not time that it came in for its share? If the housewife would use wisely the information at her hand today, it is safe to say that in six cases out of ten she could cut in half the housekeeping budget and double the comfort of living.

As conditions are, the twentieth century sees a strange phenomenon—the most vital of all processes, the raising of children, carried on under adverse conditions; human labor and life being held of as little account as in the days of building the pyramids.

Women may be trained to become the economic leaders in the body politic. It is doubtful if life will be anything but wasteful until they are trained to realize their responsibility.

The housewife was told that she must stay at home and do her work. This was preached *at* her, written *at* her, but no one of them all . . . saw the problem in its social significance, saw that the work of home-making in this engineering age must be worked out on engineering principles, and with the coöperation of both trained men and trained women. The mechanical setting of life is become an important factor, and this new impulse which is showing itself so clearly today for the modified construction and operation of the family home is the final crown or seal of the conquest of the last stronghold of conservatism, the home-keeper.

Tomorrow, if not today, the woman who is to be really mistress of her house must be an engineer, so far as to be able to understand the use of machines and to believe what she is told. Your ham-and-eggs woman was of the old type, now gone by in the fight for the right to think.

Household engineering is the great need for material welfare, and social engineering for moral and ethical well-being. What else does this persistent forcing of scientific training to the front mean? If the State is to have good citizens, productive human beings, it must provide for the teaching of the essentials to those who are to become the parents of the next generation. No state can thrive while its citizens waste their resources of health, bodily energy, time and brain power, any more than a nation may prosper that wastes its natural resources.

SOURCE 2:   Ellen Richards, *"Who Is to Blame for High Prices?"*   (1910)

Ellen Richards saw enormous possibilities for women to have an impact on society as "educated" homemakers. In this excerpt from an article in the Ladies' Home Journal, *Richards discusses the way women could solve the problem of rising prices in the early twentieth century. What is her solution? How does her discussion reflect progressive concerns?*

The American woman is today buying under the influence of hypnotic suggestion. . . .

To see things is to want them, from the infant in arms to the man of sixty years. The science of creating wants—advertising—is almost the controlling factor in modern economics of production. Man—or woman—no longer "wants but little here below"; he wants everything he sees and much of that which he reads about. Most of these things he must give money for: personal exertion will not bring them. Money must be had, and money today is not always the product of personal exertion.

From the tramp who refuses to saw wood for a meal to the housewife who declines to earn her keep by a study of household accounts, personal exertion has become distasteful. And the result? The cost of living in terms of money has increased, race suicide is charged, and society is in a turmoil generally.

It is no longer respectable to save. Thrift, counting of pennies, has gone out of fashion.

We—the great body of housekeepers—spend more money than we did ten or twenty years ago. We have more things to wear; we have better things to eat and more kinds; we have more rooms to keep clean and more things in them; we of the cities have more books and magazines, more clubs and shops. It costs a little more for clothes, for downtown luncheons, for carfares, for subscriptions and the thousand and one items of civilization. . . .

What does the social advance mean? Is it luxury, soft ease, loose morals and an envious spirit—pulling down others to climb upon them? Or is it better, stronger, happier human beings, more intellectual, less sensual?

The lesson of the ages is that work, self-denial and a look ahead are the elements of race advance. They are just as truly the elements of real social advance in a community. . . .

SOURCE: Ellen Richards, "Who Is to Blame for High Prices?" *Ladies' Home Journal*, December 1, 1910, pp. 23, 42.

The easy way means degeneracy and social ruin. If America is to stand a successful republic its women must cope with the family budget and secure good value for the money they spend. . . .

Shall the housewife employ consulting experts to tell her what to buy? . . . There are plenty of such experts on house furnishing who look after the artistic effect of their patrons' houses. Why shouldn't there be experts to advise when it comes to the question of real values from the standpoint of essential comforts? Millions of dollars of worthless knickknacks of no utility and of less than no art value are sold to American women every year. It all increases the cost of living. Not all the king's horses could make the American housekeeper buy such things once she was educated in real values as her grandmother was, as her daughters will be. She does not know, she will not think: hence she buys. . . .

The cost of living in the next few years is to be controlled not by law, not by preaching, not by the trusts, but by the careful accounting to her own conscience of the intelligent housewife willing to take pains with the expenditure of the income and ready to conserve that which she buys.

Promoters and exploiters could not have their way with informed, self-poised women. If the trusts have caused the late high prices it is because the American housewife has allowed herself to be bamboozled, browbeaten, enticed, hoodwinked and flattered into buying unnecessary things, and unnecessary costly things—because she was ignorant of relative values. . . .

American housewives have surely too much good sense to go on blindly complaining of outside forces without reforming their own habits and attempting to regain their own kingdom.

SOURCE 3:   Emma Goldman, *"Marriage and Love"*   (1917)

Emma Goldman often attacked the institution of marriage in the name of women's rights. In "Marriage and Love," published in her monthly magazine Mother Earth *in 1917, she delivers one of her most famous assaults on matrimony. What does Goldman think is wrong with marriage?*

The popular notion about marriage and love is that they are synonymous, that they spring from the same motives, and cover the same human needs. Like most popular notions this also rests not on actual facts, but on superstition.

Marriage and love have nothing in common; they are as far apart as the poles; are, in fact, antagonistic to each other. No doubt some marriages have been the result of love. Not, however, because love could assert itself only in marriage; much rather is it because few people can completely outgrow a convention. There are to-day large numbers of men and women to whom marriage is naught but a farce, but who submit to it for the sake of public opinion. At any

SOURCE: Reprinted in Emma Goldman, *The Traffic in Women and Other Essays on Feminism*, ed. Alix Kates Shulman (New York: Times Change Press, 1970), pp. 37–38, 42–44; originally from Emma Goldman, *Marriage and Love* (New York: Mother Earth Publishing Association, 1917).

rate, while it is true that some marriages are based on love, and while it is equally true that in some cases love continues in married life, I maintain that it does so regardless of marriage, and not because of it. . . .

Marriage is primarily an economic arrangement, an insurance pact. It differs from the ordinary life insurance agreement only in that it is more binding, more exacting. Its returns are insignificantly small compared with the investments. In taking out an insurance policy one pays for it in dollars and cents, always at liberty to discontinue payments. If, however, woman's premium is a husband, she pays for it with her name, her privacy, her self-respect, her very life, "until death doth part." Moreover, the marriage insurance condemns her to life-long dependency, to parasitism, to complete uselessness, individual as well as social. Man, too, pays his toll, but as his sphere is wider, marriage does not limit him as much as woman. He feels his chains more in an economic sense. . . .

The woman considers her position as worker transitory, to be thrown aside for the first bidder. That is why it is infinitely harder to organize women than men. "Why should I join a union? I am going to get married, to have a home." Has she not been taught from infancy to look upon that as her ultimate calling? She learns soon enough that the home, though not so large a prison as the factory, has more solid doors and bars. It has a keeper so faithful that naught can escape him. The most tragic part, however, is that the home no longer frees her from wage-slavery; it only increases her task.

. . . As a matter of fact, even the middle-class girl in marriage can not speak of her home, since it is the man who creates her sphere. It is not important whether the husband is a brute or a darling. What I wish to prove is that marriage guarantees woman a home only by the grace of her husband. There she moves about in *his* home, year after year, until her aspect of life and human affairs becomes as flat, narrow, and drab as her surroundings. Small wonder if she becomes a nag, petty, quarrelsome, gossipy, unbearable, thus driving the man from the house. She could not go, if she wanted to; there is no place to go. Besides, a short period of married life, of complete surrender of all faculties, absolutely incapacitates the average woman for the outside world. She becomes reckless in appearance, clumsy in her movements, dependent in her decisions, cowardly in her judgment, a weight and a bore, which most men grow to hate and despise. Wonderfully inspiring atmosphere for the bearing of life, is it not? . . .

The institution of marriage makes a parasite of woman, an absolute dependent. It incapacitates her for life's struggle, annihilates her social consciousness, paralyzes her imagination, and then imposes its gracious protection, which is in reality a snare, a travesty on human character.

If motherhood is the highest fulfillment of woman's nature, what other protection does it need save love and freedom? Marriage but defies, outrages, and corrupts her fulfillment. Does it not say to woman, Only when you follow me shall you bring forth life? Does it not condemn her to the block, does it not degrade and shame her if she refuses to buy her right to motherhood by selling herself? Does not marriage only sanction motherhood, even though conceived in hatred, in compulsion? Yet, if motherhood be of free choice, of love, of ecstasy, of defiant passion, does it not place a crown of thorns upon an innocent head and carve in letters of blood the hideous epithet, Bastard? Were marriage to contain all the virtues claimed for it, its crimes against motherhood would exclude it forever from the realm of love.

Love, the strongest and deepest element in all life, the harbinger of hope, of joy, of ecstasy; love, the defier of all laws, of all conventions; love, the freest, the most powerful moulder of human destiny; how can such an all-compelling force be synonymous with that poor little State and Church-begotten weed, marriage?

Source 4:   Emma Goldman, *"The Woman Suffrage Chameleon"* (1917)

Emma Goldman often blasted the woman suffrage movement. On what grounds does she argue against it in this excerpt from an article published in Mother Earth? *What does Goldman's opposition to World War I have to do with her argument?*

For well-nigh half a century the leaders of woman suffrage have been claiming that miraculous results would follow the enfranchisement of woman. All the social and economic evils of past centuries would be abolished once woman will get the vote. All the wrongs and injustices, all the crimes and horrors of the ages would be eliminated from life by the magic decree of a scrap of paper.

When the attention of the leaders of the movement was called to the fact that such extravagant claims convince no one, they would say, "Wait until we have the opportunity; wait till we are face to face with a great test, and then you will see how superior woman is in her attitude toward social progress."

The intelligent opponents of woman suffrage, who were such on the ground that the representative system has served only to rob man of his independence, and that it will do the same to woman, knew that nowhere has woman suffrage exerted the slightest influence upon the social and economic life of the people. Still they were willing to give the suffrage exponents the benefit of doubt. They were ready to believe that the suffragists were sincere in their claim that woman will never be guilty of the stupidities and cruelties of man. Especially did they look to the militant suffragettes of England for a superior kind of womanhood. . . .

No sooner did England join the war, for humanitarian reasons, of course, than the suffrage ladies immediately forgot all their boasts about woman's superiority and goodness and immolated their party on the altar of the very government which tore their clothing, pulled their hair, and fed them forcibly for their militant activities. Mrs. Pankhurst* and her hosts became more passionate in their war mania, in their thirst for the enemy's blood than the most hardened militarists. They consecrated their all, even their sex attraction, as a means of luring unwilling men into the military net, into the trenches and death. . . .

The arguments of the antis that woman does not need the vote because she has a stronger weapon—her sex—[were] met with the declaration that the vote will

Source: Emma Goldman, "The Woman Suffrage Chameleon," *Mother Earth*, May 1917.

*Mrs. Pankhurst: Emmeline Pankhurst, a leader of the woman suffrage movement in Great Britain.

free woman from the degrading need of sex appeal. How does this proud boast compare with the campaign started by the suffrage party to lure the manhood of America into the European sea-blood? Not only is every youth and man to be brazenly solicited and cajoled into enlisting by the fair members of the suffrage party, but wives and sweethearts are to be induced to play upon the emotions and feelings of the men, to bring their sacrifice to the Moloch* of Patriotism and War.

How is this to be accomplished? Surely not by argument. If during the last fifty years the women politicians failed to convince most men that woman is entitled to political equality, they surely will not convince them suddenly that they ought to go to certain death while the women remain safely tucked away at home sewing bandages. No, not argument, reason, or humanitarianism has the suffrage party pledged to the government; it is the sex attraction, the vulgar persuasive and ensnaring appeal of the female let loose for the glory of the country. What man can resist that? The greatest have been robbed of their sanity and judgment when benumbed by the sex appeal. How is the youth of America to withstand it?

The cat is out of the bag. The suffrage ladies have at last proven that their prerogative is neither intelligence nor sincerity and that their boast of equality is all rot; that in the struggle for the vote, even, the sex appeal was their only resort and cheap political reward their only aim.

Source 5: Emma Goldman, *"The Social Aspects of Birth Control"* (1916)

Emma Goldman became a vocal defender of birth control in the years before World War I. On what grounds does she defend the practice in this excerpt from an article published in Mother Earth?

For ages she has been on her knees before the altar of duty as imposed by God, by Capitalism, by the State, and by Morality. Today she has awakened from her age-long sleep. She has shaken herself free from the nightmare of the past; she has turned her face towards the light and is proclaiming in a clarion voice that she will no longer be a party to the crime of bringing hapless children into the world only to be ground into dust by the wheel of capitalism and to be torn into shreds in trenches and battlefields. And who is to say her nay? After all it is woman who is risking her health and sacrificing her youth in the reproduction of the race. Surely she ought to be in a position to decide how many children she should bring into the world, whether they should be brought into the world by the man she loves and because she wants the child, or should be born in hatred and loathing.

Furthermore, it is conceded by earnest physicians that constant reproduction on the part of women has resulted in what the laity terms, "female

Moloch: In the Bible, a pagan god to whom human sacrifices were offered.
Source: Emma Goldman, "The Social Aspects of Birth Control," *Mother Earth*, April 1916.

troubles": a lucrative condition for unscrupulous medical men. But what possible reason has woman to exhaust her system in everlasting child bearing?

It is precisely for this reason that woman should have the knowledge that would enable her to recuperate during a period of from three to five years between each pregnancy, which alone would give her physical and mental well-being and the opportunity to take better care of the children already in existence. . . .

Nothing so binds the workers to the block as a brood of children, and that is exactly what the opponents of Birth Control want. Wretched as the earnings of a man with a large family are, he cannot risk even that little, so he continues in the rut, compromises and cringes before his master, just to earn barely enough to feed the many little mouths. He dare not join a revolutionary organization; he dare not go on strike; he dare not express an opinion. Masses of workers have awakened to the necessity of Birth Control as a means of freeing themselves from the terrible yoke and still more as a means of being able to do something for those already in existence by preventing more children from coming into the world.

Last, but not least, a change in the relation of the sexes, though not embracing very large numbers of people, is still making itself felt among a very considerable minority. In the past and to a large extent with the average man today woman continues to be a mere object, a means to an end; largely a physical means and end. But there are men who want more than that from woman; who have come to realize that if every male were emancipated from the superstitions of the past nothing would yet be changed in the social structure so long as woman had not taken her place with him in the great social struggle. Slowly but surely these men have learned that if a woman wastes her substance in eternal pregnancies, confinements, and diaper washing, she has little time left for anything else. Least of all has she time for the questions which absorb and stir the father of her children. Out of physical exhaustion and nervous stress she becomes the obstacle in the man's way and often his bitterest enemy. It is then for his own protection and also for his need of the companion and friend in the woman he loves that a great many men want her to be relieved from the terrible imposition of constant reproduction of life, that therefore they are in favor of Birth Control.

From whatever angle, then, the question of Birth Control may be considered, it is the most dominant issue of modern times and as such it can not be driven back by persecution, imprisonment, or a conspiracy of silence.

SOURCE 6:   *Home Efficiency Table*   (1915)

The home economics movement was widely accepted by the early twentieth century and was the subject of much favorable discussion in the press. The following test was included in an article on efficiency in the home in the Independent, *a progressive-minded journal. How does it reflect the influence of the home economics movement? What role does it presume for women?*

SOURCE: Edward Earle Purinton, "Home and Efficiency," *Independent*, February 22, 1915.

HOME EFFICIENCY TABLE

FOR THE AMERICAN HOUSEWIFE AND MOTHER

DIRECTIONS. If answer is Yes, write on dotted line the number in parenthesis following each question. If answer is No, leave space blank. If neither Yes nor No, vary the figure accordingly. Find your percentage by adding column of numbers. The average grade is probably 45. It should be 95. A Table of complete values would include other questions, but this Table gives a fair estimate.

1. Do you take joy and pride in your housework? (3) ....
2. Can you finish your daily duties in eight hours? (1) ....
3. Have you ever counted and tried to cut down the number of needless steps you take in a day's work? (3) ....
4. When you are tired out, can you rest and recuperate easily and quickly? (2) ....
5. Have you time and strength in the evening to enjoy home pleasures with the family? (2) ....
6. Is your home in quiet surroundings? (3) ....
7. Do your sleeping rooms have direct exposure to morning sun? (2) ....
8. Do you keep daily records of expenses, with a modern filing system for reference? (3) ....
9. Is your grocer the best in your neighborhood—have you learned why? (3) ....
10. Do you plan your meals a week ahead, and use all the "left-overs"? (1)
11. Do you order and prepare meals on a scientific basis of nutritive value? (3) ....
12. Can you serve palatable, economical substitutes for meat? (2) ....
13. Do you know the signs of fresh meat, fish, eggs, fruits and vegetables? (2) ....
14. Has your drinking water been guaranteed pure by expert analysis? (3) ....
15. Do you buy food, clothing, furnishings, etc., on a scientific system of economy? (3) ....
16. Have you studied at least three modern schools of diet (such as Lahmann, the Lust, the Christian, or the Kellogg system)? (3) ....
17. Have you read at least three standard books on domestic science and household economy? (3) ....
18. Do you belong to a woman's club? (3) ....
19. Are you a member of the Housewives' League? (3) ....
20. Do you subscribe for one or more magazines devoted to home-making? (3) ....
21. Do you spend a day away from home at least once a month? (1) ....

22. Do you take a vacation from your family of at least two weeks every year? (3) ....
23. Have you installed a modern cleaning system, from efficient soap to vacuum cleaner? (2) ....
24. Is there an emergency medicine chest in your bathroom? (1) ....
25. Are all your windows equipped with hygienic ventilators? (3) ...   .
26. Is your lighting system powerful, while restful to the eyes? (2) ...   .
27. Have you studied the hygiene of dress? (2) ....
28. Is your doctor a teacher of health—not just a prescriber of drugs? (3) ....
29. Do you receive regularly the monthly list of publications of the U.S. Department of Agriculture? (1) ....
30. Are you thoroly informed on vocational training? (3) ....
31. Do you know where and with whom your children play? (3) ....
32. Can you answer all your children's questions, without evasion or embarrassment? (3) ....
33. Do you conduct home discussions on great questions of the day? (2) ....
34. Are you teaching your children how to earn, to save and to spend money? (3) ....
35. Can all the members of your family use their hands and brains equally well? (3) ....
36. Do the pictures and decorations in your home express sound esthetic principles? (2) ....
37. Have you developed a saving sense of humor? (3) ....
38. Are you giving your children systematic religious or ethical instruction? (3) ....
39. Do you recognize the mistakes of your early married life and are you training your children to prevent or avoid them? (3) ....
40. Is your home a haven for the poor and friendless? (3) ....

**Add up column and approximate
your grade in Home Efficiency**

Questions to Consider

1. Making reference to the primary sources, how would you compare Ellen Richards's and Emma Goldman's views of the proper role of women in society? What influences in each woman's life were most important in shaping her vision?

2. What do the lives of Richards and Goldman reveal about the constraints on women in the early twentieth century? What do the primary sources reveal about Richards's and Goldman's views of those constraints? What did both see as the ill effects of convention and public opinion?

3. Both Richards and Goldman rejected woman suffrage as a means for elevating the status of women. On what grounds did each do so? What did each woman have to do with the achievement of suffrage?

4. One historian has written that the "driving theme" of women's history at the end of the nineteenth century was women asserting "control over their own sexual lives." Judging from your understanding of the lives of Richards and Goldman, how important do you think such control was for women compared to other concerns?

5. Was Richards's or Goldman's strategy for elevating the status of women more successful? What were the main drawbacks of each?

FOR FURTHER READING

John Chalberg, *Emma Goldman: American Individualist* (New York: HarperCollins, 1991), offers a brief, engaging account of Goldman's life and ideas.

Robert Clarke, *Ellen Swallow* (Chicago: Follett Publishing Company, 1973), emphasizes Richards's work in combating pollution and provides a useful overview of her background and career.

Rosalind Rosenberg, *Beyond Separate Spheres: The Intellectual Roots of Modern Feminism* (New Haven, Conn.: Yale University Press, 1982), analyzes changing ideas about gender differences and their impact on women's struggles for equality in the early twentieth century.

Alix Kates Shulman, ed., *Red Emma Speaks: Selected Writings and Speeches by Emma Goldman* (New York: Random House, 1972), is a useful collection of Goldman's important publications and speeches.

Progressives at War:
Randolph Bourne and George Creel

As he entered the House of Representatives on the evening of April 2, 1917, President Woodrow Wilson was greeted with loud applause. Everyone in the chamber knew why he was there. A beleaguered Germany, worn down after nearly three years of war with Britain, France, and Russia, had announced only two months earlier that its submarines would strike American neutral ships trading with Britain or the other Allies. In the last month, German torpedoes had sunk four American merchant ships. Now a reluctant Wilson stood before a joint session of Congress asking that it "formally accept the status of belligerent." The somber president had no illusions about the magnitude of the task before the nation. Waging war against Germany would require far more than raising and equipping an army. The Allies and the principal Central Powers—Germany, Austria-Hungary, and Turkey—had already lost millions of men. World War I demanded, as Wilson put it, the "mobilization of all the material resources of the country." Wilson also knew that war would require the enlistment of Americans' hearts and minds. Less than two weeks after his call for American intervention, he signed an executive order creating the Committee on Public Information, the nation's first full-scale propaganda agency. Then he quickly appointed journalist, reformer, and ardent Wilson supporter George Creel to head it.

Like Wilson, Creel called himself a progressive. For nearly two decades in the early twentieth century, progressive reformers had battled many ills plaguing America's urban, industrial society. Now they saw Wilson's crusade abroad as an extension of the battle they had waged in this country to democratize politics and increase the power of the government to improve living and working conditions. Progressives like Creel believed that public power should be used to curb private interests. War would bring new opportunities to do just that. The defeat of the Central Powers, they assumed, would make the world "safe for democracy." And unprecedented wartime controls over private property would help usher in a bright progressive future for American society.

Randolph Bourne thought otherwise. As Creel eagerly sold Wilson's cause to the American people, Bourne set his impressive mind to a different task. Like

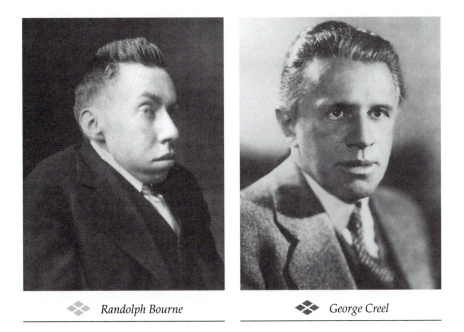

❖❖ *Randolph Bourne*   ❖❖ *George Creel*

Creel, Bourne had enthusiastically embraced many progressive assumptions about the need for social planning and the greater use of state power. Far removed from the centers of power, however, he was convinced that progressives' faith in the war's positive effects was tragically misplaced. If Creel assumed that war would further progressive reform, Bourne feared that it would overwhelm those who thought they could control its consequences. Bourne was not alone in his antiwar views. The depth of his critique, however, placed his dissent in a class by itself. No one would offer a more scathing indictment of progressive assumptions about the war—or more chilling predictions about its consequences.

"Lollipopped with Half-Truths"

In his autobiography, George Creel declared his distaste for biographies that "prattle along through infancy and adolescence." Fortunately, one can make sense of Creel's life without committing that sin. Born in Missouri in 1876, Creel was the youngest of three sons of a former Confederate officer who failed as a farmer before moving his family to Kansas City. There Creel's father drank "as an escape from his failure," while his mother ran a boarding house and imparted to young George a "fair knowledge of history and the classics." He attended high school for one year, where he wrote for the school paper. After a brief stint working at odd jobs, he went to work for the *Kansas City World* in 1894. Refusing to report on a private scandal in a prominent Kansas City family soon got him fired, but Creel had already set his sights on a larger world. Riding freight trains to New York City, he landed a job at William Randolph Hearst's *New York Journal*. It was 1898, and the Spanish-American War would soon make Hearst and the *Journal* household names. Yet Creel was not happy working for the fore-most practitioner of sensational journalism. Seeing himself as "the cheapest sort of hack," he returned to Kansas City to start the *Independent,* a weekly journal, with the backing of a New York acquaintance.

Beginning with its first issue in 1899, the *Independent* offered readers poetry, short stories, and discussions of social and economic issues. With the slogan "A Clean, Clever Paper for Intelligent People," the publication demonstrated a certain high-mindedness. As the *Independent*'s slogan suggested, Creel was no opponent of conventional morality. In fact, he later declared that he was "repelled" by communists because of their "derision" of middle-class respectability. At the same time, he was no opponent of reform, and he used the *Independent* to promote a progressive agenda. Serving as editor and publisher, Creel took on the political machine of Kansas City boss Tom Pendergast and even promoted Woodrow Wilson for the presidency in 1905, seven years before Wilson became the Democratic Party candidate. As a high school student, Creel had heard Wilson speak about "the cultivation of the mind and the reading of books" and was instantly won over by the Princeton professor. Imbued with the spirit of reform, the young editor championed everything from the regulation of public utilities to the liberation of women from a "hermetically sealed home."

After selling the *Independent* in 1909, Creel took an assignment as a writer for the *Denver Post,* where he demonstrated the same crusading zeal, campaigning for such progressive reforms as the initiative, referendum, and recall;* effective railroad regulation; an income tax; and municipal ownership of public utilities. Disillusioned by the *Post*'s halfhearted commitment to reform, Creel jumped to the rival *Rocky Mountain News,* where he did battle with Denver's political machine and, in one editorial, suggested that eleven state legislators be lynched. (At the subsequent libel trial, Creel testified that he meant exactly what he said.) When a reform mayor was elected in 1912, the newspaperman was appointed police commissioner in the new regime. Creel closed down the red-light district, rounded up prostitutes, and pushed a plan to rehabilitate them. Amid a public outcry, he took away policemen's nightsticks and guns and refused to arrest "Big Bill" Haywood and other Industrial Workers of the World* (IWW) agitators when they arrived in Denver. "Happening to believe in free speech," he declared, "I gave the wobblies the right to talk their heads off."

Such controversial policies helped end his career as commissioner after only several months. Continuing for a time as a muckraker* at the *Rocky Mountain News,* Creel supported Wilson as the "bosses' foe" in the 1912 presidential campaign. The year after Wilson's election, he quit the *Rocky Mountain News* and moved to New York. There he wrote for *Harper's Weekly, Century, Everybody's Magazine,* and other muckraking magazines and coauthored *Children in*

Initiative, referendum, and recall: Political reforms adopted in a number of states in the early twentieth century. They were intended to give voters more power by allowing them to initiate their own legislation, vote on proposed laws or amendments, and recall elected officials before their terms had expired.

Industrial Workers of the World: A radical labor union formed in 1905 whose members were nicknamed "Wobblies."

Muckraker: An investigative reporter in the early twentieth century who helped promote progressive reform by reporting on corruption in government and business.

Bondage (1914), an attack on "the great American cancer" of child labor. Creel's muckraking often supported Wilson's New Freedom* program. It also put him in touch with men who would play an important role in the Wilson administration, including Cleveland mayor Newton D. Baker, the future secretary of war. About the same time, Creel's circle of acquaintances was further broadened by his marriage to the actress Blanche Bates. The star of *Madame Butterfly, The Darling of the Gods,* and other stage hits counted among her friends Margaret Wilson, the president's daughter.

Creel took up his pen even more directly in Wilson's cause in 1916. During the president's reelection campaign, he wrote *Wilson and the Issues,* which posed the election as a choice between a "government of the people" and "the rule of the self-elected few." He was a loud defender of Wilson's secretary of the Navy, Josephus Daniels, who had come under heavy Republican attack for accusing private contractors of overcharging the Navy. During the campaign, Creel assembled a group of "publicists" and authors, including muckrakers Ray Stannard Baker, Lincoln Steffens, and Ida Tarbell,* to issue endorsements and write pamphlets. Wilson was so delighted by Creel's contributions to his campaign that he offered him a position in his administration, which Creel declined. With a growing family, "setting up a home in Washington," he later confessed, "called for more money than I had."

Creel soon changed his mind about government service. He knew that although Wilson's call for war was met with virtually unanimous approval in Congress, his support fell far short of that in the country at large. Many Americans opposed involvement in the war because of the absence of a direct German attack on the United States. Others had ethnic ties to Germany, Austria-Hungary, or even anti-British Ireland and thus disagreed with Wilson's war policy. Still others pointed to the distance of the "European war" from American shores as the reason for their opposition. Meanwhile, many socialists considered the war nothing more than a struggle between capitalist nations. By the time the United States entered the war, Creel was eager to head any government agency charged with wartime publicity. He even suggested himself for the job to Secretary Daniels, telling Daniels that any such agency should be less concerned with censorship, which he called "criminally stupid," than with efforts to "arouse ardor and enthusiasm" for the war. In April 1917, Wilson appointed him to head the Committee on Public Information (CPI) shortly after it was created.

Under Creel, the CPI worked to influence public opinion in a variety of ways. Creel and his three assistant directors—the secretaries of war, state, and the Navy—oversaw both the Foreign Section, which maintained offices in more than thirty countries, and the Domestic Section, which disseminated war news at home. Through its News Division, the CPI eventually issued some six thousand press releases. To inform the public about the government's activities during the war, it also started the *Official Bulletin,* the first daily newspaper put out

---

New Freedom: The reforms advanced by Wilson in the 1912 presidential campaign, including trustbusting and lower tariffs.

Ray Stannard Baker, Lincoln Steffens, and Ida Tarbell: Baker wrote about the plight of African Americans, Steffens exposed corruption in city government, and Tarbell took on John D. Rockefeller in an exposé of his Standard Oil Company.

by the federal government. The News Division, Creel observed, "present[ed] the facts without the slightest trace of color or bias." Typical of many press releases, however, was *Pershing's Crusaders,* a newsreel that purported to show "the very latest news of what our boys are doing in the front line trenches." Opening with a scene of two American soldiers standing beside a medieval Crusader, it declared, "The men of America are going out to save Civilization."

At the beginning of the war, Creel told Wilson that "*expression,* not *suppression,* was the real need." Later, he boasted that the American people received "a daily diet of our material." Yet Creel found that influencing news content involved more than issuing an avalanche of press releases. Less than two months after the United States entered the war, Creel also put out guidelines for coverage of the war by the press. Declaring that all "questionable" material should be voluntarily submitted to the CPI for approval, he reminded journalists that "the term traitor is not too harsh in application to the publisher, editor, or writer who wields . . . power without full and even solemn recognition of responsibilities." Although Congress placed serious curbs on free expression with the Espionage Act* in 1917 and the Sedition Act* the following year, the CPI had no statutory authority to engage in censorship. Still, as a member of the Censorship Board, established to oversee the government's numerous censorship efforts, Creel had the power to review all magazine articles prior to publication, ban publications from the mail, and recommend that editors be prosecuted. Armed with this power, he not only suppressed radical publications but also received widespread cooperation from the press.

Influencing the content of war news was one thing, but Creel envisioned an even broader role for his agency. To arouse Americans' "ardor" for the war, the CPI developed a publicity and advertising offensive that included cartoons, posters, newspaper advertisements, pamphlets, and films. Creel called on the services of hundreds of writers, journalists, academics, artists, and advertising men. In addition to Tarbell, Baker, and Steffens, Creel recruited muckrakers John Spargo* and Upton Sinclair,* reformer Jane Addams,* and movie director D. W. Griffith* to work for the CPI. While the Bureau of War Expositions displayed exhibits of captured German war equipment in 20 cities, the Bureau of State Fair Exhibits emphasized the need for wartime conservation in displays that attracted some 7 million people at 60 fairs. Meanwhile, the Four-Minute Men organized 75,000 volunteer speakers who gave four-minute talks to perhaps 400 million people on topics such as German militarism and the dangers of treason. The Division of Women's War Work mobilized women by mailing approximately 50,000 letters and producing several thousand news and feature

---

Espionage Act: Authorized jail sentences and fines for individuals found guilty of interfering with the draft or encouraging disloyalty to the United States.

Sedition Act: Extended similar penalties to those whose published writings attacked the government.

John Spargo: Investigated and wrote about child labor.

Upton Sinclair: The author of an influential exposé of the meatpacking industry (see Chapter 7).

Jane Addams: The founder of Hull House, a Chicago settlement house.

D. W. Griffith: Produced *The Birth of a Nation* (1915), a silent movie that glorified the Ku Klux Klan's efforts to overturn Reconstruction in the South.

stories to demonstrate what women could do to aid the war effort. The Bureau of Cartoons offered guidance to the nation's cartoonists, while the Picture Division and the Film Division showed Americans the government's war activities through the "exploitation of the camera."

It was with printer's ink, however, that the CPI primarily carried on its war for Americans' hearts and minds. Working through its Division of Civic and Educational Publications, which was supposed to "educate" the public about American democracy, Creel's organization blanketed the country with millions of pamphlets, posters, and advertisements designed to promote patriotism and create support for Wilson's war policy. Much of the CPI's attention was concentrated on the nation's classrooms, where youngsters could be taught, as one CPI official put it, "the more virile virtues of duty and effort and sacrifice." The CPI's main vehicle for instilling these values was the *National School Service*, a bulletin sent to thousands of schools to help teachers bring the war home to their pupils. Filled with stories about the war, the *National School Service*'s goal was to create "unswerving loyalty" among children by making "every school pupil a messenger for Uncle Sam" and every teacher "an officer of the state." And the CPI's efforts to sway students did not end there, as the nation's history teachers learned. [**See Source 1.**]

Through the Division of Civic and Educational Publications, the CPI also published some seventy-five million pamphlets and "Loyalty Leaflets." These publications were intended to promote American democratic ideals, but they often reflected a growing concern about national unity and immigrants who allegedly threatened to undermine it. *American and Allied Ideals,* written by a University of Illinois English professor, declared that unassimilated immigrants were "enemies of the American republic." Meanwhile, *Friendly Words to the Foreign Born,* written by a federal judge, warned that the problem with immigrants "is not the fact of the hyphen, but whether a man's heart is at the American end of the hyphen." Other CPI pamphlets addressed the problem of loyalty among the nation's workers with messages designed to prevent labor unrest and increase productivity. In *Why Workingmen Support the War,* for instance, University of Wisconsin economist John R. Commons declared that labor would come out of the war with a "universal" eight-hour day and "as much power to fix its own wages . . . as employers have."

CPI literature also sought to justify American involvement in the war by presenting German militarism "in all its horror." Its pamphlets pictured enemy soldiers as bloodthirsty beasts who had been "cold-bloodedly programmed" for years by their leaders. The CPI's visual images of the enemy were even more damning. If the CPI was, as Creel declared, "a vast enterprise in salesmanship," it was only natural that its chairman turned "almost instinctively" to Madison Avenue for assistance in selling the war. Dozens of advertising men, as eager to demonstrate the power of their craft as they were to promote the war, came to work for Creel's Division of Advertising. In conjunction with artists such as Charles Dana Gibson, creator of the famous Gibson girl* posters at the turn of

Gibson girl: One of the young women portrayed in posters created by Charles Dana Gibson. In contrast to the traditional portraits of corseted Victorian women, Gibson girls were often depicted enjoying athletic and outdoor activities and came to symbolize the rejection of older styles and ideas.

the century, they churned out posters and advertisements for numerous government agencies. Gibson believed that it was impossible to "create enthusiasm for the war on the basis of rational appeal." Instead, wartime art had to "appeal to the heart." Guided by such thinking, the CPI produced some of the war's most memorable propaganda images. Like many of the CPI's pamphlets, some of these images pointed to the dangers that German militarism posed to America. [**See Source 2.**] Others simply emphasized German atrocities. [**See Source 3.**]

The CPI often relied on dubious accounts of the Germans' rape, enslavement, and execution of civilians and the enemy's use of human shields. Nonetheless, Creel believed that his agency's work represented the "most sober and terrific indictment ever drawn by one government of the political and military system of another government." Ever sure of his own convictions, he entertained no doubts about his agency's efforts to create "national unity" during the war. "From the first," he said after the war, "nothing stood more clear than the confusion and shapelessness of public opinion." If anything, Creel's efforts to shape public opinion reflected perfectly his own progressive and democratic ideals. As the former muckraker observed, "Before a sound, steadfast public opinion could be formed, it had to be *informed*." And informing the public, Creel concluded, was exactly what the CPI had done. After all, he said, "a free people were not children to be . . . lollipopped with half-truths," because in a democracy, war is not just a fight of generals but also "the grim business of a whole people."

"War Is the Health of the State"

Randolph Bourne agreed with Creel that war was "grim business." Yet he rejected outright the progressive belief that World War I was a struggle to make the world safe for democracy. Instead, he focused on the war's dark reality. Far from expanding reform, the fight against Germany and its allies would only choke it off. When the war was over, he predicted, the intellectuals who supported this holy crusade would be swept aside. Creel may have believed that the war was not only for generals, but Bourne had no such faith. As much as in Germany, he argued, the conduct of war in the United States would reflect not the will of the people, but the needs of the state.

Bourne's unorthodox views arose naturally from a profound alienation whose roots reached deep into his childhood. Born in 1886 into a declining yet comfortable family in Bloomfield, New Jersey, Bourne grew up in a three-story house with large grounds that included a tennis court and a small golf course. Yet his childhood circumstances were not as fortunate as this idyllic setting might suggest. His birth was, as he later put it, "terribly messy." The umbilical cord was wrapped around his left ear, leaving it deformed. The physician's forceps did more damage, scarring his face and twisting it into a permanent grimace. Then, at age four, he was struck by spinal tuberculosis, which retarded his growth and left him afflicted with double curvature of the spine. In short, Bourne would live his life as a hunchbacked dwarf with a grossly deformed face that rarely failed to elicit initial shock.

Most of Bourne's adult friends, once they had engaged his remarkable mind, claimed they quickly forgot what one called his "misshapen body." But childhood acquaintances were often less kind, and Bourne's early years were full of despair. His condition quickly made him an outsider. "I suffered tortures," he later confessed, "in trying to learn to skate, to climb trees, to play ball, to conform in general to the ways of the world." Although he later claimed that childhood had had "nothing to offer him," young Randolph took up the piano and reading. At age two, he began to read grocery labels, and by the time he started school, he could read the Bible and other books. Nonetheless, the precocious youngster was often frustrated by the "passivity" into which he was forced. Unable to join directly in activities, he studied other people and became adept at sizing them up. He was not without friends and was even elected class president in high school. At the same time, he showed signs of increasing estrangement from his family and its environs.

The Bournes traced their ancestry back to Bloomfield's seventeenth-century Puritan founders. Embodiments of middle-class Protestant respectability, they counted themselves among the town's leading citizens. For Randolph, however, neither Bloomfield nor his family offered much stimulation. The impoverishment of both seemed to be symbolized by the family's set of classics, "stiffly enshrined behind glass doors that were very hard to open." The works of Nathaniel Hawthorne, Alfred Tennyson, and Sir Walter Scott sat there, Bourne reported, "but nobody ever discussed them or looked at them." The failure of Bourne's father to live up to Bloomfield's code of respectability reinforced Randolph's sense of alienation. Like the elder Creel, Bourne's father drank too much, paid too little attention to business, and eventually abandoned his family. Whereas Creel went on to defend conventional values, Bourne longed to escape from Bloomfield's provincialism and his family's middle-class puritanism. "I am constantly confronted there," he confided to a friend, "by the immeasurable gulf between my outlook and theirs."

Bourne's experiences after high school only deepened his disaffection. He realized that he would never enter the world of "dances and parties and social evenings and boy-and-girl attachments." He also knew that he could not attend college. Though admitted to Princeton, he could not enroll due to the family's dwindling resources. After working several months at odd jobs, he found employment working on a machine that punched out music rolls for player pianos. The mind-numbing work helped him "fix the terms" by which he saw the world. When his employer cut his pay, Bourne protested and threatened to quit. Then fear gripped him, and he returned quietly to his workbench. "This was my only skill," he confessed. When his employer's business eventually folded, Bourne had tended a machine so long that his love of literature was nearly dead. Two years spent looking for work in New York City only deepened his sense of estrangement. He endured this period of "mental torture" that arose from the "repeated failure even to obtain a chance to fail" by immersing himself in Greek and Roman classics and social criticism. His reading eventually led him to socialism.* With the enthusiasm of a convert, Bourne became convinced that he never would have embraced "this radical philosophy" were it not for his

---

Socialism: The doctrine that calls for public rather than private ownership of the means of production. Socialists in the early twentieth century often concluded that many progressive solutions to the nation's social and economic ills were inadequate.

deformity. He could now comfort himself in the knowledge that "the price has not been a heavy one to pay."

Bourne worked at more odd jobs until 1909. Then, despairing over his unfitness for "the business world," he applied for admission to Columbia University and was accepted with a scholarship, the first of many. After the deadening routine of factory work and the narrow-minded conformity of Bloomfield, Bourne found the atmosphere at Columbia liberating. "One's self respect," he declared, "can begin to grow like a weed." Delighting in "the pure pleasure of thought," he quickly caught the attention of his professors. He had little trouble making close friends, and he discovered that writing for campus publications allowed him to express his radical views. When a detective who was frequently employed by corporations to investigate labor unrest spoke to several campus clubs, for instance, an indignant Bourne lashed out. "Better a thousand times," he declared, "that Emma Goldman should address a club of students."

Such commentary soon landed Bourne a spot on the *Columbia Monthly*, a campus journal, and the next year he was named its editor. He made an even bigger splash when the *Atlantic Monthly* published his response to an article attacking youth for their vulgar tastes, poor command of English, socialist leanings, and general lack of "character." In "The Two Generations," Bourne declared that many young men faced the unpleasant prospect of "being swallowed up in the routine of a big corporation." It was understandable, he concluded, that young people had grown "impatient with the conventional explanations of the older generation." In another *Atlantic Monthly* article and in his first book, *Youth and Life* (1913), Bourne returned to a defense of his generation. Youth, he declared, would never believe that "the inertia of older people is wisdom." Arguing that youth felt an overpowering urge "toward self-expression," he advised young people to resist the destruction of the spontaneity that their elders saw as irresponsible hedonism and lack of self-control.

Bourne's call for his generation to resist conformity reflected the influence on him of John Dewey, the champion of what came to be known as "progressive education." At Columbia, Dewey launched a frontal assault on traditional conceptions of childhood and learning. Nineteenth-century methods of instruction were rooted in a long-standing view that children must be transformed into little adults. Educators went about that task with heavy doses of discipline, morality, memorization, and instruction in Greek and Latin, subjects traditionally associated with an aristocratic ideal of education. Dewey called for a more "democratic" education that recognized the individuality of children and was related to life rather than sealed off from it. Instead of making little adults in school, he argued, "for certain moral and intellectual purposes, adults must become as little children." Bourne received Dewey's ideas as manna from heaven. The Columbia educator, he believed, was "the most significant thinker in America," for his theories provided nothing less than a way to reshape conservative institutions, remove old habits of thought, and remake society. Education itself could be an instrument of reform. Rather than merely indoctrinate students and produce conformists—"the conventional bigoted man," as Bourne put it—schools could develop self-expressing individuals.

Later in the twentieth century, Bourne's views about his generation earned him a reputation as the first spokesman for a youth rebellion. For the time being, his writing helped increase his celebrity on campus and, after graduation in 1913, led to a fellowship that allowed him to travel to Europe. In England, he found a class-bound society stymied by its conservatism. In Germany, Bourne was struck by a sense of community, by the country's cleanliness and order, and by a certain "lack of critical sense" among Germans. His views about German conformity were no doubt tempered by his arrival there at a "tense and tragic moment." In the opening days of the war, Bourne stood on a street in Berlin and watched endless columns of soldiers march by. Two weeks later, he was on a ship bound for the United States, convinced that European civilization was about to be "torn to shreds."

When Bourne arrived in New York City at the end of the summer, he "never expected to be so glad to come back to America." He moved into an apartment near Greenwich Village,* where he took to wearing a black cloak that covered his hunched back. Hoping to put his experience "to some useful purpose," he also began to support himself by writing for the *Atlantic Monthly, Lippincott's Magazine,* and the *New Republic,* a progressive magazine founded in 1914. Over the next four years, Bourne wrote at least three hundred literary essays and articles on a variety of social issues, particularly Dewey's ideas on education. Increasingly, though, his writing would be bound up with the war he had only glimpsed in Berlin.

Even before 1917, Bourne was distressed by calls for military preparations, especially when they were accompanied by demands for the "Americanization" of immigrants. He was repelled by the "poison" of mindless chauvinism he had seen in Europe. Fearful that war would only bring regimentation and conformity to American life, he became a vocal champion of diversity. Responding to calls that immigrants shed their native cultures, he declared that "there is no distinctly American culture." Immigrants leavened American life with new ideas, he said, while those who insisted on "national unity" only created "hordes of men and women without a spiritual country."

After the United States' entry into the war, Bourne took up his pen against a fight he thought unjust and misguided. Much of his criticism was aimed at the progressive professors and writers who supported the war and often worked for the Committee on Public Information and other government agencies. In particular, he scorned such progressive thinkers as his onetime hero Dewey and *New Republic* editors Herbert Croly and Walter Lippmann. These intellectuals dismissed suggestions that the war would breed intolerance or that "liberty of thought and speech," as Dewey put it, "would suffer . . . in any lasting way." Instead, they justified support for American intervention with the belief that the war, like a classroom, provided a marvelous setting for remaking society. In Dewey's words, the war would demonstrate "the supremacy of public need over private possessions." In fact, it had brought unprecedented government controls to the economy. The War Industries Board, for instance, coordinated the nation's industrial production, while the Food Administration oversaw the production and distribution of foodstuffs. Meanwhile, the National War Labor Board imposed regulations on labor to make sure production continued uninterrupted. Altogether, some five thousand government agencies controlled

*__*Greenwich Village:__ A neighborhood in New York City that was a haven for writers, artists, and intellectuals.

production, rationalized industry, and enlisted private interests in the cause. Dewey and other reformers were heartened by the unprecedented opportunity these wartime agencies created to reshape society along more "scientific" and "rational" lines. Bourne countered that societies, unlike schools, were "not rational entities" and thus not suitable laboratories for social control and experimentation. He believed that linking themselves to the "beast" of war would not make these intellectuals any better able to control its ends. [**See Source 4.**]

Bourne paid a steep price for his dissent. He soon found the pages of the *New Republic* closed to him. With his ability to earn a living severely curtailed, he had to give up his apartment for a room in a basement. Though impoverished and depressed, he continued to write for the *Seven Arts,* a short-lived radical journal that was harassed by federal agents for publishing articles critical of the war. His experience led him to think even more deeply about the impact of war on society. In 1918, he began a study of the modern state, whose nature had been brought "into very clear relief" by the war. The state, he insisted, was simply "the organization of the herd to act offensively or defensively against another herd similarly organized." By coercing cooperation, war was bad for creativity and individualism but good for the state. In fact, he concluded, "war is the health of the State." [**See Source 5.**]

"Ghost in a Black Cloak"

Bourne never finished his essay on the state. Only weeks after the armistice ending World War I, he became one of the more than half million Americans carried away in the influenza epidemic of 1918. Meanwhile, the Committee on Public Information lived on until 1919, when Congress shut it down along with the other wartime regulatory agencies. The next year, George Creel published the "amazing story" of the CPI, which told how it had spread the "gospel of Americanism" and "weld[ed]" Americans into "one white-hot mass instinct." [**See Source 6.**]

Even before Creel told his agency's story, some of the effects of the CPI's work were already evident. Its efforts to heat up Americans' "instincts" had helped create the very climate of intolerance and repression that Bourne had predicted. In this atmosphere, the Wilson administration had found it easy to support the Sedition Act and other moves to repress minority opinion. Meanwhile, rising nativism—the belief that native-born Americans should be favored over immigrants—had led to numerous wartime vigilante attacks on German Americans. One of the most notorious cases of mob action took place near St. Louis in 1918 when a young German American (who had tried unsuccessfully to enlist in the U.S. Navy) was stripped, dragged through the streets, and lynched. In their zeal to achieve national unity, "patriots" across the nation attempted to eradicate all traces of German culture from American life. They removed German books from libraries and schools (and frequently burned them), demanded that orchestras stop performing the works of German composers, and even renamed such familiar items as sauerkraut (Liberty cabbage) and hamburgers (Liberty sandwiches). Nor were Germans their only targets. In the drive to create national unity, all immigrant groups were suspect in the eyes of "100 percenters." In 1917, Congress imposed a literacy test on immigrants, which was sustained over a presidential veto. Four years later, the Immigration Restriction Act established quotas that limited the number of European immigrants allowed to enter the country.

Nativism, in turn, fed rising antilabor and antiradical sentiment. After all, many workers were immigrants, and socialism seemed to many Americans a foreign ideology. As CPI chairman, Creel understood the vulnerability of workers to the no-strike policy advanced by the National War Labor Board. He even sympathized with labor's view that its sacrifices regarding wages and hours should be matched by employers' "concessions in the matter of profits." During the war, however, charges of disloyalty against workers by management proved a very effective tool in muzzling unions. Moreover, workers who *were* opposed to the war often had the full weight of government authority dropped on them. Federal authorities raided meeting halls of the antiwar IWW in 1917 and tried IWW leaders under the Espionage Act. Dozens of other dissenters met a similar fate, including socialist leader Eugene Debs, whose antiwar speech earned him a ten-year prison sentence. Such repression did not end with the armistice in 1918. The next year, the Wilson administration had federal agents round up thousands of radicals and alleged radicals and then jailed or deported them in what came to be known as the Red Scare.

By the time the Red Scare died down in 1920, the war had provoked still other unexpected responses. Creel defended both Wilson and the Treaty of Versailles* after the war, but many Americans were quickly disillusioned with Wilson's idealistic rhetoric about saving the world for democracy. In the coming years, they would conclude that the United States should stay out of other nations' conflicts. Something else had gone wrong as well. Many progressives had entered World War I with great hopes of using government to restrain private interests for the public good. In 1920, they watched as voters elected Republican presidential candidate Warren G. Harding, who promised not a golden age of reform, but "normalcy." In the coming decade, few Americans shared John Dewey's concern for "public need." Instead, many settled down to enjoy unprecedented prosperity, often by purchasing the new consumer goods pouring from the nation's factories. Suddenly, the Progressive era seemed far away.

Before Creel died in 1953 after a long career as a popular history writer and columnist, he would find new enemies to fight. He ran against former muckraker and socialist Upton Sinclair for the Democratic nomination in California's gubernatorial race in 1934. After World War II, he accused liberals of being duped by a vast communist conspiracy. Long before Creel became obsessed with the specter of communism, however, other former progressives were disturbed by something else. Entering World War I with such high hopes, they were haunted by an apparition at its end. Writer John Dos Passos described the figure this way in his 1932 novel *1919*:

> A tiny twisted . . . ghost in a black cloak
> hopping along the grimy old brick and brownstone
>   streets still left in downtown New York,
> crying out in a shrill soundless giggle:
> *War is the health of the State.*

---

*Treaty of Versailles: The treaty negotiated by Wilson and European leaders in 1919 that ended World War I, imposed heavy penalties on Germany, and created a League of Nations.

PRIMARY SOURCES

SOURCE 1:   History Teacher's Magazine *Announcement for Committee on Public Information Literature* (1917)

As part of its effort to influence school curricula, the Committee on Public Information worked closely with the National Board for Historical Service (NBHS), a group of prominent historians formed early in the war to supply "the public with trustworthy information of historical or similar nature." Working with the History Teacher's Magazine, *the NBHS advised teachers how to adapt history courses to the war and how to secure free CPI publications for the classroom. What does this source reveal about the success of the NBHS in achieving its goal?*

The Committee on Public Information

Established by Order of the President, April 4, 1917

Distribute free *except as noted* the following publications :

I. Red, White and Blue Series :

No. 1. How the War Came to America (English, German, Polish, Bohemian, Italian, Spanish and Swedish).

No. 2. National Service Handbook (primarily for libraries, schools, Y. M. C. A.'s, Clubs, fraternal organizations, etc., as a guide and reference work on all forms of war activity, civil, charitable and military).

No. 3. The Battle Line of Democracy. Prose and Poetry of the Great War. Price 25 cent. Special price to teachers. Proceeds to the Red Cross. Other issues in preparation.

II. War Information Series :

No. 1. The War Message and Facts Behind it.

No. 2. The Nation in Arms, by Secretaries Lane and Baker.

No. 3. The Government of Germany, by Prof. Charles D. Hazen.

No. 4. The Great War from Spectator to Participant.

No. 5. A War of Self Defense, by Secretary Lansing and Assistant Secretary of Labor Louis F. Post.

No. 6. American Loyalty by Citizens of German Descent.

No. 7. Amerikanische Bürgertreue, a translation of No. 6.

Other issues will appear shortly.

III. Official Bulletin :

Accurate daily statement of what all agencies of government are doing in war times. Sent free to newspapers and postmasters (to be put on bulletin boards). Subscription price $5.00 per year.

Address Requests to

Committee on Public Information, Washington, D. C.

What Can History Teachers Do Now?

You can help the community realize what history should mean to it.

You can confute those who by selecting a few historic facts seek to establish some simple cure-all for humanity.

You can confute those who urge that mankind can wipe the past off the slate and lay new foundations for civilization.

You can encourage the sane use of experience in discussions of public questions.

You can help people understand what democracy is by pointing out the common principle in the ideas of Plato, Cromwell, Rousseau, Jefferson, Jackson and Washington.

You can help people understand what German autocracy has in common with the autocracy of the Grand Mogul.

You can help people understand that democracy is not inconsistent with law and efficient government.

You can help people understand that failure of the past to make the world safe for democracy does not mean that it can not be made safe in the future.

You can so teach your students that they will acquire "historical mindedness" and realize the connection of the past with the present.

You can not do these things unless you inform yourself, and think over your information.

You can help yourself by reading the following :

"History and the Great War" bulletin of Bureau of Education.

A series of articles published throughout the year in THE HISTORY TEACHER'S MAGAZINE.

You can obtain aid and advice by writing to

The National Board for Historical Service, 1133 Woodward Building, Washington, D. C.

United States Bureau of Education, Division of Civic Education, Washington, D. C.

Committee on Public Information, Division of Educational Co-operation, 10 Jackson Place, Washington, D. C.

The Committee on Patriotism through Education of the National Security League, 31 Pine Street, New York City.

Carnegie Endowment for International Peace, 2 Jackson Place, Washington, D. C.

National Committee of Patriotic and Defense Societies, Southern Building, Washington, D. C.

The World Peace Foundation, 40 Mount Vernon St., Boston, Mass.

American Association for International Conciliation, 407 West 117th Street, New York City.

The American Society for Judicial Settlement of International Disputes, Baltimore, Md.

The Editor, THE HISTORY TEACHER'S MAGAZINE, Philadelphia.

SOURCE: Reprinted in James R. Mock and Cedric Larson, *Words That Won the War: The Story of the Committee on Public Information, 1917–1919* (Princeton, N.J.: Princeton University Press, 1939), p. 184; originally from *History Teacher's Magazine*, September 1917.

■■■

Source 2:   *An Advertisement for Publications of the Committee on Public Information* (1918)

Much of the Committee on Public Information's work attempted to illustrate that the United States could not remain isolated from the German threat. What impact do you think such propaganda had on Americans' attitudes?

THE HOHENZOLLERN DREAM

Germany is a war-made,—a war-making state.

She believes the sword the only satisfactory arbiter of international questions, blood the only food for a growing state.

With Germany in the ascendancy, war will remain the world's chief business.

The longer she is permitted to retain her "might" idea, the more ruthless her methods, the wider her conquests.

The next war will come *right* on to our own shores unless we crush the War idea—unless we crush Germany.

Know the essential war facts! Your government itself will give them to you. Any two of the following named pamphlets sent free upon request.

The President's Flag Day Speech. With evidence of Germany's plans. 32 pages.
The War Message and the Facts Behind It. 32 pages.
The Nation in Arms. 18 pages.
Why We Fight Germany.

War, Labor and Peace.
Conquest and Kultur. 160 pages.
German War Practices. 96 pages.
Treatment of German Militarism and German Critics.
The German War-Code. 16 pages.

Address, **COMMITTEE ON PUBLIC INFORMATION, 8 Jackson Pl., Washington, D.C.**

Contributed through Division of Advertising

U. S. Gov't Comm. on Public Information

This space contributed for the Winning of the War by

Source: Reprinted in Stephen Vaughn, *Holding Fast the Inner Lines: Democracy, Nationalism, and the Committee on Public Information* (Chapel Hill: University of North Carolina Press, 1980), p. 87; originally from Records of the Committee on Public Information, National Archives.

Source 3:   *"Bachelor of Atrocities"*   (1918)

The Committee on Public Information's Division of Advertising created many adver-
tisements for the Treasury Department's war bond drives. Many of these advertisements,
Creel admitted, showed " 'bloody boots,' trampled children, and mutilated women." One
of them, "Bachelor of Atrocities," was produced for college publications. What does this
source suggest about George Creel's intention to use rational appeals to mold public
opinion?

Bachelor of Atrocities

IN THE vicious guttural language of Kultur, the degree A. B. means Bachelor of
Atrocities. Are you going to let the Prussian Python strike at your Alma Mater,
as it struck at the University of Louvain?

The Hohenzollern fang strikes at every element of decency and culture and taste
that your college stands for. It leaves a track so terrible that only whispered fragments
may be recounted. It has ripped all the world-old romance out of war, and reduced
it to the dead, black depths of muck, and hate, and bitterness.

You may soon be called to fight. But
you are called upon right now to buy
Liberty Bonds. You are called upon to
economize in every way. It is sometimes
harder to live nobly than to die nobly. The
supreme sacrifice of life may come easier
than the petty sacrifices of comforts and
luxuries. You are called to exercise stern

self-discipline. Upon this the Allied Success depends.

Set aside every possible dollar for the
purchase of Liberty Bonds. Do it relent-
lessly. Kill every wasteful impulse that
America may live. Every bond you buy
fires point-blank at Prussian Terrorism.

BUY U. S. GOVERNMENT BONDS FOURTH LIBERTY LOAN

Contributed through Division of Advertising   United States Govt. Comm. on Public Information

This space contributed for the winning of the war by

Source: Reprinted in Stephen Vaughn, *Holding Fast the Inner Lines: Democracy, Nationalism, and the
Committee on Public Information* (Chapel Hill: University of North Carolina Press, 1980), p. 165;
originally from Records of the Committee on Public Information, National Archives.

SOURCE 4: Randolph Bourne, *"The War and the Intellectuals"* (1917)

In this article, written shortly after the American entry into the war, Randolph Bourne expresses his opposition to progressive intellectuals' assumptions about the war. On what grounds does he reject them?

We go to war to save the world from subjugation! But the German intellectuals went to war to save their culture from barbarization! And the French went to war to save their beautiful France! And the English to save international honor! And Russia, most altruistic and self-sacrificing of all, to save a small State from destruction! Whence is our miraculous intuition of our moral spotlessness? Whence our confidence that history will not unravel huge economic and imperialist forces upon which our rationalizations float like bubbles? . . .

The task of making our own country detailedly fit for peace was abandoned in favor of a feverish concern for the management of the war, advice to the fighting governments on all matters, military, social and political, and a gradual working up of the conviction that we were ordained as a nation to lead all erring brothers towards the light of liberty and democracy. . . .

The results of war on the intellectual class are already apparent. Their thought becomes little more than a description and justification of what is going on. They turn upon any rash one who continues idly to speculate. Once the war is on, the conviction spreads that individual thought is helpless, that the only way one can count is as a cog in the great wheel. There is no good holding back. We are told to dry our unnoticed and ineffective tears and plunge into the great work. Not only is everyone forced into line, but the new certitude becomes idealized. . . . The pacifist is roundly scolded for refusing to face the facts, and for retiring into his own world of sentimental desire. But is the realist, who refuses to challenge or criticise facts, entitled to any more credit than that which comes from following the line of least resistance? The realist thinks he at least can control events by linking himself to the forces that are moving. Perhaps he can. But if it is a question of controlling war, it is difficult to see how the child on the back of a mad elephant is to be any more effective in stopping the beast than is the child who tries to stop him from the ground.

SOURCE: Reprinted in Carl Resek, ed., *War and the Intellectuals: Essays by Randolph S. Bourne, 1915–1919* (New York: Harper & Row, 1964), pp. 7, 10, 12; originally from *Seven Arts,* June 1917.

SOURCE 5:   Randolph Bourne, *"The State"*   (1919)

In this unfinished essay, published after his death, Randolph Bourne contrasts the "State" with the nation and the government. The State, Bourne concludes, is a "mystical conception." The nation represents the people in a country, while the government is the power exercised by its leaders. What impact does the State have on individuals during a war, according to Bourne?

As the Church is the medium for the spiritual salvation of m[a]n, so the State is thought of as the medium for his political salvation. Its idealism is a rich blood flowing to all the members of the body politic. And it is precisely in war that the urgency for union seems greatest, and the necessity for universality seems most unquestioned. The State is the organization of the herd to act offensively or defensively against another herd similarly organized. The more terrifying the occasion for defense, the closer will become the organization and the more coercive the influence upon each member of the herd. . . .

The classes which are able to play an active and not merely a passive rôle in the organization for war get a tremendous liberation of activity and energy. . . . Every individual citizen who in peacetimes had no function to perform by which he could imagine himself an expression or living fragment of the State becomes an active amateur agent of the Government in reporting spies and disloyalists, in raising Government funds, or in propagating such measures as are considered necessary by officialdom. Minority opinion, which in times of peace, was only irritating and could not be dealt with by law unless it was conjoined with actual crime, becomes, with the outbreak of war, a case for outlawry. Criticism of the State, objections to war, luke-warm opinions concerning the necessity or the beauty of conscription, are made subject to ferocious penalties, far exceeding in severity those affixed to actual pragmatic crimes. Public opinion, as expressed in the newspapers, and the pulpits and the schools, becomes one solid block. "Loyalty," or rather war orthodoxy, becomes the sole test for all professions, techniques, occupations. Particularly is this true in the sphere of the intellectual life. There the smallest taint is held to spread over the whole soul, so that a professor of physics is *ipso facto* disqualified to teach physics or to hold honorable place in a university—the republic of learning—if he is at all unsound on the war. Even mere association with persons thus tainted is considered to disqualify a teacher. Anything pertaining to the enemy becomes taboo. His books are suppressed wherever possible, his language is forbidden. His artistic products are considered to convey in the subtlest spiritual way taints of vast poison to the soul that permits itself to enjoy them. So enemy music is suppressed, and energetic measures of opprobrium taken against those whose artistic consciences are not ready to perform such an act of self-sacrifice. . . .

War is the health of the State. It automatically sets in motion throughout society those irresistible forces for uniformity, for passionate cooperation with the

SOURCE: Reprinted in Carl Resek, ed., *War and the Intellectuals: Essays by Randolph S. Bourne, 1915–1919* (New York: Harper & Row, 1964), pp. 69, 70–71; originally from James Oppenheim, ed., *Untimely Papers* (New York: B. W. Huebsch, 1919).

Government in coercing into obedience the minority groups and individuals which lack the larger herd sense. The machinery of government sets and enforces the drastic penalties, the minorities are either intimidated into silence, or brought slowly around by a subtle process of persuasion which may seem to them really to be converting them. . . . Other values such as artistic creation, knowledge, reason, beauty, the enhancement of life, are instantly and almost unanimously sacrificed, and the significant classes who have constituted themselves the amateur agents of the State are engaged not only in sacrificing these values for themselves but in coercing all other persons into sacrificing them.

Source 6: *George Creel on the Committee on Public Information* (1920)

In George Creel's account of the activities of the Committee on Public Information published after the armistice, he demonstrates his firm faith in its work. On what grounds does he defend the actions of the CPI and, in particular, its efforts to arouse the "war-will" of the people?

The Committee on Public Information was called into existence to . . . plead the justice of America's cause before the jury of Public Opinion. . . . *In no degree was the Committee an agency of censorship, a machinery of concealment or repression. Its emphasis throughout was on the open and the positive. At no point did it seek or exercise authorities under those war laws that limited the freedom of speech and press.* In all things, from first to last, without halt or change, it was a plain publicity proposition, a vast enterprise in salesmanship, the world's greatest adventure in advertising.

Under the pressure of tremendous necessities an organization grew that not only reached deep into every American community, but that carried to every corner of the civilized globe the full message of America's idealism, unselfishness, and indomitable purpose. We fought prejudice, indifference, and disaffection at home and we fought ignorance and falsehood abroad. . . . We did not call it propaganda, for that word, in German hands, had come to be associated with deceit and corruption. Our effort was educational and informative throughout, for we had such confidence in our case as to feel that no other argument was needed than the simple, straightforward presentation of facts.

There was no part of the great war machinery that we did not touch, no medium of appeal that we did not employ. The printed word, the spoken word, the motion picture, the telegraph, the cable, the wireless, the poster, the sign-board—all these were used in our campaign to make our own people and all other peoples understand the causes that compelled America to take arms. All that was fine and ardent in the civilian population came at our call until more than one hundred and fifty thousand men and women were devoting highly specialized abilities to the work of the Committee, as faithful and devoted in their service as though they wore the khaki.

Source: George Creel, *How We Advertised America* (1920; reprint, New York: Arno Press, 1972), pp. 3–5.

While America's summons was answered without question by the citizenship as a whole, it is to be remembered that during the three and a half years of our neutrality the land had been torn by a thousand divisive prejudices, stunned by the voices of anger and confusion, and muddled by the pull and haul of opposed interests. These were conditions that could not be permitted to endure. What we had to have was no mere surface unity, but a passionate belief in the justice of America's cause that should weld the people of the United States into one white-hot mass instinct with fraternity, devotion, courage, and deathless determination. The *war-will*, the will-to-win, of a democracy depends upon the degree to which each one of all the people of that democracy can concentrate and consecrate body and soul and spirit in the supreme effort of service and sacrifice. What had to be driven home was that all business was the nation's business, and every task a common task for a single purpose.

QUESTIONS TO CONSIDER

1. Although both George Creel and Randolph Bourne considered themselves progressives, they held very different views about World War I. What do the primary sources reveal about those views? How did their backgrounds influence their perceptions of the war?

2. In a democracy, Creel argued, winning a war depends on the degree to which people commit "body and soul and spirit" to it. How did the Committee on Public Information attempt to elicit such a commitment? Did its efforts subvert Woodrow Wilson's goal of waging a war for "democracy"?

3. Bourne argued that the progressives who took the United States to war would not be able to control its consequences. What were the war's most important effects on American society? Did they validate Bourne's analysis?

4. Some historians have argued that as Americans grew disillusioned with World War I after the armistice, they also lost interest in reform. What does the work of Creel and the Committee on Public Information reveal about the impact of the government's efforts to control Americans' hearts and minds during the war? What role did Creel's agency play in a backlash against reform after the war?

5. Citing specific sources, explain whether Bourne or Creel offered a more cogent analysis of the war. What does their work reveal about the wisdom of Wilson's decision to take the nation to war without a direct attack on the country?

FOR FURTHER READING

George Creel, *Rebel at Large: Recollections of Fifty Crowded Years* (New York: G. P. Putnam's Sons, 1947), demonstrates Creel's ability to tell a story and provides insight into his background and activities as the head of the Committee on Public Information.

Louis Filler, *Randolph Bourne* (New York: Citadel Press, 1966), remains one of the most engaging of the many studies of Bourne's life and work.

David Kennedy, *Over Here: The First World War and American Society* (New York: Oxford University Press, 1980), provides an excellent survey of the First World War's impact on American society.

Carl Resek, ed., *War and the Intellectuals: Essays by Randolph S. Bourne, 1915–1919* (New York: Harper & Row, 1964), is a brief collection of Bourne's writings on World War I. These essays formed the basis of his reputation later in the twentieth century.

Stephen Vaughn, *Holding Fast the Inner Lines: Democracy, Nationalism, and the Committee on Public Information* (Chapel Hill: University of North Carolina Press, 1980), offers a thorough account of the CPI's efforts to control news and encourage nationalism during World War I.

Science, Religion, and "Culture Wars" in the 1920s: William Jennings Bryan and Clarence Darrow

It was hot and humid in Dayton, Tennessee, when Clarence Darrow called William Jennings Bryan to the witness stand. Bryan confidently stepped forward, took an oath, sat down, and gazed at a sea of three thousand spectators. They were gathered in July 1925 for the trial of John Scopes, the town's high school science teacher. The twenty-four-year-old Scopes stood accused of violating a new law that prohibited the teaching of evolution in the state's public schools. Sensationalism drew many curious onlookers to Dayton, but invisible and unnamed codefendants, not ballyhoo alone, explain the phenomenal public interest in the trial. To millions of Americans, Scopes stood on the side of enlightened, modern thought. To millions of others, he stood for everything threatening and dangerous to traditional values and religious ideals.

Whatever brought the spectators to Dayton, the courtroom could no longer hold them all, so the judge decided to move the proceedings to the courthouse lawn, where Bryan took his seat under a blazing afternoon sun. The sixty-five-year-old witness needed no introduction. He had been catapulted into the national spotlight in 1896 when he captured the Democratic presidential nomination with a rousing speech at his party's convention. Bryan lost the election, but remained an important figure in national politics. In coming years, he exercised his impressive oratorical skills in speeches around the country. In many of them, he denounced the theory of evolution as a "conspiracy among the atheists and agnostics against the Christian religion," and by the early 1920s he was the leader of a nationwide anti-evolution movement.

A lawyer by training, Bryan came to Dayton as a member of the prosecution team. But in an unusual move the defense called him as an "expert witness" on the Bible. Sitting in his shirt sleeves, this "defender of the faith" was an eager combatant in what he called a "duel to the death" between Christianity and science. He was not prepared, though, for Clarence Darrow. The most famous lawyer of his day, Darrow had racked up an impressive string of courtroom victories defending underdogs. Bryan may have been a peerless orator, but Darrow's ability to examine witnesses in the courtroom was unsurpassed. For two hours, the sixty-eight-year-old attorney subjected the bewildered Bryan to a

Clarence Darrow and William Jennings Bryan

withering barrage of questions. Frustrated, Bryan finally lashed out at Darrow, proclaiming that he was out to ridicule "every Christian who believes in the Bible." "We have the purpose," Darrow retorted, "of preventing bigots and ignoramuses from controlling the education of the United States."

The Scopes Trial brought face to face two leading combatants in the culture wars raging across the United States in the 1920s. While Bryan spoke for an older, rural society dominated by traditional morals and ideas, Darrow represented a modern, urban society characterized by new beliefs, manners, and values. Products of the old order, Bryan and Darrow traced their roots to the same side in this contest. But like many other Americans, they were divided by social, cultural, and intellectual currents sweeping over the nation in the early twentieth century. Thus, the two old warriors, representing millions of others, found themselves facing off in Dayton.

"The Armor of Righteous Cause"

William Jennings Bryan's very presence at the Scopes Trial was a testament to the enduring impact of his upbringing. Bryan was born in 1860 in Salem, Illinois, the fourth of six surviving children of Silas and Mariah Bryan. Planted squarely in the nation's farm belt, Salem counted some two thousand residents. Its small shops and mills served those who, as Bryan's father put it, worked up "a sweat of the face in agricultural pursuits." Young Will knew exactly what that meant. Shortly after he was born, Bryan's family moved to a farm just outside town. Earning most of his income as a lawyer and judge, Silas was only a gentleman farmer. Nonetheless, Will was subjected to his share of physical work. What he called the drudgery of farm chores left him with abiding respect for those who earned a living behind a plow.

The Bryan household was intensely religious. A devout Baptist deacon, Silas Bryan prayed three times a day and gathered the family every Sunday afternoon for hymn singing. Because Mariah was a committed Methodist, Will attended Sunday school every week at each of his parents' churches. Raised in two Protestant churches, he found it easy to join yet another. After attending a Presbyterian revival in Salem when he was fourteen, Bryan became a member of the church. Will had already imbibed a strong disdain for swearing, drinking, gambling, dancing, and other activities of "questionable moral tendency." As he later wrote, having grown up in a "Christian home," his conversion did not represent any change in "habits of life or habits of thought."

If Bryan shared his parents' Protestant piety, he also embraced his father's political views. Active in local politics, Silas was a staunch Democrat. His was the party of Thomas Jefferson and Andrew Jackson. Like these party founders, Silas firmly believed in the people's ability to govern themselves. Common people were the best judges of their own interests and possessed enough wisdom to govern themselves as they saw fit. The danger was a government that promoted the interests of the few. Along with these views, young Bryan inherited a love for politics, itself. As a twelve-year-old, Will accompanied his father while he campaigned unsuccessfully for Congress, and from then on Will's life's course was set. Like his father, Bryan had little difficulty mixing politics with piety or turning numerous political causes into moral crusades.

Exposed early on to both pulpit and stump, Bryan was attracted to oratory. He joined the debating club in high school and later participated in speech contests as a student at Illinois College in nearby Jacksonville, Illinois. Bryan was drawn to the study of law as preparation for a career in politics and after graduating at the head of his class in 1881, he went off to Union Law School in Chicago, where he continued to compete in speech contests. Degree in hand, he returned to Jacksonville two years later, married his college sweetheart Mary Baird, and settled down to practice law and enter politics. After several years, though, he was frustrated by the scant political opportunities for a Democrat in heavily Republican Jacksonville. So in 1887, he headed west with Mary and the first of their three children to settle in Lincoln, Nebraska.

It was a good choice, given Bryan's political aspirations, oratorical skills, and reverence for common people. And the timing could not have been better. By the late 1880s, many farmers were caught in a vise of overproduction, falling prices, and high debt. In 1890, their worsening plight gave birth to the Populist Party. [See Chapter 3.] The same year, Bryan took advantage of the rising agrarian unrest to win a seat in Congress. Meanwhile, his oratory gained him wider attention. Across the rural South and West, stricken farmers demanded the coinage of silver in the belief that increasing the amount of money in circulation would cause farm prices to rise. A supporter of silver, Bryan won reelection in 1892 with Populist and Democratic votes. He lost a bid to become a senator two years later, but his political career was not over. As the economy skidded into a deep depression and farmers' woes mounted, the pro-silver Bryan was flooded with invitations to speak around the country, including at the Democratic Convention in 1896.

Bryan's moment arrived at the Chicago convention. This son of Salem understood the outlook and shared the values of millions of hard-pressed rural Americans. He knew they faced a threat from powerful corporate interests centered in distant eastern cities. And he believed in their strength and virtue. He reminded the gathering that, "the humblest citizen in all the land, when clad in the armor of righteous cause, is stronger than all the hosts of error." He also demonstrated his ability to mix Protestant piety with politics. Assaulting a gold-based money system, he dramatically spread his arms wide and proclaimed, "You shall not crucify mankind upon a cross of gold!" The "Cross of Gold" speech rocked the convention hall, and the electrified delegates awarded Bryan their party's presidential nomination. In the end, however, silver and rural support could not defeat Republican William McKinley, who captured the urban, industrial Northeast with support of the gold standard and tariff policies favorable to business.

Bryan's sterling oratory kept him in the spotlight as he continued to speak out on important issues after the election. During the Spanish-American War, he was a vocal opponent of America's acquisition of overseas territory. If common people in this country were capable of governing themselves, he believed, those in Cuba and the Philippines were as well. Once more capturing the Democratic nomination in 1900, Bryan attacked imperialism in the presidential campaign. He lost to McKinley again, but continued to reach a wide audience. He returned to Lincoln to start *The Commoner*, a newspaper whose mission was to "aid the common people in protection of their rights." Its favorite targets were big business and banks, and within a year it boasted a circulation of 140,000. In coming years, Bryan reached even more people through public speaking. Most summers, he lectured before Chautauqua* gatherings in hundreds of small towns across the country. He often made the same points: the importance of faith in God and the right of the people "to have what they want in legislation." During the progressive era, many people wanted legislation that put restraints on corporate power, and in 1908 Bryan's ability to articulate these concerns won him the Democratic presidential nomination for a third time; he faced Republican William Howard Taft and once again fell short.

Bryan quickly found other crusades, though. One was a resurgent temperance movement, fed by a progressive desire to uplift people by controlling their behavior. Like many Protestants, Bryan, a lifelong teetotaler, associated alcohol consumption with sin. Non-Protestant immigrants crowding the nation's cities attached no such stigma to drink. In fact, the growing debate over alcohol in the early twentieth century reflected a deep cultural divide between middle-class, native-born, mostly rural Protestants and growing numbers of poor Catholic and Jewish immigrants in the cities. Like other temperance advocates, though, Bryan could not see religious bigotry in support for prohibition. It was just another "righteous cause," and in coming years he watched with satisfaction as Nebraska and many other rural states went dry.

Bryan approached the cause of peace with the same fervor. When Woodrow Wilson named him secretary of state in 1915, soon after the outbreak of war in

---

Chautauqua: An institution with roots in religious meetings at Chautauqua Lake in New York state. It sponsored lectures on religious and educational topics and public issues in small towns in the late nineteenth and early twentieth centuries.

Europe, he applied the Christian message of peace to diplomacy, but resigned the next year after concluding that the Wilson Wilson administration sided with the Allies. Campaigning against American entry into World War I, he defined the problem much as he had in 1896. Arrayed against the peace-loving common people were predatory concentrations of wealth headquartered in the East: the "money power" of Wall Street, the "tariff barons," and the "trust magnates," who would drag the nation to war for profit.

Bryan looked to the future with optimism when peace finally came in 1918. He called the postwar period a "glorious" time. It would be so for many Americans, especially the well-off residents of cities. Primary beneficiaries of a prolonged postwar economic expansion, they enjoyed unprecedented prosperity and wide opportunities to buy new consumer goods and indulge in new forms of entertainment. They eagerly embraced other changes as well: new technology, new values, and new standards of morality and behavior. The result was a seismic shift in American culture. Bryan and millions of other mostly rural Americans, however, were not prepared for it. One last time, therefore, the "Great Commoner" donned "the armor of righteous cause" to defend common people. This time the foe had little to do with concentrated economic power. Rather, it was the modern ideas and dangerous cultural influences emanating from eastern cities. In the 1920s, Bryan and many others targeted a concrete and potent symbol of this elusive threat to the old life: the theory of evolution. They also found a very able opponent in one of its most outspoken defenders: the man who squared off against Bryan in Dayton.

"This Village Religious Stuff"

Clarence Darrow entered the world in an Ohio village that some casual observers might easily have mistaken for Salem, Illinois. Nestled in the northeastern corner of the state, the farming community of Kinsman numbered some four hundred people when Darrow was born there in 1857. Growing up in Kinsman, he enjoyed experiences that he remembered fondly all his life: fishing, playing baseball, and tobogganing down snow-covered hills. Looking back much later on the circumstances of his birth, though, he observed that he would have chosen to be born in a "noisy city" instead of a tiny village.

He most certainly would have chosen more elevated economic circumstances. The fifth child of Amirus and Emily Eddy Darrow, the famous attorney was born to a family that traced its roots to the seventeenth-century Plymouth Pilgrims. Yet the Darrows were poor, and young Clarence, who cared little about ancestry, inherited very limited prospects. Amirus eked out a living as a carpenter and furniture maker, while Emily kept house and struggled to make the growing family's ends meet.

Clarence later realized, however, that his parents bequeathed to him something more important than economic advantage. Amirus and Emily had been drawn to one another by a love of books, and their home in Kinsman was piled high with them. Those books provided one of young Clarence's first childhood memories. "The house was small, the family large, the furniture meager," he later wrote, "but there were books whichever way one turned." Clarence became an avid reader in this environment. Here was an inheritance that eventually carried him far from Kinsman.

Like young Bryan, Darrow also inherited his father's views about politics and religion. As a student in Pennsylvania, Amirus had studied theology, apparently with the intention of becoming a minister. By the time he graduated, however, he had lost his faith, and in a sea of rural Protestant piety Amirus stood alone. "My father," Darrow observed later, "was the village infidel." He stood apart in other ways, too. In heavily Republican northeast Ohio, Amirus was a Democrat. In a Yankee culture that valued practicality and achievement, he remained unconcerned with material success. Amirus gloried in his reputation as an outsider who defied popular opinion. He had a profound impact on young Clarence, who also learned to stand up for his convictions no matter how unpopular. All his life, he would emulate his father.

The results were obvious in his experiences at school and church. For all his love of books, Clarence was not a good student. Though eager to learn, he never cared for formal schooling. Like his father, he came to view schools as institutions that instilled orthodox views, encouraged conventional morality, and suppressed independent thinking. Looking back on his own experience, he concluded that school was "an appalling waste of time." He came to feel much the same about organized religion. Despite Amirus's unorthodox views, Emily made sure that the Darrow children were marched off to church on Sundays. It was not a pleasant experience for the boy, who never forgot the "tortures of listening to an endless sermon."

Besides views about education and religion, Amirus imparted to his son a belief that he should strive to succeed and gain influence. By fits and starts, he did. After completing high school in 1873, Darrow enrolled at Allegheny College, his father's alma mater. Still only a mediocre student, he dropped out after one year, returned to Kinsman, and went to work in his father's furniture shop. He quickly discovered that carpentry did not suit him, so he tried his hand at school teaching in a nearby village. Despite his feelings toward his own formal schooling, he managed to stay for three years before he enrolled in the University of Michigan's law school, where a college degree was not yet required for admission. He stayed only one year. Concerned about the strain on his family's finances, Darrow left to study in a lawyer's office in Youngstown, Ohio, where he passed the bar examination after only several months.

At age twenty-one, he was ready to fulfill his father's dream for him. Returning to Kinsman, Darrow hung out his lawyer's shingle. He also courted Jessie Ohl, a longtime acquaintance and daughter of a prosperous mill owner. He married her in 1880. The couple soon moved to nearby Andover and then to the larger town of Ashtabula as Darrow searched for clients. Like Bryan, he got involved in the Democratic Party and developed an appetite for public speaking. Unlike Bryan, however, he grew tired of life in a "farming section with farmers' ideas." As he later put it, he "read himself out" of the countryside. So Darrow moved his family again several years later, this time to a mecca for ambitious young men in the rural Midwest: Chicago.

He could not have made a better choice. Chicago in 1887 was one of the fastest-growing cities in the country—a commercial, financial, and industrial hub of nearly a million people. It was also a focal point of many of the changes transforming American society in the late nineteenth century: industrial expansion, a flood of immigrants from southern and eastern Europe, the rise of organized labor and industrial strife, and the growing specter of political radicalism. Darrow was not in the Windy City long before its vibrant environment had, in the words of one biographer, "blown the straw out of his hair."

Darrow had no money or connections when he moved to Chicago. Within a decade, he was one of the city's best-known attorneys. More than anyone, he owed his rapid rise to John Peter Altgeld. A German immigrant, Altgeld was a Cook County judge and rising star in the Illinois Democratic machine. As Altgeld rose to the governorship in 1892, Darrow was at his side as a friend and advisor. Altgeld shared Darrow's radical sympathies and was equally contemptuous of popular opinion, as he demonstrated in 1893 when he pardoned three anarchists convicted in the fatal Haymarket Square bombing in 1886.* As Darrow worked to advance his mentor's political career, Altgeld opened doors for his young protégé with various appointments, including one as corporate attorney for the Chicago and Northwestern Railway, which had a keen interest in Chicago politics and the means to provide Darrow with financial security.

Darrow was on the railroad's payroll for six years, but guilt over his work there eventually led him to take up the cause of labor. At a time of unprecedented labor unrest, he built a thriving practice defending unions. In 1895, he successfully defended Eugene Debs, the socialist leader of the American Railway Union who was charged with criminal conspiracy during the Pullman Strike of 1894.* With Debs's acquittal, Darrow had no problem attracting clients. In 1902, the United Mine Workers union called on him to arbitrate a strike in the coal fields of Pennsylvania. Later, he won the acquittal of William "Big Bill" Haywood and two other leaders of the Western Federation of Miners accused of murdering the former governor of Idaho. In these cases and others, the cantankerous Darrow perfected his devastatingly effective courtroom style: a combination of logic and verbal abuse designed to diminish opponents and undercut their arguments.

These cases made Darrow famous, but fame took a toll on his marriage. His wife Jessie longed for a quiet, domestic life, just as she had had in Kinsman. Clarence, on the other hand, was seduced by the city. Fond of the public spotlight, he relished his growing celebrity. He reveled in opportunities to participate in lectures, debates, and dinner parties, where he discussed the great issues of the day and enjoyed new friends. His fame also offered opportunities to mingle with admiring women—and carry on adulterous affairs with some of them. Only seven years after moving from the country, Darrow filed for divorce.

In the city, Darrow found liberation from social conventions and the opportunity to flout traditional morality. Although he remarried in 1903, he preached and occasionally practiced free love. He defied conventional political views by espousing socialism and advocating numerous reforms, including black rights.

Haymarket Square Bombing: A bombing incident that occurred after police attempted to disperse a labor protest in Chicago's Haymarket Square against the McCormick reaper company. The bombing left seven people dead and resulted in the trial and conviction of eight anarchists, even though those who threw the bombs were never identified.

Pullman Strike: A strike led by Debs's American Railway Union against the Pullman Company, the manufacturer of railroad sleeping cars. The strike spread to the rails and crippled the nation's transportation system.

After taking up the cause of workers' rights, he proclaimed that labor was oppressed by an exploitive economic and political system, a view expressed during numerous trials, including his defense of three radical labor leaders accused of blowing up the *Los Angeles Times* building in 1910, killing twenty people. He also flouted conventional morality with attacks on the idea of individual responsibility for behavior. In many cases, he argued that defendants' actions were determined by their environment. That view was the basis of his defense of two young men from wealthy Chicago families, Nathan Leopold and Richard Loeb, who were accused of kidnaping and murdering a fourteen-year-old neighbor boy in 1924. Many observers called it the "crime of the century," and Darrow's clients were found guilty, but he saved them from execution by arguing that their environment had made them mentally abnormal.

Darrow's conspicuous rejection of traditional morality, politics, and ideas was matched by his vocal attacks on religion. He made his religious views public as early as 1899, when he published a pamphlet titled *Why I Am an Agnostic*. Darrow associated religion, especially evangelical Protestantism, with everything he had escaped from in leaving Kinsman. And in his mind, no one came to embody the narrow-minded and repressive religion of the countryside more than William Jennings Bryan. Darrow and Bryan actually stood on the same side of many reform causes in the early twentieth century, including the regulation of business. But since the 1890s, Darrow had maintained a simmering dislike for the Great Commoner. Political differences fed much of his animosity. Bryan's agenda for reform and his popularity in the Democratic party reflected his rural base. He appealed to voters with silver, prohibition, and piety. Darrow, on the other hand, had moved to the city and aligned himself with a big-city Democratic Party machine and industrial workers. Like many city dwellers, he associated Bryan and his moralistic appeals with provincial Protestant bigotry. After he ran unsuccessfully for a seat in Congress in 1896, Darrow blamed his defeat on Bryan, who had alienated many urban voters. In an encounter with the former Democratic presidential candidate the next year, Darrow told Bryan that he was not ready to lead his party. "You'd better go back to Lincoln," he exploded, "and study science, history, [and] philosophy . . . and quit this village religious stuff." Twenty-eight years later in Dayton, Darrow would have the opportunity to do battle with Bryan and his "village religious stuff."

The "Monkey Trial"

By the time Clarence Darrow gained nationwide fame defending the perpetrators of the "crime of the century," William Jennings Bryan's influence in politics had diminished. His influence in religious affairs, however, had soared. By 1924, Bryan marched at the head of a Protestant religious movement known as fundamentalism. Based on the doctrine of the Scripture's infallibility, fundamentalism was organized as a movement in 1919 by conservative Christians in response to "modernists" who believed that readers of the Bible had to understand its historical context and its allegorical and symbolic nature. In the early 1920s, fundamentalism brought together millions of Methodists, Baptists, and other mostly rural Protestants in a militant religious crusade centered in the southern Bible Belt. It also identified an evil to battle: Darwinian evolution.

Evolutionary theory, of course, was not new in the 1920s. The English biologist Charles Darwin first advanced his theory of evolution through natural selection in the mid-nineteenth century. Although modified by some since Darwin's day, the theory was universally embraced by scientists and widely accepted by the public in the 1920s. Already by the late nineteenth century, school textbooks had replaced the notion of man's divine creation with Darwinian explanations. Many Christian theologians, moreover, adapted their views to it. For those swept up in the fundamentalist movement, however, evolution was an outrage. It suggested a randomness to existence that contradicted a Christian worldview. More to the point, it flew in the face of a literal reading of Scripture, especially the creation accounts in the Book of Genesis.

Yet the appeal of anti-evolutionism went deeper than that. For many Americans in the 1920s, this modern idea was a highly charged unifying symbol for all that was wrong with their society. And plenty seemed to have gone wrong in the postwar Jazz Age. A revolt against traditional Victorian morality was in full swing, reinforced by such modern ideas as Sigmund Freud's* psychoanalytic theories, which many Americans understood as a call to overthrow sexual inhibitions. Respectability suddenly seemed to have been discarded in favor of loose morals and shocking behavior. In alcohol-sodden speakeasies, patrons flouted prohibition, which had been enacted nationwide with ratification of the Eighteenth Amendment in 1919. On dance hall floors, young people moved suggestively to the rhythms of shocking new music. Flappers—single and sexually free young women—openly rejected traditional Victorian ideals regarding gender, sexuality, and self-control. Dangerous "modernism," it seemed, had taken hold everywhere. [See Source 1.]

Many Americans had little difficulty locating the source of these disturbing trends. They were manifestations of the powerful new culture emanating from the nation's rapidly expanding cities, which now claimed more residents than the countryside. This urban culture's influences were everywhere: in movies, radio programs, music, and the hedonistic, live-for-the-day messages of advertising. As the locus of a pervasive new morality, urban America was more threatening than ever. Fears of the city were further heightened by other changes, such as the influx of African Americans into northern cities. Sparked by a labor shortage during World War I, this Great Migration of blacks out of the South transformed the racial makeup of urban America. It also reinforced the association between cities and such dangers as race mixing and loose morals. These fears were reflected in widespread condemnations of jazz, increasingly popular among urban whites, as too "sensuous" and "African." The urban landscape was also transformed by a new wave of immigration that washed millions of newcomers onto the nation's shores. Huddled in urban tenements, they made the city a confusing Tower of Babel to many native-born, rural Americans.

Faced with this rising threat, rural America fought back. One obvious counterattack was Prohibition. The Eighteenth Amendment was an attempt by

---

Sigmund Freud: The Austrian psychoanalyst who in the early twentieth century argued that the exploration of the unconscious mind was the key to understanding behavior and that the sex drive was the most important component of one's psychological makeup.

mostly native-born, small-town, and rural Americans to impose traditional Protestant morality on besotted, city-dwelling immigrants. In a postwar environment of rising nativism, it was also no accident that the door to massive European immigration slammed shut with the passage of the Johnson-Reed Act in 1924. The new law established annual quotas for immigration that favored northern European immigrants over non-Protestant southern and eastern Europeans. Nor was it coincidence that the Ku Klux Klan enjoyed a resurgence during the Jazz Age. Promising to battle Jews, Catholics, immigrants, "flapperism," violations of prohibition, and other manifestations of immorality, the Klan attracted millions of mainly small-town and rural Americans. **[See Source 2.]**

In the early 1920s, many Americans saw the theory of evolution as the religious counterpart to a dangerous new urban culture. Nobody reflected that view better than Bryan. The Great Commoner, of course, had been long concerned about various threats emanating from the city, including Darwinism. He believed that the idea of the survival of the fittest was a convenient argument by conservative social Darwinists* to undermine reform. Darwin's theory, he declared in 1904, was a "merciless law by which the strong crowd out and kill off the weak." He was even convinced that German militarism was fostered by the belief that a "struggle for survival" applied to nations. Most important, though, Darwinism posed a threat to Christianity. The teaching of evolution caused young people "to lose faith in the Bible." As dangerous social, cultural, and intellectual trends threatened society, defending the faith and the traditional morality it upheld was more imperative than ever. Favoring old-time religion and old-fashioned music, art, and literature, Bryan never wavered in his beliefs or cultural preferences. And like many other Americans, he believed that Darwinism undermined them all. As he declared in 1924, "All the ills from which America suffers can be traced back to the teaching of evolution."

When fundamentalists turned their attention to the teaching of evolution in the 1920s, they had a powerful champion in Bryan. And they soon had their first victory. Bills to ban the teaching of evolution were introduced by 1925 in several southern states, including Tennessee. That state's bill made it a crime to teach in the public schools "any theory that denies the story of the Divine creation of man as taught in the Bible." Although one lawmaker jokingly proposed legislation to "require teachers to teach that the world is not round," the anti-evolution bill passed in 1925. The vote in the legislature's lower house was seventy-one to five.

The American Civil Liberties Union immediately sought a case to test the law's constitutionality. Founded during World War I in response to the Wilson administration's efforts to root out antiwar dissent, the ACLU waged a broader defense of civil liberties after the war. Its attorneys saw the Tennessee law as a violation of freedom of speech and a teacher's right to work without political interference. So they placed advertisements in newspapers seeking a plaintiff. With John Scopes's cooperation, the leading citizens of Dayton responded.

Social Darwinists: Late nineteenth-century social commentators who applied Darwin's theory of evolution through natural selection to society to defend unrestricted competition and justify the position of powerful corporations and the wealthy.

Looking merely to generate publicity for their economically slumping town, they succeeded beyond their wildest dreams. Thousands of curious people, some with pet primates, and reporters from all over descended on Dayton to witness or report on the Scopes "Monkey Trial."

Public interest in the trial only increased when Bryan and Darrow entered the fray. For Bryan, it would be a chance to defend the faith. As he announced before the trial, this case boiled down to one question: "Is there a God?" For the Great Commoner, though, there was another issue, too. The man who battled to protect the people from powerful minority interests firmly believed that the majority had the right to determine what was taught to children in school and to protect them from dangerous ideas. For his part, Darrow knew this case could establish the unconstitutionality of the anti-evolution law. More important, the trial presented an opportunity to battle the "village religion" that was responsible for it. Brought to the defense by Scopes himself, Darrow had little faith in the wisdom of the people to determine what their children should be taught in school. He put his faith instead in a minority: established experts in a discipline.

In fact, each side's lead attorneys reflected the social and cultural division surrounding the battle over evolution. Two ACLU attorneys sat for the defense with the agnostic Darrow: one a Catholic, the other a Jew. All three men hailed from the big city. The two ACLU lawyers were from New York City, while Darrow's home was a city synonymous with corruption and gangsterism. One ACLU attorney was a wealthy radical; the other a successful divorce lawyer and, in the words of one southern newspaper, a "slick city fellow." Darrow, of course, had been divorced himself. And sitting beside them was young Scopes, a Kentucky native whose father, a labor organizer, had passed to his son a willingness to challenge orthodoxy. On the other side sat Bryan, ready to defend God and old-time religion. He got a standing ovation from the crowd as he entered the courtroom on the first day, but his attacks on the National Education Association, the American Library Association, and other organizations for "poisoning young minds" with "anti-Christian propaganda" made him a laughingstock to many Americans. The longtime "dry" on prohibition was in favor of immigration restriction and refused to take a stand against the Ku Klux Klan at the Democratic Convention in 1924. Beside him sat a young state attorney general who proudly proclaimed his fundamentalist faith and a retired attorney general who taunted the defense attorneys as "outsiders" and "agnostics." [**See Source 3.**]

The trial lasted seven days. The first six were occupied with jury selection and legal skirmishes on several fronts. The defense first contended that the law itself was a violation of the state constitution's separation of church and state. What Darrow called a "foolish, mischievous, and wicked act" resulted in the implementation of fundamentalist religious doctrine by the state. [**See Source 4.**] When the prosecution countered that the separation of church and state referred to a state's preference for one particular religious *denomination* over others, the judge rejected the dismissal of Scopes's indictment on constitutional grounds. The defense also argued that the anti-evolution law violated Scopes's right of free speech in the classroom, but the prosecution responded that a teacher has no such right there. If Scopes did not like the conditions laid down by his employer, Bryan declared, he was free to take a job at an "atheist school." When the defense sought to bring in experts in science and theology to testify that Christianity and evolution were compatible, Bryan argued that "the Word of God . . . does not take an expert to understand it." [**See Source 5.**] The defense was stymied again when the judge barred outside experts from testifying—a ruling that seemed to bring the trial to an end. But in a surprise move, the defense called Bryan himself to testify as an expert witness on the Bible. It wanted to demonstrate that even a fundamentalist like Bryan might not read the Bible literally and thereby prove that Scopes did not necessarily contradict scripture in teaching evolution. Darrow, of course, was determined to have Bryan demonstrate what he considered to be the narrow-minded bigotry behind the fundamentalist assault on evolution. Just as eager to defend his faith, Bryan agreed to testify, against the wishes of the other prosecutors.

When the Great Commoner took the stand on the trial's seventh day, Darrow's questioning was relentless. Zeroing in on Bryan's literal reading of scripture, Darrow laid bare Bryan's astounding ignorance of basic scientific and historical information. He asked Bryan about biblical accounts of a whale swallowing Jonah, Joshua's ability to make the sun stand still, and God's creation of the universe in six days. His searing examination forced Bryan to admit that the Bible sometimes could not be read literally—a position supporting the defense's contention that evolution did not necessarily contradict biblical accounts. When Bryan jumped to his feet and objected to his opponent's "slurring of the Bible," his flash of anger only played into Darrow's hands. Shaking his fist at the witness, Darrow shot back, "I am examining you on your fool ideas that no intelligent Christian on earth believes." [**See Source 6.**]

After two hours, with both men enraged and shouting at one another, the judge suddenly adjourned for the day. An exhausted Bryan slumped in his chair, while a throng of bystanders crowded around Darrow to congratulate him. The next morning, the prosecution refused to let Bryan go back on the stand. Darrow countered by waiving his right to a closing statement, thereby denying Bryan the opportunity to deliver his. With that, the trial was over. In coming weeks, commentators across the country would weigh in on it. [**See Source 7.**]

The verdict was anticlimactic. After deliberating for nine minutes, the jury found Scopes guilty. He was later fined $100. Still seeking a constitutional ruling on the state's anti-evolution law, the defense appealed the verdict to the Tennessee Supreme Court. But it was foiled again. Although that court overturned Scopes's conviction on a technicality, it refused to issue a broader constitutional ruling on the law, which stayed on the books until the legislature repealed it in 1967.

After the trial, Bryan lingered in Dayton to make plans for the fight against evolution. Five days later, he laid down to take a nap from which he never woke. As thousands of mourners watched the train taking the Great Commoner's body to Washington, D.C., for burial, many of them blamed the "atheists" for carrying him away. The anti-evolution movement lived on, though. The next year, 1926, Mississippi banned the teaching of evolution, and the governor of Texas moved to purge mention of evolution from that state's textbooks. Nineteen state legislatures across the nation considered anti-evolution bills in 1927. Although none of those bills passed, Arkansas passed an anti-evolution law by referendum the next year. Meanwhile, many county boards of education in the South banned the teaching of evolution in public schools. In Georgia, the Ku

Klux Klan took up the cause of removing evolutionists from the classroom. Publishers also revised science textbooks to eliminate mention of evolution from them—or began to offer two versions, one with and one without Darwin's theory. Only in 1930, when the nation's attention shifted to economic depression, did the anti-evolution movement wane.

In the face of these anti-evolution victories, Darrow battled on. In lectures and debates, he proclaimed his agnosticism and ridiculed the fundamentalists' literal reading of the Bible. He also continued to defend the theory of evolution and even served as a commentator in a movie about it in 1931. And until four years before his death in 1938 at age eighty-one, he was in court defending clients. Like his old adversary, Darrow lived long enough to see himself become a folk hero.

Neither Bryan nor Darrow, of course, survived to see the Supreme Court strike down Arkansas's ban on teaching evolution in a 1968 decision declaring it to be a violation of the First Amendment. Nor would they witness the emergence of a new anti-evolution movement in our own time. Its followers, known as "creationists," are not necessarily guided by a literal reading of Scripture, but proclaim the "intelligent design" of life by a Creator. And unlike earlier anti-evolutionists, they insist that this belief should be taught in schools *alongside* Darwinism. Eighty years after the Scopes Trial, creationists had introduced proposals challenging the supremacy of Darwinian evolution in the public schools in at least twenty states, and President George W. Bush had weighed in on the side of teaching intelligent design in school. Observing this new movement, William Jennings Bryan might be pleased. Clarence Darrow, on the other hand, would probably seek one more courtroom battle involving the teaching of religion and science in the schools.

PRIMARY SOURCES

SOURCE 1:   *A Defense of Youthful Morality*   (1926)

Changes in manners and morals, especially evident among young people in the postwar era, elicited much critical comment in the 1920s. In this source, one writer in her early twenties responds to attacks on the morality of the younger generation. Do you think the changes she discusses reflected a cultural divide that was also evident in the battle over evolution?

The syllabus of crimes charged against this "fabulous monster," the Younger Generation, might read as follows: It has exhibited a general independence of thought and action not compatible, according to its accusers, with those ideals and traditions which are the foundation of true family life. It has shown a flagrant contempt for parents and parental guidance. It has displayed, even flaunted, its disregard of morals,—indicated in its lack of manners, its dancing, its drinking,

SOURCE: Regina Malone, "The Fabulous Monster," *Forum*, July 1926, pp. 27, 28–29, 30.

its "petting," and its intimate relationships with men. It has chosen entirely to disregard religion; or, still worse, it has dared to attack the firmly established religious beliefs of its ancestors.

Let us consider these charges in detail.

Is independence a crime? Logically, an age of freedom always follows a period of artificiality and repression. . . . Is not this independence of our Youth of to-day little more than a swing of the pendulum from Victorianism, with its laughable prudery and absurd conventions, to an ultra-sophisticated and brutally frank age of Modernism? It is only by juxtaposition and contrast that either age appears exaggerated. . . .

The revolt of my generation is the natural and wholesome reaction to an age which evaded nearly every reality. It is the revolt against the patent absurdities of Victorianism. We are criticized for dispensing with that old institution— chaperonage. . . . They criticize our clothes. Consider the spectacle of my maternal grandmother setting out for a trip to Philadelphia and safeguarding her virtue by donning nineteen petticoats! . . . One by one the petticoats have been discarded. Now they are all but extinct, gone the way of the "stays" as my grandmother in her evasive manner would have termed them, and all other useless encumbrances. Now it is significant that the superficial aspects of our revolt have worked backwards. Mother, too, has discarded corsets and petticoats in imitation of daughter. She has sought and obtained political freedom. And it follows inevitably that economic and moral freedom will also come.

Which brings us to a more serious phase of the Youth question: our attitude toward sex. We no longer spell the word with a capital letter; and it is as frankly discussed as automobiles. . . . Why should our elders consider our interest in this subject a sign of unnaturalness or perversion? Should it not constitute the chief concern of those in whose hands the future generation lies? Is not this desire and ability to procreate the primary function of every human being? . . .

Finally we come to religion. The younger members of society have thrown religion overboard,—that is, religion as conceived by their elders. No longer do we believe in a Deity moulded in the form of a police inspector. But our own faith in an Infinite Being possessed of infinite comprehension is too great to leave us stranded high and dry on the rocks of unbelief. As we sought, and are finding freedom in other channels, so will we find it in religious ones.

SOURCE 2: *An "Imperial Wizard" Explains the Ku Klux Klan's Appeal* (1926)

The source below is from an article written by Hiram Wesley Evans, one of the leaders of the Ku Klux Klan in the 1920s. What does it reveal about the connection between the "culture wars" of the 1920s and other divisions in American society? Is Darwinism part of Evans's own analysis?

SOURCE: Hiram Wesley Evans, "The Klan's Fight for Americanism," *The North American Review*, March 1926, pp 38–39, 49.

The Klan . . . has now come to speak for the great mass of Americans of the old pioneer stock. We believe that it does fairly and faithfully represent them, and our proof lies in their support. To understand the Klan, then, it is necessary to understand the character and present mind of the mass of old-stock Americans. The mass, it must be remembered, as distinguished from the intellectually mongrelized "Liberals."

These are, in the first place, a blend of various peoples of the so-called Nordic race, the race which, with all its faults, has given the world almost the whole of modern civilization. The Klan does not try to represent any people but these.

There is no need to recount the virtues of the American pioneers; but it is too often forgotten that in the pioneer period a selective process of intense rigor went on. From the first only hardy, adventurous and strong men and women dared the pioneer dangers; from among these all but the best died swiftly, so that the new Nordic blend which became the American race was bred up to a point probably the highest in history. This remarkable race character, along with the new-won continent and the new-created nation, made the inheritance of the old-stock Americans the richest ever given to a generation of men.

In spite of it, however, these Nordic Americans for the last generation have found themselves increasingly uncomfortable, and finally deeply distressed. There appeared first confusion in thought and opinion, a groping and hesitancy about national affairs and private life alike, in sharp contrast to the clear, straightforward purposes of our earlier years. There was futility in religion, too, which was in many ways even more distressing. Presently we began to find that we are dealing with strange ideas; policies that always sounded well, but somehow always made us still more uncomfortable.

Finally came the moral breakdown that has been going on for two decades. One by one all our traditional moral standards went by the boards, or were so disregarded that they ceased to be binding. The sacredness of our Sabbath, of our homes, of chastity, and finally even of our right to teach our own children in our own schools fundamental facts and truths were torn away from us. Those who maintained the old standards did so only in the face of constant ridicule. . . .

We are a movement of the plain people, very weak in the matter of culture, intellectual support, and trained leadership. We are demanding, and we expect to win, a return of power into the hands of the everyday, not highly cultured, not overly intellectualized, but entirely unspoiled and not de-Americanized, average citizen of the old stock.

SOURCE 3: *A Preacher Defends Tennessee from Attack (1925)*

The author of this article was a popular fundamentalist minister who preached around the country in the 1920s against evolution and modernism. In his view, how does the defense team in the Scopes Trial reflect the threat facing Tennessee?

SOURCE: John Roach Straton, "The Most Sinister Movement in the United States," *American Fundamentalist*, December 26, 1925, pp. 8–9.

The real issue at Dayton and everywhere today is: "Whether the religion of the Bible shall be ruled out of the schools and the religion of evolution, with its ruinous results—shall be ruled into the schools by law." The issue is whether the taxpayers—the mothers and fathers of the children—shall be made to support the false and materialistic religion, namely evolution, in the schools, while Christianity is ruled out, and thereby denied their children.

And with this goes the even deeper issue of whether the majority shall really have the right to rule in America, or whether we are to be ruled by an insignificant minority—an "aristocracy" . . . of skeptical schoolmen and agnostics.

That is the exact issue in this country today. And that it is a very real and urgent issue is proved by the recent invasion of the sovereign state of Tennessee by a group of outside agnostics, atheists, Unitarian preachers, skeptical scientists, and political revolutionists. These uninvited men—including Clarence Darrow, the world's greatest unbeliever, and Dudley Malone,[1] the world's greatest religious What-Is-It,—these and the other samples of our proposed "aristocracy" of would-be rulers, swarmed down to Dayton during the Scopes trial and brazenly tried to nullify the laws and overthrow the political and religious faiths of a great, enlightened, prosperous, and peaceful people.

And the only redeeming feature in all that unlovely parade of human vanity, arrogant self-sufficiency, religious unbelief, and anti-American defiance of majority rule was the courtesy, hospitality (even to unwelcome guests), forbearance, patience, and Christlike fortitude displayed by the noble judge, and the Christian prosecuting attorneys and people of Tennessee!

There was an element of profound natural irony in the entire situation. Darrow, Malone, and the other members of the Evolutionist Bund[2] vicariously left their own communities and bravely sallied forth, like Don Quixote, to defeat the windmills and save other communities from themselves.

They left New York and Chicago, where real religion is being most neglected, where law, consequently, is most defied, where vice and crime are most rampant, and where the follies and ruinous immoralities of the rising generation—debauched already by religious modernism and a Godless materialistic science—smell to high heaven, and they went to save from itself a community where women are still honored, where men are still chivalric, where laws are still respected, where home life is still sweet, where the marriage vow is still sacred, and where man is still regarded, not as a descendant of the slime and beasts of the jungle, but as a child of God, with the wisdom and love of a divine Revelation in his hands, to guide him on life's rugged road, to give him the knowledge of a Savior from his sins, and to plant in his heart the hope of heaven to cheer him on his upward way!

And that is the sort of community which Darrow, Malone, and company left Chicago and New York to save!

Think of the illogic of it! and the nerve of it! and the colossal vanity of it!

Little wonder it is recorded in Holy Writ that "He that sitteth in the Heavens shall laugh" at the follies of men! And surely the very battlements of

---

1. Dudley Malone was a divorce attorney from New York City and a member of the defense team.
2. The Bund was a German-American political organization.

Heaven must have rocked with laughter at the spectacle of Clarence Darrow, Dudley Malone, and their company of cocksure evolutionists going down to save the South from itself!

It is all the other way around! The religious faith and the robust conservatism of the chivalric South and the sturdy West will have to save America from the sins and shams and shames that are now menacing her splendid life!

Source 4:   *Clarence Darrow Attacks the Anti-Evolution Law as Unconstitutional*   (1925)

On the second day of the trial, Clarence Darrow argued that the Tennessee law prohibiting the teaching of evolution in the state's public schools was unconstitutional. On what grounds does he argue that it violates the state constitution's guarantee of religious freedom?

The people of Tennessee adopted a constitution, and they made it broad and plain, and said that the people of Tennessee should always enjoy religious freedom in its broadest terms, so I assume, that no legislature could fix a course of study which violated that. . . .

[T]he state of Tennessee under an honest and fair interpretation of the constitution has no more right to teach the Bible as the divine book than that the Koran is one, or the book of Mormons, or the book of Confucius, or the Budda [sic], or the Essays of Emerson, or any one of the 10,000 books to which human souls have gone for consolation and aid in their troubles. . . .

What is the Bible? Your Honor, I have read it myself. I might read it more or more wisely. Others may understand it better. Others may think they understand it better when they do not. But in a general way I know what it is. I know there are millions of people in the world who look on it as being a divine book, and I have not the slightest objection to it. I know there are millions of people in the world who derive consolation in their times of trouble and solace in times of distress from the Bible. I would be pretty near the last one in the world to do anything or take any action to take it away. I feel just exactly the same toward the religious creed of every human being who lives. If anybody finds anything in this life that brings them consolation and health and happiness I think they ought to have it whatever they get. I haven't any fault to find with them at all. But what is it? The Bible is not one book. The Bible is made up of sixty-six books written over a period of about one thousand years, some of them very early and some of them comparatively late. It is a book primarily of religion and morals. It is not a book of science. Never was and was never meant to be. Under it there is nothing prescribed that would tell you how to build a railroad or a steamboat or to make anything that would advance civilization. It is not a textbook or a

Source: First seen in *The World's Most Famous Court Trial: State of Tennessee* v. *John Thomas Scopes* (National Book Co., 1925); reprinted by Da Capo Press, 1971, pp. 75, 77–78, 84.

text on chemistry. It is not big enough to be. It is not a book on geology; they knew nothing about geology. It is not a book on biology; they knew nothing about it. . . .

[Y]our life and my life and the life of every American citizen depends after all upon the tolerance and forebearance of his fellowman. If men are not tolerant, if men cannot respect each other's opinions, if men cannot live and let live, then no man's life is safe, no man's life is safe.

Here is a country made up of Englishmen, Irishmen, Scotch, German, Europeans, Asiatics, Africans, men of every sort and men of every creed and men of every scientific belief; who is going to begin this sorting out and say, "I shall measure you; I know you are a fool, or worse; I know and I have read a creed telling what I know and I will make people go to Heaven even if they don't want to go with me, I will make them do it." Where is the man that is wise enough to do it?

SOURCE 5:   *William Jennings Bryan Argues Against Expert Testimony*   (1925)

Bryan was silent during the first four days of the Scopes Trial. On the fifth day, however, he spoke against admitting expert testimony. On what grounds does he do so? How does his argument reflect broader conflicts that divided the nation in the 1920s?

[W]hile Mr. Scopes knew what the law was and knew what evolution was, and knew that it violated the law, he proceeded to violate the law. That is the evidence before this court, and we do not need any expert to tell us what that law means. An expert cannot be permitted to come in here and try to defeat the enforcement of a law by testifying that it isn't a bad law and it isn't—I mean a bad doctrine—no matter how these people phrase the doctrine—no matter how they eulogize it. This is not the place to try to prove that the law ought never to have been passed. The place to prove that, or teach that, was to the legislature. . . . And, my friends, if the people of Tennessee were to go into a state like New York—the one from which this impulse comes to resist this law, or go into any state—if they went into any state and tried to convince the people that a law they had passed ought not to be enforced, just because the people who went there didn't think it ought to have been passed, don't you think it would be resented as an impertinence? . . . The people of this state passed this law, the people of this state knew what they were doing when they passed the law, and they knew the dangers of the doctrine—that they did not want it taught to their children, and my friends, it isn't—your honor, it isn't proper to bring experts in here to try to defeat the purpose of the people of this state by trying to show that this thing that they denounce and outlaw is a beautiful thing that everybody

SOURCE: First seen in *The World's Most Famous Court Trial: State of Tennessee* v. *John Thomas Scopes* (National Book Co., 1925); reprinted by Da Capo Press, 1971, pp. 171–172, 180–182.

ought to believe in. . . . These people want to come here with experts to make your honor believe that the law should never have been passed and because in their opinion it ought not to have been passed, it ought not to be enforced. It isn't a place for expert testimony. We have sufficient proof in the book—doesn't the book state the very thing that is objected to, and outlawed in this state? . . .

The question is can a minority in this state come in and compel a teacher to teach that the Bible is not true and make the parents of these children pay the expenses of the teacher to tell their children what these people believe is false and dangerous? Has it come to a time when the minority can take charge of a state like Tennessee and compel the majority to pay their teachers while they take religion out of the heart of the children of the parents who pay the teachers? . . . Now, your honor, when it comes to Bible experts, do they think that they can bring them in here to instruct the members of the jury, eleven of whom are members of the church? I submit that of the eleven members of the jury more of the jurors are experts on what the Bible is than any Bible expert who does not subscribe to the true spiritual influences or spiritual discernments of what our Bible says.

Voice in audience, "Amen!" . . . And, when it comes to Bible experts, every member of the jury is as good an expert on the Bible as any man that they could bring, or that we could bring. The one beauty about the Word of God is, it does not take an expert to understand it. . . . That Bible is not going to be driven out of this court by experts who come hundreds of miles to testify that they can reconcile evolution, with its ancestor in the jungle, with man made by God in His image, and put here for purposes as a part of the divine plan. No, we are not going to settle that question here, and I think we ought to confine ourselves to the law and to the evidence that can be admitted in accordance with the law.

Source 6:   *Clarence Darrow Questions William Jennings Bryan on the Bible*   (1925)

On the seventh day of the Scopes Trial, Clarence Darrow called Bryan to the stand to prove that a literal reading of the Bible was absurd and, therefore, John Scopes did not violate the Tennessee law forbidding the teaching of "the Divine creation of man as taught in the Bible." Do you think that Darrow succeeded in his goal?

Mr. Darrow—How long ago was the flood, Mr. Bryan?
    A—Let me see Usher's[1] calculation about it?
    Mr. Darrow—Surely.
    (Handing a Bible to the witness.)

Source: First seen in *The World's Most Famous Court Trial: State of Tennessee v. John Thomas Scopes* (National Book Co., 1925); reprinted by Da Capo Press, 1971, pp. 288, 289, 290, 298–299, 302, 304.

1. James Ussher was a seventeenth-century Irish archbishop who calculated the date of creation as 4004 B.C.E.

A—I think this does not give it.

Q—It gives an account of Noah. . . .

The Witness—It is given here, as 2348 years B.C. . . .

Q—You are not satisfied there is any civilization that can be traced back 5,000 years?

A—I would not want to say there is because I have no evidence of it that is satisfactory.

Q—Would you say there is not?

A—Well, so far as I know, but when the scientists differ, from 24,000,000 to 306,000,000 in their opinion, as to how long ago life came here, I want them nearer, to come nearer together before they demand of me to give up my belief in the Bible.

Q—Do you say that you do not believe that there were any civilizations on this earth that reach back beyond 5,000 years?

A—I am not satisfied by any evidence that I have seen. . . .

Q—You have never had any interest in the age of the various races and people and civilization and animals that exist upon the earth today? Is that right?

A—I have never felt a great deal of interest in the effort that has been made to dispute the Bible by the speculations of men, or the investigations of men. . . .

Q—Would you say that the earth was only 4,000 years old?

A—Oh, no; I think it is much older than that.

Q—How much?

A—I couldn't say.

Q—Do you say whether the Bible itself says it is older than that?

A—I don't think the Bible says itself whether it is older or not.

Q—Do you think the earth was made in six days?

A—Not six days of twenty-four hours.

Q—Doesn't it say so?

A—No, sir.

Gen. Stewart[2]—I want to interpose another objection. What is the purpose of this examination?

Mr. Bryan—The purpose is to cast ridicule on everybody who believes in the Bible, and I am perfectly willing that the world shall know that these gentlemen have no other purpose than ridiculing every Christian who believes in the Bible.

Mr. Darrow—We have the purpose of preventing bigots and ignoramuses from controlling the education of the United States and you know it, and that is all. . . .

Q—Does the statement, "The morning and the evening were the first day," and "The morning and the evening were the second day," mean anything to you?

A—I do not think it necessarily means a twenty-four-hour day.

Q—You do not?

A—No. . . .

---

2. Tom Stewart was a young attorney general and member of the prosecution team.

Q—Then, when the Bible said, for instance, "and God called the firmament heaven. And the evening and the morning were the second day," that does not necessarily mean twenty-four hours?

A—I do not think it necessarily does.

Q—Do you think it does or does not?

A—I know a great many think so.

Q—What do you think?

A—I do not think it does.

Q—You think those were not literal days?

A—I do not think they were twenty-four-hour days.

Q—What do you think about it?

A—That is my opinion—I do not know that my opinion is better on that subject than those who think it does.

Q—You do not think that?

A—No. But I think it would be just as easy for the kind of God we believe in to make the earth in six days as in six years or in 6,000,000 years or in 600,000,000 years. I do not think it important whether we believe one or the other. . . .

Q—Now, you refer to the cloud that was put in the heaven after the flood, the rainbow. Do you believe in that?

A—Read it.

Q—All right, Mr. Bryan, I will read it for you.

Mr. Bryan—Your honor, I think I can shorten this testimony. The only purpose Mr. Darrow has is to slur at the Bible, but I will answer his question. I will answer it all at once, and I have no objection in the world, I want the world to know that this man, who does not believe in a God, is trying to use a court in Tennessee—

Mr. Darrow—I object to that.

Mr. Bryan—(Continuing) to slur at it, and while it will require time, I am willing to take it.

Mr. Darrow—I object to your statement. I am exempting you on your fool ideas that no intelligent Christian on earth believes.

The Court—Court is adjourned until 9 o'clock tomorrow morning.

SOURCE 7:   *A Black Leader Comments on the Scopes Trial (1925)*

Black historian, author, and journalist W. E. B. Du Bois commented on the Scopes Trial as the editor of Crisis, *the official publication of the National Association for the Advancement of Colored People. What meaning does he assign to the trial and its verdict? Does his commentary point to another division within American society that was revealed by the anti-evolution controversy in the 1920s?*

SOURCE: W. E. B. Du Bois, "Scopes," *Crisis*, September 1925, p. 218.

One hundred per cent Americans are now endeavoring to persuade hilarious and sarcastic Europe that Dayton, Tennessee, is a huge joke and very, very exceptional. . . . The truth is and we know it: Dayton, Tennessee, is America: a great, ignorant, simple-minded land, curiously compounded of brutality, bigotry, religious faith and demagoguery, and capable not simply of mistakes but of persecution, lynching, murder and idiotic blundering, as well as chairty, missions, love and hope.

That is America and America is what it is because we believe in Ignorance. The whole modern Nordic civilization of which America is a great and leading branch has sold its soul to Ignorance. Its leading priests profess a religious faith which they do not believe and which they know, and every man of intelligence knows, they do not and cannot believe. . . .

The folk who leave white Tennessee in blank and ridiculous ignorance of what science has taught the world since 1859 are the same ones who would leave black Tennessee and black America with just as little education as is consistent with fairly efficient labor and reasonable contentment; who rave over the 18th Amendment and are dumb over the 15th,* who permit lynching and make bastardy legal in order to render their race "pure." It is such folk who, when in sudden darkness they descry the awful faces of the Fanatic, the Fury and the Fool, try to hide the vision with gales of laughter.

But Dayton, Tennessee, is no laughing matter. It is menace and warning. It is a challenge to Religion, Science and Democracy.

QUESTIONS TO CONSIDER

1. How did the backgrounds of William Jennings Bryan and Clarence Darrow influence their positions regarding Darwinian evolution in the 1920s? How did these positions reflect their views about other important issues?

2. The trial in a small southern town of a young high school science teacher accused of teaching evolution would not at first glance seem worthy of nationwide attention. How do you explain the great interest surrounding the Scopes Trial in 1925? What do you see as its significance?

3. What broad social, cultural, and intellectual divisions among Americans do the sources reveal? How did cultural, sectional, religious, and social differences interact by the 1920s to support a fundamentalist anti-evolution movement? How did Bryan and Darrow reflect these differences?

4. William Jennings Bryan believed that the majority of people in a community had the right to determine what should be taught to their children in school. Clarence Darrow, on the other hand, believed that this should be decided by experts in a given discipline. Who do you think was correct? Are there dangers in each position? What do you think each man would say about the idea of teaching "intelligent design" alongside the theory of evolution in the nation's schools today?

---

*The Fifteenth Amendment, ratified in 1870, was intended to guarantee black males the right to vote.

FOR FURTHER READING

Robert W. Chery, *A Righteous Cause: The Life of William Jennings Bryan* (Boston: Little, Brown and Company, 1985), offers a concise overview of Bryan's life and career.

David J. Goldberg, *Discontented America: The United States in the 1920s* (Baltimore: Johns Hopkins University Press, 1999), examines numerous changes in postwar American society, including those that led to a backlash against evolution.

Edward J. Larson, *Summer for the Gods: The Scopes Trial and America's Continuing Debate Over Science and Religion* (New York: Basic Books, 1997), examines the roots of the anti-evolution movement in the 1920s that culminated in the Scopes Trial.

Roderick Nash, *The Nervous Generation: American Thought, 1917–1930* (Chicago: Ivan R. Dee, 1990), provides an overview of intellectual and cultural currents during the 1920s.

Kevin Tierney, *Darrow: A Biography* (New York: Thomas Y. Crowell, 1979), is a comprehensive, though highly readable, account of Darrow's life.

CHAPTER

7

Politics and the Big Screen
in the Great Depression:
Upton Sinclair and Louis B. Mayer

As the curtains parted and the lights dimmed, the Friday night patrons at Hollywood's El Portal theater settled back in their seats. Tonight's feature was *Chained*, starring Joan Crawford and Clark Gable. This Metro-Goldwyn-Mayer (MGM) release offered moviegoers a few hours of relief from the grim reality of life in 1934. The story of a young American woman who falls in love with an Argentine rancher on a cruise to South America, the movie portrayed lives that most Americans could only dream about. As usual, the El Portal's patrons sat through a cartoon and newsreel before the main feature. Tonight, however, they were also treated to a political short titled *California Election News*. The five-minute feature was a reminder that the gubernatorial election was only a few weeks away.

Normally, of course, a California governor's race was a subject unworthy of the big screen. These were not normal times, though. Since late 1929, the Great Depression had thrown millions of Americans out of work. Five years later, many of its victims continued to stand in relief lines, find shelter in shantytowns, and roam the nation's highways and railroads. In California, closed banks, foreclosed farms, shuttered businesses, and shattered lives stood as testaments to the Depression's devastation. So did the sudden political rise of a socialist named Upton Sinclair, who had won the Democratic Party's nomination for governor in 1934. Sinclair had been catapulted to fame with the publication of *The Jungle* (1906), his shocking Progressive era exposé of the meatpacking industry. Later, he had moved to southern California, where he wrote a stream of novels. Now he was on the verge of winning the governorship on a platform called End Poverty in California (EPIC), which proposed state-run enterprises, steep taxes on the rich, and a tax on the motion-picture industry.

California's movers and shakers were alarmed. Louis B. Mayer, for one, was terrified at the prospect of a Sinclair victory. Like Sinclair, Mayer had been born poor. The head of MGM, however, was no socialist. A Republican Party state chairman, Mayer lived with his wife and daughters in a huge Santa Monica home overlooking the Pacific. As the most powerful movie mogul in Hollywood, he ran his studio with a tyrant's grip on his stars and an industry captain's cold eye on the bottom line. Mayer wanted Sinclair stopped, and as the boss of

♦ Upton Sinclair   ♦ Louis B. Mayer

Hollywood's most successful studio, he was determined to bring the anti-Sinclair message right into California's movie theaters. Tonight, long before Clark Gable got the girl, the El Portal's patrons would be among the first to see and hear it.

As a map of the Golden State flashed on the screen and strains of "California, Here I Come" filled the theater, the *California Election News* narrator introduced himself as the "Inquiring Cameraman." His job, he explained, was to travel all over California and talk with voters. The faces of laborers, women, and businessmen appearing on the screen, he said, were not actors. "I don't rehearse them," he intoned, "I'm impartial." As even the dimmest viewer could see, these Californians' political preferences fell into a neat pattern. An African American in an old car, a Hispanic with shifty eyes, and an elderly man with no front teeth all pledged their support for Sinclair or "St. Clair." They were quickly countered by respectable-looking voters: an African American standing in front of a house, an elderly woman in a suburban yard, two men in suits. All of the anti-Sinclair voters declared that the Democratic candidate and his EPIC plan were dangerous and radical. Later, some amused EPIC supporters were sure that some of the "Inquiring Cameraman's" voters were actors. Yet laughter would be a feeble defense against the likes of Louis B. Mayer. His studio's political short was the first attempt to use the enormous power of big-screen images to defeat a political candidate. And in the midst of one of the most vitriolic gubernatorial campaigns in American history, it was merely a preview of more to come.

"Movie Writing . . . Inevitably Becomes Trash"

If Upton Sinclair had a more worrisome enemy than Louis B. Mayer, it was Sinclair himself. By 1934, he had denounced the capitalist system as bankrupt, Wall Street as "bond slavery," and bankers as "parasites." He also had assaulted nearly every major institution in American life: colleges ("manned by intellectual prostitutes"), religion ("a mighty fortress of graft"), marriage ("prostitution"), medicine ("a thousand dollars [for] a few minutes work"), and the press ("the business of presenting the news of the day in the interest of economic privilege"). Even the Boy Scouts ("more warlike every day") were not immune. At least Sinclair realized that he was his own worst enemy. "I have written so much," he confessed during the campaign, "and not always temperately." He was also self-aware enough to understand the source of his attitudes toward money and power. "I diagnose my psychology," he declared in his *Autobiography*, "as that of a 'poor relation.'" It was his lot "from earliest childhood," he explained, "to live in the presence of wealth which belonged to others."

The "others" in Sinclair's case were his maternal grandfather, a railroad treasurer, and his aunt and her banker husband, members of Baltimore's business elite. Descended from a long line of naval officers, Sinclair's father looked and acted every bit the southern gentleman. In reality, though, he was a failed New York City salesman and a drunk who frequently disappeared, leaving Upton and his mother sleeping in hovels. The youngster's financially strapped parents periodically sent him to live in Baltimore, where he learned firsthand the difference between wealth and poverty. In his relatives' luxurious homes, Sinclair quickly came to resent his inferior position. He found his snobbish uncle insufferable and resolved "never to 'sell out' to that class."

Sinclair's parents reinforced his early prejudices. His father worshiped the Confederate general Robert E. Lee and other "Virginia gentlemen" because they rose above mere moneygrubbing, while his mother condemned even tea or coffee consumption. From them, young Upton inherited a lifelong abhorrence of business and alcohol—and a broad Puritan streak. With an ascetic's self-discipline, he subsisted for most of his life on rice and raw fruits and vegetables. Through all of it, he also displayed an amazing capacity for work. His mother also instilled in him a love of reading. In his uncle's library, young Sinclair found plenty of unread books, which provided an escape from both poverty and snobbery. They also left him with a rich imagination and an ability to spin a tale.

In 1892, the precocious fourteen-year-old entered the College of the City of New York, the same year he wrote and sold his first short story. Writing fourteen hours a day, Sinclair made enough money to move into his own apartment when he was seventeen. After graduation, he studied literature at Columbia University while supporting himself as a magazine writer. He was quickly disenchanted with both hack writing and graduate school, however. Convinced that he had the ability to write a great novel, he spent an entire summer holed up in a cabin by a lake in Quebec, where he wrote up to sixteen hours a day. By fall, he had a manuscript—and a bride. The eighteen-year-old daughter of family friends happened to be at the same lake that summer with her mother. Later that year, Meta Fuller and Upton Sinclair, then twenty-two, were married.

The couple's marriage began amid dreams of literary success, but they were soon dashed. When publishers rejected his manuscript, Sinclair immediately set to work on a novel about greed and unhappiness in high society. When publishers rejected it as well, Meta left with their infant son to live with her parents, convinced that her husband needed to find a real job. Living alone in an attic in New York, the desperate Sinclair ground out two more novels. The first earned no royalties. The second, a merciless attack on the rich, no publisher wanted. In his hour of despair, Sinclair found salvation. Introduced by an editor to a small circle of wealthy socialists, he was a ready convert. Though no stranger to social inequality, his reading had left him ignorant of socialism and its call for public ownership of the means of production. "It was like the falling down of prison walls about my mind," he declared. With financial support from his new friends, Sinclair finished another book while living in a tent. A romantic novel set in the years before the Civil War, it sold poorly, too. The book's treatment of slavery's horrors, however, intrigued the editor of an influential socialist weekly. When he asked Sinclair to write an exposé of modern-day wage slavery, the struggling author quickly agreed.

Published in 1906, *The Jungle* changed Sinclair's life. The book became a bestseller as stunned readers ignored its socialist message and concentrated instead on the vivid descriptions of conditions in meatpacking plants. (In the novel, one worker falls into a vat and ends up as sausage.) The book helped spur the passage of the Pure Food and Drug Act in 1906, which prevented the sale of mislabeled or adulterated foods and drugs. Muckraking, though, had never been Sinclair's intention. Rather, he had spent seven weeks in Chicago's stockyards and slaughterhouses to provide a realistic setting for a story about capitalism's exploitation of workers. As he later put it, he had aimed at Americans' hearts and hit them "in the stomach." Nonetheless, at twenty-seven, Sinclair was famous, and for the first time in his life, he was also flush with money.

Determined to realize a utopian vision, he used the royalties from *The Jungle* to establish a cooperative community of some forty like-minded writers, professors, and artists in New Jersey. Unfortunately, Sinclair's investment went up in smoke when the place burned down four months later. Sinclair soon joined a single-tax community* in Alabama, but communal living put a further strain on his marriage. At the New Jersey and Alabama communities, both Upton and Meta had extramarital affairs, and in 1911 the couple finally divorced. By then, Sinclair had been converted again. In 1909, he had visited a sanatorium run by Bernarr Macfadden, the Progressive era's leading prophet of fitness. While Macfadden convinced him of the value of vegetarianism and fasting, Sinclair fell in love with another "patient," a Mississippi judge's daughter named Mary Craig Kimbrough. Despite his belief that marriage was merely a middle-class convention, in 1913 he married Mary Craig, a union that lasted until her death nearly five decades later. The couple's interest in health and fitness soon brought them to southern California, already home to many cultists and health faddists. They settled in Pasadena, where "Craig" dabbled in real estate while Upton pecked out an endless stream of books on his typewriter.

None of Sinclair's later works matched the success of *The Jungle*, but he never shied away from attacks on powerful, even sacred, institutions. Thus he wrote exposés of churches, the press, schools, and the arts—all institutions, he believed, corrupted by capitalism. At the same time, Sinclair eagerly sought wealth and social acceptance. An avid tennis player, he enjoyed this "leisure-class recreation" at a socially exclusive Pasadena tennis club, even though off the court he

---

Single-tax community: A community that imposed a tax on the appreciated value of real estate. The single tax had been proposed by the late-nineteenth-century reformer Henry George and had sparked a popular reform movement.

was shunned by fellow members. Rejected by Pasadena's gentry, Sinclair kept company with a group of wealthy socialists that included actor Charlie Chaplin, one of Hollywood's richest men.

In Hollywood, he again found himself on the fringes of wealth and power, slighted yet longing to break in. *The Jungle* had been made into a silent film, and although it had not been a box-office success, it had left him with a nagging desire to hit it big in the movies. The feeling intensified when studios showed interest in some of his later work. In fact, much of Sinclair's work was for MGM, which paid him twenty thousand dollars for *The Wet Parade* (1931) and ten thousand dollars to develop a plot and characters for another proposed movie. Even so, Sinclair felt that the studio executives were shunning him, and he believed their motives were political. The "masters of capitalist drama and screen," he complained, repeatedly broke contracts because of his socialist message—or forced him to break them when they "set to work to undo my efforts."

Like a scorned lover, he claimed not to desire what he could not have. "I refuse to do movie writing," he said, "because it inevitably becomes trash." Yet for decades, Sinclair actually sought such work, and at the outset of the Depression, he even bought a foreclosed Beverly Hills mansion to be closer to Hollywood. Determined that the big screen would be his ticket to success, he invested in a failed movie venture with the Russian filmmaker Sergei Eisenstein in the early 1930s. Later, he accepted twenty thousand dollars from William Fox to write the film producer's biography. Sinclair's anti-Semitic account pictured Hollywood as a bastion of Jewish gangsters. That did not prevent him, however, from giving his unlisted telephone number—one of his most guarded secrets—to a Jewish studio executive named Irving Thalberg in the hopes of getting more work. Thalberg, as it happened, was the right-hand man of another Jewish studio executive, Louis B. Mayer.

"More Stars . . . Than in Heaven"

In 1934, Mayer, the head of MGM, was the highest-paid corporate executive in the country. This son of an immigrant peddler had come a long way. Although his energies were not directed to intellectual pursuits, like Sinclair he worked incessantly. As one early acquaintance testified, "He rarely slept. . . . and he rarely ate without talking business." More than anything, though, Mayer understood motion pictures, the public, and the economics of the film industry.

Like many other Jewish immigrants, Mayer's parents came to the United States to escape czarist Russia. They arrived in steerage in 1888 with their three children. Louis, the middle child, was three years old. Shortly after arriving in New York, the family left for Canada, where Mayer's father worked as a door-to-door peddler and then as a scrap-metal dealer. Before long, he had an assistant. Less interested in book learning than in making money, Louis left school at age twelve to pull a wagon through the streets of St. John, New Brunswick, and collect metal. Two years later, the new sign above the business—J. MAYER & SON—indicated that the boy had already become a partner. The ambitious Louis prodded his father to take on larger salvaging jobs, including wrecked ships. By 1900, Mayer & Son had merged with an American salvage outfit, and Louis had become its northeastern representative. The job gave him the opportunity to travel throughout New England and see a larger world. Determined to leave St. John, he moved to Boston in 1904, taking a job with another scrap-metal merchant. Not long after that, he also found a bride, Margaret Shenberg.

Quickly striking out on his own, Mayer bought his own scrap-metal operation in Brooklyn, New York, only to see it wiped out in the Panic of 1907.* Discouraged and now the father of two daughters, he moved back to Boston to live with Margaret's parents and look for another line of work. He found one at a nickelodeon called the Hub. Nickelodeons showed short, inexpensive silent features—entertainment that even the working class could afford. And unlike the scrap-metal business, they did not appear to be affected by recession. After spending time at the Hub studying programs and films, he scraped together $600 to lease a vacant theater in Haverhill, a factory town north of Boston. Nickelodeons were frequently associated with suggestive entertainment, and everything about Mayer's venture seemed unsavory. Located in a seedy part of town, the rundown property had been the home of traveling burlesque shows. Yet Mayer thought that movies shown in the right setting could attract the middle class—and those who aspired to join it. The workers from Haverhill's numerous factories and mills, he believed, would be willing to pay for inexpensive, respectable entertainment.

Repaired, repainted, and renamed the Orpheum, the theater opened in late 1907. Like other theaters of the day, it booked moving pictures and vaudeville acts, and Mayer made sure that the theater, the images on its screen, and its live performances were clean. His hunch about his patrons' cultural aspirations paid off. By the end of the first year, Mayer had grossed $25,000. Within four years, he had opened a second Haverhill theater, a movie palace that seated twenty-five hundred people and cost $150,000 to build. Soon he had a monopoly on all of the city's theaters and had taken his movie houses into several nearby towns.

By then, Mayer realized that the future of the theater business was not vaudeville but motion pictures. He also knew that exhibitors had little control over the kinds of films produced or their rental rates. Exhibition, he discovered, was a low-margin proposition. The real money was in the other two segments of the business: production and distribution. In a succession of quick moves starting in 1913, Mayer climbed up the motion-picture chain, first getting into distribution and then into production. In 1915, he secured the New England distribution rights to *The Birth of a Nation,* D. W. Griffith's huge hit about the post–Civil War redemption of the South at the hands of the Ku Klux Klan. Mayer pocketed $150,000 from the deal—enough to persuade him to liquidate his theater interests and break into producing, potentially the most profitable end of the business. In 1917, he set up his own production company. His first picture, *Virtuous Wives,* was a big hit, and he immediately began work on a second film, *In Old Kentucky,* which was to be largely shot outdoors. Most of the other film producers had already set up studios in southern California, where the climate permitted year-round outdoor filming. *In Old Kentucky* was all the impetus Mayer needed to join them. In 1918, he moved his family in quick succession from Haverhill to Boston to a bungalow near the Hollywood district of Los Angeles.

For the next five years, Mayer's modest four-stage studio churned out comedies and melodramas. The films did well, but Mayer was constrained by

---

Panic of 1907: An economic downturn brought on by the collapse of the stock market and several bank failures.

the economics of the rapidly growing movie industry. As weekly theater attendance reached into the tens of millions, increasing competition had driven up the big stars' salaries. For instance, Charlie Chaplin was already under contract with another studio for a million dollars a year. To justify such huge contracts, studios had to put their stars in a lot of films—a difficult proposition for a small company like Louis B. Mayer Pictures. Meanwhile, large theater operators such as Marcus Loew, who had built a chain of more than one hundred theaters in the Northeast, were under increasing pressure to maintain a steady flow of films into their theaters. As in other major industries, the solution was to achieve economy through vertical integration* and consolidation.

By the early 1920s, theater operators had moved into distribution and production, while producers had moved into exhibition. Mayer fell "victim" to this consolidation wave in 1925, when he sold his company to Marcus Loew's production company for seventy-six thousand dollars. Like many motion-picture pioneers, Loew had started out in vaudeville. In 1920, the theater operator had bought Metro Pictures Corporation, a struggling production company. Four years later, he had combined it with Goldwyn Pictures, another fledgling outfit whose most notable feature was its trademark Leo the lion and the halo scroll reading *Ars Gratia Artis* (Art for Art's Sake). Already impressed by Mayer's operation, Loew turned to the young producer to run the new company, naming him first vice president and head of production at Metro-Goldwyn-Mayer (MGM). Mayer would get a weekly salary of fifteen hundred dollars and 10 percent of the studio's profits. Meanwhile, his young assistant, Irving Thalberg, became second vice president.

Although he now worked for someone else, Mayer was still in charge. After a ceremony at the company's new Universal City studios, where he read congratulatory telegrams from President Calvin Coolidge and Secretary of Commerce Herbert Hoover, Mayer got down to the business of producing movies. After all, Loew's expanding theater chain had nearly a quarter of a million seats to be filled every day. Mayer organized the studio into numerous departments and film production into an assembly line. Every assistant producer and department head was answerable to the studio head. Mayer also controlled the kinds of movies that MGM made. The films that filled seats, he believed, had strong characters whom viewers could root for and relate to. Moviegoers did not want to be confused or threatened, and they did not want their values challenged. Just like Haverhill's Orpheum theater, MGM's films would be clean: Adultery, lewdness, and infidelity were invariably condemned. "I'll never make anything that I wouldn't take my daughters to see," Mayer said.

Above all, MGM's boss also knew that big-name stars filled theater seats. In the silent film era, his studio's stable included Lillian Gish, Greta Garbo, Lon Chaney, and Lionel Barrymore. After MGM switched to sound production in 1929, it laid claim to Judy Garland, Katharine Hepburn, and Spencer Tracy, as well as Joan Crawford and Clark Gable. By the early 1930s, MGM advertised that its films contained "more stars than there are in heaven." These big-name stars often commanded princely salaries and lived like royalty. Marion Davies's dressing room on the MGM lot, for instance, was a fourteen-room "bungalow."

Vertical integration: A form of business organization in which one firm controls all steps in the production process, from securing the raw materials to distributing the finished product.

By the 1930s, this star system helped make Hollywood the third-biggest source of news in the nation—after New York City and Washington, D.C.—as studios released tidbits about their stars' lives to a ravenous public.

The glitter surrounding the stars also hid the dictatorial control that Mayer and other studio heads exercised over them. The stars, Mayer realized, were the studios' biggest asset. That meant they needed to be controlled. Contracts tied stars to a studio for seven years and gave it total control over their performances and roles. More than any other studio boss, Mayer rid his studio of performers who showed independence. His control extended to the stars' private lives. Responding to a growing public outcry about Hollywood's lax moral standards, the studios imposed censorship on themselves in 1930 with the establishment of a production code. Will Hays, president of the Motion Picture Producers and Distributors of America, administered the code. In this atmosphere, Mayer would not tolerate even a hint of public scandal among his stars.

If no movie boss was more powerful than Mayer, no company prospered more under the studio system than MGM. By the early 1930s, Hollywood was dominated by five major firms that turned out the vast majority of motion pictures, cooperated on movie distribution, and controlled the most lucrative theaters. Of the so-called Big Five, MGM was the biggest and most profitable. Mayer's rationalized production system and absolute control proved a winning formula even in the depths of the Depression. Between 1930 and 1933, his studio produced nine of the twenty-four top-grossing films. Mayer spent lavishly, pouring on average far more money into each film than any other studio. He also knew that Depression era movie audiences wanted to be entertained with fantasy, not reminded of their troubles. Although Warner Brothers and a few other studios produced gangster, crime, and other "social problem" films in the 1930s, MGM studiously avoided movies that dealt with the decade's social and economic issues. Rather, Mayer's studio was a dream factory that produced films conveying glitz, glamour, and luxury. [See Source 1.]

While MGM churned out celluloid fantasies, the Depression's stark reality was becoming all too clear. Between 1929 and 1932, the nation's economic output plummeted nearly 50 percent, more than fifty-five hundred banks went under, and unemployment swelled from only 3 percent to 25 percent. Not heavily industrialized in the early twentieth century, California initially felt the Depression's effects less than many other areas. By 1934, however, even the Golden State had withered under its impact. In that year, more than 400,000 Californians were unemployed, 1.5 million were on public relief or private charity, and thousands of desperate migrants streamed into the state every week. Many of these newcomers were former tenants or sharecroppers from the South who had been run off the land, victims of a prolonged agricultural slump. Others were victims of the drought that had turned much of the high plains into the Dust Bowl. These poor refugees—"Okies," as many Californians called them—usually found conditions in the Golden State little better than those they had fled. By 1934, there were not enough agricultural jobs to go around. Those lucky enough to find work in the fields often labored for as little as fifteen cents an hour. No wonder labor unrest and violence had spread from the state's farms to its canneries and docks in the past year.

By 1934, the Depression was even hitting uncomfortably close to the movie studios' star-studded lots. Since 1929, movie attendance had decreased by about twenty-five million, and thousands of movie houses had turned out their lights for good. At the same time, labor organizing spread to Hollywood, as hard times spawned a renewed interest in unions among workers nationwide. Membership in the Screen Actors Guild, a union formed in 1933 to battle the "professional slavery" of the studio contract system, grew dramatically in just its first year. Writers quickly followed suit by reviving the Screen Writers Guild, with several MGM writers taking the lead. Confronted with growing labor agitation, the studio heads were alarmed, and MGM even placed a number of its employees under surveillance, suspicious that they might be communists. Making matters worse, by the fall of 1934, Upton Sinclair appeared headed for victory in the governor's race.

"Nonsense Often Rules the Roost"

Only the year before, some disgruntled California Democrats had persuaded Sinclair to challenge the state party's conservative establishment by running for governor. The author launched his campaign in characteristic fashion, by writing *I, Governor of California: And How I Ended Poverty*, a futuristic story about a governor named Upton Sinclair. In this "true story of the future," Sinclair ends poverty in California by taking over idle farmland and factories and turning them over to cooperatives owned by unemployed farmers and workers. As the story made clear, production for use rather than profit was the heart of Sinclair's End Poverty in California (EPIC) program. Sinclair also called for the repeal of the sales tax, steeply graduated income and property taxes, and stiff taxes on public utilities. In addition, needy individuals over age sixty would be able to collect a monthly pension of fifty dollars. In a series of pamphlets produced during the campaign, Sinclair further defined the EPIC program. He made clear that it was not just a temporary relief measure but a way to restructure the economy of California permanently through the introduction of socialism. [**See Source 2.**]

Sinclair's platform quickly gained widespread support among Californians disillusioned by the failure of FDR's New Deal to bring economic recovery. It was especially popular in the southern part of the state, where many recent transplants from the Midwest had settled. Many were lower-middle-class and elderly and had looked forward to a warm and comfortable retirement. The Depression had taken away their jobs and, as banks and insurance companies went under, their retirement nest eggs as well. With their golden dreams shattered, these people found an outlet for their increasing disaffection by rushing into any number of reform movements. Thousands of them joined the Utopian Society of America, an organization dedicated to promoting a technocracy.* Others flocked to the movement led by Francis Townsend, a retired Long Beach physician and former midwesterner whose Townsend Plan proposed to rescue the elderly with a two-hundred-dollar monthly pension. Organized in early 1934, Townsend's movement spread rapidly through southern California and beyond. By the end of the year, it would claim a half million followers nationwide.

Utopians and Townsendites provided the EPIC movement with a large, enthusiastic, well-organized constituency. Many small farmers, blue-collar workers, and academics—and even some studio employees—were attracted to the EPIC

Technocracy: A society in which the government and economy are controlled by technocrats—scientists and engineers.

crusade as well. By the summer of 1934, Sinclair's supporters had organized more than a thousand EPIC clubs, which held picnics, auctions, rummage sales, and other fundraisers. They also had registered 350,000 Democratic Party voters. In the August primary, Sinclair shocked the state's Democratic establishment—and himself—when the accelerating EPIC bandwagon crushed his opponent, George Creel, Woodrow Wilson's propaganda chief during World War I. (See Chapter 5.) Meanwhile, the winner of the Republican primary—archconservative incumbent Frank Merriam—had generated little excitement, even among Republicans, and Sinclair had outpolled him by nearly a hundred thousand votes.

Like most other Californians, Louis B. Mayer was surprised by Sinclair's sudden popularity. Only two years before, during the filming of Sinclair's book *The Wet Parade,* the MGM boss had ordered "that bum" kept off the studio's lot. After learning of Sinclair's victory, Mayer told reporters that if Sinclair won in the November election, "chaos" would reign in the state. "I am a Republican," he added, "only because I believe a Republican administration is better for the business and economic condition of our country." Mayer was not ready to concede the defeat of the economic system just yet. First, he quickly drafted his own employees into the anti-Sinclair cause by deducting one day's wages a week from the biggest stars down to the stagehands. Next, he rallied other studio bosses to support the effort to stop the EPIC movement. Through MGM, they were linked to an anti-Sinclair front organization called United for California. It brought together Mayer, *Los Angeles Times* publisher Harry Chandler, the head of the huge agricultural cooperative Sunkist, and the bosses of other big firms such as Southern California Edison, Southern Pacific, and Standard Oil of California. United for California raised several hundred thousand dollars, much of it from Hollywood studios. Then, with the assistance of Lord & Thomas, an advertising agency brought in to run the Merriam campaign, it began to wage all-out war on Sinclair. Lord & Thomas had previously convinced millions of Americans to consume California citrus products. Now, for the first time, an ad agency would run a political campaign. Bankrolled by United for California, the agency began filling the airwaves with anti-Sinclair radio spots, while anti-Sinclair groups blanketed the state with millions of pamphlets and leaflets. **[See Source 3.]**

To Sinclair, Mayer represented everything that was evil about a studio system dominated by the "masters of big business and special privilege." Now he had a chance to defy the studio boss. When Mayer issued a statement during the campaign that the studios would move to Florida if Sinclair won the election, the Democratic candidate dismissed the threat as "bunk." Then he countered Mayer with a threat of his own: Once elected, he would get the state into the movie business. Such pronouncements only made his opponents' task easier. The novice Democratic candidate also said too much in public, as when he jokingly remarked that if he were elected, "half the unemployed of the United States will come to California." Raising the frightening specter of an invading army of unemployed people, the anti-Sinclair forces skillfully played on middle-class fears of social unrest and class conflict. For instance, the *Los Angeles Examiner* and other newspapers ran a picture of homeless people arriving in California by train in anticipation of a Sinclair victory. Readers did not know that the photo was a fake—a still from *Wild Boys of the Road,* a 1933 Warner Brothers movie about young men who rode the rails during the Depression.

Meanwhile, Mayer's assistant Irving Thalberg also worked to thwart the Sinclair movement. The result was *California Election News,* a series of film shorts that looked and sounded like newsreels but were merely anti-Sinclair propaganda. After the first *California Election News* trailer appeared in theaters in mid-October, some irate patrons protested. That did nothing, however, to stop the "Inquiring Cameraman" series. The second installment hit theaters later that month. It followed the format of its predecessor, but it lacked any subtlety at all. One man in the film said that he was going to vote for "St. Clair" because he "is the author of the Russian government." He was countered by an auto mechanic, wearing a bow tie and spotless clothes, who said, "Mr. Merriam will support all the principles America has stood for."

The Sinclair campaign protested that the *California Election News* shorts contained fake footage and that the Inquiring Cameraman created copy "to suit himself," but MGM kept roaring. The third film arrived in theaters the weekend prior to the election. This one abandoned the man-on-the-street format to present a shocking exposé of hobos invading California. It was filled with scenes of men riding the rails, although some of the images were much sharper than others, a hint that they were probably cuts from feature films. Then it took viewers into the "jungle" of a "hobo camp." As the camera passed over the "hobos" (or movie extras), the narrator said ominously, "Look at them. Listen to them, and *think.*" **[See Source 4.]**

In the face of this barrage, Sinclair's campaign sputtered. California's newspapers lined up uniformly against the Democratic candidate and frequently reminded their readers of Mayer's threat to pull the motion-picture industry out of the state if Sinclair won. **[See Source 5.]** The *Los Angeles Times* ran virtually no news stories on Sinclair's campaign, while emitting a daily drumbeat of anti-Sinclair editorials. A "maggot-like horde of Reds," it warned in one, was supporting the Sinclair campaign. "They are termites . . . secretly and darkly eating into everything that the American heart has held dear and sacred." Denied access to the state's media, the candidate was forced to campaign mostly at rallies of the faithful. They were no match for the frightening images that too many Californians saw in newspapers and on the big screen. When the votes were counted, Sinclair had lost. More than 879,000 voters had cast ballots for him, but more than 1,138,000 had voted for Merriam.

It did not help that Sinclair had failed to gain FDR's support. The president already had a wary eye on Francis Townsend and the other leaders of Depression-era crusades. By 1934, right-wing Michigan radio priest Charles Coughlin had won a large audience with calls for social justice. Meanwhile, Louisiana populist demagogue Huey Long had amassed a huge nationwide following with his Share Our Wealth program, which proposed to combat the Depression's effects with soak-the-rich taxes and wealth redistribution. Given these men's threats to his own popularity, Roosevelt was not about to go out on a limb for the eccentric Sinclair. The failure of George Creel and other California Democratic leaders to endorse their party's candidate also did not help. In addition, Sinclair had failed to persuade the Progressive Party candidate, who garnered more than 300,000 votes, to withdraw. Finally, Sinclair had refused to counter the charges leveled against him by his opponents. The accusations were merely "nonsense," he told a Screen Writers Guild organizer. "But nonsense," the writer replied, "often rules the roost."

"We Did Win"

On election night, Mayer threw a bash attended by some of Hollywood's biggest celebrities. The studio boss declared jubilantly that the "voters of California have made a fearless choice between radicalism and patriotism." Sinclair, too, met the election outcome in fitting fashion: He wrote a book about it. Titled *I, Candidate for Governor: And How I Got Licked*, it was a "revelation of what money can do in American politics [and] what it will do when its privileges are threatened."

Even though Mayer had helped defeat Sinclair, the nature of his victory became less clear as time went on. The MGM lion, of course, still roars on the big screen, while motion pictures remain a powerful form of popular cultural expression. Moreover, advertising and public relations have come to play an increasing role in American political campaigns as the line between entertainment and news becomes ever more blurred. The power of Mayer and other studio moguls, however, would diminish in the next two decades. Buoyed by the pro-labor Wagner Act,* studio employees began to win independence from the bosses' iron grip. Later, as fear of communist subversion grew in the late 1940s, Hollywood became the target of congressional investigators. Although Mayer and other bosses solidified their reputations as redbaiters with blacklists against alleged communists, the "red scare" in Hollywood demonstrated the studios' vulnerability to outside political pressures. So did a major antitrust decision by the Supreme Court in 1948 that ordered the studios to get out of the film exhibition business, a ruling that hit MGM especially hard. Within a few years, the rise of television would further erode the studios' power. By the early 1950s, even the once mighty MGM saw its sales and profits slump.

The demise of the studio system was paralleled by the deterioration of Mayer's personal life. Although MGM's films frequently upheld the sanctity of marriage, Mayer was not a faithful husband, and in 1946 Margaret Mayer sued for divorce. About the same time, when his young girlfriend decided to marry another man, Mayer took an overdose of sleeping pills. Although he remarried several years later, Mayer was increasingly out of touch with changing popular tastes in films. Six years before he died in 1957, MGM ousted its one-time master.

Meanwhile, Sinclair continued to churn out books until a few years before he died in 1968. Right after the California election, he attempted to take EPIC nationwide, but the crusade soon collapsed as unemployment began to decline with the help of the New Deal programs. Yet EPIC had left its mark. While governor, Frank Merriam signed a state income tax, one of the planks in EPIC's platform. Furthermore, the New Deal responded to EPIC and other popular movements by embracing a raft of new programs, including Social Security, steeper taxes on the rich, and massive work relief. Perhaps Sinclair had all that in mind when he answered a reporter's question in 1958 about how California would be different had he won in 1934. "We did win," he replied. "We gave California and all the other states an exciting awareness of what democracy really is."

---

*Wagner Act: Legislation passed in 1935 that bolstered the right of labor unions to organize and bargain collectively for wages and benefits.

PRIMARY SOURCES

SOURCE 1:   *Publicity Poster for* Grand Hotel   (1932)

By the 1930s, MGM's movies had a recognizable style. Stages, often in a sleek art deco style, were bathed in brilliant lighting that helped create a glossy look. Close-ups of stars were filmed with "Rembrandt lighting," a type of backlighting that helped lend an air of glamour to the characters. Few MGM movies better captured "the Studio Age formula for movies" than Grand Hotel *(1932), the story of love and intrigue involving an ambitious stenographer (Joan Crawford) and guests at a posh hotel. What do you think this movie advertising poster for that film conveyed to audiences in the early 1930s? Does it reflect the movie studio system? Does it reflect the reality of American life at the time?*

SOURCE: GRAND HOTEL © 1932 Turner Entertainment Co. An AOL Time Warner Company. All rights reserved. Reprinted in Tino Balio, *History of the American Cinema* (New York: Charles Scribner's Sons, 1990), V, 186.

SOURCE 2:   Upton Sinclair, *"EPIC Answers"*   (1934)

Following is an excerpt from one of four pamphlets that Sinclair published before the 1934 California gubernatorial election. What are his solutions to the Depression?

In our State of California we have now more than a million persons dependent upon public charity for their existence. Many of our counties are already bankrupt. Our State will be more than a hundred million dollars "in the hole" by the end of 1934, and bankruptcy has only been averted by the Federal Government stepping in to take the burden of feeding the hungry. The Federal Government is now supporting the banks, the insurance companies, the railroads, the great industrial corporations; the home-owners, the farmers, the veterans, the unemployed. Bankruptcy for the Federal Government is only a question of months.

To this problem there can be but one solution. It is necessary to put the unemployed at productive labor. A million people in California must be made self-sustaining. They must have access to the land to grow their own food; they must have access to the factories to produce their own clothing and building materials, out of which to make their own homes. We must take them off the backs of the little tax-payers, and stop forcing the latter out of their homes and off their ranches. There must be prompt action, for the crisis is desperate and the next breakdown may lead to attempts at revolt and civil war. . . .

The destitute people cannot get land or factories or raw materials for themselves. This can only be done by the credit of the State. The EPIC plan proposes that the State shall purchase the idle land and factories at the present bankruptcy prices, and shall immediately institute a State system of production and exchange, whereby the unemployed may produce what they consume.

The "subsistence homesteads" now proposed as a solution of the problem constitute a step backward. When men live on small farms and produce only what they themselves consume, they can never escape poverty and drudgery. Modern production is mass production, both on farms and in factories. It requires great tracts of land, costly machinery, and expert direction.

The EPIC plan proposes that the State of California shall set up land colonies in which the unemployed farm workers shall live and produce the food required by the million destitute persons in our State. Operating thus upon a large scale, the farm workers can live in what will amount to new villages, with all the advantages of modern civilization: kitchens and cafeterias operated by the community, a social hall with opportunities for recreation, a church, a school-house, a store, a library, a motion picture theatre, etc. . . .

The factories will be great productive units owned and managed by the State. There also will be social buildings with kitchens, cafeterias, lecture halls, libraries, etc. The State will maintain a system of distribution, whereby the food is brought into the cities and the manufactured products are taken out to the land colonies, and all the products of the system are made available at cost. Those who produce will receive the full social value of their product, so they

SOURCE: Upton Sinclair, "EPIC Answers," pp. 3–4, 5–6 in Upton Sinclair, *The EPIC Plan for California* (1934).

will be able to buy what they have produced, and for the first time consumption will balance production. . . .

People are now losing their homes and ranches because they can no longer pay their taxes. The tax system of the State is to be revised, and all homes occupied by the owners and ranches operated by the owners, which are assessed at less than $3000, are to be exempted from taxation. Taxes on the more valuable properties will be graduated, increasing at the rate of one-half of one per cent for each $5000 of additional value.

It is proposed to repeal the State sales tax, which is a tax on poverty, and to raise a portion of the money by means of a State tax upon stock exchange transactions. New York State imposes a tax of 4 cents per share on stock transfers, and there is no reason why California could not do the same. It is estimated that a million shares change hands in our State every gambling day. Let Wall Street pay the sales tax!

Next it is proposed to impose a State income tax. In the United States today an income of $25,000 per year pays 10%. In England, France, and Germany, such an income pays 30% to 40%. So there is ample margin for a graduated State income tax. It is also proposed to increase the State inheritance tax in the higher brackets, taking 50% of those great fortunes which are unearned and which are a menace to our society.

Finally, it is proposed to impose a graduated tax upon idle and unused land. Our cities and towns are ringed around with vacant lots held by speculators. If a person owns a lot assessed at not more than $1000, and wishes to build a home upon that lot, there will be a State building loan fund to make this possible. But persons who are holding large tracts of land out of use will be taxed for it, the tax being graduated according to the valuation held by each individual.

It is also proposed to include a tax on privately owned public utility corporations and banks, which are shamefully undertaxed at present.

The remainder of the EPIC program has to do with those persons who are unable to work. It promises that needy persons over sixty years of age who have lived three years within the State, shall receive a pension of $50 per month. It promises the same for the blind and disabled, and for the widowed mothers of dependent children. If there are more than two children, it proposes to add $25 per month for each additional child.

Source 3:   *Anti-Sinclair Leaflet*   (1934)

Anti-Sinclair forces flooded California with millions of leaflets. What fears does this example reflect?

SOURCE: Reprinted in Greg Mitchell, *The Campaign of the Century: Upton Sinclair's Race for Governor of California and the Birth of Media Politics* (New York: Random House, 1992), between pp. 332 and 333.

SOURCE 4:   *California Election News, No. 3*   (1934)

"Bums" get off a train in MGM's third installment of the "Inquiring Cameraman" series. Can you think of an example of similar political advertising from our own time?

SOURCE: Reprinted in Greg Mitchell, *The Campaign of the Century: Upton Sinclair's Race for Governor of California and the Birth of Media Politics* (New York: Random House, 1992), between pp. 332 and 333; originally from University of Southern California Newsfilm Library.

SOURCE 5:   *Anti-Sinclair Cartoon*   (1934)

In this cartoon showing Louis B. Mayer preparing to leave California, readers are re-
minded of the movie industry's importance to the state. The newspaper headline in the
cartoon refers to California senator William McAdoo. Do you think the threat illus-
trated here was real?

THAT'S THE QUESTION

QUESTIONS TO CONSIDER

1. Although Upton Sinclair's and Louis B. Mayer's politics were very different, in
   some ways the two men were much alike. How would you compare Sinclair and
   Mayer? What are the most important factors in each man's life for understanding
   his public or political activities?

SOURCE: Department of Special Collections, University of California Library, Davis, California.
Reprinted in Upton Sinclair, *I, Candidate for Governor: And How I Got Licked* (1934; reprint, Berkeley: University of California Press, 1994), p. 171.

2. What do the rise and work of Mayer and MGM reveal about the forces that helped shape the motion-picture industry in the early twentieth century? Do the films that MGM produced in the early 1930s reflect those forces?

3. What were the goals of Sinclair's EPIC campaign? Given the circumstances in the 1930s, were they realistic?

4. Why did Sinclair lose the California governor's race in 1934? What do the actions of Mayer and the other opponents of Sinclair's campaign reveal about some of the forces that limited reform in the 1930s? Are the same forces at work in campaigns today?

5. Considering modern American politics and society, as well as the issues in the 1934 California election, do you think Sinclair was correct in arguing that he and his supporters actually did win?

FOR FURTHER READING

Scott Eyman, *The Life and Legend of Louis B. Mayer* (New York: Simon and Schuster, 2005), provides a comprehensive account of Mayer's rise and fall.

Leon Harris, *Upton Sinclair: American Rebel* (New York: Thomas Y. Crowell Company, 1975), is a sympathetic treatment of Sinclair that concentrates on his life through the 1934 campaign.

Greg Mitchell, *The Campaign of the Century: Upton Sinclair's Race for Governor of California and the Birth of Media Politics* (New York: Random House, 1992), is a highly readable day-by-day account of the 1934 election, emphasizing the groundbreaking aspects of the anti-Sinclair campaign.

Robert Sklar, *Movie-Made America: A Cultural History of American Movies* (New York: Random House, 1994), explores motion pictures as a form of cultural expression related to important political, economic, and social developments.

Robert H. Stanley, *The Celluloid Empire: A History of the American Movie Industry* (New York: Hastings House, 1978), offers a brief overview of the development of moviemaking as a business dominated by large corporations.

Racism and Relocation During World War II: Harry Ueno and Dillon Myer

As Harry Ueno slept on the night of December 5, 1942, he was blissfully unaware that his life was about to take a turn for the worse. Ueno was one of
the roughly 120,000 Japanese and Japanese Americans confined in internment
camps during World War II. He was awakened when three jeeps loaded with
military police (MP) pulled up in front of his barracks at California's Manzanar
Relocation Center. Startled by the MPs' arrival, Ueno jumped from his bed
when he heard a bang at the door and the demand that he get dressed. Earlier
that evening, another Japanese-American internee had been beaten inside Manzanar by a group of masked men. It was no random act of violence. Home to
more than 10,000 people of Japanese ancestry, Manzanar had been wracked by
tensions among the internees. Many internees, including the assault victim,
urged cooperation with the policy of internment. Other internees resented both
the policy and its supporters. As Ueno approached his barracks door, he was
about to become the focus of that division.

The MPs took Ueno to the Manzanar police station, where he was interro-
gated about the beating for the next two hours. Then he was driven in handcuffs
to the jail in nearby Independence, California. The next afternoon, the Manzanar police chief drove Ueno back to the internment center, where he was thrown
in jail with five or six other Japanese internees. As Ueno looked outside his jail
window that evening, he noticed a large number of internees milling around.
They had gathered to demand that camp authorities set Ueno free. The next day
was the first anniversary of the Japanese attack on Pearl Harbor, and as the
crowd grew bigger, he heard a sergeant exhort the MPs to "remember Pearl
Harbor!" Then he saw the MPs put on gas masks and begin to throw tear gas
canisters into the crowd. As smoke filled the air, Ueno heard five or six shots at
close range. From farther away came the sound of machine gun fire. When the
smoke cleared, he saw one man lying facedown on the ground.

The Manzanar Riot left two men dead and ten others wounded. It was the
deadliest outbreak of violence in any of the nation's ten internment camps. It
was also the kind of incident that Dillon Myer was determined to avoid. Myer
was the head of the War Relocation Authority (WRA), the federal agency that

❖ *Harry Ueno (center, rear)*	❖ *Dillon Myer*

administered the internment camps. A career bureaucrat in the federal government, he wanted no trouble in his facilities. Moreover, Myer was actually sympathetic to the Japanese Americans under the WRA's wartime control. He realized that camp disturbances like the one at Manzanar only reinforced anti-Japanese sentiment and the public perception that his agency needed to be tougher on the internees. Thus he had little use for "troublemakers."

Ueno seemed to be just that. He was accused of beating a fellow internee, and his arrest had sparked the deadly violence. In Myer's mind, Ueno needed to be dealt with swiftly. Although Ueno was never charged with any crime, he would be hauled off to isolation centers in Utah and Arizona. Later, he would be confined to another such center holding thousands of allegedly disloyal Japanese and Japanese Americans. Seeking release from criminal confinement, Ueno met resistance at every turn. In the minds of Myer and many Japanese-American internees, he was a dangerous agitator who threatened the future of all Japanese Americans.

"Once a Jap, Always a Jap"

Harry Ueno was a very unlikely troublemaker. Before the war, he had lived quietly in Los Angeles with his wife and three children. Never one to shy away from hard work, he had labored diligently at a variety of jobs in the fruit and vegetable business. For a time, he had run a small fruit stand near Hollywood frequented by movie stars and even studio boss Louis B. Mayer (See Chapter 7). Ueno had quickly learned that Mayer and the other movie people were hard to please, so he had tried to have a variety of produce in stock even when it was out of season. Always he had been careful to mind his own business.

Few Japanese and Japanese Americans in California had such an opportunity to brush up against Hollywood producers and movie stars. But in another way, Ueno was typical of many West Coast Japanese and Japanese Americans before World War II. As did many of the roughly 47,000 Issei* and 79,000 Nisei* in the United States, Ueno had a lot of experience growing or marketing agricultural produce. Up and down the West Coast's fertile valleys, Japanese immigrants had begun to succeed as small farmers in the early twentieth century. Although many of them had originally come to Hawaii and the mainland as farm laborers in the late nineteenth century, they had always aspired to farm their own land. Frequently, they had worked modest plots of marginal land and managed to produce bountiful harvests. In 1920, people of Japanese descent represented only 2 percent of California's population, but they produced 92 percent of the state's strawberries, 80 percent of its celery, and 66 percent of its tomatoes.

Like many Japanese-American families, the Uenos got their start in agriculture. Harry Ueno's parents had moved from Hiroshima to the island of Hawaii around 1897 to work as agricultural laborers. When Harry was born in 1907, the second of three sons, his parents were working on a sugar plantation. Within a few years, however, his father was leasing land to grow his own sugar cane and watermelons. Achieving a measure of prosperity, he sent eight-year-old Harry back to Hiroshima to be educated. The boy lived with his grandparents for seven years until his father and mother also returned to Japan. By then, Harry felt alienated from his parents, and he moved to Tokyo, where he delivered morning and evening newspapers and attended school during the day. After earning only food and shelter for six months, he moved back home. "I was thinking," Ueno later recalled, "'What to do? I must do something for myself.'" Two months after enrolling in a course to become a member of the merchant marine, he was on a ship bound for the United States.

By the time the freighter arrived in the Pacific Northwest in 1923, Ueno had decided that he was not cut out to be a sailor. At Tacoma, Washington, the last American port of call, he jumped ship and went to work in a sawmill. He was surprised by the large number of Japanese workers in the mill's labor camp. He discovered that many of them were illegal aliens and that their biggest fear was a raid by immigration officials. His camp quarters even had a trapdoor, and a couple of times he found himself escaping under the house to avoid arrest. Still only sixteen, he did not realize that being born in Hawaii had automatically made him an American citizen.

Ueno worked for three years at the sawmill before heading east to join his brother in Milwaukee. After working in Milwaukee for a time, the brothers moved to Chicago. As a Kibei—American born but educated in Japan—Ueno spoke little English. By contrast, his brother had been educated in the United States and spoke little Japanese. After a few years, Ueno split with his brother and headed back to the West Coast. At first, he worked with a cousin on a farm in Stockton, California, and then he returned to Washington State. Once again, he found work in a sawmill, which employed about 150 other Japanese. Ueno

---

Issei: First-generation immigrants from Japan who were not citizens of the United States and were referred to as Japanese.

Nisei: Second-generation Japanese who had been born in the United States, were American citizens, and were referred to as Japanese Americans.

worked ten hours a day, six days a week. At the onset of the Depression, when white workers started to unionize, Japanese workers were not allowed to join the union and were shut out of the mills. So Ueno went back to California. In San Francisco, he met Yaso Taguchi, a young woman whose family had emigrated from Japan in 1923. They were married in 1930.

The Uenos moved to Los Angeles, settled down, and had three sons. Harry Ueno quickly found work in the produce business. After running his own business for a couple of years, he worked for a market in the Hollywood area, and then as a buyer and manager for a market in Beverly Hills. Unlike many other Japanese-American families, the Uenos did not live in the Little Tokyo section of Los Angeles, but in another area close to downtown that was restricted to whites by a zoning ordinance. The Uenos were allowed to live there only because their landlady went to court three times to get them exempted from the zoning law. Although Ueno had contacts in Little Tokyo and went there occasionally to shop, he did not "mix in with any politics." Nor was he a member of the Japanese American Citizens League, the most prominent Japanese-American organization. Although his family was Buddhist, Ueno never went to the Buddhist temple in Los Angeles, and he sent his children to a Catholic school. He did not even belong to a *kenjinkai,* an association based on members' ties to their ancestral homes.

As a Kibei, Ueno had little in common with the Nisei, even though they were of the same generation. "The Kibei kind of withdrew," he later recalled. "They couldn't communicate good enough." Thus, even though most Japanese were forced by restrictive real-estate covenants and zoning laws to live in enclaves apart from white society, Ueno was doubly alienated, by both his Japanese ancestry and his Japanese education. As he later put it, "I just lived mostly by myself."

Whether Issei, Nisei, or Kibei, of course, the Japanese experienced isolation in American society because of deep-seated anti-Asian racism. Immigrants from across the Pacific had long been the targets of both periodic vigilante violence and discriminatory laws. In 1882, Congress had barred the Chinese from further immigration into the country, a ban extended to the Japanese in 1924. Since the late nineteenth century, American law had prevented Asians from becoming naturalized citizens. On the West Coast, long a hotbed of anti-Asian racism, immigrants from China, Japan, Korea, and the Philippines were frequently the targets of discrimination. California slapped these unwelcome immigrants with exclusion, and restrictive zoning laws, as well as laws preventing land ownership by aliens. Fired by fears of cheap foreign labor, many Americans in the early twentieth century viewed the Japanese as a menace. Although they remained a minuscule portion of California's population, their growing numbers seemed evidence to many whites of a Japanese plot to take over the West Coast. Meanwhile, the very success of Issei farmers left them vulnerable to baseless accusations that they were driving white farmers off the land.

Pearl Harbor quickly brought anti-Japanese prejudice to a boil in the Golden State and elsewhere. In the days after the attack, many West Coast residents expressed doubts about the loyalty of the Japanese and Japanese Americans in their midst. Race set the Japanese apart in a way that it did not differentiate Americans of German or Italian extraction. Thus suspicions about disloyalty among those of German or Italian ancestry were dealt with on more of an individual basis. By contrast, people of Japanese descent were condemned as a group. As the *Los Angeles Times* put it shortly after Pearl Harbor, a "Japanese American born of Japanese parents . . . grows up to be a Japanese, and not an American."

Such assumptions led to a rising anti-Japanese hysteria. It was fed by newspaper editors, politicians, and some military leaders. California governor Culbert Olson, for instance, claimed in a statewide radio address shortly after Pearl Harbor that Japanese residents were preparing to aid the enemy. About the same time, an influential columnist wrote that "the Pacific Coast is in imminent danger of a combined attack from within and without." False rumors fanned fears of sabotage and espionage. One report maintained that Japanese Americans in Hawaii had aided the attack on Pearl Harbor. Another story spread in the press and on radio claimed that class rings from American colleges had been found on some of the Japanese pilots shot down at Pearl Harbor. Speaking in Seattle less than two months after the attack, one journalist said that if the city were bombed, "you will be able to look up and see some University of Washington sweaters on the boys doing the bombing!" The absence of any evidence of sabotage or spying by longtime Issei, Nisei, or Kibei did not matter. In fact, to some observers, it only confirmed the danger that the Japanese posed. In defiance of logic, lack of sabotage seemed proof of a conspiracy to commit it.

By early 1942, numerous civilian and military officials were calling for the evacuation of the Japanese from the West Coast. "We cannot run the risk," the mayor of Los Angeles announced in early February 1942, "of another Pearl Harbor episode in Southern California." Members of Congress quickly agreed. One California congressman warned that the Japanese represented a "national threat." A congressman from Mississippi declared, "Once a Jap, always a Jap." In the middle of February, the entire West Coast congressional delegation sent President Franklin Roosevelt a unanimous recommendation to "evacuate all persons of Japanese lineage" from California, Washington, and Oregon. In the face of the mounting hysteria, few in the Roosevelt administration questioned the legality or morality of removing American citizens from their homes and placing them in relocation camps. Responding to the growing calls for evacuation, Roosevelt signed Executive Order 9066 on February 19, 1942. The order allowed the secretary of war to establish military zones along the West Coast and exclude any citizen or alien from them. In other words, it permitted the evacuation of the entire Japanese population. On the same day that FDR signed the evacuation order, Army intelligence reported that "mass evacuation [was] unnecessary." Although some members of the armed forces supported evacuation, the decision for internment had clearly been driven by politics, not military necessity.

The next month, FDR signed another executive order creating the War Relocation Authority, an independent government agency responsible for running the internment centers. Starting that spring, Japanese and Japanese Americans were ordered by the War Department to assembly centers—facilities along the West Coast that could accommodate large crowds. From there they were moved to internment centers, which were scattered from eastern California to Arkansas. There, behind barbed wire and under the constant observation of armed guards, Harry Ueno, his family, and most of the other evacuees would live for nearly four years. Like Ueno, two-thirds of them were American citizens.

For Ueno, the months after the attack on Pearl Harbor were embittering. Like many other Japanese Americans, he "could see [hatred] in people's eyes." He also learned how quickly hatred could turn into doubts about loyalty. A few days after the Japanese attack on Pearl Harbor, a neighbor told Ueno that the "Japs" were cruel and inhuman. He replied that "this country is the same way too." Then he told the woman that a Japanese doctor in the Los Angeles area who had recently been taken in for questioning by the Federal Bureau of Investigation (FBI) had later been found dead in his jail cell. The doctor, he declared, had been killed by the FBI. Within hours, two FBI agents appeared at Ueno's door wanting to know the source of his information. Then they took him downtown for questioning. The harassment by the FBI continued right up to the night before Ueno's evacuation, when agents told him that he would go to jail unless he gave them a name.

At the same time, Ueno was annoyed by the response of the Japanese American Citizens League (JACL) to the growing anti-Japanese sentiment. Founded in 1929, the JACL was the largest and most powerful Japanese-American organization. What would now be called a civil rights organization, the Nisei-dominated JACL promoted the assimilation of Japanese immigrants into American society. After the attack on Pearl Harbor, it went out of its way to demonstrate Japanese-American loyalty to the United States. For instance, it put up a large banner outside a Los Angeles drugstore declaring it to be the headquarters of the Anti-Axis Committee.* Such actions dismayed Ueno, who wondered what the JACL was trying to prove. Later, when two JACL witnesses testified that a small group of Issei fishermen were spies for the Japanese navy, he was incensed. The JACL's leaders, Ueno said later, should have defended these "innocent victims of war."

In May 1942, the Ueno family left Los Angeles on a bus for Manzanar on the eastern slope of the Sierra Nevada. They were told to take whatever they could carry, except food and cooking utensils. The family departed their home with three or four suitcases. Originally scheduled to go to the Santa Anita Assembly Center (a racetrack near Los Angeles), they were instead transported by bus directly to Manzanar, a trip of some two hundred miles across southern California's Mojave Desert. Years later, Ueno recalled feeling that "it was open season for 'Jap hunting'" and that the camp would provide protection for them. Even though he found the conditions there austere, he later said, "We tried to make the best of the situation."

"Kind of Dirty Work"

If Harry Ueno lived much of his life estranged from his environment, Dillon Myer could not have fit more perfectly into his. Myer was raised on what he called "a typical corn belt farm of 135 acres in central Ohio." Like the Myer family itself, his childhood experiences were firmly fixed in the rural Midwest. When he was born in 1891, the farm had already been in the family for nearly sixty years, and the Myers had established themselves as one of the leading families in the small community of Hebron. Dillon's grandfather, of German extraction, had purchased the land after migrating from Maryland. An only child,

Anti-Axis Committee: The Axis was the alliance formed by Germany, Italy, and Japan in 1940. The JACL was obviously trying to prove its loyalty to the United States.

Dillon's father stayed on the farm and married a woman of Scots-Irish descent. The second of the couple's four children, Dillon experienced a remarkably conventional rural upbringing filled with "plenty of food and many homey pleasures." Farm chores were punctuated by fishing in the summer, rabbit and quail hunting, and family gatherings around the fire in the winter. Later, as a teenager, Dillon would attend dances at a lakeside park.

Like almost everyone else they knew, the Myers were churchgoing people. The family attended the local Methodist Episcopal church, where Dillon's father served as an officer. Every day at home, Dillon later recalled, his father "sat at the head of the table and always gave the blessing." He also disapproved of Sunday baseball games and did not hesitate to give a tardy Dillon his first switching when he was only five. At the same age, Dillon was assigned his first farm chore, collecting eggs. Later, he took on milking and wood-splitting duties. Meanwhile, his mother drummed into him the importance of correct spelling and good posture. Along with his brother and younger sisters, he walked more than a mile to a one-room country school. And like countless children in the late nineteenth century, he learned to read from William Holmes McGuffey's school readers, whose lessons were laced with Protestant morality. In short, Dillon Myer's childhood world was narrow, strict, and provincial. Yet he was never alienated from it. He demonstrated little youthful rebelliousness or inclination to challenge authority. In fact, classmates kidded him about being "the good little boy."

If Myer rebelled at all as a youth, it was by rejecting his father's wish that he become a Methodist minister. As a high school freshman, he was impressed by the salary and free living quarters provided to the manager of a nearby farm. So in 1910, he enrolled in the College of Agriculture at Ohio State. During his senior year, he was offered a job as an agronomy instructor at the University of Kentucky. Disgusted after he was twice denied a raise, he left for Evansville, Indiana, in 1916 to become a county agricultural agent. It was Myer's first step into a growing agricultural bureaucracy. Part of the national Cooperative Extension Service established by Congress in 1914, county agents shared the latest agricultural techniques and information with farmers. It was a perfect training ground for young Myer. Reporting to the county school board and township trustees, he learned the importance of making the right contacts. After another brief stint as a county extension agent in Ohio, he became a district supervisor. While in that position, he met another county agent, named Jenness Wirt, a clothing and interior decorating specialist in the extension service, and they were married in 1924.

In the coming years, Myer worked his way up in the government bureaucracy. Even the onset of hard times in the early 1930s did not slow his rise. In 1933, Ohio's extension director asked Myer to supervise the New Deal's Agricultural Adjustment Administration (AAA) programs in the state. Created in 1933, the AAA sought to lift farm prices by cutting agricultural output. Myer proved an energetic and effective administrator and was soon promoted to work at AAA headquarters in Washington, D.C. When the Supreme Court found the AAA unconstitutional in 1936, he moved to the Soil Conservation Service (SCS), established in response to the spread of the Dust Bowl. The SCS was part of the Department of Agriculture, headed by Henry A. Wallace. (See

Chapter 9.) Myer quickly gained Wallace's attention and was promoted to assistant chief of the SCS. As Myer put it later, much of his work "had to do with the tough problems that nobody else wanted to handle." It was, he admitted, "kind of dirty work," but the farm boy turned bureaucrat proved very adept at it. Besides, it paid well. For a man who was able to recall decades later exactly how much he made in his various government positions, that was an important consideration. In fact, he had taken the SCS position only after threatening to quit if his salary was not increased to sixty-five hundred dollars—more than 97 percent of all Americans earned in 1935.

Myer was asked to take on another kind of "dirty work" when he was appointed director of the new War Relocation Authority in June 1942. Since its creation by FDR's executive order earlier that year, the WRA had been headed by future president Dwight Eisenhower's younger brother, Milton Eisenhower, who happened to have been Myer's boss at the SCS. Eisenhower was deeply troubled by the injustice of Japanese relocation, as were many others in the Agriculture Department who had developed close contacts with West Coast Japanese farmers. Unable to carry out his WRA assignment in good conscience, Eisenhower had taken a job in the Office of War Information. During a dinner party, he told Myer that he should accept the WRA assignment only if he could "sleep and still carry on the job." Myer took the job, he later said, "with an open mind." With the exception of "two boys" in his class at Ohio State, he explained, he "didn't know any Japanese."

When Myer took over the WRA, relocation was largely accomplished. He had had nothing to do with the decision to uproot the Japanese and Japanese Americans from their homes and place them in internment camps. Rather, he was charged with merely maintaining the policy. Nearly two decades later, he would claim to have believed that only selective Japanese evacuation was justified. He also would confess that he had had "little information" about the Japanese on the West Coast and little knowledge about the reasons for the evacuation. Very soon, though, he had found out that "most of the reasons were phony." Yet in testifying before a subcommittee of the House Un-American Activities Committee in 1943, Myer defended mass evacuation. [**See Source 1.**] And unlike Milton Eisenhower, the new WRA head apparently slept quite soundly. Long after he accepted the appointment, Myer said, "[I am never] bothered when it comes to carrying on a job that I feel I am responsible for."

"To Live . . . in a Free and Equal Society"

About the same time that Myer was taking over the WRA, the Uenos were settling into their new home at Manzanar. Arriving at night, they were handed sackcloth and told to stuff it with hay to make a mattress. Then they were assigned to a room with three other families. The families were separated by a sheet hung as a partition. Bathrooms were communal, and meals were taken in a mess hall. Ueno joined a work detail cutting sagebrush to make room for camp expansion. He was later transferred to a mess hall, where he found many other Kibei. Educated in Japanese preparatory schools, Kibei had "no special skill," Ueno recalled, "just basic training for college." Thus they were often assigned to work in the camp kitchens. In the mess, Ueno heard widespread complaints about shortages of meat and sugar, a vital wartime commodity. He and the other internees attributed the problem to embezzlement by white camp administrators. He told the mess steward and the assistant director of the camp that he would report them to the FBI if they did not follow up on his complaints. That fall, he decided to organize a union so that the internees' grievances could be heard. The Mess Hall Workers' Union gained the approval of camp authorities, including the director, Ralph Merritt. Ueno also won the backing of many internees, more than twelve hundred of whom signed a petition supporting the union.

Ueno later contended that his union was concerned only with improving conditions in the mess halls, yet his sudden activism also seemed related to Japanese-American politics. Not all of the internees at Manzanar welcomed Ueno's efforts. That was especially true of certain members of the Japanese American Citizens League—Nisei who sought to cooperate with camp administrators. Some of them had already formed the Fair Employment Practices Committee, headed by an internee named Fred Tayama. Ueno was convinced that it was nothing more than a front for Manzanar's administrators. At the same time, Nisei internees had formed a JACL-dominated commission to help govern the camp. One of its members was Joe Masaoka, whose brother was the JACL's national secretary. Another was Togo Tanaka, a leader of the JACL in Los Angeles who had urged cooperation with authorities during the evacuation from southern California. Ueno believed that these internees "were not for the people in the camp but more for the benefit of the administration."

The Mess Hall Workers' Union was short-lived. On December 5, 1942, a small group of masked men beat Fred Tayama, who accused Ueno of having participated in the attack. Although Ueno claimed that he had been at a Parent Teacher Association meeting that night, Manzanar authorities picked him up and hustled him off to jail. The next evening, as Ueno looked on from the Manzanar jail, several thousand internees gathered to hear about his fate. Suddenly, the crowd got out of control. As Ueno looked on, MPs dispersed the crowd, but not before twelve people had been shot, two fatally. **[See Source 2.]** The Manzanar Riot brought an end to the Mess Hall Workers' Union, which was quickly disbanded. It was also the beginning of a long ordeal for Ueno.

Along with seven other internees, including five other members of his union, Ueno was transported later that night to the jail in Bishop, California. After four days, they were taken to the jail in Lone Pine, sixty miles to the south. Unable to talk or write to his wife, Ueno was held there for a month before he received a notice from Dillon Myer. According to Ueno, it said, "We're going to move you to someplace with a little more open space, and we're going to have a quick hearing for your case." Shortly after, Ueno and the others were taken to a depot, where they were placed on a train bound for Moab, Utah. There they were held in an old Civilian Conservation Corps* camp. Later, they were joined by internees from other centers who were also considered "undesirables." At Moab, the WRA routinely censored the letters that Ueno sent to his family and friends at Manzanar. **[See Source 3.]** Meanwhile, he demanded to know when

---

Civilian Conservation Corps: A program created in 1933 as part of the New Deal to employ young, out-of-work men on conservation projects.

Myer was going to have a hearing. He also complained about his treatment. After a heated argument with the camp director over censorship of the mail, his lack of a hearing, and the "harsh regulations," Ueno was ready to renounce his American citizenship and return to Japan with his family. "I thought that the only way I could get all my freedom and happy living was in Japan," he declared. "Also, I wanted my children to live and grow in a free and equal society."

It would be a long time before Ueno got his freedom. Myer never arranged for a hearing. When Ueno requested a transfer to an alien internment camp, the WRA chief turned him down, claiming that U.S. citizens could not be transferred to such facilities. Instead, Ueno and five other prisoners were sent to the Leupp Isolation Center near Winslow, Arizona, where there were about 80 Japanese prisoners and 150 guards. By the time Ueno arrived, he had given up hope for a hearing. When the Leupp Isolation Center closed at the end of 1943, Ueno was moved once again. Still charged with no crime, he found himself at the Tule Lake Segregation Center in northeastern California, where several pro-Japanese and radical groups were interred. Determined to keep quiet and keep to himself, Ueno was accused by other internees of being both pro-Axis and procommunist. As he later put it, he was "getting it from both ends."

"Champion of Human Rights"

Dillon Myer felt that he was getting it from both ends, too. Committed to "carrying on" the job for which he was now responsible, Myer preferred what he once called "a middle-ground approach" to dealing with the Japanese and Japanese Americans. Thus he defended the mass evacuation while shielding the WRA from critics who believed that it did not go far enough. As a seasoned administrator, he knew that harsh treatment of "troublemakers and agitators" such as Harry Ueno could play an important role in defending his agency from assault.

Myer's "middle ground," however, was not just the policy of a cautious bureaucrat. It also reflected his view that America's "Japanese problem" could be solved only by their complete assimilation into what he called America's "melting pot." The easiest way to achieve that, Myer believed, was to break down the Japanese community through dispersion. **[See Source 4.]** Shortly after taking over the WRA, therefore, he began relocating Nisei internees outside the internment camps to communities across the country. Although Ueno and other Kibei were excluded from the program, it eventually placed thirty-six thousand internees in communities as far away as the East Coast. Their first steps toward assimilation were to fill out a detailed questionnaire and then submit to an interview by WRA staff. **[See Source 5.]** A man who had little understanding or appreciation of Japanese culture, Myer wished to see any remnants of it eradicated as quickly as possible. Perhaps that explains his reaction to the vegetable and flower gardens planted by internees at the Poston Relocation Center in Arizona. According to one government official, they were "gardens of ancient Japanese beauty," but to Myer they were "the worst thing I have come on in all my inspections of the camps."

Myer's views dovetailed perfectly with those of the JACL, which had fought to assimilate the Nisei into American society by eradicating any trace of

Japanese culture among them. Before the war, it had called on its members to eliminate "those mannerisms and thoughts which mark us apart, aside from our physical characteristics." Once relocation began, the JACL called it a "humane and democratic resettlement." Naturally, the WRA director felt comfortable working with the JACL. He conferred often with Mike Masaoka, the organization's national secretary and brother of Ueno's rival at Manzanar, Joe Masaoka.

Myer's policy of "leniency" toward the Nisei alarmed the WRA's critics. Their worst fears about the Japanese had been confirmed by the Manzanar Riot. Many of them believed that Myer's agency was, in the words of one California congressman, "coddling" the internees. Their suspicions were heightened when agents of the House Un-American Activities Committee (HUAC) raided the JACL's national headquarters and seized papers revealing Masaoka's contacts with Myer. By 1943, the WRA had become the target of separate HUAC and military affairs subcommittee investigations. Under growing assault, Myer skillfully fended off his critics by cracking down on "bad" Japanese internees. In 1943, the WRA began segregating internees deemed dangerous, disloyal, or "potentially disloyal." The new policy reflected a belief shared by Myer and many other Americans that "unassimilated" Japanese posed a fundamental threat to American security. Kibei like Harry Ueno, who had spent part of their lives in Japan, were its prime targets. A WRA memorandum in 1942 had already identified the Kibei as "the potentially most dangerous" of the Japanese Americans. Despite the "protection afforded them by the Bill of Rights," the memo concluded, many Kibei should be placed in "custodial detention."

That, of course, is exactly where the WRA had put Harry Ueno after the Manzanar Riot. By early 1943, Myer longed to put more "hardboiled boys" in the "same place." He realized, however, that moving Japanese and Japanese Americans into internment camps was one thing but placing American citizens in jail only because they had lived for a time in Japan was quite another. He also knew that no law made greater allegiance to Japan than to the United States a crime. The courts were unlikely to accept a WRA policy of putting Kibei in prison and holding them there indefinitely. The key was finding a way to prove their "disloyalty" and then hope that the courts went along. In fact, Myer was correctly anticipating the Supreme Court's thinking on internment. In 1944, in *Korematsu v. United States,* the Court would uphold the right of the federal government to order the mass evacuation of Japanese Americans from the West Coast during a military emergency. Later that same year, however, in *Ex parte Endo,* the Court would rule that the WRA did not have the authority to hold "loyal" citizens indefinitely.

Myer soon got an opportunity to weed out "disloyal" internees from the camps and hold them for the duration of the war. It came when Secretary of War Henry Stimson moved in 1943 to create a segregated Nisei combat unit, later known as the 442d Regimental Combat Team. All draft-age Nisei males had to register for the draft and be administered a loyalty oath. As Myer realized, that oath could be given to all internees and used to screen out "disloyal or potentially disloyal individuals." Myer's plan eventually netted about twelve thousand internees. As a WRA press release put it, "It is believed to be the first time that any group in the country has been sorted and segregated on the basis of

National loyalty." By removing the "bad apples" from the camps, Myer countered criticism about WRA "coddling" of "pro-Japanese" internees. At the same time, he reassured a concerned public that their communities would not be endangered by his program to disperse and assimilate "loyal" internees around the country. The segregation program, however, came at a price. The "disloyals" were sent to the Tule Lake Segregation Center for the duration of the war. Unfortunately, the Tule Lake camp had been built to accommodate thousands fewer internees than the WRA sent there. In 1943, internees went on strike to protest their conditions, including cramped quarters and inadequate food and fuel. Violence surrounding the protest left one internee dead and resulted in the imposition of martial law.

One of the "incorrigible troublemakers" sent to Tule Lake was Harry Ueno. He did not realize that he and many other Kibei were pawns in Myer's effort to carry out a "middle-ground approach" to internment. Sent to Tule Lake after the riot there, he had learned enough to keep a low profile in his new home. Nonetheless, he was one of the last internees to leave the last WRA camp to close after the war. Unlike more than forty-seven hundred other internees, nearly two thousand of them American citizens, Ueno was not repatriated to Japan because he had never formally renounced his citizenship. And by the time he was released in March 1946 from Tule Lake, he had heard enough discouraging reports about conditions in Japan to changed his mind about returning there.

Ueno found himself starting life all over again. Yaso Ueno, released from Manzanar only a month before, had already moved to San Jose, where Harry joined her. Together, they began to rebuild their lives. It was not easy. Altogether, internees had lost perhaps as much as $2 billion in homes and property. After the war, prejudice against the Japanese remained strong. Even returning Japanese-American veterans frequently encountered derision and discrimination. Like many other former internees, though, Ueno never complained publicly about his treatment. As he had before the war, he quietly went about his business. The family moved to the central California coast, where they worked for several years "about twenty-nine days out of thirty" and saved as much as they could. Then they returned to San Jose, where they grew strawberries. "When you are working for someone else," Ueno told his children, "you never get a chance to make yourself any headway."

By that time, Dillon Myer had come to be revered by many Japanese Americans. They had not forgotten how he had worked to shield Nisei internees from harsher treatment. Like most other Americans, they shared his ideal of assimilation. With his resettlement program, Myer had worked to fulfill both the JACL's and his own visions of Americanization through the elimination of native culture. In 1946, the organization presented Myer with a citation at a banquet held in New York City. "TO DILLON S. MYER," the citation read, "American and champion of human rights and common decency."

Later, Myer brought the same assimilationist assumptions to his job as head of the Bureau of Indian Affairs (BIA). As BIA chief in the early 1950s, Myer sought to break down the Indians' attachment to their traditional culture. He stressed the importance of sending Indian children away to school "in order to get them off the reservation complex and milieu." Indian reservations proved to be far more difficult to manage, however, than internment camps. Myer's attempt in 1952 to gain increased police power over reservation Indians was met with quick protests, and he had no organization comparable to the JACL to come to his defense. The next year, he was terminated as BIA chief.

Myer held other government posts until he retired in 1964. About the same time, his assumption about the need to "Americanize" nonwhite minorities would come under mounting assault. By the late 1960s, the civil rights, Indian rights, and Chicano rights movements forced many Americans to reassess long-standing attitudes about race and culture. The decision to intern Japanese and Japanese Americans during World War II also came under growing attack. Six years after Myer died and forty-six years after Americans of Japanese ancestry were uprooted from their homes simply for having been born Japanese, Congress finally moved to right the wrong. In 1988, it formally apologized for the "grave injustice" of internment and gave each survivor of the camps, including Harry Ueno, twenty thousand dollars.

PRIMARY SOURCES

SOURCE 1:   Dillon Myer, *"Constitutional Principles Involved in the Relocation Program"* (1943)

In July 1943, Dillon Myer presented this statement on Japanese exclusion from the West Coast to a subcommittee of the House Un-American Activities Committee. On what grounds does he justify evacuation?

We believe, in the first place, that the evacuation was within the constitutional power of the National Government. The concentration of the Japanese-Americans along the West Coast, the danger of invasion of that Coast by Japan, the possibility that an unknown and unrecognizable minority of them might have greater allegiance to Japan than to the United States, the fact that the Japanese-Americans were not wholly assimilated in the general life of communities on the West Coast, and the danger of civil disturbance due to fear and misunderstanding—all these facts, and related facts, created a situation which the National Government could, we believe, deal with by extraordinary measures in the interest of military security. The need for speed created the unfortunate necessity for evacuating the whole group instead of attempting to determine who were dangerous among them, so that only those might be evacuated. That same need made it impossible to hold adequate investigations or to grant hearings to the evacuees before evacuation.

SOURCE: Reprinted in Richard Drinnon, *Keeper of Concentration Camps: Dillon S. Myer and American Racism* (Berkeley: University of California Press, 1987), p. 38; originally from Japanese American Evacuation and Resettlement Study, 67/14, T1.02, Bancroft Library, University of California, Berkeley.

SOURCE 2:   *"Rifles Cow Manzanar Japs After Fatal Riots"*
(1942)

This front-page story from the Los Angeles Times *two days after the Manzanar Riot provides an account of the disturbance that left two Japanese internees dead. What attitudes does it reveal about Japanese Americans?*

MANZANAR, Dec. 7. — Cowed by the ready guns of the Army's military police after a riot yesterday during which one Japanese was killed and nine[1] other pro-Axis residents of the camp bent on "banzai-ing" the first anniversary of the Nipponese sneak attack on Pearl Harbor were wounded, the 10,000 occupants of this huge reception center were quiet today under martial law enforced by augmented troops.

Other would-be celebrants of the grim event which hurled America into war reposed in an Owens Valley community jail, while still others were reported under arrest in barracks within the center six miles south of Independence. . . .

According to Ralph P. Merritt, manager of the center, the disturbance was precipitated Saturday night by Japanese inmates who wished to celebrate the anniversary of the Pearl Harbor attack.

Shouting "Pearl Harbor, banzai, banzai!" an estimated 1000 pro-Axis Japanese, many of whom are Kibei, or natives of Japan, demonstrated in a firebreak and hooted down Japanese-American Nisei (second-generation Nipponese) who protested their antics.

Remonstrator Beaten

Fred Toyama [sic], secretary of the Los Angeles Japanese-American Citizens League, who attempted to dissuade the demonstrators from their wild celebration, was beaten so severely he was hospitalized outside the inter[n]ee area because irate Kibei attempted to wrest him from the doctors ministering to his serious wounds.

Harry Ueno, said to be an Axis-sympathizer, who was jailed following the Saturday-night disturbance, was removed to the Inyo County Jail at Independence. . . .

Mob Numbers 4000

When authorities refused to free Ueno, a mob estimated at 4000 demonstrated wildly.

Then, when a large portion of the crowd moved menacingly toward the troops, the soldiers tossed tear-gas bombs. This proved of little effect because of

1. The final toll was two dead and ten wounded.

a wind which wafted the fumes away, and the mob resumed its forward surge. Stones, clubs and other missiles were hurled at the troops.

Capt. Martin Hall, in command of the police, ordered the mob to halt. After several commands were ignored and the barrage of missiles threatened to maim the police, Capt. Hall reluctantly gave the order to fire.

Ten Rioters Fall

Ten rioters collapsed under the volley and the remainder retired to their quarters under the officer's orders.

Merritt said that about 4000 inmates were Japan-born, and 400 others, although born in this country, were pro-Axis, having been educated in Japan and indoctrinated with Japanese militarism. . . .

Manzanar Blooming

Manzanar is a model community of neat prefabricated wooden barracks, a 150-bed hospital, mess halls, laundries, recreation halls and administration buildings. It occupies a 5800-acre site on the west side of the valley and, under labor by thousands of occupants, has begun to [appear as] a pleasant, blooming area of trees, gardens and flowers.

The riot here followed by two weeks a similar flare-up by Poston Relocation Center evacuees near Parker, Ariz., when the camp administration was overthrown and authority defied. At Poston, as here, loyal Japanese-Americans attempted to prevent disloyal outbreaks.

SOURCE 3:   *Censored Letters of Harry Ueno*   (1943)

While incarcerated at the Moab Isolation Center in Utah, Ueno wrote letters to his wife and friends at Manzanar. What do these letters, censored by the War Relocation Authority, reveal about Ueno's state of mind? About the WRA?

Among the letters received from subject UYENO [sic] were several containing matters of [relevant] information. . . . There are being set forth hereinafter excerpts from these letters written by UYENO to his wife, YASOKO UYENO, who still resides at the Manzanar Relocation Center. In one letter UYENO states:

"A few detainees might be released from here and returned to Manzanar but I can't trust them except for one or two persons, and as

SOURCE: Reprinted in Kunitomi Embrey, Arthur A. Hansen, and Betty Kulberg Mitson, *Manzanar Martyr: An Interview with Harry Y. Ueno* (Fullerton: Oral History Program, California State University, 1986), appendix 24; originally from Ueno Papers, Collection 1555, 67/14, t1.02. Reprinted by permission of the Department of Special Collections, Charles E. Young Research Library, University of California, Los Angeles.

I have mentioned in my last letter, 'The honest person will not be able to be released from this camp.' . . .

". . . Only one way we can see the future is wait till the end of war. It might solve itself. We understand the American democracy by Lieutenant Colonel's inquiry. I told him that I'm very glad to be a Japanese. Asked the question 'Do you have a desire to go out if there is a good job?' I answered him that no matter how much money is piled on me, I will not participate to the war effort and am thinking of the Japanese. I wish you have the same intention like I have."

In a letter dated March 29, 1943 to his wife, UYENO [stated:]

"Today I received your letter of March 27, 1943. I have learned that you did not receive No. 6 and No. 7 as yet. I may safely say that the government dares to do so. It is outrageous to confiscate or detain our legal mail on which the letters have stamps on them. This action which we are seeing before our eyes is called the democracy. The democracy is what they are praising is as different as light and darkness. This is what we call a thief that has some truth in him. Remember this, YASOKO.

"We have asked so many times, why are we segregated from the others and detained in jail for such a long time? But they cannot give us an exact answer for our question. They tortured us because we have a citizenship. If we tried to expatriate our citizenship, they insist that we cannot do such actions while we are staying in the mother-land. I think this problem can be solved in the past war because we know who is translating our letters.

"Our victory is approaching day by day is the day we are able to settle and solve our problems. I will wait till then. . . . The victims who gave their lives on December 6th gave us a chance to observe the democracy of the United States of America.

"I realize that I am a happy fellow to be a Japanese. I tried to sign up on repatriation application, but they do not have such a form in here. I asked to have them bring those forms here so I might be able to sign up as soon as it comes. If you have a chance to do so you do it. I would like to renounce the children's citizenship too."

In his letter of April 8, 1943, UYENO stated:

"Non-suffering life will not know a pleasure of life. When I think of the expeditioned soldiers' families, our existing circumstances are the heaven. How hardship it is, I think we should bear. I believe you have sufficiently determined about your mind. . . .

In a letter dated April 9, 1943, UYENO states:

"Yesterday two fellows and today two fellows were compulsory transferred from our room to the others where the moderate party stay in. The remainder are those who expatriated a citizenship of American to the authority. I suppose you do understand our spirit. We became the pure Japanese and living with Japanese spirit. We are entirely different than those who praise Japanese victory and thinking of

Japanese and doubtfully wondering their citizenship with worrying that America might win the war. I believe the man should have their faith and should die with their faith then that what we will call them as a true man. . . .

"I hope to let the Manzanarians see our daily life and situation of ours. It is an easy thing to be born as a Japanese but it is a[s] hard to live as a real Japanese. We, the remainders of eight fellows, will fight as Japanese and live as Japanese. Of course, we expect and determine that there are many privations and obstacles en route to our future life. It might happen that we might be segregated to the other camp and might be placed under the extra vigilance over us. If it occurred we cannot help it. Our spirit cannot apologize us if we act cowardly. Also I feel ashamed toward those who died as our sacrifice. . . .

"We selected the way we are taking at the present time. We will fight to the last man and overcome. Living for pride and [dying] for pride is good enough and if the person complain such guy should fall to the kingdom of dogs."

In the last letter dated April 10, 1943, UYENO stated:

"We are the first class nation of the world. Our spiritual civilization overcomes those of the Americans. Our existing circumstances is the situation before the bayonets and the privilege is denied but when the time comes they will understand. We are all the victims of fraudulent doctrine. There is the cause why Japan rised with her arms. They haven't any privilege and valuation to pursue the gold to us. You endure and live strongly as Japanese woman even if we have to die for the spirit of Japanese; after all we are Japanese. We will die silently, I hope so."

Source 4: *Dillon Myer on Japanese Resettlement* (1943)

In 1943, Dillon Myer was questioned by Senator Edwin C. Johnson of the Senate Military Affairs Subcommittee on War Relocation Centers. What assumptions does Myer reveal about his program to resettle Japanese-American internees outside the camps?

SENATOR JOHNSON: Is it your underlying idea that the Jap, no matter how long he is here, will finally merge with our citizenship the same as any white man?

MR. MYER: My underlying idea is that since these people are going to continue to be American citizens, they will have to merge into our economy and be accepted as part of it, otherwise we are always going to have a racial problem.

SOURCE: Reprinted in Richard Drinnon, *Keeper of Concentration Camps: Dillon S. Myer and American Racism* (Berkeley: University of California Press, 1987), pp. 56–57; originally from Senate Military Affairs Subcommittee, 20 January 1943, 78th Cong., 1st sess., 55–56.

SENATOR JOHNSON: Of course, you know that no Pacific States allow intermar-
riage. They are always going to be brown men. Do you think they will finally merge and just be accepted in every way like a white man?

MR. MYER: Well, I can't predict that. I can say this, that there are a good many
hundreds of the youngsters of college age and many who have gone to college in the past who have been accepted in the professions and otherwise.

Now, I think that you will find, other than color, that after about four or
five generations these people will be living under the same standards as
any other American citizens. They won't know anything else. I don't know
what the ancestry of all the people around this room is. I know what my
own is. We have been a melting pot of the nations here and we have accepted these people.

SOURCE 5: *War Relocation Authority Questions for
Resettlement Applicants* (1943)

*When the War Relocation Authority began Dillon Myer's program to resettle internees
in 1943, it subjected those who wished to live and work outside the camps to a rigorous
screening process. What do the questions asked of applicants reveal about administrators' cultural and racial assumptions?*

Before questioning you any further, we would like to ask if you have any objection to signing a Pledge of Allegiance to the United States.

Will you assist in the general resettlement program by staying away from
large groups of Japanese?

Will you try to develop such American habits which will cause you to be accepted readily into American social groups?

Are you willing to give information to the proper authorities regarding any
subversive activity . . . both in the relocation centers and in the communities in
which you are resettling?

Would you consider an informer of this nature an "Inu"? (Stool-pigeon)

Will you conform to the customs and dress of your new home?

Have you been associated with any radical groups, clubs, or gangs which
have been accused of anti-social conduct within the center?

Can you furnish any proof that you have always been loyal to the United
States?

SOURCE: Reprinted in Richard Drinnon, *Keeper of Concentration Camps: Dillon S. Myer and American
Racism* (Berkeley: University of California Press, 1987), p. 53; originally from RG 107, National
Archives.

QUESTIONS TO CONSIDER

1. What factors led to Japanese internment during World War II? What role did racism play in the treatment of Japanese Americans during the war?

2. Harry Ueno's background was different from that of many Japanese Americans. What does his story reveal about internment? About the Japanese-American community? How did Ueno's background shape his response to internment?

3. Dillon Myer claimed many years after World War II that he did "the best possible job under difficult circumstances." What were the circumstances or factors that led Myer to impose such strict measures against Ueno and other "troublemakers" in the internment camps? To understand Ueno's fate, is it necessary to understand Myer's own history?

4. How would you characterize Myer's policies as head of the War Relocation Authority? Do you agree with the Japanese American Citizens League's description of Myer at the end of the war?

FOR FURTHER READING

Roger Daniels, *Prisoners Without Trial: Japanese Americans in World War II* (New York: Hill and Wang, 1993), provides a concise overview of the decision to evacuate Japanese Americans and their experiences in the internment camps.

Richard Drinnon, *Keeper of Concentration Camps: Dillon S. Myer and American Racism* (Berkeley: University of California Press, 1987), is a critical treatment of Myer as director of the War Relocation Authority and later the Bureau of Indian Affairs.

Kunitomi Embrey, Arthur A. Hansen, and Betty Kulberg Mitson, *Manzanar Martyr: An Interview with Harry Y. Ueno* (Fullerton: Oral History Program, California State University, 1986), offers an account of Ueno's early life and his experiences as an internee.

Dillon Myer, *Autobiography* (Berkeley: University of California, 1970), is an oral history detailing Myer's life and career, including his experiences as director of the War Relocation Authority.

John Tateishi, *And Justice for All: An Oral History of the Japanese American Detention Camps* (New York: Random House, 1984), presents brief oral histories of numerous Japanese-American internees, including Harry Ueno.

CHAPTER

❖ ❖

9

Confrontation and Compromise in the Cold War: James Byrnes and Henry A. Wallace

As Henry A. Wallace looked out at his audience in New York City's Madison Square Garden in September 1946, he feared for the future. The vice president under Franklin Roosevelt and now Harry Truman's secretary of commerce, Wallace was convinced that the United States and the Soviet Union were on the brink of war. The partners in World War II now faced off across a divided Europe. Their relationship, once cooperative, was engulfed in suspicion. Wallace was convinced that war between the two nations could be avoided, but that could happen only if the Truman administration rejected the dangerous policy of confrontation with the Soviets advocated by Secretary of State James Byrnes.

A wily political infighter, Byrnes was sure that Wallace was a dreamer. The former South Carolina senator saw himself as a hardheaded realist. He was convinced that the Soviet Union would have to be dealt with forcefully. And, he feared, the commerce secretary's ideas were dangerous. Thrown together as allies against Nazi Germany, the United States and the Soviet Union had entered a marriage of convenience. But now that Germany was defeated, Byrnes believed that the Soviets loomed as the new threat. Headed by dictator Joseph Stalin, the Soviet Union was a communist—and officially atheistic—state. It proclaimed the doctrine of worldwide communist revolution. Already it had established several communist states in Eastern Europe. The United States, Byrnes insisted, had to follow a "get tough" policy that met Soviet expansion with diplomatic and military force. Using the threat of war might force cooperation from the Soviets, but caving in to them would surely lead to war itself.

Wallace was equally convinced that he was the realist. Thus, as the commerce secretary launched into his Madison Square Garden address, he told his audience that the United States had to pay a "just price" for peace. If it took a belligerent stance against the Soviets, they would respond in a similar fashion. As each side became increasingly suspicious of the other, a war worse than the previous one would inevitably follow. The only way to build a lasting peace was to unite the nations of the world. American policy toward the Soviet Union should be based on trade agreements and economic aid, not diplomatic bluster, military threats, and atomic bombs. "He who trusts in the atom bomb," he

167

James Byrnes   Henry Wallace

declared, "will sooner or later perish by the atom bomb." By the time he sat down, Wallace had delivered the most important speech of his career. And although he did not realize it, he had set off a firestorm. Within days, Byrnes and Wallace were engaged in a dramatic showdown. In the balance, both believed, was the peace of the world.

"This Must Not Be"

Henry A. Wallace would not have denied that he was idealistic. Yet he would certainly have protested against any accusation that he was impractical. He was, after all, a midwestern farmer, born in Iowa in 1888. As a result, his political views were shaped by agricultural concerns. In 1895, his father and grandfather (both named Henry Wallace) began publishing a farm journal that came to be called *Wallaces' Farmer*. The journal advocated pro-farm political issues and discussed the latest scientific and mechanical advances in farming. It also provided the Wallace family with prosperity and a solid reputation among the farmers of the Midwest. Both staunch Republicans, Henry's grandfather worked in Theodore Roosevelt's administration, and his father served as secretary of agriculture under Warren Harding and Calvin Coolidge. After graduating from Iowa State College in 1910 with a degree in animal husbandry, young Henry went to work on *Wallaces' Farmer*. He married and had three children. When his father left Iowa to work in Washington in 1921, Henry took over as editor of the journal.

The young Wallace became a leading voice for farmers in the 1920s. Years before the onset of the Depression, agriculture was in a severe slump. Wallace used his position to protest the low prices for agricultural products. He called for government action to raise farm prices and promoted efficiency on the farm to enable farmers to help themselves. He also founded the first hybrid corn company in the country. Hybrid crops were designed to increase yields, and Wallace was sure the application of science to agriculture would result in greater production. Eventually, his call for government intervention on behalf of farmers led to his break with the Republican Party. In 1928, he became a Democrat. Four years later, he supported Franklin Roosevelt for president and was rewarded for his help when FDR named him secretary of agriculture.

During the Great Depression, Wallace became the national leader of pro-farm politics. He promoted government programs that would revolutionize American agriculture by increasing the federal government's role in farming, including control over production and prices. This meant centralized planning, which to conservatives smacked of socialism. His actions, especially the move to slaughter millions of farm animals and limit crop acreage when many Americans were going hungry, made him one of the most controversial figures of the New Deal. Before the Depression was over, he even rejected the capitalist free-market economy of his grandfather and father in favor of a planned economy.

By the end of the 1930s, Wallace was a leader of the Democratic Party's liberal wing, which promoted more federal regulation and more government to control the economy. He wanted government regulations to establish better conditions for factory workers, which made him a hero to organized labor. As a prominent New Dealer and a prolific writer who had published many books, he also appealed to intellectuals. Because of his popularity with these groups, he was the clear choice for vice president when Roosevelt ran for a third term in 1940. The conservative southern wing of the Democratic Party opposed Wallace, arguing that he was a socialist. Roosevelt, however, fought hard for his nomination, and when FDR won the election, Wallace became vice president of the United States.

When World War II started, Wallace began to speak out more about his vision for America's role in the world. After the United States defeated Germany and Japan, he believed, it should work to set up an international organization that would regulate trade, raise living standards, and prevent future wars. Someday, he was sure, the world would have one government and the common man would be free and prosperous. Indeed, he believed that the United States was about to embark on what he called the "Century of the Common Man."

Wallace's international views convinced James Byrnes and other conservative Democrats that he was a dreamer. If given the chance, they believed, he would destroy capitalism at home and abroad, weaken the American military, threaten national sovereignty, and destroy the Democratic Party. As another presidential election approached in 1944 and Roosevelt's health declined, conservative Democrats feared that Wallace might soon become president. Determined to prevent that, they pushed Byrnes as an alternative to Wallace. Although labor leaders and the influential first lady, Eleanor Roosevelt, continued to support Wallace, Roosevelt's reelection was not as certain as it had been in 1940. Thus he did not want to alienate the conservatives in his own party. Northern liberals, however, strenuously objected to the southerner Byrnes. When conservatives compromised by suggesting Harry Truman, a more moderate senator from Missouri, Wallace's fate was sealed. After FDR won his fourth term in 1944 with Truman as his running mate, Wallace became secretary of commerce.

Wallace lost the vice-presidency at a crucial time. When FDR died a few months after his inauguration in early 1945, Truman became president. The war in Europe was virtually over, and it would be left to Truman to conclude the war in the Pacific. It also would be Truman's job to deal with the Soviet Union after the war's end.

Since 1941, the Soviets had been allies of the United States in World War II, but it was not an easy relationship. Earlier in the war, while the Soviets were suffering enormous losses on the eastern front, the British and Americans had repeatedly postponed an invasion of France, which would have greatly relieved the Soviet position. A naturally suspicious Stalin feared that his Western partners were deliberately stalling until Germany and the Soviet Union wore each other down. Nonetheless, Roosevelt remained convinced that he could get along with Stalin, and he was hopeful that the two nations would continue to cooperate after the war. In fact, that hope was reinforced early in 1945 when Roosevelt, Stalin, and British prime minister Winston Churchill met at Yalta in the Soviet Union. At the Yalta Conference, the "Big Three" made plans for an international organization called the United Nations, which would work to maintain peace through collective security. Stalin also promised to enter the war against Japan three months after the war in Europe was over, and Allied leaders pledged to establish governments in liberated Europe responsible to the will of the people through "free elections."

Under Truman, FDR's personal diplomacy was quickly replaced by confrontation. When Truman became president, the Soviets had already "liberated" much of Nazi-occupied Eastern Europe. They also had established a Soviet puppet government in Poland. The United States and Great Britain had earlier excluded the Russians from a role in forming a new government in Italy—the first country in Europe to be liberated from enemy hands. FDR understood that the language of the Yalta agreements was vague and that it actually gave Stalin great latitude in Eastern Europe. But Roosevelt was gone, and some of Truman's advisers believed that the Soviets' quick move to establish communist regimes in Eastern Europe was evidence that Stalin had gone back on his word.

Henry Wallace also was alarmed. Just before Germany surrendered in May 1945, Wallace noted in his diary that "more and more it begins to look like the psychology is favorable toward our getting into war with Russia.* This must not be." Wallace knew he had to speak out. It was highly unusual for a commerce secretary to express his view on foreign policy publicly, but he was convinced that he, not Truman, should have succeeded Roosevelt. Furthermore, as secretary of commerce, he believed that he had a legitimate voice in foreign affairs. After all, economics was the key to diplomacy, and trade relations could be the means of preventing another war. That was especially true now because the Soviet Union had been economically devastated by the war and the United States could use economic aid to assist its World War II ally. The more Wallace

Russia: Technically, one of the fifteen republics that made up the Soviet Union. The names *Russia* and *Soviet Union* had been used interchangeably since the creation of the Soviet state after the Russian Revolution of 1917.

spoke out, though, the more it was apparent that many of his criticisms were directed at the man charged with overseeing foreign policy for the president—the new Secretary of State, James Byrnes.

"Give It to Them with Both Barrels"

James "Jimmy" Byrnes was a superb politician. A pragmatic dealmaker who always put what was achievable ahead of what was desirable, he won a reputation as a man who could get things done. He skillfully used his humble origins to appeal to the common man, but rather than rock the boat, he pursued conservative policies on economics and race. Born in 1882 in Charleston, South Carolina, James F. Byrnes was the son of a clerk and a seamstress. The family's difficult financial situation was made much worse by the death of Jimmy's father before Jimmy was born. His mother would somehow provide for her own invalid mother as well as a sister, niece, daughter, and young son. By the time Jimmy was fourteen, the family's difficult financial circumstances forced him to drop out of school and go to work as a messenger for a law firm. He continued his education informally and then decided to become a lawyer himself. He passed the bar in 1903 and settled down to practice in Aiken, South Carolina, where he married and became increasingly interested in politics.

His own political career began in 1908 when he won election to the office of public prosecutor. In 1910, he was elected to the U.S. House of Representatives, where he served for more than a decade. There he quickly established his reputation as a practical politician who was willing to compromise to help pass legislation. He also made powerful friends, including Franklin Roosevelt, who was then serving as assistant secretary of the Navy. A white supremacist, Byrnes shared the racial attitudes of the early-twentieth-century white South. Although he supported segregation, he denounced the Ku Klux Klan when it reemerged after World War I. In the 1920s, the Klan was not only antiblack but also anti-Catholic and anti-immigrant. Although Byrnes had converted to the Episcopalian faith, his family was Irish Catholic. He refused to have anything to do with anti-Catholic politics, which helped lead to his defeat in his overwhelmingly Protestant congressional district in 1924. Byrnes then returned to the practice of law, but six years later, he ran for the U.S. Senate. By then, the Klan's popularity had collapsed and the Depression had set in, and Byrnes was elected.

He quickly became an influential member of the Senate. His election had been partly due to the financial backing of Bernard M. Baruch, a fellow South Carolinian who had made a fortune in stock speculation on Wall Street. After Baruch and Byrnes became friends in the early 1930s, the financier put Byrnes in control of his vast campaign contributions to fellow Democrats. As Byrnes doled out these funds, his own influence increased. Meanwhile, during the Depression, his power in the Senate grew as he carefully balanced fiscal conservatism with the growing need for individual relief. In the process, he became a leader of the conservative wing of the Democratic Party in the Senate. Often southerners, these men defended racial segregation in the South, favored less government regulation of business, and distrusted the growth of federal power at the expense of the states. This position often pitted Byrnes against his old friend FDR, whose New Deal called for federal controls on the economy and a vast expansion of federal power. Yet Byrnes, ever the pragmatist, insisted that governing was "really a matter of policy, not principle," and he never lost FDR's trust and support. Indeed, Byrnes was a fiscal conservative when federal money was spent in other states, but he became much more liberal when South Carolina was involved.

After the outbreak of World War II in 1939, Roosevelt and Byrnes became staunch allies. In fact, Byrnes was Roosevelt's man in the Senate, especially when it came to battling strong opposition to American involvement in the war. In 1940, Byrnes even set aside his own unfavorable ideas about the liberal Wallace to help persuade conservative delegates at the 1940 Democratic convention to accept the agriculture secretary as FDR's running mate. For his loyalty, Roosevelt rewarded Byrnes with an appointment to the Supreme Court in 1941. He served on the Court for a year, then resigned to accept Roosevelt's offer to head the Office of Economic Stabilization and, later, the Office of War Mobilization (OWM), agencies designed to boost production and oversee the distribution of war materiel. Although these agencies carried out the very centralized economic planning that Byrnes opposed, he agreed to lead them in the name of winning the war. His actions as OWM director soon earned him the nickname "Assistant President," so pervasive were the agency's controls over the nation's economy.

By 1944, Byrnes was in a powerful position to challenge Henry Wallace for the privilege of being FDR's running mate. Given his dedicated service, Byrnes had reason to believe that the president would choose him. Like other Democratic conservatives, he disdained Wallace's politics. He also believed that the next vice president would eventually be president, either by winning the office in 1948 or inheriting it if Roosevelt died. Roosevelt wanted to keep the southern base of his party happy, but he feared that Byrnes would be unpopular with organized labor and that his segregationist views would cost the Democrats African-American votes in the North. Byrnes also had another political liability: his Catholic background. In the end, of course, FDR compromised, ousting Wallace in favor of Truman, who seemed palatable to both liberal and conservative factions of the party.

Just as FDR did not forget the ousted Wallace, however, he did not forget Byrnes. In early 1945, Byrnes traveled with the president to meet Churchill and Stalin at the Yalta Conference. In fact, Byrnes's presence at Yalta helped make him a player in American foreign policy. When Roosevelt died that April, Truman named Byrnes secretary of state. "He'd been to Yalta," Truman said later, explaining his choice. Yet Truman, who had virtually no experience in foreign affairs, had another reason for asking Byrnes to take the job. As the new president wrote in his diary, he wanted someone who was "hard hitting," not "smart boys in the State Department," to advise him on foreign policy. Byrnes would not hesitate to speak his mind.

Byrnes's advice started with the atomic bomb. Roosevelt had told him all about the top-secret Manhattan Project to develop an atomic bomb, and it was Byrnes who informed Truman of the details of the program shortly after Truman became president. Throughout World War II, Byrnes had urged Roosevelt to pursue a "hard war" policy that used all the resources the United States could muster to inflict the maximum amount of damage and win the war quickly.

Now he pushed Truman to use the atomic bomb, arguing that since it had cost about two billion dollars to build, the public would want it to be used. Further, he was convinced that using the bomb would hasten the end of the war, make an invasion of Japan unnecessary, and save countless American lives. He also knew that using the bomb had another advantage. As he told Truman, it would put the United States "in a position to dictate our own terms at the end of the war." In other words, it would send a clear message to the Soviet Union that the United States was willing to use whatever force it took to win. Byrnes knew, of course, that the Soviets were set to come into the war against Japan in early August, but he was alarmed by the way the Soviets were exerting their authority in Eastern Europe. He believed that using the bomb would give the United States tremendous leverage in diplomatic relations with them.

Truman agreed with Byrnes. But after the United States used two bombs to end the war with Japan, the Soviets did not seem any more willing to accede to American demands. Meeting with the Soviet foreign minister V. M. Molotov shortly after Japan surrendered, Byrnes protested the tightening of Soviet control over the governments of the Eastern European nations of Romania and Bulgaria. He insisted that the Soviets' actions violated the agreement at Yalta to conduct "free elections" in liberated nations. Yet Molotov was unmoved. He pointed out, for instance, that the Americans had excluded the Soviet Union from participating in the postwar occupation of Japan. When Byrnes got home, he reported that the Soviets were "welching" on the Yalta agreements. The United States, he went on, was facing a "new Russia, totally different than the Russia we dealt with a year ago."

The Truman administration seemed divided on Soviet actions in Eastern Europe and thus on what to do about them. Secretary of the Navy James Forrestal and Truman's chief of staff, William D. Leahy, for instance, believed that Stalin's actions in Eastern Europe were driven by a desire for expansion and that the Soviets could not be trusted. Others, including Truman, believed that difficulties with the Soviets could be overcome and that the two powers might reach some accommodation. Differences were "inevitable," Truman said in October 1945, but he hoped that they could be worked out "if we [give] ourselves time." Byrnes agreed. In Congress, he had gotten things done by being flexible, and he had not given up on working with the Soviets. Thus, when he met with Stalin in Moscow at the end of 1945, Byrnes was willing to compromise. In exchange for Byrnes's promise of access to American atomic research in the future, the Soviets promised to support a proposed United Nations commission that would inspect nations' nuclear facilities. Byrnes also got the Soviets to place a few noncommunists in the Romanian and Bulgarian governments in exchange for American diplomatic recognition of those regimes and a token Soviet role in the postwar occupation of Japan. This agreement did nothing to weaken Soviet control in Eastern Europe, but the secretary of state was elated. He believed that it signaled the continuation of cordial relations between the United States and the Soviet Union. The conference in Moscow, he later said, had helped "restore 'peace on earth.'"

When Byrnes returned from Moscow, he came under heavy fire from Republicans in Congress and administration officials who wanted no compromises at all with the Soviets. They believed that Byrnes, as one of them put it, had "given far too much away to the Russians." By early 1946, Truman agreed. The president was very close to Leahy, who had argued for no concessions to Soviet demands and who had sharply criticized Byrnes after the Moscow meeting. Truman also had an eye on the opinion polls, which demonstrated that in just months, the public's willingness to trust the Soviets had dropped dramatically. In addition, Truman was miffed that Byrnes had announced the Moscow agreement without informing him. Later, he told his secretary of state that he "would not tolerate a repetition of such conduct."

Another Soviet action further hardened Truman's views about the Soviets. During World War II, Great Britain and the Soviet Union had moved troops into Iran to make sure that country's rich oil fields did not fall into enemy hands. Each nation had promised to remove its forces six months after the end of the war. By early March 1946, however, Soviet forces had not yet withdrawn. The continued occupation, Truman told Byrnes, was "an outrage." Like many Americans, the president had drawn a lesson from the diplomacy leading up to World War II. Diplomatic efforts to prevent war by caving in to Germany's demand for territory in neighboring Czechoslovakia in 1938 had failed to head off war. Now Soviet actions in Eastern Europe and Iran had led Truman to conclude that appeasing the Soviets would not work either. "Unless Russia is faced with an iron fist and strong language," he informed Byrnes, "another war is in the making." He added, "I'm tired of babying the Soviets."

At the same time, Truman had another justification for a hard-line policy against the Soviets. It came from an American diplomat named George F. Kennan. While stationed in Moscow, Kennan sent the State Department a long diplomatic telegram arguing that Soviet conduct in the world was driven not by a desire to achieve harmonious relations with the rest of the world but by the Soviet system of government. Rejecting the idea that Soviet actions in Eastern Europe stemmed from legitimate concerns for security, Kennan argued that the Soviets had a "neurotic view of world affairs" created by the need to prop up their ruthless regime at home. In other words, the Soviets were building an empire in Eastern Europe to ensure that the Soviet Union remained united and to keep those at the top in power. The implications were clear: Soviet expansionism had to be contained. **[See Source 1.]** Kennan's analysis was widely read in the administration, and it also struck a chord with the president and his advisers who had been skeptical of Soviet actions in Eastern Europe all along. It provided the administration with the intellectual framework to justify an uncompromising stance toward the Soviets. From now on, the Soviets were not a shaky ally but the enemy.

Byrnes quickly reflected the emerging administration consensus regarding the Soviets. With Soviet forces continuing to occupy northern Iran, Byrnes believed that the Soviets were preparing to launch an invasion of the country. Referring to both diplomatic and military force, he said, "We'll give it to them with both barrels." As American officials devised a plan to encircle the Soviet Union with a permanent ring of military bases, Byrnes made it clear in a series of speeches that the United States would consider using military force to defend Iran. Then he took the matter to the United Nations, which sparked a Soviet walkout. A week later, however, the Soviets agreed to pull their troops out of Iran.

For the United States—and for Byrnes—the Iran crisis was a turning point. Combined with earlier developments in Eastern Europe and Kennan's analysis, events in Iran made it increasingly difficult for Byrnes, Truman, and most other administration officials to believe that Soviet actions were driven by legitimate security needs. When it came to the Soviet Union, Byrnes remarked shortly after the Iranian crisis, "American opinion was no longer disposed to make concessions on important questions." From now on, those would have to come from the Soviets. Nowhere would that be clearer than in Germany. Occupied by the United States, the Soviet Union, Great Britain, and France, Germany remained divided in late 1946. Unable to come to terms with the Soviet Union on the reunification of the country, Byrnes announced a new policy in September. If Germany could not be entirely reunified, he said in a speech in Stuttgart, the United States would move to reunify the western zones. Under no circumstances would the United States allow Germany to fall under Soviet influence. "As long as there is an occupation army in Germany," he told his German audience, "American forces will be part of that occupation army." The United States was now prepared to accept a divided Germany—and a divided world. [See Source 2.]

"The Tougher We Get"

Henry Wallace watched with alarm the hardening relations between the United States and the Soviet Union. He was not alone. Many officials, often with ties to the Roosevelt administration, were dismayed at the Truman administration's harsh rhetoric and uncompromising stance toward the Soviets. They had witnessed FDR's diplomacy with Stalin and hoped that some accommodation could be reached preserving the "Grand Alliance" after the war. Former ambassador to the Soviet Union Joseph E. Davies called the breakdown in relations "tragic." Senator Claude Pepper of Florida said that Soviet actions were the result of their fears of growing British and American hostility toward them. Even FDR's son James Roosevelt said that the Truman administration had not fairly informed the American people of the Soviet views on foreign relations. No one, however, was more outspoken than Henry A. Wallace. The Soviets, he believed, had legitimate security concerns in Eastern Europe. He opposed any increase in the military power of the United States in response to the Soviet occupation of the area. Such military muscle flexing would only provoke Soviet fears. In the spring of 1946, he sent two long letters to Truman arguing that the Soviets had reasonable grounds to fear the United States and calling on the president to take steps to promote trade between the two nations. He also began speaking out publicly, warning Americans of the dangers of an atomic arms race.

These pronouncements made Jimmy Byrnes irate. By March 1946, the secretary of commerce was the lone holdover from Roosevelt's cabinet in the Truman administration. Wallace had the support of farmers, organized labor, and intellectuals. Many members of these groups disliked the more conservative Truman, and the president knew it. He needed Wallace, at least through the November elections. Thus he could afford to ignore Wallace's policy recommendations, but he could not afford to muzzle him. In fact, he wanted Wallace to campaign for the Democrats. Ironically, although Wallace had less and less influence in the administration, his position remained secure, and he was free to influence administration policy by swaying public opinion.

Wallace delivered his first major campaign address at Madison Square Garden in September only six days after Byrnes's Stuttgart speech. Wallace declared that the United States had "no more business in the *political* affairs of Eastern Europe than Russia [had] in the *political* affairs of Latin America, Western Europe and the United States." In a jab at Byrnes's intervention in the Iranian crisis, he said that American foreign policy was "purchasing oil in the Near East with the lives of American soldiers." Instead of military posturing, he called for a diplomatic policy that addressed Soviet fears—one emphasizing trade and economic assistance. A hard line, he insisted, was no way to build peace. Getting tough never worked, "whether for schoolyard bullies or businessmen or world powers." "The tougher we get," he predicted, "the tougher the Russians will get." **[See Source 3.]**

When he read about Wallace's address several days later, Byrnes was livid. He was especially incensed by Wallace's remark that Truman had reviewed the commerce secretary's Madison Square Garden address two days before and had agreed with it. Two days after the speech, however, the president said, in the face of a growing controversy about the administration's foreign policy, that he had approved only Wallace's right to deliver the speech, not the content. Several days later, when Wallace said that he intended to give more speeches on foreign policy, Byrnes sent Truman an ultimatum in which he threatened to resign if Wallace was not muzzled. Truman now had to choose between his link to the liberals in the Democratic Party and the spokesman for the administration's hard-line foreign policy. Letting Byrnes go could open Truman up to the charge that he was soft on communism only two months before the congressional elections. And, of course, it meant repudiating the very policy he had endorsed and believed to be correct. Several days later, he fired Wallace.

Byrnes had his victory, but he did not enjoy it for long. Never popular with organized labor, the secretary of state soon came under attack from the powerful Congress of Industrial Organizations (CIO). The CIO had become a force in the late 1930s by successfully targeting millions of workers in the automobile, steel, and tire and rubber industries. Its support was crucial to the political success of Truman and the Democrats. Two days after Wallace's speech, Truman received a telegram from the CIO's leadership condemning Byrnes as an enemy of democracy abroad and calling for his resignation. At the same time, liberals began to attack Byrnes for his views on segregation.

These attacks, however, were not as damaging as those from Republican and administration hard-liners, who criticized Byrnes for being soft on communism. In 1945, Byrnes had defended a State Department employee named John Service who had been accused of passing secret documents to a magazine critical of U.S. foreign policy. Service and several others involved in the case had been exonerated by a grand jury, and the charges against them had been dropped. Nonetheless, without realizing it, Byrnes had opened himself up to the charge of not being sufficiently vigilant in protecting the State Department from subversives. As the United States entered into a worldwide struggle against communism, it was tempting for politicians to exploit the issue of communist subversion at home for political gain. That was especially true by 1946, in the wake of the publicity surrounding the Service case and several other cases of alleged spying. Indeed, Republicans would make significant gains in the congressional elections that year by accusing the Democrats of not doing enough to root out subversives in the United States. (See Chapter 10.) Suddenly, Byrnes was a political liability to Truman.

At the same time, Truman had come to depend on new men in the administration. Presidential aide Clark Clifford, Undersecretary of State Dean Acheson, and Chief of Staff William Leahy supported an even more confrontational approach toward the Soviets than Byrnes now pursued. Clifford advised Truman in a confidential report in September 1946, for instance, that the United States had to be prepared "to wage atomic and biological warfare, if necessary" against the Soviet Union. Earlier, Clifford had joined Byrnes in calling for Wallace's head, and now he was working to turn the president against Byrnes. He even implied that the secretary of state was appeasing the Soviets beneath the surface of his "get tough" policy. In poor health and aware that he was being forced out, Byrnes resigned his cabinet post in early 1947.

As Byrnes's career demonstrates, both Republicans and Democrats had learned how explosive charges about being soft on communism could be. In addition, virtually anyone was now open to suspicion. That would be especially clear within two months after Byrnes's departure, when the president announced the Truman Doctrine in a dramatic speech before Congress. It was the first expression of what came to be known as the containment policy—a sweeping American commitment to contain the expansion of communism on a global scale. The Truman Doctrine committed the United States to assisting any nation resisting Soviet-backed aggression and would serve as the foundation for American foreign policy for the next four decades of cold war with the Soviet Union. **[See Source 4.]** As it happened, the initial drafts of Truman's address quoted Byrnes's statement during the Iranian crisis that the United States would not let "coercion or pressure" on other nations go unchallenged. At Clifford's insistence, Byrnes's name and remarks were excised from the speech. Thus his name would not be associated with the policy he had helped devise.

"Is This America?"

Once Wallace and Byrnes left the Truman administration, they would become thorns in the president's side. In 1948, Wallace abandoned the Democratic Party and ran as the Progressive Party's candidate for president. He advocated his long-held plans for an international government and called for domestic reform that would curb the excesses of capitalism and bring prosperity to all Americans—and the rest of the world as well. Most of all, he attacked Truman's foreign policy of containment. This policy, he said, went against the American principles of liberty, equality, and self-government. A creation of big business and the military, the policy represented American imperialism. **[See Source 5.]**

By appealing to liberals, organized labor, farmers, and even radicals, Wallace threatened to draw enough votes from Truman to swing the election to Republican candidate Thomas Dewey. But Truman campaigned vigorously, ferociously attacking Wallace for his communist ties. Labor leaders, worried about communist influence in their unions, refused to support Wallace and began expelling radicals from their organizations. Meanwhile, the Democrats created an anticommunist organization called Americans for Democratic Action, which attacked Wallace and accused him of being a front for the communist movement. Wallace's political fortunes took another blow when he traveled in the South and called for civil rights for African Americans. He was soon the target of angry crowds, which sometimes pelted him with rotten fruits and vegetables. At one point, surrounded by a shouting mob, Wallace turned to a bystander and asked, "Are you an American? Is this America?"

By 1948, the rising political star of the 1930s had become a pariah. In November, Wallace received only 2.4 percent of the vote, while Truman scored a dramatic come-from-behind victory over Dewey. After the election, Wallace continued to oppose Truman's cold war policies, but his career as an office seeker was over. He contented himself with a private life devoted to reading, writing, and agricultural science. Meanwhile, his hybrid corn company thrived, and, ironically, he became a wealthy capitalist. Until his death in 1965, he enjoyed a comfortable retirement on his farm in New York.

Jimmy Byrnes also became a harsh critic of the Truman administration after leaving the cabinet. His attacks came from the other end of the political spectrum. After his resignation, Byrnes returned to South Carolina, where he served as governor from 1951 to 1955. Still a supporter of segregation, he attacked the Truman administration on another front: the growing battle over civil rights. In 1948, Truman had run for reelection on a civil rights platform, after moving to desegregate the armed forces. Byrnes also blasted Truman's support of national health insurance, increased unemployment benefits, and greater federal subsidies for public housing, measures Byrnes associated with a "welfare state." Eventually, he abandoned the Democratic Party, and in 1960 he endorsed Republican Richard Nixon for president. By the time he died in 1972, Byrnes had become an important figure in the Republican Party by helping it break the traditional Democratic hold on the South.

Henry Wallace and Jimmy Byrnes shared strangely similar fates. They had both narrowly missed making it to the presidency, and each believed that he would have made a better president than Truman. In addition, both had been let go by Truman. Yet they were very different men. Wallace was a visionary whose idealistic views about international cooperation led him to put principles above compromise. Byrnes was a realist, a pragmatic wheeler-dealer willing to give in for the sake of agreement. The two men had very different views of and plans for the post–World War II world and U.S. relations with the Soviet Union. Wallace believed that if the United States addressed legitimate Soviet security concerns, the two nations could continue to cooperate. Byrnes believed that the United States had to use force against the Soviet Union to prevent the spread of communism, protect American interests, and make the Soviets more cooperative. In his view, a practical cold war policy involved a balance of military and diplomatic threats. Yet as the United States began a worldwide crusade against communism, neither man's approach was acceptable. Neither Wallace's idealism nor Byrnes's willingness to compromise fit with the growing American consensus about Soviet motives. In the cold war mindset already fixed by the late 1940s, the ability to demonstrate ideological purity was more important than skill at fashioning political compromises. Thus, in their own ways, Wallace and Byrnes were two of the early victims of the long cold war.

PRIMARY SOURCES

SOURCE 1:   George F. Kennan, *"The Long Telegram"*   (1946)

As an attaché at the American embassy in Moscow, George F. Kennan cabled his "long telegram" to the State Department in Washington, D.C., in February 1946. His analysis of the Soviet government and its behavior in foreign affairs was widely read in the Truman administration and did a great deal to shape the administration's foreign policy toward the Soviets. What are Kennan's views of the Soviets? What are the implications for American policy?

[W]e have here [in the Soviet Union] a political force committed fanatically to the belief that with US there can be no permanent *modus vivendi*,* that it is desirable and necessary that the internal harmony of our society be disrupted, our traditional way of life be destroyed, the international authority of our state be broken, if Soviet power is to be secure. This political force has complete power of disposition over energies of one of world's greatest peoples and resources of world's richest national territory, and is borne along by deep and powerful currents of Russian nationalism. In addition, it has an elaborate and far flung apparatus for exertion of its influence in other countries, an apparatus of amazing flexibility and versatility, managed by people whose experience and skill in underground methods are presumably without parallel in history. Finally, it is seemingly inaccessible to considerations of reality in its basic reactions. For it, the vast fund of objective fact about human society is not, as with us, the measure against which outlook is constantly being tested and re-formed, but a grab bag from which individual items are selected arbitrarily and tendenciously to bolster an outlook already preconceived. This is admittedly not a pleasant picture. Problem of how to cope with this force [is] undoubtedly greatest task our diplomacy has ever faced and probably greatest it will ever have to face. It should be point of departure from which our political general staff work at present juncture should proceed. It should be approached with same thoroughness and care as solution of major strategic problem in war, and if necessary, with no smaller outlay in planning effort. I cannot attempt to suggest all answers here. But I would like to record my conviction that problem is within our power to solve—and that without recourse to any general military conflict. And in support of this conviction there are certain observations of a more encouraging nature I should like to make:

SOURCE: Reprinted in Thomas H. Etzold and John Lewis Gaddis, *Containment: Documents on American Policy and Strategy, 1945–1950* (New York: Columbia University Press, 1978), pp. 61–62; originally from *Foreign Relations of the United States: 1946* (Washington, D.C.: Government Printing Office, 1946), VI, 696–709.

**Modus vivendi:* Manner of getting along.

1. Soviet power, unlike that of Hitlerite Germany, is neither schematic nor adventuristic. It does not work by fixed plans. It does not take unnecessary risks. Impervious to logic of reason, and it is highly sensitive to logic of force. For this reason it can easily withdraw—and usually does—when strong resistance is encountered at any point. Thus, if the adversary has sufficient force and makes clear his readiness to use it, he rarely has to do so. If situations are properly handled there need be no prestige-engaging showdowns.
2. Gauged against Western World as a whole, Soviets are still by far the weaker force. Thus, their success will really depend on degree of cohesion, firmness and vigor which Western World can muster. And this is factor which it is within our power to influence.

SOURCE 2: *James Byrnes Restates American Policy Toward Germany* (1946)

James Byrnes laid out his views regarding a still-divided Germany in a major speech in Stuttgart, Germany, in September 1946. Notice that Byrnes does not make any direct accusations against the Soviets but alludes to certain problems that have arisen under the joint-occupation arrangement. What are they? How does he justify the American action to create a partially reunified Germany? How does the new American policy for Germany reflect a firmer approach toward the Soviets?

I have come to Germany to learn at first hand the problems involved in the reconstruction of Germany and to discuss with our representatives the views of the United States Government as to some of the problems confronting us.

We in the United States have given considerable time and attention to these problems because upon their proper solution will depend not only the future well-being of Germany but the future well-being of Europe. . . .

The carrying out of the Potsdam Agreement* has . . . been obstructed by the failure of the Allied Control Council* to take the necessary steps to enable

SOURCE: James F. Byrnes, "Restatement of U.S. Policy," *Department of State Bulletin,* September 15, 1946, pp. 496, 497–498, 499, 500.

Potsdam Agreement: The agreement reached at a meeting of Stalin, Churchill, and Truman in Potsdam, Germany, in the summer of 1945. A major issue dividing the participants at the Potsdam Conference was postwar reparations—that is, the right of the Allies to remove assets from their German zones of occupation to pay for war damages. The agreement allowed the Western Allies to ship German industrial equipment from their zones to the Soviets. In return, the Soviets agreed to ship food from their heavily agricultural zone in the east to the western zones of occupation.

Allied Control Council: A council composed of representatives from the United States, Britain, France, and the Soviet Union to control postwar Germany. In reality, the military commanders in the four nations' zones of occupation had more power than the council.

the German economy to function as an economic unit. Essential central German administrative departments have not been established, although they are expressly required by the Potsdam Agreement.

The equitable distribution of essential commodities between the several zones so as to produce a balanced economy throughout Germany and reduce the need for imports has not been arranged, although that too is expressly required by the Potsdam Agreement.

The working out of a balanced economy throughout Germany to provide the necessary means to pay for approved imports has not been accomplished, although that too is expressly required by the Potsdam Agreement.

The United States is firmly of the belief that Germany should be administered as an economic unit and that zonal barriers should be completely obliterated so far as the economic life and activity in Germany are concerned.

The conditions which now exist in Germany make it impossible for industrial production to reach the levels which the occupying powers agreed were essential for a minimum German peacetime economy. Obviously, if the agreed levels of industry are to be reached, we cannot continue to restrict the free exchange of commodities, persons, and ideas throughout Germany. The barriers between the four zones of Germany are far more difficult to surmount than those between normal independent states.

The time has come when the zonal boundaries should be regarded as defining only the areas to be occupied for security purposes by the armed forces of the occupying powers and not as self-contained economic or political units.

That was the course of development envisaged by the Potsdam Agreement, and that is the course of development which the American Government intends to follow to the full limit of its authority. It has formally announced that it is its intention to unify the economy of its own zone with any or all of the other zones willing to participate in the unification. . . .

We favor the economic unification of Germany. If complete unification cannot be secured, we shall do everything in our power to secure the maximum possible unification. . . .

From now on the thoughtful people of the world will judge Allied action in Germany not by Allied promises but by Allied performances. The American Government has supported and will continue to support the necessary measures to de-Nazify and demilitarize Germany, but it does not believe that large armies of foreign soldiers or alien bureaucrats, however well motivated and disciplined, are in the long run the most reliable guardians of another country's democracy. . . .

Security forces will probably have to remain in Germany for a long period. I want no misunderstanding. We will not shirk our duty. We are not withdrawing. We are staying here. As long as there is an occupation army in Germany, American armed forces will be part of that occupation army. . . .

While we shall insist that Germany observe the principles of peace, good-neighborliness, and humanity, we do not want Germany to become the satellite of any power or powers or to live under a dictatorship, foreign or domestic. The American people hope to see peaceful, democratic Germans become and remain free and independent.

Source 3:   Henry A. Wallace, *"The Way to Peace"*   (1946)

Henry Wallace's Madison Square Garden speech in September 1946 marked a break with the Truman administration's foreign policy and led to his resignation from the cabinet. How does he challenge the policies of Truman and Byrnes? How does he propose to deal with the Soviets?

During the past year or so, the significance of peace has been increased immeasurably by the atom bomb, guided missiles and airplanes which soon will travel as fast as sound. Make no mistake about it—another war would hurt the United States many times as much as the last war. We cannot rest in the assurance that we invented the atom bomb—and therefore that this agent of destruction will work best for us. He who trusts in the atom bomb will sooner or later perish by the atom bomb—or something worse. . . .

[W]e are reckoning with a force which cannot be handled successfully by a "Get tough with Russia" policy. "Getting tough" never brought anything real and lasting—whether for schoolyard bullies or businessmen or world powers. The tougher we get, the tougher the Russians will get.

We must not let our Russian policy be guided or influenced by those inside or outside the United States who want war with Russia. This does not mean appeasement.

We most earnestly want peace with Russia—but we want to be met half way. We want cooperation. And I believe that we can get cooperation once Russia understands that our primary objective is neither saving the British Empire nor purchasing oil in the Near East with the lives of American soldiers. We cannot allow national oil rivalries to force us into war. All of the nations producing oil, whether inside or outside of their own boundaries, must fulfill the provisions of the United Nations Charter and encourage the development of world petroleum reserves so as to make the maximum amount of oil available to all nations of the world on an equitable peaceful basis—and not on the basis of fighting the next war.

For her part, Russia can retain our respect by cooperating with the United Nations in a spirit of openminded and flexible give-and-take.

The real peace treaty we now need is between the United States and Russia. On our part, we should recognize that we have no more business in the *political* affairs of Eastern Europe than Russia has in the *political* affairs of Latin America, Western Europe and the United States. We may not like what Russia does in Eastern Europe. Her type of land reform, industrial expropriation, and suppression of basic liberties offends the great majority of the people of the United States. But whether we like it or not the Russians will try to socialize their sphere of influence just as we try to democratize our sphere of influence. This applies also to Germany and Japan. We are striving to democratize Japan and our area of control in Germany, while Russia strives to socialize eastern Germany. . . .

Under friendly peaceful competition the Russian world and the American world will gradually become more alike. The Russians will be forced to grant

Source: Henry A. Wallace, "The Way to Peace," *Vital Speeches of the Day,* October 1, 1946, pp. 738–741.

more and more of the personal freedoms; and we shall become more and more absorbed with the problems of social-economic justice.

Russia must be convinced that we are not planning for war against her and we must be certain that Russia is not carrying on territorial expansion or world domination through native communists faithfully following every twist and turn in the Moscow party line. But in this competition, we must insist on an open door for trade throughout the world. There will always be an ideological conflict—but that is no reason why diplomats cannot work out a basis for both systems to live safely in the world side by side. . . .

In the United States an informed public opinion will be all-powerful. Our people are peace-minded. But they often express themselves too late—for events today move much faster than public opinion. The people here, as every-where in the world, must be convinced that another war is not inevitable. And through mass meetings such as this, and through persistent pamphleteering, the people can be organized for peace—even though a large segment of our press is propagandizing our people for war in the hope of scaring Russia. And we who look on this war-with-Russia talk as criminal foolishness must carry our message direct to the people—even though we may be called communists because we dare to speak out.

I believe that peace—the kind of peace I have outlined tonight—is the basic issue, both in the Congressional campaign this fall and right on through the Presidental election in 1948. How we meet this issue will determine whether we live not in "one world" or "two worlds"—but whether we live at all.

Source 4: Harry S. Truman, *The Truman Doctrine* (1947)

Harry Truman chose to follow a forceful policy toward the Soviet Union, a policy that included the concept of containment. He outlined this policy in what came to be known as the Truman Doctrine. How does he define the challenge facing the United States? What are the implications for the United States?

The gravity of the situation which confronts the world today necessitates my appearance before a joint session of the Congress.

The foreign policy and the national security of this country are involved.

One of the primary objectives of the foreign policy of the United States is the creation of conditions in which we and other nations will be able to work out a way of life free from coercion. This was a fundamental issue in the war with Germany and Japan. Our victory was won over countries which sought to impose their will and their way of life, upon other nations.

To ensure the peaceful development of nations, free from coercion, the United States has taken a leading part in establishing the United Nations. The United Nations is designed to make possible lasting freedom and independence

Source: *Public Papers of the Presidents of the United States: Harry S. Truman, 1947* (Washington, D.C.: Government Printing Office, 1963), pp. 176–180.

for all its members. We shall not realize our objectives, however, unless we are willing to help free peoples to maintain their free institutions and their national integrity against aggressive movements that seek to impose upon them totalitarian regimes. This is no more than a frank recognition that totalitarian regimes, imposed upon free peoples, by direct or indirect aggression, undermine the foundations of international peace and hence the security of the United States.

The peoples of a number of countries of the world have recently had totalitarian regimes forced upon them against their will. The Government of the United States has made frequent protests against coercion and intimidation, in violation of the Yalta agreement, in Poland, Rumania, and Bulgaria. I must also state that in a number of other countries there have been similar developments.

At the present moment in world history nearly every nation must choose between alternative ways of life. The choice is too often not a free one.

One way of life is based upon the will of the majority, and is distinguished by free institutions, representative government, free elections, guarantees of individual liberty, freedom of speech and religion, and freedom from political oppression.

The second way of life is based upon the will of a minority forcibly imposed upon the majority. It relies upon terror and oppression, a controlled press and radio, fixed elections, and the suppression of personal freedoms.

I believe that it must be the policy of the United States to support free peoples who are resisting attempted subjugation by armed minorities or by outside pressures.

I believe that we must assist free peoples to work out their own destinies in their own way.

I believe that our help should be primarily through economic and financial aid which is essential to economic stability and orderly political processes. . . .

The free peoples of the world look to us for support in maintaining their freedoms.

If we falter in our leadership, we may endanger the peace of the world—and we shall surely endanger the welfare of this Nation.

Great responsibilities have been placed upon us by the swift movement of events.

I am confident that the Congress will face these responsibilities squarely.

Source 5:   Henry A. Wallace, *"The Path to Peace with Russia"* (1946)

Henry Wallace expressed his dissatisfaction with the Truman administration's foreign policy in speeches and articles, including this article published in the liberal New Republic *in 1946. How does Wallace challenge James Byrnes's policies? What alternatives does he propose?*

Source: Henry A. Wallace, "The Path to Peace with Russia," *New Republic*, September 30, 1946, pp. 401–402, 403, 404, 405.

How do American actions since V-J Day* appear to other nations? I mean by actions the concrete things like $13 billion for the War and Navy Departments, the Bikini [Island] tests of the atomic bomb and continued production of bombs, the plan to arm Latin America with our weapons, production of B-29's and planned production of B-36's, and the effort to secure air bases spread over half the globe from which the other half of the globe can be bombed. I cannot but feel that these actions must make it look to the rest of the world as if we were only paying lip-service to peace at the conference table. These facts rather make it appear either (1) that we are preparing ourselves to win the war which we regard as inevitable or (2) that we are trying to build up a predominance of force to intimidate the rest of mankind. How would it look to us if Russia had the atomic bomb and we did not, if Russia had 10,000-mile bombers and air bases within a thousand miles of our coast lines and we did not?

Some of the military men and self-styled "realists" are saying:

"What's wrong with trying to build up a predominance of force? The only way to preserve peace is for this country to be so well armed that no one will dare attack us. We know that America will never start a war."

The flaw in this policy is simply that it will not work. In a world of atomic bombs and other revolutionary new weapons, such as radioactive poison gases and biological warfare, a peace maintained by a predominance of force is no longer possible. . . .

Insistence on our part that the game must be played our way will only lead to a deadlock. The Russians will redouble their efforts to manufacture bombs, and they may also decide to expand their "security zone" in a serious way. Up to now, despite all our outcries against it, their efforts to develop a security zone in Eastern Europe and in the Middle East are small change from the point of view of military power as compared with our air bases in Greenland, Okinawa and many other places thousands of miles from our shores. We may feel very self-righteous if we refuse to budge on our plan and the Russians refuse to accept it, but that means only one thing—the atomic-armament race is on in deadly earnest. . . .

WHY RUSSIA DISTRUSTS THE WEST

I should list the factors which make for Russian distrust of the United States and of the Western world as follows: The first is Russian history, which we must take into account because it is the setting in which Russians see all actions and policies of the rest of the world. Russian history for over a thousand years has been a succession of attempts, often unsuccessful, to resist invasion and conquest—by the Mongols, the Turks, the Swedes, the Germans and the Poles. The scant thirty years of the existence of the Soviet government has in Russian eyes been a continuation of their historical struggle for national existence. . . . Then, in 1941, the Soviet state was almost conquered by the Germans after a period during which the Western European powers had apparently acquiesced in the

*V-J Day: August 15, 1945, the day that fighting between the United States and Japan in World War II officially ended.

rearming of Germany in the belief that the Nazis would seek to expand eastward rather than westward. The Russians, therefore, obviously see themselves as fighting for their existence in a hostile world. . . .

Our interest in establishing democracy in Eastern Europe, where democracy by and large has never existed, seems to her an attempt to rëestablish the encirclement of unfriendly neighbors which was created after the last war and which might serve as a springboard of still another effort to destroy her.

If this analysis is correct, and there is ample evidence to support it, the action to improve the situation is clearly indicated. The fundamental objective of such action should be to allay any reasonable Russian grounds for fear, suspicions and distrust. We must recognize that the world has changed and that today there can be no "one world" unless the United States and Russia can find some way of living together. . . .

Two-way Trade

It is of greatest importance that we should discuss with the Russians in a friendly way their long-range economic problems and the future of our coöperation in matters of trade. The reconstruction program of the USSR and the plans for the full development of the Soviet Union offer tremendous opportunities for American goods and American technicians. . . .

Many of the problems relating to the countries bordering on Russia could more readily be solved once an atmosphere of mutual trust and confidence is established and some form of economic arrangements is worked out with Russia.

Questions to Consider

1. Citing specific sources, how would you compare the foreign policy positions of Henry Wallace and James Byrnes? In what ways did each man's views about foreign policy after World War II reflect his experiences or views about other issues prior to that time? Given the circumstances at the end of the war, whose position was more realistic?

2. Very shortly after World War II, the Truman administration developed a containment policy that was directed against the Soviet Union. What was that policy? What circumstances or ideas shaped it? What was Byrnes's role in its development?

3. Although Wallace and Byrnes had very different views about how the United States should deal with the Soviet Union after World War II, both met similar fates in the Truman administration. What does the career of each man reveal about the various influences on postwar foreign policy? To what extent did domestic political considerations influence American foreign policy in the early stages of the cold war? What do the fates of Wallace and Byrnes reveal about the impact of foreign policy on American politics at the beginning of the cold war?

4. Do you think relations between the United States and the Soviet Union would have turned out differently if Wallace or Byrnes had been chosen as Franklin Roosevelt's running mate in 1944? How so?

For Further Reading

John C. Culver and John Hyde, *American Dreamer: A Life of Henry A. Wallace* (New York: W. W. Norton & Company, 2000), is a recent and engaging biography of Wallace.

John Lewis Gaddis, *Now We Know: Rethinking Cold War History* (Oxford: Oxford University Press, 1997), offers a post–cold war evaluation of the long conflict between the United States and the Soviet Union.

Melvyn Leffler, *A Preponderance of Power: National Security, the Truman Administration, and the Cold War* (Stanford, Calif.: Stanford University Press, 1992), is a comprehensive treatment of the origins of the cold war.

David Robertson, *Sly and Able: A Political Biography of James F. Byrnes* (New York: W. W. Norton & Company, 1994), is a recent and thorough examination of Byrnes's life and political career.

Politics and Principle in the Second Red Scare: Joseph McCarthy and Margaret Chase Smith

Margaret Chase Smith trembled as she stood to speak on the floor of the United States Senate. Part of her doubted that she should do this. As a freshman senator, she knew that she was expected to keep quiet. Of ninety-six senators in 1950, she was the only female. Worse, she was about to criticize the actions of a colleague. In the past several months, fellow Republican Joseph McCarthy had gained nationwide attention with shocking charges about Communist subversives working in the federal government. At first, Smith took the Wisconsin senator's allegations very seriously. Like most Americans, she feared the specter of worldwide Communism—and the dangers of Communist spies in the government. But the more she listened to McCarthy, the more she doubted him. Meanwhile, people's reputations were being ruined, and none of her colleagues had condemned McCarthy's actions on the Senate floor. In the end, she believed she had to do it.

As Smith glanced around the chamber, she spotted a glaring McCarthy directly behind her. She knew he would not like what she was about to say and would find some way to punish her. But she was determined not to let him intimidate her. Nervously, she began: "I speak as a Republican. I speak as a woman. I speak as a United States Senator. I speak as an American." Then she went on to observe that some "of us who shout the loudest about Americanism" ignore "some of the basic principles of Americanism," including the rights to criticize, protest, and hold unpopular ideas.

Smith's address stirred many observers, but it did nothing to silence McCarthy. In fact, he was only at the beginning of a spectacular senate career. In coming years, Americans heard many more alarming charges from him about Communist subversion. By the time his career was over, so were those of many other Americans—individuals accused of Communist sympathies or associations. And by then, his name had become synonymous with the post–World War II anticommunist hysteria.

McCarthy, of course, did not start the postwar anticommunist hysteria that came to be known as McCarthyism. In fact, ever since the Red Scare of 1919, the

❖❖ *Joseph McCarthy*   ❖❖ *Margaret Chase Smith*

threat of Communist subversion had periodically provoked deep fears in Americans. During the Great Depression, the American Communist Party and the various front organizations that it sponsored drew thousands of members, and Communists became active in labor unions supported by the New Deal. Prodded by conservative and anti-union groups, Congress established the House Un-American Activities Committee (HUAC) in 1938 to respond to charges that Communists had infiltrated the federal government. HUAC investigations fought the New Deal by focusing on Communist influence in unions and federal agencies, but concerns about subversion subsided when the United States entered a wartime Grand Alliance with the Soviet Union. As World War II gave way to the Cold War, however, anticommunism moved to the center stage of American politics. Through the late 1940s, the issue stayed there as young Congressman Richard Nixon and members of HUAC investigated alleged Communist influence, from Washington, D.C., to Hollywood. Those investigations and the publicity that Federal Bureau of Investigation Director J. Edgar Hoover gave to the alleged threat of Communist subversion played a large role in promoting a second red scare. They also set the stage for McCarthy, the most vocal anticommunist politician by the early1950s, to exploit it.

If McCarthy did not start the post–World War II anticommunist hysteria, Smith was not alone in attacking him. For a time, though, she was perhaps the most prominent politician in the nation to speak up against him. In so doing, she too played a unique role in this red scare and, like McCarthy, highlights important aspects of it. Together, these two colleagues and adversaries illustrate factors that fostered this scare, kept it alive, and finally led to its demise.

Tail-Gunner Joe

The man who sat glowering behind Margaret Chase Smith started life in circumstances that made it unlikely he would land in the United States Senate only thirty-nine years later. Joseph R. McCarthy was born in the tiny settlement of Grand Chute in central Wisconsin, the grandson of a poor Irish immigrant and son of a farmer. On their modest farm, McCarthy's parents raised a small herd of cows and five sons and two daughters. By the time Joseph was born in 1908, the McCarthys had moved from a log cabin to a white clapboard house without electricity or plumbing. Although stories abound regarding Joe's childhood, little is known for sure. Also of Irish descent, his mother was a devout Catholic and apparently uneducated. By all accounts, his no-nonsense father worked incessantly. Neighbors remember young Joe as strong, energetic, and extroverted. Like his father, he was a hard worker. He was also an excellent student. He attended a one-room school, where his teacher was impressed by his sharp mind and keen memory, and let him sit in on the older students' lessons.

McCarthy's native intelligence seemed matched only by his energy and ambition. Dropping out of school at fourteen to help out his father, young Joe soon grew tired of farm work. His mother constantly encouraged her youngest son to be somebody and by age sixteen he was ready to strike out on his own. Renting an acre from his father, he raised chickens and within a year had a thriving business. Although it eventually failed when he was laid low by flu, the determined McCarthy rebounded quickly. After talking his way into a job as a grocery store manager in a nearby town, he introduced aggressive marketing and soon racked up the biggest sales in the chain. When not at work, he found time to attend high school. Twenty years old when he enrolled, he worked at an accelerated pace and finished in a year. Now consumed by the desire for an education, he headed off in 1930 to attend Catholic Marquette University in Milwaukee.

The ambitious McCarthy thrived at Marquette. Outgoing and friendly, he was elected senior class president. Few of his classmates seemed as devoted to the Catholic faith. Few, too, could match his energy. To earn money, he worked numerous jobs, from cook to service station manager. He also made money gambling. He played poker without fear, aggressively raising the stakes even on poor hands until his opponents folded. McCarthy even arm wrestled for money. When not gambling, he boxed. In all these extracurricular activities, he seemed to demonstrate a trait that many who knew him later would recognize: what one biographer called "exaggerated masculinity."

McCarthy left Marquette with a law degree five years after he entered. With little time to study, he had succeeded with dogged determination. And he was motivated by his new plan: He would enter politics. Heading to Waupaca, a small county seat near his hometown, he set up a one-man law practice in 1935. He was friendly and aggressive in both pursuing clients and handling their cases. The next year, he ran unsuccessfully for district attorney as a staunch New Deal Democrat. When he ran for a nonpartisan judgeship for the Appleton district three years later, though, the outcome was different. McCarthy outpolled the incumbent by outhustling him. By election day, he had talked to practically every eligible voter. He won many of them over with informal, neighborly charm. He also put out advertisements that deliberately misstated his opponent's age and deceived voters about his pay. At twenty-nine, McCarthy took a seat on the bench.

When the United States entered World War II, McCarthy realized that a war record would help him win higher office, so he enlisted in the Marines in 1942 and shipped off to the South Pacific to serve as an intelligence officer. For nearly three years, he debriefed pilots after they returned from bombing runs. By 1943, however, Wisconsin newspapers began to carry stories about McCarthy's exploits as a tail gunner who flew on dangerous missions. According to one report, he fired off more bullets on a single mission than any other Marine in history. In reality, McCarthy and many other Marines often went along on routine flights to relieve their boredom. On one such trip, eager to break the record for most ammunition used on a flight, McCarthy had fired numerous rounds into coconut trees. When he returned, the public relations officer wrote up a press release about his record for newspapers back home. On another mission, McCarthy falsely claimed, he was wounded by enemy fire. He actually broke his foot in a hazing incident on board one flight. When a *Milwaukee Journal* reporter later uncovered the real story of McCarthy's war "wound," McCarthy called the paper "pro-Communist." By then, however, his war record did not matter. The legend of Tail-Gunner Joe was embedded in the minds of Dairy State voters.

McCarthy came home to a hero's welcome in 1945. Having switched parties years before, he ran for the Republican nomination for the Senate in 1946. After winning the backing of wealthy conservatives who saw an opportunity to defeat the liberal incumbent, McCarthy entered the primary with a large campaign war chest. Some of the money was used to produce campaign literature emphasizing the candidate's combat experience. "Yes, folks," declared one advertisement, "CONGRESS NEEDS A TAIL-GUNNER." Meanwhile, McCarthy campaigned in his usual dogged style. When the votes were tallied, he had won.

McCarthy sounded a new theme in the general election. With the backing of ultraconservative *Chicago Tribune* publisher Colonel Robert McCormick, McCarthy emphasized the "disloyalty" of the Democratic Party and attacked his Democratic rival as "Communistically inclined." At one campaign rally, he pledged to remove "the vast number of Communists from the public payroll." Like other Republicans running for office in 1946, McCarthy tapped into some voters' repugnance for the New Deal, which conservatives like McCormick equated with Communism. At the same time, many Americans were frustrated by the onset of the Cold War and the seeming inability of the Truman administration to deal with what appeared to be a growing Soviet threat in Europe. In 1946, Republicans made large gains in Congress. One of the party's new senators was Tail-Gunner Joe, who had gotten his first lesson in anticommunism's potency as a political issue.

For the next three years, though, Wisconsin's new senator was just another anti–New Deal Republican. His voting record reflected those views—as well as his ties to powerful corporate interests. He took up the cause of the real estate lobby. He also championed the decontrol of sugar prices and received financial backing from Pepsi-Cola, a company in desperate need of sugar after the war. Before long, he had a new nickname on Capitol Hill: the Pepsi-Cola Kid.

At the same time, McCarthy began to strike colleagues as rude and disrespectful of the Senate's procedures and customs. Many observers noted his often disheveled appearance and his rumpled, ill-fitting clothes. He gambled, drank heavily, and developed a reputation as a womanizer. He also struck many acquaintances as boorish. "He is ignorant, crude, boastful," said one, "unaware of either intellectual or social refinements." It was an image McCarthy went out of his way to cultivate now that he mixed with people from a different world. In his elevated circumstances, the self-made former boxer and ex-Marine relished his lowbrow, tough-talking masculine image. In the minds of voters, he knew, it set him apart from opponents he routinely characterized as soft and unmanly.

If McCarthy's colleagues dismissed the brash senator as inconsequential, that assessment soon changed. Halfway through his term, he faced sagging support in Wisconsin. Searching for an issue to boost his popularity in late 1949, he turned to one he had used before: Communism. Speaking in Madison, he said the city's liberal *Capital-Times* newspaper was spreading "the Communist Party-line propaganda." Later, he told Republican gatherings that the State Department was "honeycombed and run by Communists" and that "Christian nations" were losing the war with Communism. At the time, such charges made perfect political sense. Democrats made a remarkable comeback in 1948 with the Truman administration's anti-Soviet containment policy and attacks on Republican economic and social policies. Republicans now had only one obvious response: stepped-up attacks on Democrats as soft on Communism at home. Many of McCarthy's fellow Republicans may have been skeptical about his charges regarding subversion in the government, but they were not about to muzzle him. As one Republican Senator told him, "Joe, you're a real SOB. But sometimes it's useful to have SOBs around to do the dirty work."

It mattered little that the threat of Communist subversion was enormously exaggerated by 1950. Although many Americans were attracted to the Communist Party or its numerous front organizations during the Depression, the party's membership and appeal had diminished considerably by 1946. And even though some Communists stole secrets, they had never been in a position to influence American foreign policy or undermine the nation's ability to defend itself. In fact, most of the suspected Communists in the government had been fired or quit their jobs after the passage in 1939 of the Hatch Act, which barred Communists from government jobs.

In the face of American setbacks in the Cold War and several well-publicized spy cases, however, the dangers of Communist subversion seemed real enough. Americans had only recently watched half of Europe fall behind the Iron Curtain. Frustrated and fearful, they took seriously the notion that the United States was losing the Cold War because it had not done enough to root out Communists at home. A frightening train of events bolstered that idea. In 1945, accusations regarding stolen classified documents led to the arrest of several journalists and a prominent State Department official. Responding to growing concern about subversives in the government and the effective Republican accusation in the 1946 elections that Democrats were soft on Communism, the Truman administration created a loyalty program the next year. This massive internal security effort to screen government employees found little evidence of spying. Yet it seemed to confirm the fears of many Americans that Communist subversion posed a serious threat to the nation. Spy charges leveled in 1948 against a former State Department official named Alger Hiss, who had attended the Yalta Conference* in 1945 as an aide to Franklin Roosevelt, only reinforced these fears. The fall of China to Communists in 1949 and the Soviet detonation of an atomic bomb the same year raised them even further. Then, in early 1950, Hiss's conviction seemed to seal the case. As many Americans asked how the United States could have "lost" Eastern Europe and China to the Communists, this and other spy cases suggested a ready answer: Communist subversion at the highest levels of the government was responsible.

Against this backdrop, Joe McCarthy stepped forward with shocking revelations and hit political pay dirt. Only three weeks after Hiss's conviction, he delivered a speech in Wheeling, West Virginia, that warned of the dangers of espionage facing the nation. Borrowing freely from a recent address of Richard Nixon, he went on to attack the Truman administration and its secretary of state, Dean Acheson. Then he added something new and stunning. He claimed to have "here in my hand" a list of 205 names of known Communists working in the State Department. In coming days, McCarthy made a similar claim in speeches across the country. **[See Source 1.]** He also warned that the failure of the Truman administration to open the department's loyalty files immediately "will label the Democratic Party as being the bedfellow of international Communism." By the time he returned to Washington, D.C., McCarthy's shocking charges had made headlines. A United States senator claimed to have hard evidence that a Communist underground had burrowed into the government and the Truman administration was covering it up. Tail-Gunner Joe did not realize it yet, but he was about to become the leading actor in a growing red scare.

"Paralyzed With Fear"

Margaret Chase Smith had much in common with Joe McCarthy. Both were relative newcomers to the Senate, sat on the Republican side of the aisle, hailed from small towns, and rose from meager circumstances. In the clublike atmosphere of the Senate, both considered themselves outsiders. Yet Smith also differed from her Wisconsin colleague in fundamental ways. The product of a small-town New England upbringing, Smith was raised in Skowhegan, Maine. She never considered the woolen and textile mill center on the Kennebec River anything but home. Like Mainers in general, most of the town's five thousand residents could easily list the personal qualities they valued most: frugality, honesty, practicality, common sense, and independence. In a long public career, this daughter of Skowhegan seemed the very embodiment of these simple Yankee virtues. They firmly rooted Smith in her hometown throughout her life, even as they carried her far from her humble beginnings there.

Smith was born in 1897, the oldest of George and Carrie Chase's four children. George made only a sporadic living as a barber, and Carrie was forced to work as a waitress, store clerk, and stitcher at a shoe factory. She even took in

*_Yalta Conference_: A meeting in 1945 between Franklin Roosevelt, British Prime Minister Winston Churchill, and Soviet leader Josef Stalin to discuss the fate of postwar Europe.

laundry and ironing for neighbors. As the oldest child, Margaret helped out by waiting tables, performing temporary domestic work, and clerking at a store. In the process, she learned the value of thrift and hard work. She knew that her grandfather faithfully saved fifty cents of his weekly pay and died with $10,000 in the bank and holding the deed to the Chase family home. She also imbibed the lessons about work and money from her grandfather's set of Horatio Alger* stories, which became her favorite books. She learned, too, that she wanted a better life, a desire that kept her in school. Like many girls, she studied commercial subjects such as shorthand and typing, a practical choice given the increasing demand for female office workers in the early twentieth century.

Although college was the obvious way to rise in life, family finances prevented it. In a way easily recognized by Horatio Alger's readers, however, pluck and luck soon offered another path for Margaret to better her circumstances. For several years, she worked part-time as a telephone operator. One night she took a call from a Clyde Smith. The two supposedly talked for some time, and that one call turned into many more. Recently divorced, Smith was a prominent businessman, Skowhegan town selectman, and Maine state senator. Carrie Chase reminded her daughter that Smith was old enough to be her own husband. Margaret also knew that he had a reputation for liking the girls, especially younger ones. Before long, though, Smith was seeing Margaret and her family a lot. He also offered her a temporary job in the assessor's office. Then after a brief stint as a schoolteacher and two more years at the phone company, Margaret landed a job as general office assistant at a newspaper. All the while, Smith (himself a partner at the newspaper) hovered nearby.

At the same time, Margaret found another avenue for advancement. She helped organize a local branch of the Maine Federation of Business and Professional Women's Clubs (BPW). With few professional or business opportunities for women in the 1920s, the club offered important support for ambitious working women. It provided Margaret opportunities for public speaking and to hone her office and organizational skills. With abundant energy and a sharp eye for details, she blossomed in the BPW. In a few years she was president of the local branch and by 1925 president of the Maine State Federation. As she traveled, spoke, and organized on the BPW's behalf, Chase broadened her horizons and gained self-confidence. Since the BPW often lobbied the legislature, it also offered her a political education—and an opportunity to become involved in the Republican party. By 1930, she was elected a Maine State Republican Committeewoman.

The same year, Chase's life changed dramatically when she married Clyde Smith and moved into his thirty-two-room mansion. She insisted that she be known as Margaret Chase Smith to retain her own identity. She would need it, for her marriage was far from perfect. Clyde expected a well-managed household. As Margaret put it later, he wanted "his soup on the table when he came in." And he never lost his eye for women. Her one consolation was the opportunity her marriage offered to further her political education. As Smith worked his way from the state senate to the governor's executive council and then to the House of Representatives, Margaret was with him at every step. She brought

Horatio Alger: The author of a series of children's tales in the nineteenth century whose youthful male protagonists begin life in humble circumstances and rise up with "pluck and luck": hard work, thrift, and perseverance combined with good fortune.

along her organizational and political skills. Campaigning with him, she kept track of names, typed letters, and mixed with local politicians. After he won his seat in Congress, Margaret served as his chief aide and office assistant. When poor health limited his trips back to Maine, she often went in his place to make speeches, visit party officials, and meet constituents.

Margaret also took note of her husband's strategy for political success. Maine was a rock-ribbed Republican state. The major political division was between the party's moderates and conservatives. Clyde Smith was a moderate Republican who supported workmen's compensation, limits on child labor, and a state old-age pension program. Proud of their own self-reliance, Mainers were not fond of New Deal social welfare programs. When he ran for Congress in 1936 in the midst of the Depression, though, Smith bet they would support someone who demonstrated compassion for the down and out. He was right. Margaret did not realize it, but this moderate stance would work for her, too. By late 1939, Clyde Smith's health had deteriorated, and doctors confirmed that he was suffering from late-stage syphilis. Before he died in 1940, he urged Margaret to run for his seat, and that spring she won a special election to fill his unexpired term.

If Clyde Smith's political career taught Margaret important lessons, she learned another at the very outset of her own. German forces had rolled over most of Europe by 1940, and Maine's new representative talked up the importance of national defense. When she ran for re-election later that year, she prevailed in part because her strong support for preparedness helped blunt gender-oriented attacks from her male Republican primary challenger, who declared that the coming of war required a "militant" representative in Congress and that "a flick of the wrist and a smile won't do it." Smith never wavered from her strong support for the military and national defense. Within two years she won a spot on the House Committee on Naval Affairs, where she gained a reputation for expertise in military affairs. When World War II gave way to the Cold War, she endorsed the Truman Doctrine* announced in 1947 and the Marshall Plan* proposed in 1948, the two pillars of the Truman administration's Cold War containment policy. From the beginning, Smith neutralized concerns about her gender among conservative Maine voters. No one would ever attack *her* as weak on national defense or the Cold War.

As only one of seven female representatives in 1940, Smith entered a masculine world on Capitol Hill. She decided to ignore discrimination and worked to be taken seriously by her colleagues. She never tried to be one of the boys and always wore conservative attire topped off by a fresh rose in her lapel—her fashion trademark. With her frank honesty and deeply ingrained sense of integrity, she also took advantage of the longstanding assumption that women were more moral than men. Besides her independence, and plainspoken honesty, Mainers loved her frugality. She sold her late-husband's mansion and moved into an unadorned wood frame house. Meanwhile, she faithfully minded constituents' concerns, making sure she answered every letter the same day it arrived. She

Truman Doctrine: A policy that the United States would assist any nation facing the threat of Communist takeover from the outside or within.

Marshall Plan: A massive economic relief program for Western European nations intended to lessen the appeal of Communism.

also knew that her image of integrity permitted her to defy her party. A moderate on social issues, she frequently broke Republican ranks on labor, education, and social welfare legislation. As the *New York Times* later put it, "if she had been born in any other state except Maine she'd be a Democrat."

With wide support among Maine voters, Smith won three more terms in the House and then captured a Senate seat in 1948. At age fifty-one, she was the first female Republican Senator and the only woman in the chamber. Denied a position on the powerful Armed Services Committee, she was assigned to the Expenditures Committee. There, she turned to the ranking Republican on the committee for a spot on its investigations subcommittee. Joe McCarthy agreed to give it to her. She found her Wisconsin colleague pleasant, but was disturbed to learn that he had talked to reporters about supposedly confidential deliberations among several members of the subcommittee. Nonetheless, when McCarthy began speaking out about subversion in the State Department in early 1950, she took his charges seriously enough to go to the Senate floor to listen.

Like millions of other Americans, Smith believed the problem of domestic spying was real. In fact, she initially believed that McCarthy was "on to something disturbing and frightening." But her fear soon turned to dismay and disgust. When he handed her copies of the evidence he waved around in the Senate chambers, she noted that the information the documents contained was not relevant to the cases at hand. As she said later, "I began to wonder whether I was as stupid as I thought." In fact, McCarthy's charges about Communists in the State Department were based on old files that had been thoroughly investigated. McCarthy did not know that many of the subjects had already been fired and that Communists had been lumped together in these investigations with such "security risks" as homosexuals and alcoholics.

Listening to the tough-talking Tail-Gunner, Smith began to hear a loudmouth. As one of the few women in Congress, she had learned that decorum and respect for rules paid off. Clearly, McCarthy had not. Above all, though, she was disturbed by his methods. Smith had suffered smears during her own Senate campaign in 1948, including the accusation that she was soft on Communism. She understood how reckless charges could destroy people's reputations. She was especially concerned after McCarthy pointed to his first "security risk," a woman who was an acquaintance of Smith. McCarthy charged that this former member of a United Nations committee on women belonged to twenty-eight "Communist front organizations." Smith did not believe the charges and, in fact, they quickly fell apart—as did his charges against several prominent Foreign Service officers, but not until after the accusations had destroyed their reputations and careers.

Smith had no interest stoking public fears for political gain. As a congresswoman, she voted against making HUAC a permanent House committee because she saw how its members could destroy people for their own political benefit. Congressional investigating committees like HUAC generated enormous publicity for their members, who were not bound by the courts' procedures guaranteeing due process and were free to denounce witnesses and ruin their lives. Such behavior was common during HUAC's investigations of alleged Communist influence in Hollywood in the late 1940s. By the time anticommunist investigators were done there, more than two hundred actors, producers, screen writers, and other studio employees had lost their jobs and were blacklisted, which prevented them from seeking employment elsewhere in the motion picture industry. Meanwhile, many more government employees, and those in the radio, television, and other industries nationwide, experienced a similar fate. Smith knew that under such lax procedures it was easy for anyone who held dissenting views to become a target. Expressing unconventional ideas could easily become synonymous with treason. **[See Sources 2 and 3.]**

Smith was not alone in perceiving dangers in McCarthy's charges. Democrats in Congress saw political peril in them as well. Shortly after McCarthy spoke out, the Senate's Democratic majority created a special committee headed by conservative Maryland Democrat Millard Tydings to look into his accusations. Meanwhile, some editorial writers and others also questioned McCarthy's tactics and findings. But no one really seemed prepared to stop him. In a couple of months, he had gone from an obscure senator to a national figure whose face graced the covers of major news magazines. Public opinion polls showed widespread support for him. McCarthy could confidently proclaim that nothing would prevent him from exposing the "egg-sucking phony liberals" or the "Communists and queers" in the State Department. Just as confidently, he could dismiss the Tydings Committee as a Democratic party effort to whitewash the Truman administration's wrongdoings.

Now appalled by McCarthy's dirty work, Smith was dismayed that none of her Republican colleagues had spoken up on the Senate floor to denounce his tactics. Believing that he had the Senate "paralyzed with fear," she decided to do it. After drafting a statement, she quietly rounded up six other moderate Republican Senators to sign it. Then she strode into the Senate chamber to read her "Declaration of Conscience." Without mentioning McCarthy by name, she declared that the Senate had been debased to a "forum of hate" and individual reputations had been sacrificed "for selfish political gain." **[See Source 4.]**

"Have You No Sense of Decency?"

Fifteen minutes after Smith started, she sat down. She fully expected that McCarthy would stand to offer a rebuttal. Instead, he sat through her speech whitefaced and then left the Senate floor without saying a word. Smith quickly heard from many other people, though. After her Declaration was picked up by the press, letters of praise flooded her office. One newspaper declared that her speech had the "ring of Lexington, of Valley Forge, of the Gettysburg address." *Newsweek* magazine even put her on its cover. "Senator Smith: A Woman Vice President?" read the accompanying caption. But not all the reaction was favorable. One Massachusetts paper, for instance, condemned Smith for failing to see that McCarthy was responsible for bringing attention to "this Communist issue." And the day after her speech, Smith heard from McCarthy on the Senate floor. The fight against those who "are attempting to betray this country shall not stop," he declared, "regardless of what any individual or group in this Senate . . . may say or do." Later, he labeled Smith and her cosigners "Snow White and her Six Dwarfs."

McCarthy had good reason to go on the offensive. Smith's Declaration may have stirred positive editorial comment, but it had little impact on her colleagues. Smith hoped that her statement would elicit wide support in the Senate. McCarthy, though, was too valuable to Republicans, and five of Smith's six cosigners soon abandoned her. Meanwhile, few Democrats wanted to be charged with being soft on Communism. And timing was again on McCarthy's side. Only weeks after Smith denounced McCarthy's behavior, Communist North Korean forces launched a massive invasion of South Korea. Under the auspices of the United Nations, Truman quickly committed American troops to the conflict. But the Communists were again on the march in Asia. Three weeks later, the Tydings Committee released its report, which concluded that McCarthy's allegations were a "fraud and a hoax." Only three days after that, however, another espionage bombshell exploded. Julius Rosenberg, who had earlier worked on the Manhattan Project to develop the atomic bomb, was arrested for spying. Gains made by Republicans in the elections later in 1950 strengthened McCarthy's hand even more. One of the Senate Democrats who lost that year was Millard Tydings, who went down to defeat after a vicious campaign supported by the Wisconsin senator. By then, the Korean war was descending into stalemate. After American commander Douglas MacArthur publically criticized Truman for not seeking victory by attacking China, the president, who feared such a move would provoke an even bigger war, fired MacArthur for publically criticizing the commander-in-chief. In early 1951, MacArthur came home a hero to millions of Americans who believed that limited war against Communism represented appeasement.

With the momentum of events shifting his way, McCarthy began to play for bigger stakes. He called Truman a son of a bitch for firing MacArthur and declared that he should be impeached. Then he launched a renewed attack on the State Department, which he said was the root cause of the country's Cold War setbacks. His first target was Secretary of State Dean Acheson. Like the convicted Alger Hiss, Acheson was well-bred and highly educated. He spoke with an English accent and exuded an air of refinement. The secretary and "his lace handkerchief crowd" made inviting targets for McCarthy, who sensed that such attacks played well with folks back home. McCarthy now charged that Acheson had "betrayed us." Then he moved on, declaring that former Secretary of State George Marshall was involved in an "immense" conspiracy. Marshall was a hero of World War II and architect of the Marshall Plan to rebuild Western Europe to prevent Communist expansion after the war, but McCarthy declared that he bore responsibility for the loss of Eastern Europe and for the "sellout" of China under Truman. Marshall, he declared, was a "willing instrument of the Hisses and the Achesons, . . . the misguided men who let American boys die to make America safe for Communism."

When he was criticized for such charges, the former boxer punched back. He compared critical newspapers to the *Daily Worker*, the American Communist Party publication. He defended his "brass-knuckle" methods by reminding audiences that the fight against the Reds required such tactics. And he could always charge that Democrats who criticized him were only attempting to whitewash the failure of the Truman administration to root out Communists from the government.

McCarthy—and his allies—could also enlist assumptions about gender, which associated masculinity with toughness and women with the home, to undermine critics. McCarthy frequently cited his Marine training, declaring, "We weren't taught to wear lace panties and fight with lace hankies." In 1952, Smith herself was the target of a gender-based McCarthyite attack with the publication of a book titled *USA Confidential*, written by two best-selling authors. Their sensationalist account of the "shockingly corrupt under-life of America" declared that lesbianism was the result of "Marxist teaching" and the State Department was "more than thirty percent faggot." In one chapter titled "Reds in Clover," the authors called Smith one of the nation's "left-wing apologists," a consort of pro-Communists, and "a lesson why women should not be in politics." **[See Source 5.]**

Smith promptly filed a libel suit and later trial testimony established that one of the authors talked with McCarthy and that Smith was included in the book because of her Declaration. Yet McCarthy and his allies knew what they were doing. Given the hold of the postwar era's domestic ideology, which defined women's proper place in the home, it was easy to imply that those who defied traditional gender roles were, if not Communists themselves, subversive of the status quo. It mattered little that Smith's anticommunist rhetoric was often as strident as McCarthy's, as when she advocated dropping the atomic bomb on North Korea to "stop the Red murderers." Such heated rhetoric was no match for McCarthy's clever use of masculinity. It was a useful political weapon, he knew, in his battle against alleged Communists—or his lone female colleague in the Senate.

As Margaret Chase Smith also learned, McCarthy also knew how to defend himself by wielding senatorial power. After reading her Declaration, Smith got a lesson about his growing clout when Republican Senate leaders stripped two of her committee assignments. At the same time, McCarthy bumped Smith from his investigations subcommittee and replaced her with Richard Nixon, who had earlier gained nationwide fame as a member of HUAC and now sat in the Senate. McCarthy bored in on Smith again in 1951 when she served as a member of a committee looking into his role in the campaign against Millard Tydings in Maryland. When the committee's final report characterized McCarthy's behavior as dishonest, he retaliated by calling Smith a "puny" politician and accusing her of launching "one of the most vigorous attacks . . . upon my exposure of Communists."

Nonetheless, Smith continued to stand up to McCarthy. She declared on the Senate floor that opposition to Communism was not his "exclusive possession" and that differing with him on tactics did not make one a Communist. "I shall not permit intimidation," she announced, "to keep me from expressing my honest convictions." McCarthy responded to these attacks by supporting another Republican candidate when Smith ran for re-election in 1954. Backed by Texas oil millionaires close to McCarthy, Smith's primary challenger called Smith too "weak-willed" to fight the "ominous clouds of atheistic, international Communism." In fact, he sounded so much like the Wisconsin senator on the stump that reporters called him "Junior McCarthy." The contest gained nationwide attention as the first election in 1954 to show, as one magazine put it, "how the voters feel about 'McCarthyism.'" When their votes were counted, Mainers demonstrated that they resented McCarthy's interference and still valued Smith's independence. She won by a five-to-one margin.

It was a sign of things to come. After winning his own landslide re-election in 1952, McCarthy seemed invincible. Yet for all his charges, he had not uncovered a single subversive. And with Republican Dwight Eisenhower as president and Republicans in control of Congress by 1953, McCarthy's political usefulness had suddenly diminished. Most Republicans had little interest in continued charges about Communist subversion with their party now running the government. McCarthy, however, was not about to give up on the issue that had catapulted him to national prominence.

Instead, he launched his last crusade to root out the Communists. As the new chairman of the Senate Committee on Government Operations, McCarthy turned first to the Government Printing Office in 1953. The subversion there, he suggested, was "worse than the Hiss case." He investigated the Voice of America, an arm of the State Department that beamed radio broadcasts on four continents to counter Communist propaganda. Then he went on to the department's Overseas Library Program, charging that books written by "Communist authors" sat on its shelves in overseas nations. By the time these investigations were over, more people had lost their jobs, at least one had committed suicide, and books were pulled from libraries and many of them burned. **[See Source 6.]**

Then McCarthy made a fatal mistake: He took on the United States Army. After investigating allegations of spying at an Army base in New Jersey, he charged that the Army was unable to counter "the deliberate Communist infiltration of our Armed Forces." In doing so, he incurred the wrath of military brass and Eisenhower, a former Army general. And in early 1954, McCarthy handed them a weapon to use against him. Army officials knew that a member of his legal staff named Roy Cohn had intervened repeatedly on behalf of a friend and former McCarthy staff consultant to get him preferential treatment in the Army. When McCarthy refused to fire Cohn, the Army released a report accusing McCarthy of also intervening numerous times on behalf of Cohn's friend. Now McCarthy would become the victim of his own weapon: a Senate investigation conducted by his own Government Operations Committee.

The televised Army-McCarthy Hearings started in April 1954. Before they ended, millions of Americans had tuned in. On their TV screens, they saw McCarthy bully witnesses at first hand. Toward the end of the hearings, McCarthy rashly accused a young assistant of Joseph Welch, the Army's chief counsel at the hearings, of Communist leanings. It was clear he had gone too far, and Welch cut into him: "Little did I dream you could be so reckless and so cruel," Welch declared. "Have you no sense of decency?" After the hearings, much of McCarthy's public support evaporated. Before the end of the year, the Senate voted on a resolution to censure McCarthy for "unbecoming" conduct, a reprimand one step short of removal. The vote was 67–22. One of the Republicans who voted for censure, of course, was Margaret Chase Smith.

By late 1954, McCarthy's four years in the national spotlight were over. Although he continued his attacks in speeches, he was now largely ignored by the press and shunned in the Senate. Just the year before, McCarthy had married a member of his Senate staff, abandoning his erratic bachelor's life. But he still drank heavily despite deteriorating health, and in 1957 died of cirrhosis of the liver. By then, McCarthyism had mostly died out too. In its wake lay thousands of victims: those in government, business, academia, and Hollywood who lost jobs or reputations. McCarthy had never been alone in exploiting Communism, and he did not start the episode that came to bear his name, but he could claim a fair number of those victims.

One of them was Smith, although the price she paid was not very steep compared to many others. In fact, she would go on to enjoy a career as long and steady as McCarthy's was short and volatile. Sitting in the Senate until 1972, Smith won a seat on the powerful Armed Services Committee and became one of the Senate's most ardent Cold Warriors. At the same time, she continued to be lauded for her honesty and integrity. Smith never remarried, and until she died in 1995 she never lost her reputation for independence.

All the while, though, she never examined basic Cold War assumptions. Protesting only McCarthy's methods, not his goals, she never doubted the threat of internal subversion. The American Communist Party, she declared in 1953, was "a subversive organization working to place us under domination of Communist Russia." Ignoring the First Amendment, she even introduced a bill to prevent the distribution of "Communistic propaganda." Likewise, she never doubted the logic of the American Cold War containment policy. As that war continued long after McCarthyism ended, Smith never questioned the need for American military intervention abroad in the name of containing Communism. She was unwavering, for instance, in her support for the American commitment to Vietnam. As she declared in 1968, "we are in Vietnam to stop the Communists from conquering the world." Many Mainers would come to disagree with that assessment and in 1972 she lost her seat in the Senate to an antiwar Democrat, partly for that reason. Unlike Joe McCarthy, Smith never exploited the fear of Communism. But she never asked if it was realistic either. And for that, she finally paid another price.

PRIMARY SOURCES

SOURCE 1: *McCarthy Assaults the State Department* (1950)

No copy exists of the speech that Joseph McCarthy delivered in Wheeling, West Virginia, in which he asserted that he had 205 names of subversives working in the State Department. In another speech only days later, McCarthy claimed to have fewer names. He put that version of his speech into the Congressional Record. *How does McCarthy characterize his targets in this speech? What does it reveal about the basis of his appeal?*

At war's end we were physically the strongest nation on earth and, at least potentially, the most powerful intellectually and morally. Ours could have been the honor of being a beacon in the desert of destruction, a shining living proof

SOURCE: Senator Joseph McCarthy, speech, *Congressional Record*, Senate, 81st Cong., 2nd sess., February 20, 1950, pp. 1954, 1957.

that civilization was not yet ready to destroy itself. Unfortunately, we have failed miserably and tragically to arise to the opportunity.

The reason why we find ourselves in a position of impotency is not because our only powerful potential enemy has sent men to invade our shores, but rather because of traitorous actions of those who have been treated so well by this Nation. It has not been the less fortunate or members of minority groups who have been selling this Nation out, but rather those who have had all the benefits that the wealthiest nation on earth has had to offer—the finest homes, the finest college education, and the finest jobs in Government we can give.

This is glaringly true in the State Department. There the bright young men who are born with silver spoons in their mouths are the ones who have been worst. . . .

I have in my hand 57 cases of individuals who would appear to be either card carrying members or certainly loyal to the Communist Party, but who nevertheless are still helping to shape our foreign policy.

One thing to remember in discussing the Communists in our Government is that we are not dealing with spies who get 30 pieces of silver to steal the blueprints of a new weapon. We are dealing with a far more sinister type of activity because it permits the enemy to guide and shape our policy. . . .

This brings us down to the case of one Alger Hiss who is important not as an individual any more, but rather because he is so representative of a group in the State Department. It is unnecessary to go over the sordid events showing how he sold out the Nation which had given him so much. Those are rather fresh in all of our minds. . . .

If time permitted, it might be well to go into detail about the fact that Hiss was Roosevelt's chief adviser at Yalta when Roosevelt was admittedly in ill health and tired physically and mentally. . . .

Of the results of this conference, Arthur Bliss Lane of the State Department had this to say: "As I glanced over the document, I could not believe my eyes. To me, almost every line spoke of a surrender to Stalin."

As you hear this story of high treason, I know that you are saying to yourself, "Well, why doesn't the Congress do something about it?" Actually, ladies and gentlemen, one of the important reasons for the graft, the corruption, the dishonesty, the disloyalty, the treason in high Government positions—one of the most important reasons why this continues is a lack of moral uprising on the part of the 140,000,000 American people. In the light of history, however, this is not hard to explain. . . .

As you know, very recently the Secretary of State proclaimed his loyalty to a man guilty of what has always been considered as the most abominable of all crimes—of being a traitor to the people who gave him a position of great trust. The Secretary of State in attempting to justify his continued devotion to the man who sold out the Christian world to the atheistic world, referred to Christ's Sermon on the Mount as a justification and reason therefor, and the reaction of the American people to this would have made the heart of Abraham Lincoln happy.

When this pompous diplomat in striped pants, with a phony British accent, proclaimed to the American people that Christ on the Mount endorsed communism, high treason, and betrayal of a sacred trust, the blasphemy was so great that it awakened the dormant indignation of the American people.

He has lighted the spark which is resulting in a moral uprising and will end only when the whole sorry mess of twisted, warped thinkers are swept from the national scene so that we may have a new birth of national honesty and decency in Government.

SOURCE 2: *HUAC Investigates Subversion in Hollywood (1947)*

In 1946, the House Un-American Activities Committee turned its attention to Communist influence in Hollywood movie studios. Many of the witnesses, including actor Ronald Reagan, were friendly. Ten of them, however, were not. All of the so-called Hollywood Ten, including screenwriter Ring Lardner, were on the political left and some of them were or had been Communists. All of them would be sent to jail for contempt of Congress. All were also blacklisted and lost their jobs. What does this testimony reveal about HUAC's methods?

STRIPLING:[1] Mr. Lardner, the charge has been made before this committee that the Screen Writers Guild which, according to the record, you are a member of, whether you admit it or not, has a number of individuals in it who are members of the Communist Party. This committee is seeking to determine the extent of Communist infiltration in the Screen Writers Guild and in other guilds within the motion-picture industry.

LARDNER: Yes.

STRIPLING: And certainly the question of whether or not you are a member of the Communist Party is very pertinent. Now, are you a member or have you ever been a member of the Communist Party?

LARDNER: It seems to me you are trying to discredit the Screen Writers Guild through me and the motion-picture industry through the Screen Writers Guild and our whole practice of freedom of expression.

STRIPLING: If you and others are members of the Communist Party you are the ones who are discrediting the Screen Writers Guild.

LARDNER: I am trying to answer the question by stating first what I feel about the purpose of the question which, as I say, is to discredit the whole motion-picture industry.

CHAIRMAN: You won't say anything first. You are refusing to answer this question.

LARDNER: I am saying my understanding is as an American resident—

CHAIRMAN: Never mind your understanding. There is a question: Are you or have you ever been a member of the Communist Party?

SOURCE: Ring Lardner Jr., testimony, House Committee on Un-American Activities, *Hearings regarding Communist Infiltration of the Hollywood Motion-Picture Industry,* 80th Cong., 1st sess., October 30, 1947.

1. Robert Stripling, the committee's chief counsel.

LARDNER: I could answer exactly the way you want, Mr. Chairman—

CHAIRMAN: No—

LARDNER: (continuing). But I think that is a—

CHAIRMAN: It is not a question of our wanting you to answer that. It is a very simple question. Anybody would be proud to answer it—any real American would be proud to answer the question, "Are you or have you ever been a member of the Communist Party"—any real American.

LARDNER: It depends on the circumstances. I could answer it, but if I did I would hate myself in the morning.

CHAIRMAN: Leave the witness chair.

LARDNER: It was a question that would—

CHAIRMAN: Leave the witness chair.

LARDNER: Because it is a question—

CHAIRMAN: (pounding gavel). Leave the witness chair.

LARDNER: I think I am leaving by force.

CHAIRMAN: Sergeant, take the witness away.

(Applause.)

Source 3:   Red Channels *Exposes "Reds"*   (1950)

In 1950, three former FBI agents published Red Channels, *a book listing people in the entertainment industry who were allegedly Communists or Communist sympathizers. Such a listing often spelled disaster for a career. One of those included in* Red Channels *was playwright Arthur Miller, who was later called to testify before HUAC and then indicted for contempt of Congress for refusing to provide another writer's name to the committee. Still later, Miller claimed that HUAC's chairman, Democrat Francis Walter, had been willing to call off the whole thing if Miller could get his wife, actress Marilyn Monroe, to be photographed with Walter while shaking his hand. What activities or affiliations earned Miller a listing in the book?*

Arthur Miller

Playwright—"Death of a Salesman," "All My Sons"

	Reported as:
American Youth Congress	Signer of call. Official proceedings, 1/28 30/38.
Book Find Club	Writer. *Book Find News*, 5/46, p. 7; 1/46, p. 3.
	Author of Club selection. *Book Find News*, 1/46, p. 3.

SOURCE: *Red Channels* (New York: American Business Consultants Inc., June 1950), p. 111.

Civil Rights Congress	Signer. Statement in defense of Eisler. *Daily Worker*, 2/28/47, p. 2. Signer. Statement defending Communist Party. *Daily Worker*, 4/16/47, p. 2. Speaker, "Abolish America's Thought Police." *Daily Worker*, 10/6/47, p. 8.
Committee of Welcome for the Very Rev. Hewlett Johnson	Member. *Daily Worker*, 9/22/48, p. 5.
International Workers Order	Defender of tax exemption for IWO. *Fraternal Outlook*, 11/48, p. 6.
Jewish Life	Contributor. *Jewish Life*, publication of Morning Freiheit Assocation, 3/48, p. 7.
Mainstream and *New Masses*	Speaker at rally to defend Howard Fast, 10/16/47. *New Masses*, 10/28/47, p. 2.
National Council of the Arts, Sciences and Professions	Signer for Wallace. *Daily Worker*, 10/19/48, p. 7. Member, Initiating Committee. Writers for Wallace. *Daily Worker*, 9/21/48, p. 7. Co-chairman. Performance, "The Journey of Simon McKeever," and "I've Got the Tune," Carnegie Hall, 6/21/49. Official program. Sponsor. Committee to Abolish the House Un-American Activities Committee. *NY Journal-American* 12/30/48.
New York Council of the Arts, Sciences and Professions	Speaker. Rally against the "Foley Square Convictions", 10/27/49. *Daily Worker*, 10/24/49, p. 5.
Progressive Citizens of America	Sponsor. Program, 10/25/47. . . .

Source 4:   Margaret Chase Smith, *"Declaration of Conscience"*   (1950)

In June 1950, Margaret Chase Smith stood on the Senate floor and read her condemnation of McCarthy. What is the basis of her attack on him? What is her own view about subversives in the government?

Source: William C. Lewis Jr., ed., *Declaration of Conscience: Margaret Chase Smith* (Garden City, New York: Doubleday & Company, Inc., 1972), pp. 13–14, 15–16.

I speak as briefly as possible because too much harm has already been done with irresponsible words of bitterness and selfish political opportunism. I speak as simply as possible because the issue is too great to be obscured by eloquence. I speak simply and briefly in the hope that my words will be taken to heart.

I speak as a Republican. I speak as a woman. I speak as a United States Senator. I speak as an American.

The United States Senate has long enjoyed worldwide respect as the greatest deliberative body in the world. But recently that deliberative character has too often been debased to the level of a forum of hate and character assassination sheltered by the shield of congressional immunity.

It is ironical that we Senators can in debate in the Senate directly or indirectly, by any form of words, impute to any American who is not a Senator any conduct or motive unworthy or unbecoming an American—and without that non-Senator American having any legal redress against us—yet if we say the same thing in the Senate about our colleagues we can be stopped on the grounds of being out of order.

It is strange that we can verbally attack anyone else without restraint and with full protection and yet we hold ourselves above the same type of criticism here on the Senate Floor. Surely the United States Senate is big enough to take self-criticism and self-appraisal. Surely we should be able to take the same kind of character attacks that we "dish out" to outsiders.

I think that it is high time for the United States Senate and its members to do some soul-searching—for us to weigh our consciences—on the manner in which we are performing our duty to the people of America—on the manner in which we are using or abusing our individual powers and privileges.

I think that it is high time that we remembered that we have sworn to uphold and defend the Constitution. I think that it is high time that we remembered that the Constitution, as amended, speaks not only of the freedom of speech but also of trial by jury instead of trial by accusation.

Whether it be a criminal prosecution in court or a character prosecution in the Senate, there is little practical distinction when the life of a person has been ruined.

The Democratic Administration has completely confused the American people by its daily contradictory grave warnings and optimistic assurances—that show the people that our Democratic Administration has no idea of where it is going.

The Democratic Administration has greatly lost the confidence of the American people by its complacency to the threat of communism here at home and the leak of vital secrets to Russia through key officials of the Democratic Administration. There are enough proved cases to make this point without diluting our criticism with unproved charges.

Surely these are sufficient reasons to make it clear to the American people that it is time for a change and that a Republican victory is necessary to the security of this country. Surely it is clear that this nation will continue to suffer as long as it is governed by the present ineffective Democratic Administration.

Yet to displace it with a Republican regime embracing a philosophy that lacks political integrity or intellectual honesty would prove equally disastrous to this nation. The nation sorely needs a Republican victory. But I don't want to see the Republican Party ride to political victory on the Four Horsemen of Calumny—Fear, Ignorance, Bigotry, and Smear.

I doubt if the Republican Party could—simply because I don't believe the American people will uphold any political party that puts political exploitation above national interest. Surely we Republicans aren't that desperate for victory.

SOURCE 5:   *Margaret Chase Smith Feels McCarthy's Sting* (1952)

In their exposé U. S. A. Confidential, *two pro-McCarthy journalists attacked numerous people, including leading politicians. One of them was Margaret Chase Smith, who would eventually win a retraction and a cash settlement from the publisher. What does this excerpt reveal about the way attitudes toward gender and such reforms as the New Deal intersected with anti-Communism in the early 1950s?*

There are cliques and factions and wings and blocs among the Reds, as there are among Democrats, Republicans, unions and Wall Street trusts. Some are orthodox Stalinists. Others are Trotskyites.[1] Some are nationalists. Like Tito,[2] they practice communism but do not want it directed from an outside source. These "native" Communists are the most insidious. They preach against Russia but work for a revolution they will run themselves. All these forms are closer to each other than they are to us, as honest Republicans and Democrats are for the American way despite policy differences.

Holding up the rear, like a huge infantry, are the millions of "intellectual" Socialists and welfare-staters, the Americans for Democratic Action, the Fair Dealers, the liberals and progressives, etc. Among them are shrewd and ambitious politicians like Hubert Humphrey, Warren Magnuson, Wayne Morse and F. D. Roosevelt, Jr., as well as stunted visionaries like Margaret Chase Smith. . . .

The last time we were in Washington she was making one of her typical boneheaded speeches. A Senate doorman couldn't stand it any longer. When she reached the high point of her peroration, he sniffed and remarked about the lone female, "There's too many women in the Senate!" She is a lesson in why women should not be in politics. When men argue matters of high policy they usually forget their grudges at the door. She takes every opposing speech as a personal affront and lies awake nights scheming how to "get even." She is sincere—but a dame—and she reacts to all situations as a woman scorned, not as a representative of the people. She is under the influence of the coterie of left-wing writers and reporters who dominate Washington and they praise her so assiduously she believes it.

SOURCE: Jack Lait and Lee Mortimer, *U.S.A. Confidential* (New York: Crown Publishers, Inc., 1952), pp. 53, 87.

1. Followers of Russian Communist leader Leon Trotsky, who opposed Josef Stalin after the death of Soviet leader Vladimir Lenin and was later exiled and assassinated.
2. Marshall Josip Broz Tito was the Communist leader of Yugoslavia after World War II.

Maggie is pals with Esther Brunauer[3] and made a trip to Europe with her, fare paid by the State Department. Mrs. Brunauer is now under suspension from the department as a security risk. Her husband was suspended by the Navy on the same grounds. Maggie traveled with her after the original charges were presented to the Tydings whitewash committee.

SOURCE 6:   *McCarthy Investigates Overseas Libraries (1953)*

As the chairman of a Senate Government Operations Subcommittee on Investigations, Joseph McCarthy accused the State Department's Information Program of stocking its overseas libraries with books written by Communist authors. After State Department official Theodore Kaghan criticized McCarthy's probe, he was called before his committee and later fired. How does McCarthy attack Kaghan in this excerpt from the hearings?

THE CHAIRMAN. So that we have this picture completely clear, I assume it is agreed that the public affairs officer, a man in your position, should have available the works of Communists, so that you can tell what they are doing, what they are thinking, and can have enough knowledge so that you can fight communism. And we are speaking about these books on the shelves. We are speaking about books not on the shelves of some private library for the public affairs officers, but books for the general public of Germany. Is that right?

MR. KAGHAN. That is right.

THE CHAIRMAN. So these Communists books are not books merely for your benefit or something for men allegedly fighting communism. They were available for the German people in our libraries with our approval.

MR. KAGHAN. Yes, they were.

THE CHAIRMAN. And you say you have taken the works of how many authors off the shelves?

MR. KAGHAN. When I left there were 4 or 5 authors off. They may be more now. Possibly half a dozen before I left. When I directed someone to take them off, that order would go to the man in charge of the American Houses, who was in charge of the libraries, and he would remove the books. . . .

---

3. Esther Brunauer was a State Department official who lost her job for her alleged Communist affiliations. McCarthy charged that she and Smith had traveled together to a United Nations conference in Italy, shared a hotel room, and discussed Brunauer's Communist sympathies. In fact, Smith met Brunauer only briefly at the conference and barely knew her.

SOURCE: United States Senate, 83rd Congress, 1st sess., Permanent Subcommittee on Investigations of the Committee on Government Operations, *Hearings*, pp. 190, 199–200.

THE CHAIRMAN. Let me ask you: Did you write a play, Beyond Exile?

MR. KAGHAN. The name is familiar; yes.

THE CHAIRMAN. Does this play consist largely of a series of conversations between a father and son?

MR. KAGHAN. Sir, I don't remember what that play was about.

THE CHAIRMAN. Well, I will refresh your recollection, then, if I may. Here is one of the speeches made by the son to the father. And this consists largely of a running argument, the father trying to convince the son he should not be a Communist, the son trying to convince the father that he should be a Communist. Let us take the finale of this play. The son says:

> Well, that's a fine how-do-you-do. It isn't enough that my father has to be a capitalist, but he's got to come out openly and betray his employees, just like all the other dirty capitalists. Do I have to come here and tell my own father that he is a slavedriver, an exploiter of labor, an enemy to civilization?

And the father, finally, in the close, has this to say. He says:

> Peter, Peter, for God's sake listen to me, Peter. You were right, do you hear, you were right! I have been all wrong, Peter.

Would you say that that would make good anti-Communist propaganda?

MR. KAGHAN. No, sir. It sounds pretty corny, now.

THE CHAIRMAN. Is it merely corny? Is not that the Communist Party line right down to the last period?

MR. KAGHAN. One of those statements would be the Communist Party line, yes. One of the characters that said that, apparently—

THE CHAIRMAN. What part of this would not be the Communist line? The son arguing with the father that he should be a Communist, pointing out that the father is a dirty capitalist, an exploiter of labor, and the father ending by saying: "You were right, do you hear, you were right! I have been all wrong, Peter."

Is that not Communist propaganda?

MR. KAGHAN. That would be Communist propaganda if that is what the whole play ends up with and is about. I don't recall what the play is about.

THE CHAIRMAN. Would you like to review that play and give me your view of it?

MR. KAGHAN. If you wish; yes, sir.

THE CHAIRMAN. Yes; I would like to have you do it.

I think this is what we will let you do. We will be going over your plays. Just so there will be no claim that we have taken the material out of context, I believe you should review these plays of yours and come back here tomorrow morning, and tell us which ones you consider are Communist-line plays and which ones are not; whether you think we have been unfair to you in reading the excerpts that we have.

Now let me ask you this question. If you today felt the same as you felt in 1939, would you think that you were a proper man to head this information program?

MR. KAGHAN. No, sir. . . .

QUESTIONS TO CONSIDER

1. What do the essay and primary sources in this chapter reveal about the factors that led to the rise of a red scare in the late 1940s and early 1950s? What do they reveal about its impact?

2. What was Joseph McCarthy's role in this red scare? Why did he have the impact that he did? Is "McCarthyism" an accurate label for this episode?

3. What does this chapter reveal about McCarthy's motives and methods? What does it reveal about the sources of his appeal?

4. How would you explain why Margaret Chase Smith was the lone Republican to speak out on the Senate floor against McCarthy in 1950? What did her background and political situation have to do with it? What do Chase and McCarthy reveal about the role of gender in the second red scare?

5. What was Margaret Chase Smith's criticism of McCarthy? Was it valid? Did it go far enough? Why was it not effective in 1950? What changed by 1954 to make his censure possible?

FOR FURTHER READING

Richard M. Fried, *Nightmare in Red: The McCarthy Era in Perspective* (New York: Oxford University Press, 1990), provides a useful overview of the anticommunist crusade after World War II.

Elaine Tyler May, *Homeward Bound: American Families in the Cold War Era* (New York: Basic Books, 1988), explores the Cold War's impact on family life and the role of women.

David M. Oshinsky, *A Conspiracy So Immense: The World of Joe McCarthy* (New York: The Free Press, 1983), offers a detailed and engaging account of McCarthy's rise, methods, and downfall.

Janann Sherman, *No Place for a Woman: A Life of Senator Margaret Chase Smith* (New Brunswick, New Jersey: Rutgers University Press, 2000), is one of several recent biographies of the Maine senator.

Stephen J. Whitfield, *The Culture of the Cold War* (Baltimore: Johns Hopkins University Press, 1996), provides a useful and often entertaining overview of anticommunism's impact on popular culture after World War II.

From Black Protest to Black Power: Roy Wilkins and Fannie Lou Hamer

The very thought of Fannie Lou Hamer made Roy Wilkins furious. As executive secretary of the National Association for the Advancement of Colored People (NAACP), Wilkins led the largest civil rights organization in the United States. He possessed power and influence and even had the ear of President Lyndon Johnson. In August 1964, Wilkins had come to the Democratic National Convention in Atlantic City to celebrate Johnson's nomination as the Democrats' candidate for president. The NAACP leader believed that nothing should tarnish the event—or diminish the president's chances in the fall election. He certainly was not going to let an uneducated daughter of a Mississippi sharecropper bring down the president of the United States.

That, Wilkins feared, was exactly what Hamer and others in the Mississippi Freedom Democratic Party (MFDP) might end up doing. Along with other southern civil rights activists, Hamer had organized the MFDP only months earlier. They hoped to seat its delegates at the Atlantic City convention as a protest against the exclusion of blacks from primary elections by Mississippi's regular Democratic Party. Like the other MFDP delegates in Atlantic City, Hamer had grown tired of the conditions that African Americans faced in Mississippi. She had been denied the right to vote because of the color of her skin and been beaten for her involvement in civil rights organizing. Now she believed that the Democratic convention should acknowledge that Mississippi's Democratic Party delegates represented only the state's white voters. Wilkins, however, was convinced that such a move would drive southern delegates right out of the convention and into the arms of the Republicans. That would be a stunning setback for the civil rights movement and the position of blacks in American society.

Wilkins was no stranger to racial discrimination, and while working for the NAACP, he had fought numerous civil rights battles. He was well aware of the conditions in Mississippi. During a demonstration in Jackson in 1963, Wilkins had been arrested along with NAACP field secretary Medgar Evers. Less than two weeks later, Evers had been gunned down outside his home. Still, Wilkins was distrustful of the direct-action techniques of some of the younger civil rights activists. He put his faith in legal and political action as the best way to achieve gains for African Americans. That approach, he realized, often involved compromise.

Roy Wilkins   Fannie Lou Hamer

Hamer and the other MFDP delegates saw things differently. They had challenged the South's racial caste system and suffered greatly for it. As one MFDP delegate put it, "We have been treated like beasts in Mississippi. They shot us down like animals." Thus, when Lyndon Johnson offered the MFDP delegation only two seats at the convention as a compromise, Hamer was incensed. "We didn't come all this way for no two seats," she announced. It was not the response Wilkins wanted to hear. "You don't know anything, you're ignorant, you don't know anything about politics," he said as he confronted Hamer on the convention floor. "You people have put your point across, now why don't you pack up and go home?" Hamer and the other MFDP delegates, though, were not going anywhere.

"Never . . . Turn Your Back on a Crumb"

Roy Wilkins was not about to apologize to the MFDP delegates for the power he wielded by 1964. Nor would he listen for long to lectures about Mississippi's virulent racism. In fact, he had only to look to his own father to see its crippling effects. Born in St. Louis, Missouri, in 1901, Wilkins was the son of a college-educated porter who had fled Mississippi after hitting a white man who had called him a "nigger." Fearful that he would be lynched, William Wilkins and his wife, Mayfield, had taken the train north to St. Louis that very night. William soon found work at a brick kiln, and the couple moved into a flat in a black neighborhood, where Roy was born a year later. St. Louis was not Mississippi, but Jim Crow* was enforced in the city's schools, restaurants, and theaters. When he was old enough, Roy began his education at a segregated school. By then, William and Mayfield had had two more children, a boy and a girl, but they had found little happiness. William was soured by his dirty, low-paying job, and Mayfield soon died of tuberculosis. Realizing that William could not raise his three children alone, Roy's aunt and uncle took six-year-old Roy and his younger brother and sister to live with them in St. Paul, Minnesota.

In the home of Sam and Elizabeth Williams, Roy found a very different environment from the one he had known in St. Louis. Sam was the chief steward on the Great Northern Pacific Railroad president's private car. The Williamses owned a home in an integrated neighborhood, and they shared the middle-class outlook of their Scandinavian and German immigrant neighbors. They also instilled in the Wilkins children the value of thrift and hard work. From Sam, Roy learned "that the world was not the universally hostile place my own father had taken it to be." At the same time, Sam Williams had no illusions about the position of blacks in American society. Like many other members of the small but growing black middle class, he joined the NAACP, which W.E.B. Du Bois and a number of white progressives founded in 1909 to fight racial discrimination. Du Bois's magazine, the *Crisis,* came into the Williams home every month. In it, Du Bois called on an educated black elite—the "talented tenth"— to take the lead in improving the status of African Americans. Not surprisingly, Sam Williams drilled into the Wilkins children the importance of education. "You should go to school," he told Roy, "and be the best."

Wilkins's grammar school and high school in St. Paul were integrated, and he got along easily with white classmates. Originally intent on becoming an engineer, he fell in love with books in high school. He was editor of the school's literary magazine, president of the literary society, and editor of the yearbook. After graduating in 1919, he headed to the nearby University of Minnesota still relatively innocent about race. His innocence was shattered the next year when sixteen black roustabouts attached to a traveling circus were accused of raping a young white woman in Duluth. The day after they were arrested, a mob of five thousand whites descended on the jail, smashed through a thick brick wall with a battering ram, seized three of the suspects, and lynched them on nearby light poles as they pleaded for their lives. No evidence linked any of the roustabouts to the rape. The cases against eleven of them were dismissed, and one was found innocent. The remaining man, found guilty and sentenced to thirty years in prison, was freed after several years of legal work by the NAACP. For the first time in his life, Wilkins found himself thinking of black people "as a very vulnerable *us*—and white people as an unpredictable *them.*" A little later, he joined Du Bois's organization.

At about the same time, Wilkins decided on a career in journalism. He worked on the college paper as its first black reporter and later became editor of a local black weekly, where he denounced black separatist Marcus Garvey's Universal Negro Improvement Association and even Du Bois's growing interest in

Jim Crow: The South's rigid system of legal racial segregation of public facilities. Extending from railroad cars to drinking fountains, Jim Crow had been established in the late nineteenth century and upheld by the Supreme Court in *Plessy* v. *Ferguson* in 1896.

pan-Africanism.* Du Bois, he observed, should "use his time and talents" fighting the "evils" of lynching, disfranchisement, and segregation rather than waste them on promoting the unity of American blacks and Africans. Wilkins had already developed a deep hostility not only toward segregation but also toward self-segregation. Thinking back to his old St. Paul neighborhood, he later said, "For me, integration is not an abstraction."

Segregation still was, but after his graduation in 1923, that quickly changed. Taking a job as managing editor of the *Kansas City Call*, another black weekly, Wilkins got his first full introduction to Jim Crow. Kansas City was, as he later put it, "a Jim Crow town right down to its bootstraps." Neighborhoods, schools, hospitals, theaters, and even the stands in the Kansas City Blues baseball stadium were racially divided. For years, the city's major daily newspaper refused to run any pictures of African Americans. To attend a vaudeville show, Wilkins had to use an alley entrance and climb the stairs leading to the Jim Crow roost—the last row of seats in the highest gallery of the theater. He found such indignities "infuriating." For the next eight years in the pages of the *Call,* he denounced police brutality, neighborhood "improvement" associations that prevented blacks from moving into white areas, a school district that provided dilapidated schools for African-American students, and Jim Crow stores and restaurants.

When not agitating against Kansas City's color line, Wilkins wooed a social worker named Aminda "Minnie" Badeau. She had come to Kansas City in 1928 to work for the local chapter of the National Urban League. Influenced by the self-help philosophy of Booker T. Washington,* the Urban League was dominated by more prosperous middle-class blacks who wished to assist their fellow African-American city dwellers. Badeau was from an old St. Louis family, and like Sam and Elizabeth Williams, her parents owned a home in an integrated neighborhood. Wilkins found her not only beautiful but also well informed and intelligent. The two hit it off immediately and were married in 1929.

By then, Wilkins was more interested in fighting "Jim Crow's hard knocks" than in reporting about them. He also had grown weary of Kansas City's racial atmosphere. His opportunity to leave came in 1931, when the new executive secretary of the New York City–based NAACP asked Wilkins to be his assistant. Walter White had met Wilkins on a trip to Missouri and was impressed by the young editor's campaign against Jim Crow. Under White, Wilkins did "a little bit of everything": lectured, organized new branches, raised money for the organization's "Depression-dry" treasury, and even worked on the NAACP's legal cases. One of them, the 1931 Scottsboro case, involved nine young black men who were convicted of raping two white women on a train near Scottsboro, Alabama. Even though the evidence against them was questionable, eight of the men were sentenced to death, and the ninth was given a life sentence. The case gave Wilkins his first taste of white justice in the South.

*Pan-Africanism: Cultural or political unity or cooperation among African states or people of African descent.

*Booker T. Washington: A black leader who preached self-help, counseled blacks to temporarily accept second-class citizenship, and helped found the Tuskegee Institute, a vocational school for blacks, in the late nineteenth century.

Meanwhile, the NAACP's investigation of black workers employed by the U.S. Army Corps of Engineers provided Wilkins's first exposure to the economic oppression of southern blacks. In the early 1930s, Wilkins discovered that blacks employed on a levee construction in Mississippi were paid as little as ten cents an hour for a twelve-hour shift. As a result of the investigation, the Corps of Engineers raised black workers' pay by as much as a dime an hour. It was not much, but it doubled what some of the men were earning. The investigation also proved to Wilkins that pressure on the government could result in changes, even if small.

In the 1930s and 1940s, in the face of continued white vigilante action against blacks in the South, the NAACP fought unsuccessfully to get the Roosevelt administration to support antilynching legislation. During World War II, Wilkins pressed the administration without success to desegregate the armed services. Yet he remained convinced that working "from on high in the Congress and Supreme Court" would eventually bring an end to discrimination and Jim Crow. In 1954, the year before he was named NAACP executive secretary, the civil rights organization won a huge legal victory. In *Brown* v. *Board of Education*, the Supreme Court ruled that segregation in public schools was unconstitutional and that states must move to end it "with all deliberate speed." The case, initiated by the NAACP and argued before the Court by Thurgood Marshall, confirmed Wilkins's faith in working "from on high."

Many blacks, however, were becoming increasingly impatient with the slow progress of civil rights. As whites moved to block desegregation, the Eisenhower administration did little to stop them. At the same time, Congress seemed unwilling to move on civil rights. In 1957, for instance, it gutted a civil rights bill pushed by the NAACP by removing a provision that would have allowed the Justice Department to sue in school desegregation and other civil rights cases. In the face of such resistance, some blacks embraced a new tactic: direct action. In 1955, an NAACP secretary named Rosa Parks was arrested for refusing to give up her seat to a white passenger on a bus in Montgomery, Alabama. Her action sparked a nearly yearlong boycott of the city's segregated buses by black riders. Several years later, members of an NAACP youth council sat down at a number of Oklahoma City segregated lunch counters and demanded to be served. By 1960, college students in Greensboro, North Carolina, and other southern cities also were "sitting in."

Initially, Wilkins supported this kind of direct action. The Montgomery bus boycott's roots had been in black churches, and the boycott had been led by Martin Luther King Jr. and other black ministers, but the NAACP had provided legal assistance. Later, Wilkins directed local NAACP branches to support the sit-ins. All the while, Wilkins preferred to work quietly behind the scenes. Influence in the corridors of power was more important, he believed, than action in the streets. Thus legal battles had to be the NAACP's main focus. Inevitably, he knew, there would be many disappointing compromises. In 1957, for example, as Wilkins had deliberated whether to accept a watered-down version of the civil rights bill, Senator Hubert Humphrey of Minnesota had helped him make up his mind. "Roy," he had said, "if there's one thing I've learned in politics, it's never to turn your back on a crumb." Wilkins had supported the bill. Later, he said, "If I had spurned [the bill], we might have been waiting outside the bakery for a much longer time." In the 1960s, however, Wilkins realized that many blacks were no longer willing to accept mere "crumbs."

"Now We're Tired of Waitin'"

In 1960, Fannie Lou Hamer knew nothing about Roy Wilkins, the NAACP, or their patient legal work. She was, however, painfully aware of the conditions she faced in Sunflower County, Mississippi. Hamer was born in the hill country of central Mississippi in 1917, the youngest of Jim and Lou Ella Townsend's twenty children. When she was two, her parents moved to a plantation in Sunflower County about twenty-five miles from the Mississippi River. Like most of the other poor blacks in the Mississippi Delta, they picked cotton. Six-year-old Fannie Lou started working in the fields when a plantation owner asked her if she would like to pick cotton so she could buy treats. That week, she picked thirty pounds of cotton. Only later did she realize that she had been trapped. "I never did get out of his debt again," she recalled later. After sixth grade, she left school to work full-time in the fields. She walked between the rows of cotton with a limp, probably from a broken leg that had not been set properly when she was a baby. She would drag a cotton sack behind her for much of her life.

Even with the children's help, the Townsends never got ahead. As share-croppers, they owed the white landowner half of their crop, plus whatever provisions they had borrowed. The family lived in a wooden shack without heat, electricity, running water, or indoor plumbing. Like other black sharecroppers, they lacked the education to know when the owner had cheated them. As Fannie Lou grew up, Mississippi consistently spent less on educating blacks than any other state. In 1950, Sunflower County did not have one four-year black high school.

As bad as the family's circumstances were, the Townsends' lives differed little from those of other poor blacks in Mississippi. In this notorious stronghold of white supremacy, most blacks worked for low wages in the fields and homes of white people. Meanwhile, they were denied justice in the courts and the right to vote. If need be, they were kept in their place with violence. The year Fannie Lou was born, more than eighty blacks were lynched in Mississippi. Things had changed little by 1955, when the badly beaten body of Emmett Till, an African-American teenager from Chicago who was visiting relatives in Mississippi, was found in the Tallahatchie River. Till had supposedly made a pass at a white woman, and the two men who had abducted him were acquitted.

In 1944, Fannie Lou married a sharecropper named Perry Hamer. The couple moved to a plantation in Ruleville, where they lived in a small house with running water and a broken toilet. Fannie Lou considered the house "decent," until one day, when she was cleaning the boss's house, she saw that the family dog had its own bathroom. "I just couldn't get over that dog having a bathroom," she recalled, "when [the owner] wouldn't even have the toilet fixed for us." Despite their poverty, the Hamers took in two girls to raise as their own.

Fannie Lou Hamer's deep religious faith helped her endure the poverty and racial hatred all around her, as well as the trauma resulting from what she called "a knot on my stomach." Hamer entered a hospital in 1961 for an operation to remove a uterine tumor and discovered later that doctors also had performed a hysterectomy without her permission. When she asked for an explanation, the doctor "didn't have to say nothing—and he didn't." A decade later, the sterilization of poor black women in the South would be taken up in the courts, but in the early 1960s, legal action was unthinkable. "I would have been taking my hands and screwing tacks in my own casket," Hamer said. The experience left her feeling helpless, angry, and bitter.

When civil rights organizers associated with the Student Nonviolent Coordinating Committee (SNCC, pronounced "snick") arrived in Sunflower County the next year, Hamer was ready to join their crusade. SNCC had been founded in 1960 by students involved in the early sit-ins in North Carolina and elsewhere in the South. They rejected the policies of Martin Luther King Jr. and other black ministers who had formed the Southern Christian Leadership Conference (SCLC) in 1957 after the Montgomery bus boycott. Instead, SNCC's young activists encouraged local black people to act on their own. By 1962, much of SNCC's grass-roots organizing was devoted to a voter registration drive in Mississippi. The Voter Education Project brought together representatives from a reluctant NAACP and the Congress of Racial Equality (CORE), which had earlier launched the Freedom Rides to desegregate the South's interstate bus system. It also brought civil rights organizers into a state previously overlooked by the NAACP and other civil rights organizations.

One of the Voter Education Project's targets was Sunflower County, which had a reputation as one of the most antiblack counties in the state. In 1962, virtually all of the county's roughly fifteen thousand voting-age blacks were excluded from the voting booth, and whites there were not about to let them in. When civil rights workers showed up in the delta, the mayor of Ruleville declared that anyone attending a voter registration school "would be given a one-way ticket out of town." If that did not stop potential voters, local authorities "would use whatever [means] they had available." Such threats did not faze the SNCC organizers. SNCC leader James Forman told blacks that they could vote people out of office and get rid of bad police officers if they would only register to vote. As Hamer listened to Forman speak at a meeting in the Williams Chapel Baptist Church in Ruleville, she remembered that one of Ruleville's cops was the brother of a man suspected of killing Emmett Till seven years before. When the SNCC representatives asked who would be willing to register to vote, she raised her hand.

Four days later, Hamer was on a rented bus with seventeen other people headed to the county courthouse. When they arrived, they were greeted by a crowd of gun-toting whites. Inside, Hamer was required to take a literacy test based on the Mississippi Constitution. She flunked. "I knowed as much about [it] as a horse knows about Christmas Day," she said later. When she returned home, the owner of the plantation where she worked told her to take her name off the registration forms if she wanted to stay there. "I didn't go down there to register for you," she replied. "I went down to register for myself." Evicted from the plantation, Hamer packed her bags and headed to town with her two girls, leaving her husband behind. She stayed with friends for several days, then, fearful that she might be killed, moved in with relatives in Tallahatchie County.

By the time she returned to Ruleville later that fall, a black municipal employee had been fired because his wife had attended voter registration classes, the Williams Chapel Baptist Church had lost its tax-exempt status, two black-owned laundries had been shut down, shots had been fired into the house where

Hamer had stayed before leaving town, and her husband had been evicted from the plantation. Hamer had already heard about the sit-ins elsewhere in the South, and she knew that black and white Freedom Riders had been met with fire-bombs and mob violence. She was ready to join SNCC. Voter Education Project director Robert Moses was impressed by Hamer's personal sacrifice and realized that she was exactly the kind of person who could help carry on SNCC's campaign long after its student volunteers had left the community.

Living on a ten-dollar monthly stipend, Hamer served as a SNCC field secretary, worked on voter registration, and taught citizenship classes. After spending long hours studying the Mississippi Constitution, she finally passed the literacy test. Meanwhile, the harassment of Hamer and other civil rights workers continued. After attending a civil rights workshop in 1963, she and six other participants were arrested in Winona, Mississippi, for going into the "whites only" section of a bus terminal. Thrown into jail for four days, Hamer was brutally beaten by two black prisoners who were threatened by the white guards. Bruised and swollen, she left the jail with a permanent loss of feeling in her arms and an even greater desire to fight the oppression of African Americans.

Increasing numbers of African Americans now shared her determination. By 1963, a growing civil rights movement was sweeping the South. Earlier, the Kennedy administration had intervened with force to protect black protesters from violence. About the same time Hamer was released from jail, President John Kennedy called on Congress to pass a sweeping civil rights bill that would end segregation in public accommodations and discrimination in employment. Two months later, Martin Luther King Jr. delivered his famous "I Have a Dream" speech during the March on Washington. These events led to a growing awareness of the civil rights movement, but conditions in Mississippi remained unchanged. By the end of 1963, SNCC's voter education campaign had little to show for its efforts. Given the state's brutal record, Roy Wilkins and many other civil rights leaders believed that SNCC's focus on Mississippi was folly. In 1964, however, Hamer and SNCC would turn the spotlight on the state.

First, Robert Moses and other SNCC members launched Mississippi Freedom Summer, which called for recruiting a thousand white college students to work on voter registration in the state. Violence directed against affluent white civil rights workers, they reasoned, would capture the attention of a nation that had generally ignored atrocities committed against blacks. Despite a death threat against her, Hamer served as a Freedom Summer organizer, and in the end, the program had exactly the effect that SNCC organizers had anticipated: The press began to pay more attention to conditions in Mississippi, especially after the murders of three civil rights workers, two of whom were white.

Meanwhile, Hamer and other SNCC activists had already made plans to get the nation's attention in another way. Earlier in 1964, they had formed the Mississippi Freedom Democratic Party (MFDP) to challenge the state's white Democratic Party. Hamer was among its first political candidates. Running for Congress against an incumbent, she was determined to demonstrate that blacks could participate in politics. "We've been waiting all our lives, and still gettin' killed, still gettin' hung, still gettin' beat to death," she told a reporter in June. "Now we're tired of waitin'." Although she and the other MFDP candidates were trounced in the Democratic primary, she and other party organizers had already set their sights on another goal: unseating the segregationist Democratic Party delegates at the party's national convention later that summer in Atlantic City. Doing so would force the nation to acknowledge the horrible conditions in Mississippi.

" 'Cause They're Not Leading Us"

When Roy Wilkins arrived in Atlantic City in late August 1964, he knew that the election of Lyndon Johnson later that fall represented the best hope for achieving progress in civil rights. Despite being a Texan with a long segregationist voting record, Johnson had quickly taken up the cause of civil rights after the assassination of President Kennedy in late 1963. LBJ, who had succeeded Kennedy, had called on Congress to pass the sweeping civil rights act proposed by the late president. While Wilkins had lobbied on Capitol Hill, Johnson had cajoled and threatened enough reluctant members of Congress into passing the Civil Rights Act of 1964 just weeks before the Democratic National Convention. Calling for an end to discrimination in employment and public accommodations, the act was a huge blow to Jim Crow. An elated Wilkins called it the "Magna Carta for the race."

Meanwhile, the Republicans had already nominated Barry Goldwater as their presidential candidate. An outspoken conservative, Goldwater opposed the Civil Rights Act. He was also in favor of states' rights, the very position that white southerners battling desegregation had embraced to prevent federal action on civil rights. For the first time since the end of Reconstruction, a Republican presidential candidate threatened to steal the Democratic Party's base in the South. By appealing to pro-segregation voters, he might even win the election. In 1964, the NAACP broke a long tradition of nonpartisanship by opposing Goldwater. For Wilkins, the decision to endorse LBJ was easy. Deciding what to do about the MFDP's challenge to Mississippi's regular Democrats was much more difficult. The regular Mississippi Democratic delegation represented everything that his organization opposed. The state's blacks had no hand in choosing any of its delegates, and it was led by a governor who described the NAACP as "niggers, alligators, apes, coons, and possums." At the same time, a floor fight over the seating of MFDP delegates at the convention would embarrass the party and LBJ. It would also drive southern Democrats right into Goldwater's arms. Yet an outright rejection of the MFDP was politically risky. Race riots had recently erupted in several cities, and demonstrators from nearby Philadelphia and New York, angry over the treatment of the MFDP at the convention, could embarrass Johnson and fuel a white backlash against civil rights.

Wilkins was in a difficult spot. How could he reconcile the MFDP's moral high ground with the practical necessities of politics? The situation called for a moderate course, one that would appease both sides. Wilkins would offer his support to the MFDP before the Democratic National Committee's Credentials Committee, which certified the legitimacy of the convention's delegates. At the same time, he would work for a compromise with the MFDP over the seating of their sixty-eight delegates. He hoped that would keep peace on the convention floor and in the streets.

Wilkins's calculations did not account for the influence of Fannie Lou Hamer. Also called to testify before the Credentials Committee, Hamer was the star witness. Sitting at a table in front of more than a hundred committee members, reporters, and television cameras that carried her message nationwide, Hamer told an electrifying tale of beatings and oppression. **[See Source 1.]** Johnson's forces finally offered the MFDP two at-large seats* and the rest of the biracial delegation the status of nonvoting "honorary guests." Wilkins and Martin Luther King Jr. told the delegates to accept the offer, but Hamer was unyielding. Some of the delegates agreed with Wilkins and King, arguing that they should take the offer and claim a "moral victory." In response to those calling for compromise, Hamer retorted, "What do you mean, moral victory? We ain't got nothin'." One of the two delegates who had been offered an at-large seat suggested that the delegates listen to leaders who knew more about politics than Hamer. "Tell me what leaders you talking about," she demanded. ". . . But now don't go telling me about somebody that ain't been in Mississippi for two weeks . . .'cause they're not leading us."

Hamer "carried the delegation," and the MFDP delegates voted to reject the compromise. As Wilkins had hoped, the white Mississippi delegation was officially seated, and the Democrats avoided a nasty fight on the convention floor. Yet that did not prevent most of the state's regular delegation from walking out of the convention anyway. Nor did it prevent LBJ from losing Mississippi and six other Deep South states in the November election—a development that marked the beginning of the end of the solidly Democratic South. The fight over the MFDP at the convention had other long-lasting consequences as well. By the time Hamer and some of the other MFDP delegates left Atlantic City, they were thoroughly disillusioned with the traditional black leaders who seemed so eager to accept compromises. Hamer referred to them as "tom* teachers and chicken-eating ministers." She was particularly disgusted with Wilkins and the NAACP. "There ain't nothing I respect less than the NAACP," she declared. After the Democratic convention, Hamer took a brief trip to West Africa that was sponsored by the black entertainer Harry Belafonte. In Africa, she saw blacks running their own businesses and even their own countries. When she returned to Mississippi, she began to talk less about civil rights and more about the need to build institutions at the local level to help blacks help themselves.

Hamer's new attitude paralleled that of many civil rights workers. SNCC members were especially disillusioned with the slow pace of economic and social change for blacks, and they were embittered by political compromises. Despite the passage of major civil rights legislation, most African Americans continued to live in poverty and suffer from discrimination. Rejecting appeals to the goodwill of whites as the best way to gain civil rights, they began to call for black control of their own institutions. In 1966, a disillusioned MFDP member and SNCC activist named Stokely Carmichael gave this new approach a name. "We been saying freedom for six years and we ain't got nothin'," he declared. "What we gonna start saying now is 'Black Power!'"

*At-large seats: Seats not connected to a particular state, district, or delegation. By offering at-large seats, Johnson refused to acknowledge the MFDP's claims that its delegates were legitimate representatives of the state party.

*Tom: A reference to a patient and humble slave named Tom, the main character in Harriet Beecher Stowe's antislavery novel *Uncle Tom's Cabin* (1852).

"Black Power" meant different things to different people. For many blacks, it clearly involved the rejection of Lyndon Johnson, the liberal white allies of the civil rights movement, and traditional civil rights leaders such as Roy Wilkins and Martin Luther King Jr. Both Hamer and Carmichael accused Wilkins of selling out blacks. For a growing number of increasingly militant blacks, however, Black Power involved a rejection of nonviolence. That idea had special appeal in northern ghettos, where many residents also began to demand community control of neighborhoods and businesses in the late 1960s. The growing frustration with peaceful protests and police brutality helps explain the appeal of organizations such as as the Black Panthers. Founded in Oakland, California, in 1966 by two college-educated activists named Huey Newton and Bobby Seale, the Black Panthers symbolized growing black militance in the minds of many whites. Conspicuously displaying their weapons, Seale and Newton spoke frequently about the need for armed revolt.

Though no Black Panther, Fannie Lou Hamer had been converted to the cause of Black Power even before Carmichael had coined the term. After the 1964 Democratic National Convention, she was thoroughly disillusioned with the white-dominated power structure. In 1966, she began to express support for Carmichael and speak at rallies that promoted black separatism. She was never able to go as far as Robert Moses, however, who declared that he would not have anything to do with white people again. Nor did she agree with SNCC when it decided in 1968 to kick whites out of the organization. Although she agreed with Black Power advocates about the need for black self-determination, she did not believe that separating themselves from whites was the best way for blacks to achieve a larger voice in government. African-American communities needed to control their own educational, economic, and political institutions. Appealing to whites in positions of power to help blacks did not work. **[See Source 2.]**

For Hamer, Black Power was a practical guide for action in her own community. As the civil rights movement fragmented in the face of growing black militance, Hamer was promoting alternative institutions that would further black economic self-reliance. By 1965, she was devoting much of her energy to the Mississippi Freedom Labor Union (MFLU). A union of domestic workers, truck drivers, and laborers, the MFLU promoted black ownership of homes, businesses, and land before falling victim to internal squabbling and shaky finances in 1966. Several years later, she helped found the Freedom Farm Cooperative to provide poor blacks and whites in Sunflower County with food and homes. The cooperative lasted for only five years, but during that time, it purchased nearly seven hundred acres and built seventy low-cost homes.

As Hamer's focus narrowed on helping what she called the "everyday" people of her county, her political concerns broadened. While Roy Wilkins and many other civil rights leaders continued to defend LBJ's policies in the Vietnam War, she criticized the war, in which blacks were fighting and dying in numbers disproportionate to those for whites. She also began to address the plight of black women. In 1971, she joined National Organization for Women founder Betty Friedan and feminist Gloria Steinem in establishing the National Women's Political Caucus. (See Chapter 13.) All the while, she continued to work on voter registration, building the MFDP, and getting blacks elected to office. Despite her harsh words for the NAACP, in 1968 she joined with it and other liberal, pro-integration groups to challenge the regular Mississippi Democrats once again. This time, the insurgents were successful. When Hamer addressed the Democratic National Convention in 1968, she was greeted with a standing ovation. She also continued to speak around the country on her understanding of Black Power. "I am not fighting for an all black world," she told a Seattle audience in 1969, "just like I am not going to tolerate an all white world." Two years later, she ran for a seat in the Mississippi state senate on a platform that reflected her broadened concerns. [**See Source 3.**] Although she lost the election, Hamer lived long enough to see more black elected officials in Mississippi than in any other state in the South and nearly 60 percent of eligible blacks registered to vote. She died in 1977.

" 'Black Power' . . . Mean[s] . . . Black Death"

If the 1964 Democratic convention was a turning point for Fannie Lou Hamer, it was a preview of difficult times ahead for Roy Wilkins. To be sure, his loyalty to LBJ was vindicated again in 1965, when the president signed the Voting Rights Act, which provided new guarantees and protections for black voters. Only days later, however, Wilkins watched helplessly as the Watts section of Los Angeles erupted in a race riot that lasted for six days and claimed thirty-four lives. The race riots in Watts and other cities in the late 1960s were an indication that desegregating the South was not the only civil rights battle. Millions of blacks still faced inadequate housing, low incomes, and poor job opportunities— problems unlikely to be solved by getting rid of Jim Crow and opening up the voting booth. "Suddenly," Wilkins said, "we found ourselves in the middle of a two-front war."

Wilkins would confront the war on this second "front" for the rest of his career. Unfortunately, he was not adequately prepared to fight it. As race riots and Martin Luther King Jr.'s assassination in 1968 brought an end to the civil rights era, the NAACP's program seemed to offer little hope to poor blacks. Caught off guard, Wilkins confessed that "no one was really prepared with a strategy or workable program" for dealing with the dire economic and social conditions among the nation's blacks. [**See Source 4.**] Nor was he prepared for the challenge to his leadership posed by many young blacks impatient with the slow progress of achieving equality. By 1966, Wilkins's main battle was not with white segregationists but with blacks who were increasingly alienated from the NAACP. Attacked as an "Uncle Tom," Wilkins was convinced that "Black Power" was an empty, dangerous slogan that would provoke a white backlash against civil rights. The "rhetorical excesses of the black power people," he charged, had made it easier for Congress to kill additional civil rights legislation. "'Black power,'" he said in an address at the NAACP's annual convention in 1966, "can mean in the end only black death." [**See Source 5.**]

After the speech, Wilkins was a marked man. In 1967, members of a small group called the Revolutionary Action Movement were arrested for plotting to assassinate him. The following year, a faction of younger NAACP members revolted against his leadership, charging that he was out of touch with the concerns of most African Americans. When they called for the organization to come out against the Vietnam War, Wilkins countered that "mingling" the civil rights and antiwar movements would only weaken the cause. Although he faced numerous challenges, in the end he won the battle and held on to his position for another decade. Until he stepped down in 1979, he continued to wage his "two-front war." One front was against growing white opposition to desegregation; the other was against Black Power advocates who promoted what he called "reverse Jim Crow." **[See Source 6.]** He never lost faith in the NAACP's goal of integration and legal equality for blacks, and after his retirement he noted with pride, "The NAACP is still with us." The same could not be said of some of the other civil rights organizations. Nor did Wilkins ever lose faith in the American legal system. "We have believed in our Constitution," he wrote in his autobiography, completed just before his death in 1981. "We have believed that the Declaration of Independence meant what it said."

PRIMARY SOURCES

SOURCE 1: *Testimony of Fannie Lou Hamer Before the Credentials Committee of the Democratic National Convention* (1964)

As part of the Mississippi Freedom Democratic Party's effort to get recognition at the Democratic National Convention in 1964, Fannie Lou Hamer offered the Credentials Committee moving testimony based on her experience in Mississippi. As LBJ watched Hamer on television, according to one witness, he "went right up the wall." Then he hastily called a news conference that preempted the live broadcast of her testimony. What does Hamer's testimony reveal about conditions in Mississippi? About the reasons for her influence in the MFDP?

Mr. Chairman, and the Credentials Committee, my name is Mrs. Fannie Lou Hamer, and I live at 626 East Lafayette Street, Ruleville, Mississippi, Sunflower County, the home of Senator James O. Eastland, and Senator Stennis.

It was the 31st of August in 1962 that 18 of us traveled 26 miles to the county courthouse in Indianola to try to register to try to became first-class citizens. We was met in Indianola by Mississippi men, Highway Patrolmen and they allowed two of us in to take the literacy test at the time. After we had taken the test and started back to Ruleville, we was held up by the City Police and the State Highway Patrolmen and carried back to Indianola where the bus driver was charged that day with driving a bus the wrong color.

After we paid the fine among us, we continued on to Ruleville, and Reverend Jeff Sunny carried me the four miles in the rural area where I had worked as a time-keeper and sharecropper for 18 years. I was met there by my children,

SOURCE: Reprinted in Peter B. Levy, ed., *Documentary History of the Modern Civil Rights Movement* (New York: Greenwood Press, 1992), pp. 139–141.

who told me the plantation owner was angry because I had gone down to try to register.

After they told me, my husband came, and said the plantation owner was raising cain because I had tried to register and before he quit talking the plantation owner came, and said, "Fannie Lou, do you know—did Pap* tell you what I said?" And I said, "Yes, sir." He said, "I mean that. . . . If you don't go down and withdraw . . . well—you might have to go because we are not ready for that." . . .

And I addressed him and told him and said, "I didn't try to register for you. I tried to register for myself."

I had to leave that same night.

On the 10th of September, 1962, 16 bullets was fired into the home of Mr. and Mrs. Robert Tucker for me. That same night two girls were shot in Ruleville, Mississippi. Also Mr. Joe McDonald's house was shot in.

And in June, the 9th, 1963, I had attended a voter registration workshop, was returning back to Mississippi. Ten of us was traveling by the Continental Trailways bus. When we got to Winona, Mississippi, which is Montgomery County, four of the people got off to use the washroom. . . . I stepped off the bus to see what was happening and somebody screamed from the car that four workers was in and said, "Get that one there," and when I went to get in the car, when the man told me I was under arrest, he kicked me.

I was carried to the county jail and put in the holding room. They left some of the people in the booking room and began to place us in cells. I was placed in a cell with a young woman called Miss Euvester Simpson. After I was placed in the cell I began to hear sounds of licks and screams. I could hear the sounds of licks and horrible screams, and I could hear somebody say, "Can you say, yes, sir, nigger?" "Can you say yes, sir?"

And they would say horrible names. She would say, "Yes, I can say yes, sir." . . . They beat her, I don't know how long, and after a while she began to pray and asked God to have Mercy on those people. And it wasn't too long before three white men came to my cell. One of these men was a State Highway Patrolm[a]n and he asked me where I was from, and I told him Ruleville; he said, "We are going to check this."

And they left my cell and it wasn't too long before they came back. He said, "You are from Ruleville all right," and he used a curse word, he said, "We are going to beat you until you wish you was dead."

I was carried out of that cell into another cell where they had two Negro prisoners. The State Highway patrolmen ordered the first Negro to take the blackjack. The first Negro prisoner ordered me, by orders from the State Highway Patrolmen, for me to lay down on a bunk bed on my face, and I laid on my face.

The first Negro began to beat, and I was beat by the first Negro until he was exhausted, and I was holding my hands behind at this time on my left side because I suffered polio when I was six years old. After the first Negro had beat until he was exhausted the state Highway Patrolman ordered the second Negro to take the blackjack. The second Negro began to beat and I began to work my feet, and the State Highway Patrolmen ordered the first Negro who had beat to

---

*Pap: Hamer's husband, Perry.

set on my feet to keep me from working my feet. I began to scream and one white man got up and began to beat me in my head and tell me to hush.

One white man—my dress had worked up high, he walked over and pulled my dress down and he pulled my dress back, back up. . . .

All of this on account we want to register, to become first-class citizens, and if the freedom Democratic Party is not seated now, I question America, is this America, the land of the free and the home of the brave where we have to sleep with our telephones off the hooks because our lives be threatened daily because we want to live as decent human beings, in America?

Source 2:   *Fannie Lou Hamer on the Lessons of the Democratic National Convention*   (1967)

In her autobiography, Fannie Lou Hamer discusses what she learned from her experiences at the Democratic National Convention in 1964. How do her conclusions put her at odds with Roy Wilkins and the approach of the NAACP in achieving civil rights?

In 1964 we registered 63,000 black people from Mississippi into the Freedom Democratic Party. We formed our own party because the whites wouldn't even let us register. We decided to challenge the white Mississippi Democratic Party at the National Convention. We followed all the laws that the white people themselves made. We tried to attend the precinct meetings and they locked the doors on us or moved the meetings and that's against the laws they made for their ownselves. So we were the ones that held the real precinct meetings. At all these meetings across the state we elected our representatives to go to the National Democratic Convention in Atlantic City. But we learned the hard way that even though we had all the law and all the righteousness on our side—that white man is not going to give up his power to us.

We have to build our own power. We have to win every single political office we can, where we have a majority of black people. . . .

The question for black people is not, when is the white man going to give us our rights, or when is he going to give us good education for our children, or when is he going to give us jobs—if the white man gives you anything—just remember when he gets ready he will take it right back. We have to take for ourselves.

Source: Reprinted in Clayborne Carson et al., *The Eyes on the Prize Civil Rights Reader: Documents, Speeches, and Firsthand Accounts from the Black Freedom Struggle, 1954–1990* (New York: Viking Press, 1991), pp. 178–179; originally from *To Praise Our Bridges: An Autobiography of Mrs. Fanny* [sic] *Lou Hamer* (Jackson, Miss.: KIPCO, 1967).

Source 3:   *Fannie Lou Hamer's Platform*   (1971)

In 1971, Fannie Lou Hamer ran as an Independent for the Mississippi senate on a plat-
form that reflected her economic and political goals. What does this platform reveal
about the differences between Hamer's and Roy Wilkins's concerns?

I, Mrs. Fannie Lou Hamer, representing ALL people of Sunflower County, am
running for state senate. If I am elected, I will do my uttermost to carry out my
duties as State Senator.

My platform consist[s] of the following:

Welfare

1) Welfare legislation is necessary to provide 100 per cent of need rather than
27% and to require that Black Workers are hired in policy making positions.

2) Legislation to change law which prohibits counties from recieving [sic] Federal Funds to set up housing for poor and elderly.

3) Erect legislation for State Medical Aid program for poor of all ages under
Federal law which provides for Medical program.

Voter Registration and Election Law

4) Mobile Voter Registration

5) Change law to permit registration after 6 months residence and to permit registration up to one month before election

6) Support MFDP court action to change election law:

    a) Independent[s] qualify one month before general election

    b) Voting in party primary shouldn't disqualify an Independent Candidate.

    c) Lower voting age to 18.

Source: "Fannie Lou Hamer's Platform" from the Fannie Lou Hamer Papers, Amistad Research
Center, Tulane University. Used by permission. Reprinted in Chana Kai Lee, *For Freedom's Sake:*
The Life of Fannie Lou Hamer (Urbana: University of Illinois Press, 1999), p. 169.

Source 4: *Poverty Rates, by Race and Family Relationship,* 1959–1999

Poverty rates for blacks, compared to those for whites, remained high in the late twentieth century. The graph below shows the percentage of each group living in poverty. What does it suggest about the success or failure of the NAACP's approach to improving the position of blacks in American society by achieving legal equality?

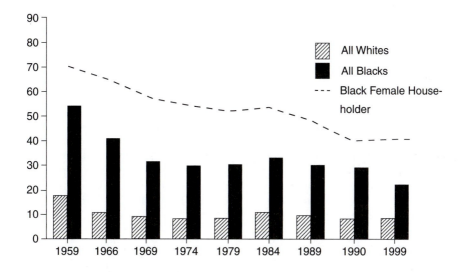

Source: 1959–1989 from Peter B. Levy, ed., *Documentary History of the Modern Civil Rights Movement* (New York: Greenwood Press, 1992), p. 249; 1990 and 1999 from *Historical Statistics of the United States; Statistical Abstract of the United States* (Washington, D.C.: Government Printing Office, 2000), p. 43.

Source 5: Roy Wilkins, *"Sail Our N.A.A.C.P. Ship 'Steady as She Goes'"* (1966)

In 1966, Roy Wilkins denounced "black power" in his keynote address to the NAACP's annual convention. In this excerpt, on what grounds does he judge it to be dangerous and misguided?

Source: From Keynote Address given by Roy Wilkins in 1966 at NAACP Convention. Reprinted in Sondra Kathryn Wilson, ed., *In Search of Democracy: The NAACP Writings of James Weldon Johnson, Walter White, and Roy Wilkins (1920–1977)* (New York: Oxford University Press, 1999), p. 424.

No matter how endlessly they try to explain it, the term "black power" means anti-white power. In a racially pluralistic society, the concept, the formation and the exercise of an ethnically-tagged power, means opposition to other ethnic powers, just as the term, "white supremacy" means subjection of all non-white people. In the black-white relationship, it has to mean that every other ethnic power is the rival and the antagonist of "black power." It has to mean "going-it-alone." It has to mean separatism.

Now separatism, whether on the rarefied debate level of "black power" or on the wishful level of a secessionist Freedom City in Watts, offers a disadvantaged minority little except the chance to shrivel and die.

The only possible dividend of "black power" is embodied in its offer to millions of frustrated and deprived and persecuted black people of a solace, . . . quite apart from its political and economic implications.

Ideologically it dictates "up with black and down with white." In precisely the same fashion that South Africa reverses that slogan.

It is a reverse Mississippi, a reverse Hitler, a reverse Ku Klux Klan.

If these were evil in our judgment, what virtue can be claimed for black over white? If, as some proponents claim, this concept instills pride of race, cannot this pride be taught without preaching hatred or supremacy based upon race?

Though it be clarified and clarified again, "black power" in the quick, uncritical and highly emotional adoption it has received from some segments of a beleaguered people can mean in the end only black death. Even if, through some miracle, it should be enthroned briefly in an isolated area, the human spirit, which knows no color or geography or time, would die a little, leaving for wiser and stronger and more compassionate men the painful beating back to the upward trail.

We of the N.A.A.C.P. will have none of this. We have fought it too long. It is the ranging of race against race on the irrelevant basis of skin color. It is the father of hatred and the mother of violence.

It is the wicked fanaticism which has swelled our tears, broken our bodies, squeezed our hearts and taken the blood of our black and white loved ones. It shall not now poison our forward march.

We seek, therefore, as we have sought these many years, the inclusion of Negro Americans in the nation's life, not their exclusion. This is our land, as much as it is any American's—every square foot of every city and town and village. The task of winning our share is not the easy one of disengagement and flight, but the hard one of work, of short as well as long jumps, of disappointments and of sweet successes.

SOURCE 6:   Roy Wilkins, *Standing Fast*   (1982)

Roy Wilkins continued to battle black separatism until the end of his tenure as head of the NAACP. In this excerpt from his autobiography, he decries what he sees as the harmful consequences of embracing black separatism. Does this source also hint at why Wilkins reacted to Fannie Lou Hamer and other grass-roots participants in the Mississippi Freedom Democratic Party as he did?

I had one last battle of my own with a new form of black power. This time the issue was separate dormitories, dining halls, and black-studies programs for Negro college students. The issue presented a terrible problem. I had been against black apartheid all of my life, and I welcomed activism on campus. I was completely in favor of the study of black history and culture, for racial pride, for reconstructing a history that had been left to die from ignorance or outright hostility. But I also thought the call for separateness, for isolation, for retreating from the rest of the campus was a sign of weakness, not strength. Just when white America thought it must at last give in and open the doors of opportunity and equality in education wider and wider, a small group of vociferous young Negroes—including, of all people, some Negro college students—began chanting, "Ve vant to be alone."

I saw the whole business as a shameful, self-inflicted form of reverse Jim Crow, and I fought it. Common sense dictated that if black college kids were going to have to go out and make it in white America, they had better learn what the white kids learned. The pretentiousness of some of those early black-studies programs was ridiculous. I'm no stuffed shirt, but I do believe that all Americans should be able to speak English properly. One day I was standing in a line and a young professor walked up and shook my hand. He said he was head of the black-studies department of a university not far away. "Mr. Wilkins," he said, "I want to ax you a question."

I couldn't believe my ears. I stopped him right there. "You're teaching our children black history and you don't even know how to pronounce a simple three-letter word?" I asked.

"That's just the way I talk," he told me, an edge coming into his voice.

"Well, you talk *wrong*," I snapped.

I still feel that way. It is not "axing" anyone too much to know how to pronounce "ask." What I said about reverse Jim Crow in those days probably cost me more than anything else I had said since my black-power–black-death speech in Los Angeles in 1966, but it had to be done. By all means let us have black studies, but as a strengthening supplement, as a means toward, not as a substitute for, understanding the world around us. I didn't want black children to become mesmerized by dashikis while the white kids were thinking about space suits.

SOURCE: Roy Wilkins and Tom Mathews, *Standing Fast: The Autobiography of Roy Wilkins* (New York: Viking Press, 1982), p. 335. Copyright © 1982 by Amanda Wilkins, executrix of the Estate of Roy Wilkins. Used by permission of Viking Penguin, a division of Penguin Putnam Inc., p. 424.

Questions to Consider

1. How would you compare Roy Wilkins's and Fannie Lou Hamer's approaches to achieving civil rights for blacks? In what ways did their methods and goals reflect their backgrounds and experiences?

2. By the middle of the 1960s, Hamer and other advocates of Black Power had denounced the moderation and compromises of Wilkins and the NAACP. Years later, however, Wilkins could declare that the NAACP "is still with us." What were the achievements and limitations of Hamer's and Wilkins's methods? Which leader do you think was more effective? Why?

3. If you had been a member of the Credentials Committee at the Democratic National Convention in 1964, what would your position have been regarding the seating of the Mississippi Freedom Democratic Party delegation at the convention? If you had been a MFDP delegate, what would your position have been regarding Lyndon Johnson's offer of only two at-large seats at the convention? Was Wilkins right in encouraging the delegates to accept the offer, or was Hamer right in urging them to reject it?

4. What do this chapter's essay and sources reveal about the reasons for the popularity of Black Power among many African Americans by the late 1960s? How do you think Hamer would have responded to Wilkins's assertion that Black Power was merely a slogan rather than a program? Do you agree with Wilkins?

5. If Wilkins and Hamer had the opportunity to examine American society and race relations today, do you think either of them would feel vindicated? What circumstances or problems do you think each would point to as signs of progress or failure?

For Further Reading

Chana Kai Lee, *For Freedom's Sake: The Life of Fannie Lou Hamer* (Urbana: University of Illinois Press, 1999), is an overview of Hamer's life and a useful discussion of her local organizing efforts after the 1964 Democratic convention.

Kay Mills, *This Little Light of Mine: The Life of Fannie Lou Hamer* (New York: Penguin Books, 1993), provides a gripping account of the conditions that Hamer confronted in her battle for black equality in Mississippi.

Charles M. Payne, *I've Got the Light of Freedom: The Organizing Tradition and the Mississippi Freedom Struggle* (Berkeley: University of California Press, 1995), examines the fight for black equality in Mississippi by focusing on the role of Fannie Lou Hamer and other grass-roots organizers.

John A. Salmond, *"My Mind Set on Freedom": A History of the Civil Rights Movement, 1954–1968* (Chicago: Ivan R. Dee, 1997), is a concise treatment of the civil rights struggle from the *Brown* v. *Board of Education* decision to the assassination of Martin Luther King Jr.

Robert Weisbrot, *Freedom Bound: A History of America's Civil Rights Movement* (New York: W. W. Norton & Company, 1990), is an overview of the modern civil rights movement, including grass-roots struggles and the efforts of national civil rights organizations.

Roy Wilkins, *Standing Fast: The Autobiography of Roy Wilkins* (New York: Viking Press, 1982), details Wilkins's rise as the leader of the nation's largest civil rights organization and offers a defense of his policies.

The Battles of Vietnam:
Robert McNamara and Jan Barry

R obert McNamara was livid. By late 1967, the secretary of defense was no
stranger to protests against the war in Vietnam. But one protest launched in
November caught his eye and raised his ire like few others. It took the form of
a full-page advertisement in the *New York Times*. Headlined "Vietnam Veterans
Speak Out," it declared that the nation's military involvement in Vietnam was
"unjustifiable and contrary to the principle of self-determination on which this
nation was founded." Antiwar demonstrations had been growing steadily in
the last two years, including one that drew 50,000 people right outside McNamara's Pentagon office window. But the defense secretary realized that this
protest was especially dangerous. By virtue of their military service, the sixty-
five veterans who signed the advertisement threatened to give the antiwar
movement legitimacy in the minds of many Americans. That very day, McNamara called the FBI and demanded an investigation of those responsible for it.

The advertisement was the work of a small outfit called Vietnam Veterans
Against the War. Founded only a month earlier by a twenty-four-year-old
named Jan Barry, the fledgling organization sought to end the war in Southeast
Asia by educating the public about it. After starting the VVAW in his New York
City living room, Barry had worked hard to round up signatures and collect
money for the ad. Driven by convictions based on his own experience in Vietnam, he believed that veterans of the war there, once organized, could be its
most effective opponents.

When Barry entered the service, few Americans challenged their nation's
commitment in Vietnam or the assumptions behind it. John Kennedy was president, and the United States was engaged in a global struggle against Communism whose roots dated to Harry Truman's containment policy in 1947. By the
early 1960s, that Cold War struggle had entered a new and dangerous phase,
characterized by a growing nuclear arms race with the Soviet Union and rising
unrest in the Third World, the nonindustrialized nations in Latin America,
Africa, and Asia. At the outset of his presidency, Kennedy urged Americans to
"bear any burden" in the defense of freedom around the world. Convinced that
the Third World represented the new Cold War battleground, it was easy for
Kennedy and advisers to see the small conflict between the government of

Robert McNamara   Jan Barry

South Vietnam and Communist insurgents as a case of expansionism by the So-viets or their Chinese Communist surrogates, which required an American response.

The result was the longest war in American history. As Secretary of Defense for seven years, Robert McNamara was one of its principal planners. In fact, the Vietnam war became so closely identified with him that it was often referred to as "McNamara's war." A man of legendary mental abilities and managerial skills, he often left those around him awestruck. McNamara applied his im-pressive talents to managing a small conflict in far-off Vietnam, which few Americans knew or cared about. A central goal of his efforts was to make sure that it stayed a relatively little war and minor concern for Americans. Under McNamara's management, though, the conflict in Vietnam turned into a very large war. By 1967, thousands of Americans and tens of thousands of Viet-namese lay dead, and the war had come home to the United States. As the growing protests at home demonstrated, Vietnam was no longer a minor concern.

Jan Barry's tour of duty ended before McNamara guided the Johnson ad-ministration's massive escalation of American forces in the mid-1960s. It also ended before many of the American forces there came to be made up primarily of working-class, often nonwhite, draftees. In coming years, though, Barry's conclusions about the war would be shared by many of these veterans, even as his organization came to mirror social divisions among them. Although Jan Barry never met Robert McNamara, few veterans offered an earlier critique of the war that McNamara did so much to shape. And few did more to help erode public support for it. If McNamara reveals much about why and how the United States fought there, Barry reveals much of what McNamara missed about Vietnam. Together, their stories illuminate what went wrong in Vietnam—and why the war there came home to the United States.

"We're Winning This War"

People marveled at Robert McNamara's remarkable mind. They often marveled more that he arose from such unremarkable circumstances. McNamara was born in San Francisco in 1916 and grew up across the bay in Oakland in a struggling middle-class household. His father, the son of a poor, Irish Catholic immigrant, was a man of iron self-discipline and obsessive frugality. As a manager for a San Francisco wholesale shoe company, his chief concern was providing for his family, especially during the hard times of the Depression. McNamara's mother was the daughter of a more prosperous Presbyterian family, and she raised her son and daughter in her faith. Convinced her son was special, she also instilled in him a strong sense of purpose and a burning ambition to succeed.

McNamara took his first step in that direction in 1933 when he headed off to the nearby University of California at Berkeley. With a love for numbers and logic, he considered majoring in mathematics, but wanted to study something more practical. Economics was the answer, and he excelled at it. By his senior year, he was elected to an elite academic society, traveled in the school's top social circles, and came to know the university's president. When he graduated in 1937, he turned down the option of graduate school and instead chose a more lucrative way to exercise his knack for numbers. He went east to attend Harvard Business School.

At Harvard, McNamara specialized in statistical control, an academic field that fit him perfectly. It had been developed several decades earlier to provide data that allowed managers to measure their company's performance and make financial projections. Statistical control saved companies money by eliminating even the smallest inefficiencies. Above all, it gave them the means to centralize control over far-flung and diverse operations. The flaw was its assumption that only managers at the top, not the rank-and-file workers, had enough information to make decisions. But running a company by the numbers represented rational business management in the 1950s.

Mastery of statistical control propelled McNamara to the top of powerful organizations in business and government. After a brief stint with a San Francisco accounting firm and an equally brief courtship of an old Berkeley acquaintance named Margy Craig, McNamara—twenty-four and married to Craig—returned to Harvard to teach accounting. He did not stay long. With the United States in World War II, the Army Air Corps came calling in 1942. It wanted McNamara and other faculty to devise a statistical control system to track the massive amount of materiel needed to fight an air war. It was a huge task, and again McNamara excelled, demonstrating an enormous appetite for work and an ability to get things done. McNamara's wartime experience left him with a key lesson: Statistical data was power. Using statistical analysis, for instance, military planners analyzed the combat experience of B-17s and B-24s, found the B-17 more successful, and altered production of the bombers accordingly. One could derive important truths from numbers, even the best way to fight a war.

After the war, McNamara used his mastery of numbers to control an entire organization. Faced with the unhappy prospect of supporting a growing family on a professor's salary, he joined a group of former Army statistical control men who sold their services to the struggling automobile manufacturer Ford. The company had suffered for years under the dictatorial control of its founder Henry Ford, but had just been taken over by grandson Henry Ford II. McNamara and the others modernized Ford's management, devising detailed inventory and financial control systems. Before long people were talking about the company's "Whiz Kids"—the young managers who had used tools of modern finance to save an American business icon. The most ambitious of the Whiz Kids, McNamara quickly rose through the company ranks to comptroller, division vice president, and then president.

McNamara was president of Ford for a month. John Kennedy, elected president of the United States in 1960, was impressed by McNamara's obvious talents and asked him to be his secretary of defense. Kennedy was eager to attract the "best and brightest" people in the country to his administration, and McNamara was just as eager for public service. Detroit provided him a nice living, but never a home for his intellect and ambition. He wanted more out of life than debates about the size of tail fins and bumpers. When Kennedy summoned the nation to commit itself to higher purposes, he heard the call.

McNamara immediately set out to strengthen the nation's defense by applying rational management techniques. Planning and accounting systems replaced the whims of military brass. Resources were allocated only after the military determined its missions and assessed the best means to carry them out. Forceful, decisive, self-assured, and always in command of the facts, McNamara shouldered aside generals and brought to the tradition-encrusted Pentagon a managerial revolution that attracted wide attention in the press. McNamara, concluded *Business Week*, was a "prize specimen" of a new breed of business manager who could move easily from one area into another.

One area was foreign policy. McNamara had no experience in this field, but as the new administration turned to the battle against Communism in the Third World, the hard-charging secretary of defense emerged as one of its most powerful members. His role in one Third World hot spot sped his rise. In 1959, Communist Fidel Castro came to power in Cuba. In 1961, the Kennedy administration tried to overthrow Castro by launching an invasion at the Bay of Pigs of Cuba by CIA-trained Cuban refugees. The next year, the Soviet Union installed medium-range nuclear missiles on the island, intending to counter a massive, McNamara-initiated buildup of American long-range missiles. In the resulting face-off with the Soviets, known as the Cuban Missile Crisis, McNamara was a forceful advocate for a carefully controlled American response, including the enforcement of a naval blockade around Cuba. That show of force got the Soviets to remove the weapons in exchange for an American pledge not to invade the island again. McNamara had helped stand down the Soviets, giving rise to his reputation as a brilliant crisis manager. Meanwhile, he took a lasting lesson from the experience: The thoughtful application of force elicited a favorable reaction from the other side. Future Cold War crises could be resolved with carefully modulated responses. In a perilous world of nuclear arms, such rational crisis management was far less dangerous than solutions often advanced by liberals, who were too reluctant to use any force, and Pentagon brass, who were too eager to use excessive force. It was a lesson that McNamara would apply to another Cold War crisis halfway around the world in Vietnam.

Compared to Cuba, the problem in Vietnam seemed insignificant at first. Snaking along the South China Sea, the country had been a French colony until 1954, when France was defeated by a Vietnamese independence movement led by Communist Ho Chi Minh. Under the peace settlement, Vietnam was temporarily divided, with nationwide elections to be held within two years. Ho then set up a Communist government in North Vietnam with its capital at Hanoi. With American help, a non-Communist but hardly democratic government arose in South Vietnam under Ngo Dinh Diem, backed by the United States as a bulwark against the spread of Communism. By 1961, however, the corrupt and unpopular Diem regime confronted a growing insurgency launched by the Vietcong (South Vietnamese Communists) in the countryside. The Vietcong posed a small threat at first, but Diem's military was unable to counter it.

Faced with the prospect of Diem's fall, Kennedy acted. The president and his advisors had not forgotten the devastating attacks on Democrats launched by Joseph McCarthy and other Republicans in the early 1950s for "losing" China to the Communists, (see Chapter 10), and they were determined to avoid similar charges now over Vietnam. Nor did they question the domino theory, the idea advanced in the early 1950s by Dwight Eisenhower, who likened Vietnam to the first of a row of dominos. If it fell to Communism, according to this theory, a chain reaction of falling countries would ensue. It was a simple—some would later say simplistic—image that elevated Vietnam's strategic significance in the minds of American leaders. In 1961, the United States stepped up American assistance to Diem, including military equipment and advisers. With his forces doing the actual fighting, Vietnam would be a model of counterinsurgency war. It would show how the United States could fight against Communist "wars of liberation" in the Third World.

When the Kennedy administration entered this military partnership with Diem, McNamara began to play a decisive role in Vietnam. Volunteering to look after the guerrilla war there, he made his first trip to the country in 1962. McNamara showed little interest in the political, social, or economic conditions of the Vietnamese or their history or culture. He put his faith in the power of numbers to yield objective information. He came away impressed by the progress Diem's forces were making against the Vietcong, even though the trip lasted only forty-eight hours. When asked later if staying longer might have changed his outlook, he replied, "Absolutely not."

Although followed by many others, that first trip demonstrated some of the flaws in McNamara's optimistic and arrogant approach to the war. Before he left for Vietnam, he sent a list of detailed questions he wanted answered. After he arrived, American military leaders at every stop told him what he wanted to hear. He learned that 1,300 strategic hamlets—villages designed to be safe from the Vietcong guerrillas—had been built by the Diem government with American assistance. In fact, only a handful were built, often through the forced relocation of villagers from ancestral homes. At one briefing, he saw maps—altered for his visit—indicating that Communist-controlled areas in the country had shrunk. He heard that Diem had 170,000 troops facing only 20,000 insurgents, numbers that did not explain why Diem's forces were having such difficulties subduing the Vietcong. The body count—the ratio of dead friendly to unfriendly soldiers—seemed encouraging too. This statistic came to be associated with McNamara's handling of the war, but also called for skepticism. With American aid and individual promotions on the line, it was too tempting for South Vietnamese and American military personnel to fudge the numbers. Some counterinsurgency experts in Vietnam realized that the challenge there was to capture the "hearts and minds" of the peasants, a mostly nonmilitary task that was impossible to quantify. Smitten with statistics, McNamara counted enemy bodies and saw only progress. "Every quantitative measurement we have," he declared, "shows that we're winning this war."

Yet it was not so. As the Vietcong insurgency continued to grow, so did the American military commitment. By the fall of 1963, the United States had 15,000 advisers in Vietnam. There only to train the South Vietnamese to fight, some of them were killed on patrols against the guerrillas. McNamara would report in 1963 that "the corner has definitely been turned toward victory," but away from his statistics there was little real evidence of that. By the end of the year, Kennedy realized that the political situation in Vietnam would make victory unlikely. Only weeks before his assassination in late 1963, he approved a coup against the unpopular and corrupt Diem regime in which the South Vietnamese leader was killed. But changing the government did not improve the political situation. In coming years, South Vietnam would be governed by a string of rulers who were no more able than Diem to gain popular support.

Meanwhile, McNamara continued as defense secretary under Lyndon B. Johnson. Kennedy's successor had little experience in foreign affairs and was primarily interested in getting his Great Society* enacted. Like other Americans, he had learned from World War II that appeasement only invited further aggression. Infatuated with his defense secretary's abilities, LBJ placed him in charge of Vietnam. In fact, McNamara had already turned pessimistic about South Vietnam's progress against the Vietcong. Rather than reassess his basic assumptions about the war, however, he now concluded that deeper American military commitment was necessary. Instead of assessing the commitment of the Vietnamese on both sides, asking whether Ho was only doing the Soviet Union's or China's bidding or had more compelling motives, and examining whether the United States could win militarily, McNamara would serve LBJ by trying to carefully manage the war's escalation so as to create few political ripples at home. **[See Source 1.]**

The opportunity to escalate was not long in coming. In August 1964, the military reported that two American naval vessels cruising in the Gulf of Tonkin off the coast of North Vietnam had been fired on by North Vietnamese patrol boats. LBJ quickly persuaded an outraged Congress to pass the Tonkin Gulf resolution, which gave the president a free hand to wage undeclared war in Vietnam. Only later did Americans learn that the resolution was based on faulty intelligence that a publically unwavering McNamara actually doubted. Soon, the United States began a bombing campaign against North Vietnam, a move intended to encourage Ho to stop supplying the growing insurgency in the south. Johnson and McNamara picked the targets at weekly luncheons. Guided by the lesson of the Cuban Missile Crisis, McNamara wanted controlled escalation, not the massive use of

---

Great Society: The sweeping domestic program launched in 1964 that resulted in new civil rights laws and numerous social welfare programs, including job training, child care, and medical assistance for the elderly and poor.

force favored by the military. *Limited* force would move Ho to cut back military assistance to the Vietcong without provoking Chinese intervention and a wider war.

Instead, McNamara got a much bigger war. The bombing campaign never led to Chinese intervention, but it failed to deter the North Vietnamese, who responded by sending their own ground forces into the south. That made the commitment of American combat troops imperative. They began arriving in the spring of 1965. By the end of the year, the United States had nearly 185,000 ground troops in Vietnam. Still thinking quantitatively, McNamara supported the military's strategy of simply grinding down the enemy. To expedite a war of attrition, he backed a massive bombing campaign, in which huge B-52 bombers rained fifty powerful conventional bombs at a time on "suspected enemy concentrations." He approved the use of napalm firebombs and herbicides that stripped bare jungle vegetation to remove the guerrillas' cover. He seemed unconcerned about the effects of these weapons on civilians. Banking on superior numbers and technology to turn the tide, he never considered the war's impact on the hearts and minds of the Vietnamese.

"Devastating the Shit Out of These . . . People"

The experience of many Americans in Vietnam demonstrated the limits of McNamara's approach to war and the flawed assumptions of American policymakers. One of those Americans was a nineteen-year-old Army enlistee named Jan Barry.[1] The son of an automobile mechanic, Barry was born in Ithaca, New York, in 1943. Shortly afterward, the family moved to the nearby town of Interlaken. Reflecting later on his childhood, Barry said he was a "stereotypical kid in a rural area." He joined the Boy Scouts, delivered newspapers, and worked at gas stations, on farms, and at a veterinarian's office. In high school, he played sports, participated in class plays and in band, and did well academically. "I grew up in a society," he said later, "in which I didn't realize that there were any limitations."

Later, Barry realized the limits imposed on his childhood environment. "Even the movies of the 1950s," he declared, "can't do justice to the deadening effect of the culture of this country." When he graduated from high school in 1961, "we had no idea you could question anything. No matter what the government did, there wasn't even the thought that you could question whatever it was." Military service, on the other hand, seemed fascinating. World War II was fresh in the minds of most Americans, including Barry's father, who had served in the Navy during the war. Barry grew up hearing "all the World War II stories of my family . . . plus those of the society at large." He was especially intrigued by *The Long Gray Line*, a television program in the 1950s about life at the West Point military academy. All this left him with a "romantic fixation" on a military career. Failing to get an appointment to West Point, he enlisted in the Army in 1962.

Barry arrived in Vietnam on Christmas eve that year. After completing radio school at Fort Benning, Georgia, he had opted for service in Vietnam when a friend told him that between combat pay and overseas pay he could "really clean up." Looking for "an adventure in Asia," Barry knew very little about Vietnam. When he went to the library before deployment there, he found only

1. Barry was born Jan Barry Crumb, but later took the pen name Jan Barry. He is known by that name in published works on the antiwar movement.

references to French Indochina. Nor did he learn anything about it in his Army training, which was focused on war with the Soviet Union. That turned out to be a blessing. As Barry later put it, in 1962 "people . . . had to find out for themselves what was going on." He would do just that.

Barry was assigned to a small, crude base camp at Nha Trang, a former French resort on the coast of the South China Sea. There he helped maintain the planes that flew supplies to outposts of the Special Forces, the counterguerrilla forces that the Kennedy administration deployed to train the South Vietnamese Army to fight the Vietcong. The United States had only about 11,000 advisory and support troops in Vietnam and, as Barry later observed, "there probably weren't more than five hundred in any one place." When he arrived at Nha Trang, he quickly got the impression that the Americans were not taking the war seriously. He was met by a drunken commander of quarters who promptly took him to town to bar hop. After Barry made his way back to the base camp, he woke the next morning in a room filled with drunken soldiers.

Barry would see a lot more that left him unimpressed with the American involvement in Vietnam. He became convinced that most of the Americans he met had no clue as to why they were in Vietnam and could not have located it on a map. Worse still, they knew little about its history or culture and had little respect for its people. Most of the Americans referred to the Vietnamese by derogatory terms such as "slopes" or "gooks." Barry, however, began to realize that he had "more of an affinity with the Vietnamese people than with Americans." He came to know the servants who worked at the base camp. He made friends with students who were aware of the repressive nature of the South Vietnamese government. He went into the homes of Vietnamese friends and met their families. He learned that many of them were "scared to death of the Saigon government" and feared for their own lives. Warned that some South Vietnamese soldiers would just as soon shoot American military personnel, he also saw little to respect in the "nasty" allies of the United States in the South Vietnamese Army. Then in 1963, Barry witnessed an antigovernment demonstration, the first of several in Nha Trang. And he watched as South Vietnamese soldiers "turn[ed] loose tanks and machine guns." As he observed later, "This was supposed to be our arsenal of democracy."

At the same time, he developed a growing respect for the Vietcong as resourceful and dedicated fighters that, like the war, the Americans were not taking seriously enough. Early one morning, Barry and the other men at the base camp were "blown out of bed" after Vietcong guerrillas sneaked through the barbed wire and blew up the airplanes. Although the guards began shooting with "no idea what they were shooting at," Barry and the other men at the base camp could not get to their weapons because they were locked up and the soldier with the key was "downtown shacked up with his girlfriend."

Talks with seasoned veterans also shaped Barry's views about the enemy and the American mission in Vietnam. Many of them, he learned, came back from the field disillusioned and convinced that the Vietcong had legitimate grievances against the government. As one of them put it to him, "we're supporting the wrong side." In Barry's mind, the rationale for American involvement in Vietnam gradually gave way. As he declared later, "We were devastating the shit out of these little people, and for what purpose?" **[See Source 2.]**

Although Barry left Vietnam in the fall of 1963 with the feeling that he was "being had," he was not ready to leave the military. In fact, he was still intent on getting into West Point, and the following spring he was accepted. He was the first student there who had been in Vietnam. His experiences in the war, however, eventually led him to question his commitment to the military. He envisioned returning to "an impossible situation" in Vietnam as a platoon leader. He also thought about spending "another thirty years of my life involved in things where we can't tell the public the truth." When he heard about the alleged attack on American warships in the Tonkin Gulf in August 1964, he did not believe that it had actually happened. As Barry's doubts about a war that "made no sense whatsoever" kept building, he finally realized that he "was in the wrong place." In 1965, he dropped out of West Point.

Barry thought little about protesting the war, though. To finish his enlistment, he had to serve with an infantry unit in Alabama, training for helicopter assaults in Vietnam. The Johnson administration was deploying the first regular combat troops to Vietnam, but Barry quickly found out that fellow infantrymen did not "want to hear about anything." Discharged in 1965, Barry headed home, moved to Manhattan the next year, and got a job at the New York Public Library. Still deeply troubled by the war, he continued to read widely about it and, as he had in Vietnam, talked to a lot of people, including reporters who had interviewed returning veterans. They told him that these vets were "more bitter than you are." Already, the antiwar movement had expanded dramatically. Beginning with teach-ins at colleges across the nation in 1965 in response to the draft and the Johnson administration's escalation of the war, the movement had grown to include a wide mix of men and women. In 1967, antiwar demonstrations in New York, Washington, D.C., and other cities drew thousands of participants.

Barry was not yet one of them. He could not imagine marching in the streets "making a fool of myself." But that would change in the spring of 1967 when antiwar activists launched a massive Spring Mobilization to protest the war with rallies across the nation. In New York City, some 300,000 people marched from Central Park to the United Nations, where they listened to antiwar speeches, including one delivered by Martin Luther King Jr. That demonstration drew hundreds of veterans, mostly from World War II and the Korean War, who were members of a group called Veterans for Peace in Vietnam. At the time, few Vietnam veterans had spoken out against the war. Most of them still supported it, and those who did not usually kept quiet. Seeking to meet other veterans opposed to the war, Barry went to the rally and found himself walking with a small group of other Vietnam vets under a banner that proclaimed "VIETNAM VETERANS AGAINST THE WAR!"

Marching that day, Barry felt the little group's impact. Hostile bystanders who yelled at the protesters were often silenced by the sight of Vietnam veterans protesting the very war in which they had fought. "You heard this sea change in the crowd," Barry recalled. He was now ready to do more, but he had no idea who his fellow Vietnam vets were when they disbanded at the end of the march. After several frustrating weeks making phone calls and writing letters, Barry rounded up five of them and founded the Vietnam Veterans Against the War. The others then elected him president.

Barry and the other VVAW members were animated by a strong sense of purpose. They were convinced that as people learned more about the war they would turn against it. "You change the public attitude in this country, things change," Barry later declared. "It wasn't any grander than that." And as McNamara approved the Pentagon's ever-larger troop requests, the organization had an ever-expanding pool of potential members. In early 1967, American forces in Vietnam jumped to 380,000. By the end of the year, they numbered more than a half million.

Yet Barry and the VVAW faced daunting obstacles. Overshadowed by more flamboyant and radical antiwar student protesters, VVAW members were ignored by the media. Contacting Vietnam veterans also proved frustrating. When the organization did locate them, they were often reluctant to join. As one early recruit declared, "A veteran, after two years of organization, doesn't want to be part of any organization again." Others, Barry discovered, were doubtful that collective action against the war would do any good. All the while, members of the VVAW were in an unenviable position. Like other war protesters, antiwar veterans were frequently attacked as traitors. At the same time, they were sometimes scorned by other antiwar Americans as "baby killers" for fighting in an "unjust" war against innocent civilians. When Barry attended one peace group meeting, for instance, a woman asked him, "And how many babies did you kill?"

The appearance of the *New York Times* advertisement in late 1967 was a turning point for the VVAW. Letters and calls from interested veterans flooded the organization's New York office. Newspapers and radio and television stations contacted it. And it got the attention of officials in the government. One was Senator Ernest Gruening, one of only two senators to vote against the Tonkin Gulf Resolution, who offered to meet with Barry and other VVAW leaders to help persuade the Senate Foreign Relations Committee to conduct hearings on the war.

Other officials, including FBI director J. Edgar Hoover and, of course, McNamara, were far less pleased. A rabid anti-Communist, Hoover believed that Communist agents had targeted the antiwar movement, and his bureau was already busy monitoring and infiltrating it. In fact, when McNamara requested an investigation of the VVAW after the publication of its *New York Times* ad, the FBI had already conducted a two-month investigation of the group and concluded that its leaders had no known ties to Communist groups. Meanwhile, McNamara's concern about the VVAW had less to do with a fear of Communist subversion than his own growing doubts about the war itself.

"Over 335,000 of Our Buddies Have Been Killed Or Wounded"

To many Americans opposed to the war, Robert McNamara represented an alliance of Pentagon "warmongers" and war-profiteering corporations. He seemed the very symbol of a technological war waged by a military-industrial establishment run by men with perfectly combed hair. Despite his continued upbeat pronouncements about the war, though, he knew by the fall of 1967 that he had guided the United States into a hopeless swamp. For a while, he held out hope for an acceptable diplomatic settlement, but now he did not even believe that was possible. He realized the North Vietnamese, unlike the Soviets in the Cuban Missile Crisis, were not going to respond in a "rational" way to the increased application of American force. In October, McNamara proposed an end to the escalation of American troops and the fruitless bombing of North Vietnam. The time had come, he concluded, to turn more of the fighting over to South Vietnamese forces and find a way out. Unfortunately, he also believed that the antiwar movement would only erode American morale and steel the enemy's resolve and thus make *any* diplomatic settlement impossible. And it did not help that Vietnam veterans had now organized against the war. As he declared to LBJ, the war's unpopularity "generates patience in Hanoi." **[See Source 3.]**

McNamara never informed the public, however, of his belief that the war could not be won. Nor did he level with his troops that the sacrifice asked of them would not lead to victory. In fact, McNamara never seriously considered the war's impact on his own troops. For years, he had received feedback in statistics generated by the military: body counts, kill ratios, and bomb tonnages. Armed with these numbers, the stat control Whiz Kid-turned war manager believed that he understood a technological war of attrition better than the soldiers slogging through Vietnamese villages, rice paddies, and jungles. He had little idea of the corrosive impact on young troops of a guerrilla war against an elusive enemy who easily blended into the civilian population. Those asked to fight in "McNamara's war," found themselves engaged in a seemingly endless succession of patrols, ambushes, and firefights. In the words of one veteran, Vietnam was "an exhausting, indecisive war of attrition in which we fought for no cause other than our own survival." **[See Source 4.]**

Nor did McNamara consider the military draft's impact on the composition of American forces or the morale of the troops. Because mostly white college students were exempt from the draft, the ranks of American soldiers by the late 1960s were filled disproportionately with working-class and poor draftees, often black or Hispanic. The civil rights movement, racial violence at home, and outspoken opposition to the war by such prominent black figures as Muhammad Ali, who refused to serve in the armed forces, and Martin Luther King Jr. spilled over to Vietnam in growing racial consciousness and rising racial tensions among American troops. As morale sank, drug abuse among draftees rose. They also became more willing to defy their commanding officers, often white and college-educated. By 1968, cases of desertion, insubordination, and even fragging—draftees killing their own officers with fragmentation grenades—increased dramatically. The nation's social divisions and racial tensions, in short, had come to the battlefield. **[See Sources 5 and 6.]**

At the same time, a growing division over the war among Americans brought the conflict in Vietnam home to the United States. In 1968, Communist forces launched a massive military campaign known as the Tet Offensive. A well-coordinated North Vietnamese and Vietcong attack during the Tet (Vietnamese New Year's) holiday, it was aimed at Saigon and numerous provincial capitals in South Vietnam. American forces eventually repelled the offensive and inflicted heavy casualties on the Communist forces, but the enemy had demonstrated enormous offensive power. In just a few weeks, the heavy fighting undermined McNamara's and Johnson's optimistic predictions about the war and led many Americans to conclude that McNamara, Johnson, and military leaders had deliberately misled them. With the death toll rising and victory nowhere in sight, many more Americans now saw their nation's involvement in Vietnam as a terrible mistake. A month after the Communist offensive and after rejecting disengagement, Johnson relieved McNamara of his duties.

After Tet, the antiwar movement exploded, sparking more protests, increasing violence, and political turmoil. Faced with rising opposition to the war, LBJ announced shortly after McNamara's departure that he would not seek re-election in 1968. That June, antiwar Democratic presidential candidate Robert Kennedy was gunned down in Los Angeles after winning the California primary. Later that summer, police launched a bloody assault on antiwar demonstrators at the Democratic Convention in Chicago, watched live by millions of shocked television viewers. That fall, Republican Richard Nixon, appealing to growing disillusionment with the war and widespread unease at rising violence at home, narrowly defeated Johnson's vice president, Hubert Humphrey, in the presidential race with a promise to end the war and restore "law and order."

For the next four years, Nixon worked to achieve what he called "peace with honor." His strategy called for "Vietnamizing" the war by gradually withdrawing American forces, turning over more of the fighting to the South Vietnamese, and negotiating with the North Vietnamese. The goal was to secure a "decent interval" between complete American withdrawal and South Vietnam's inevitable fall—a period long enough for people not to associate one with the other. But this interval would be created only if the North Vietnamese allowed South Vietnamese military forces to stand for a time against the Vietcong. To achieve that, the enemy had to be convinced that Americans retained the will to carry on the fight. Like McNamara, Nixon and his top aides feared that the antiwar movement only boosted the enemy's patience.

Yet Nixon's moves to achieve a "decent interval" only stoked antiwar sentiment further. To persuade the North Vietnamese to withdraw their own troops from the south, Nixon stepped up McNamara's massive bombing of North Vietnam. To root out alleged Communist sanctuaries in Cambodia, he ordered an American invasion of that country in the spring of 1970. Meanwhile, revelations in 1971 that American soldiers had massacred civilians at the village of My Lai in South Vietnam in 1968 turned more Americans against the war. So did the publication in 1971 of the *Pentagon Papers*, a secret Defense Department study ordered by McNamara in 1967 that revealed the deception by American leaders regarding the war.

After these events, Barry's organization moved to the forefront of the antiwar movement. In late 1970, the VVAW began numerous meetings around the country in which veterans testified about atrocities committed in Vietnam. These gatherings brought new recruits to the organization. So did a VVAW advertisement in *Playboy* magazine in late 1970 that boldly proclaimed, "Over 335,000 of Our Buddies Have Been Killed Or Wounded." By early 1971, the VVAW had nearly ten thousand members and chapters in every state.

Yet Barry and other leaders were frustrated. The organization's atrocity investigations had drawn only limited media attention, and Nixon's Vietnamization policy had convinced many Americans that the war was ending.

After the widespread protests against the invasion of Cambodia in the spring of 1970, the antiwar protests on campus and elsewhere began to subside, even though more than 330,000 American troops still fought in Vietnam in early 1971. At one meeting, Barry recalled, VVAW members were "hollering and screaming" at one another as they debated what to do when a recent VVAW recruit named John Kerry suggested that the group's members march on Washington to take their case to Congress. That April, twenty-three hundred of them, some in wheelchairs, gathered at the Capitol to launch what the VVAW called "a limited incursion into the country of Congress." During the week-long protest, many of the veterans threw away their war medals and ribbons, and Kerry himself spoke before the Senate Foreign Relations Committee against what he called a "barbaric" war. Carried live to a nationwide televison audience, that testimony was the culmination of a long effort to bring Vietnam vets before the committee that had started when Barry met with Senator Ernest Gruening after the publication of the VVAW's *New York Times* ad in 1967.

The VVAW's "incursion" into Washington, D.C., Kerry's testimony, and the massive antiwar rally that brought perhaps a half million protesters to the Capitol Mall a few days later, finally put the media spotlight on Barry's organization. Nightly television newscasts led with the veterans' protest. Because veterans were at the center of this protest, press commentary was overwhelmingly favorable. Afterward, membership soared.

At the same time, the VVAW became a high-profile target for the Nixon administration. In fact, no antiwar group caused more concern in Nixon and his top aides, who knew that its members, unlike student antiwar protesters, could not be labeled draft dodgers. As McNamara had earlier, Nixon and his aides turned to the FBI, which infiltrated and harassed the VVAW. By 1972, that infiltration led to the indictment of several VVAW members for allegedly conspiring to disrupt the Republican Convention that summer.

In the end, though, divisions among veterans themselves were a bigger threat to the VVAW than was government harassment. By the early 1970s, the organization's membership reflected the growing numbers of draftees from poor and working-class backgrounds. As the VVAW grew, it attracted more working-class recruits, who resented the participation of former officers. Disgusted by in-fighting in the organization, Barry insisted that members set aside their differences and focus on educating the public as "moral witnesses" against the war, but many militant new recruits disagreed. As one VVAW member put it, Barry's "moral witness [approach] was completely out of sync with the gritty, blue-collar temper of the antiwar veteran." By 1971, many veterans were far more angry than Barry and other VVAW organizers had been in 1967. That year, more than twenty-five thousand military personnel were dishonorably discharged. According to one Army survey, nearly half of all troops were engaged in illegal drug use. Many of them would have little patience with educating Americans one by one about the war.

Race and gender divisions also worked against the VVAW, which never recruited more than 1 percent of all Vietnam veterans. When the group's membership peaked at roughly twenty-five thousand in late 1971, half of its members were white males from blue-collar backgrounds. Although Latinos and blacks joined the VVAW and several became leaders in it, the organization re-cruited relatively few nonwhites and very few women. Many Hispanic veterans were caught up in issues affecting their own community, particularly the long strike by César Chávez's United Farm Workers' Union against the growers in California. Many antiwar black veterans were drawn to the Black Panther Party, while others perceived that the VVAW ignored racial issues. As one black vet-eran told a VVAW gathering, "you ain't got no black people behind you, be-cause you forgot about racism, man." Many of the roughly 11,000 female veterans who served in Vietnam often felt unwelcome as well. When one Army nurse came to a VVAW meeting to help plan a march on the White House, she was told that she could not participate in the protest because she was not a vet. When she countered that she served in Vietnam, a VVAW member told her that she "didn't look like a vet" and that Nixon and the media would accuse the group of "swelling the ranks with non-vets." She left the meeting and never joined the organization.

Frustrated by the VVAW's internal politics, Barry stepped down as the group's president in 1971. When the Nixon administration officially ended American involvement in the war in 1973 with the signing of the Paris Peace Accords,* he left the organization he had founded seven years earlier. The VVAW would live on until the end of the century fighting for veterans' rights, but he was convinced that its usefulness had ended. Barry, who pursued a ca-reer in journalism and later became an antinuclear activist, could leave with some satisfaction. By then, fifty-eight thousand Americans and maybe a million Vietnamese lay dead. Perhaps more than any other antiwar group, however, the VVAW had helped erode public support for the war, making it more difficult for American leaders to prolong the fighting and exact an even higher toll.

When South Vietnam fell to Communist forces just two years after the peace agreement, Robert McNamara was serving as president of the World Bank, the international bank established by the United States and other nations to extend loans to developing countries. Appointed by Lyndon Johnson when he stepped down as defense secretary, McNamara served there until 1981, as the bank became controversial for its role in saddling poor countries with high debt. He rarely spoke about the Vietnam war. In his memoir published in 1995, though, he wrote that American leaders were "terribly wrong" and had gotten involved in a country they knew nothing about, a confession condemned by many angry critics. McNamara, they insisted, had waited far too long to speak out.

---

*Paris Peace Accords: The agreement signed by representatives of the United States, North Vietnam, and South Vietnam that provided for an end to American military involve-ment in Vietnam, but did not require North Vietnamese troops to withdraw from the south.

PRIMARY SOURCES

SOURCE 1:   *Robert McNamara Assesses the Situation in Vietnam* (1964)

Robert McNamara's memorandum to Lyndon Johnson in March 1964 summarized the situation in Vietnam and recommended specific actions to assist the government of South Vietnam in its growing conflict with Vietcong guerrillas. What does this excerpt from that memo reveal about McNamara's assumptions regarding the stakes in Vietnam? What actions does he recommend if the situation there should deteriorate further?

We seek an independent non-Communist South Vietnam. We do not require that it serve as a Western base or as a member of a Western Alliance. South Vietnam must be free, however, to accept outside assistance as required to maintain its security. This assistance should be able to take the form not only of economic and social measures but also police and military help to root out and control insurgent elements.

Unless we can achieve this objective in South Vietnam, almost all of Southeast Asia will probably fall under Communist dominance (all of Vietnam, Laos, and Cambodia), accommodate to Communism so as to remove effective U.S. and anti-Communist influence (Burma), or fall under the domination of forces not now explicitly Communist but likely then to become so (Indonesia taking over Malaysia). Thailand might hold for a period with our help, but would be under grave pressure. Even the Philippines would become shaky, and the threat to India to the west, Australia and New Zealand to the south, and Taiwan, Korea, and Japan to the north and east would be greatly increased.

All of these consequences would probably have been true even if the U.S. had not since 1954, and especially since 1961, become so heavily engaged in South Vietnam. However, that fact accentuates the impact of a Communist South Vietnam not only in Asia, but in the rest of the world, where the South Vietnam conflict is regarded as a test case of U.S. capacity to help a nation meet a Communist "war of liberation." . . .

We are now trying to help South Vietnam defeat the Viet Cong, supported from the North, by means short of the unqualified use of U.S. combat forces. We are not acting against North Vietnam except by a very modest "covert" program operated by South Vietnamese (and a few Chinese Nationalists)—a program so limited that it is unlikely to have any significant effect. . . .

The key elements in the present situation are as follows:

A. The military tools and concepts of the GVN*/US effort are generally sound and adequate. Substantially more can be done in the effective employment of military forces and in the economic and civic action areas. These

SOURCE: John P. Glennon, ed., *Foreign Relations of the United States, 1964–1968* (Washington, D.C.: United States Government Printing Office, 1992), I, pp. 154, 155, 159.

*Government of South Vietnam.

improvements may require some selective increases in the U.S. presence, but it does not appear likely that major equipment replacement and additions in U.S. personnel are indicated under current policy.

B. The U.S. policy of reducing existing personnel where South Vietnamese are in a position to assume the functions is still sound. . . . However, the U.S. should continue to reiterate that it will provide all the assistance and advice required to do the job regardless of how long it takes. . . .

We have given serious thought to all the implications and ways of carrying out direct military action against North Vietnam in order to supplement the counterinsurgency program in South Vietnam. . . .

This program would go beyond reacting on a tit-for-tat basis. It would include air attacks against military and possibly industrial targets. . . . Before this program could be implemented it would be necessary to provide some additional air defense for South Vietnam and to ready U.S. forces in the Pacific for possible escalation.

The analysis of the more serious of these military actions . . . revealed the extremely delicate nature of such operations, both from the military and political standpoints. There would be the problem of marshalling the case to justify such action, the problem of Communist escalation, and the problem of dealing with the pressures for premature or "stacked" negotiations. We would have to calculate the effect of such military actions against a specified political objective. That objective, while being cast in terms of eliminating North Vietnamese control and direction of the insurgency, would in practical terms be directed toward collapsing the morale and the self-assurance of the Viet Cong cadres now operating in South Vietnam.

SOURCE 2:   *Jan Barry Assesses the Situation in Vietnam* (1997)

In an oral history of the Vietnam Veterans Against the War, Jan Barry discussed what led him to question the American rationale for fighting in South Vietnam. What does the excerpt below reveal about factors regarding the war that were overlooked by Robert McNamara in the early 1960s?

I spent an awful lot of time talking to officers and sergeants about the military. Here I am with people who were through some of the worst shit in World War II and Korea. The top professionals the military's got to send out to this end of the world are shaking and scratching their heads. This was crazy. This did not make any sense compared to their previous experience.

The ones who were the real gung-ho professionals, who were out there pressing it, came back very disillusioned. They kept saying, "We're backing the wrong side. The other side is raising the right issues on behalf of the people

SOURCE: Richard Stacewicz, *Winter Soldiers: An Oral History of the Vietnam Veterans Against the War* (New York: Twayne Publishers, 1997), pp. 90–91.

here, and the side we're backing is a dictatorship." One day, I was speaking to a Special Forces sergeant, and he said, "I been out there; we're supporting the wrong side." He said, "These [NFL forces] out there, who are from the south, that didn't come from anyplace else, are responding to these legitimate grievances that these people have against the Saigon government." He explained the whole thing to me. He put the pieces together. He says, "When you go out there, these villagers' only protection is the NLF against this police state in Saigon. What we're here for is the palace guard of a police state." He did not like to be a protector of a police state, which was the first time anybody ever said that in so many words. I had enough understanding of things to understand that part of it, and you could see for yourself that in essence, we were supporting this rotten dictatorship.

It became very clear that what was being claimed in Washington and out of Saigon headquartes had nothing to do with what we could see for ourselves. McNamara [Robert McNamara, secretary of defense] and various other VIPs would come through, and there were warnings that no one was to tell these people what was really going on. I had also heard from people who had been stationed in South Korea, Turkey, and other places that this was not unusual, that we had two different agendas: one for the public and what the real agenda was.

Slowly, one by one by one, everything was undermined as to the presumed reasons we were there. We were devastating the shit out of these little people, for what purpose? After some of them became your friends, you had to think about what was your purpose. We weren't in any way helping these people.

SOURCE 3: *McNamara Offers a Bleak Assessment* (1967)

In May 1967, McNamara wrote another memorandum for Johnson that revealed his growing doubts about a positive outcome from American military actions in Vietnam. On what basis does he draw his conclusions? How do they compare to the assessment in Source 1?

The Vietnam war is unpopular in this country. It is becoming increasingly unpopular as it escalates—causing more American casualties, more fear of its growing into a wider war, more privation of the domestic sector, and more distress at the amount of suffering being visited on the non-combatants in Vietnam, South and North. Most Americans do not know how we got where we are, and most, without knowing why, but taking advantage of hindsight, are convinced that somehow we should not have gotten this deeply in. All want the war ended and expect their President to end it. Successfully. Or else.

This state of mind in the U.S. generates impatience in the political structure of the United States. It unfortunately also generates patience in Hanoi. . . .

SOURCE: John P. Glennon, ed., *Foreign Relations of the United States, 1964–1968* (Washington, D.C.: United States Government Printing Office, 1992), V, pp. 424, 425, 426, 437.

The "big war" in the South between the U.S. and the North Vietnamese military units (NVA) is going well. We staved off military defeat in 1965; we gained the military initiative in 1966; and since then we have been hurting the enemy badly, spoiling some of his ability to strike. "In the final analysis," General Westmoreland said, "we are fighting a war of attrition." In that connection, the enemy has been losing between 1500 and 2000 killed-in-action a week, while we and the South Vietnamese have been losing 175 and 250 respectively. . . .

Regrettably, the "other war" against the VC is still not going well. Corruption is widespread. Real government control is confined to enclaves. There is rot in the fabric. Our efforts to enliven the moribund political infrastructure have been matched by VC efforts—more now through coercion than was formerly the case. So the VC are hurting badly too. . . .

Hanoi's attitude towards negotiations has never been soft nor openminded. Any concession on their part would involve an enormous loss of face. . . . They seem uninterested in a political settlement and determined to match U.S. military expansion of the conflict. . . . Hanoi appears to have concluded that she cannot secure her objectives at the conference table and has reaffirmed her strategy of seeking to erode our ability to remain in the South. The Hanoi leadership has apparently decided that it has no choice but to submit to the increased bombing. There continues to be no sign that the bombing has reduced Hanoi's will to resist or her ability to ship the necessary supplies south. Hanoi shows no signs of ending the large war and advising the VC to melt into the jungles. The North Vietnamese believe they are right; they consider the Ky regime to be puppets; they believe the world is with them and that the American public will not have staying power against them. . . .

The war in Vietnam is acquiring a momentum of its own that must be stopped. Dramatic increases in U.S. troop deployments, in attacks on the North, or in ground actions in Laos or Cambodia are not necessary and are not the answer. The enemy can absorb them or counter them, bogging us down further and risking even more serious escalation of the war.

SOURCE 4: *A Marine Describes a Technological War of Attrition* (1977)

Philip Caputo was a Marine lieutenant in Vietnam in 1965. His memoir, A Rumor of War, *describes his experiences there. What does this source reveal about the impact of the American counterguerrilla strategy in Vietnam on the soldiers fighting there?*

Everything rotted and corroded quickly over there: bodies, boot leather, canvas, metal, morals. Scorched by the sun, wracked by the wind and rain of the monsoon, fighting in alien swamps and jungles, our humanity rubbed off of us as the protective bluing rubbed off the barrels of our rifles. We were fighting in the

SOURCE: Philip Caputo, *A Rumor of War* (New York: Henry Holt and Company, Inc., 1977), pp. 229–230.

cruelest kind of conflict, a people's war. It was no orderly campaign, as in Europe, but a war for survival waged in a wilderness without rules or laws; a war in which each soldier fought for his own life and the lives of the men beside him, not caring who he killed in that personal cause or how many or in what manner and feeling only contempt for those who sought to impose on his savage struggle the mincing distinctions of civilized warfare—that code of battle-field ethics that attempted to humanize an essentially inhuman war. According to those "rules of engagement," it was morally right to shoot an unarmed Vietnamese who was running, but wrong to shoot one who was standing or walking; it was wrong to shoot an enemy prisoner at close range, but right for a sniper at long range to kill an enemy soldier who was no more able than a prisoner to defend himself; it was wrong for infantrymen to destroy a village with white-phosphorus grenades, but right for a fighter pilot to drop napalm on it. Ethics seemed to be a matter of distance and technology. You could never go wrong if you killed people at long range with sophisticated weapons. And then there was that inspiring order issued by General Greene: kill VC. In the patriotic fever of the Kennedy years, we had asked, "What can we do for our country?" and our country answered, "Kill VC." That was the strategy, the best our best military minds could come up with: organized butchery. But organized or not, butchery was butchery, so who was to speak of rules and ethics in a war that had none?

SOURCE 5: *A Black Soldier Sees Another Enemy*   (1984)

Richard Ford III served in South Vietnam in 1967 and 1968. After volunteering for reconnaissance patrols, the Army sent him to a Special Forces school at Nha Trang, Jan Barry's former base. There, Ford and six other African American soldiers trained together. In the following excerpt from an oral history about black soldiers in Vietnam, he recalls their experience at Nha Trang. What does his account reveal about racial tensions among American troops in Vietnam?

I didn't believe Nha Trang was still part of Vietnam, because they had barracks, hot water, had mess halls with three hot meals and air conditioning. Nha Trang was like a beach, a resort. They was ridin' around on paved streets. They be playing football and basketball. Nobody walked around with weapons. They were white. And that's what really freaked me out. All these white guys in the rear.

They told us we had to take our weapons to the armory and lock 'em up. We said naw. So they decided to let us keep our weapons till we went to this show.

It was a big club. Looked like 80 or 90 guys. Almost everybody is white. They had girls dancing and groups singin'. They reacted like we was some kind of animals, like we these guys from the boonies. They a little off. I don't know if I was paranoid or what. But they stare at you when you first come in. All of us

SOURCE: Wallace Terry, *Bloods: An Oral History of the Vietnam War by Black Veterans* (New York: Random House, 1984), pp. 38–39, 40–41.

got drunk and carryin' on. I didn't get drunk, 'cause I didn't drink. And we started firin' the weapons at the ceiling. Telling everybody to get out. "Y'all not in the war." We was frustrated because all these whites were in the back having a big show. And they were clerks. Next thing I know, about a hundred MPs all around the club. Well, they took our weapons. That was all. . . .

In the field most of the guys stayed high. Lot of them couldn't face it. In a sense, if you was high, it seemed like a game you was in. You didn't take it serious. It stopped a lot of nervous breakdown. . . .

We had a medic that give us a shot of morphine anytime you want one. I'm not talkin' about for wounded. I'm talkin' about when you want to just get high. So you can face it.

In the rear sometimes we get a grenade, dump the gunpowder out, break the firing pin. Then you'll go inside one of them little bourgeois clubs. Or go in the barracks where the supply guys are, sitting around playing bid whist and doing nothing. We act real crazy. Yell out, "Kill all y'all motherfuckers." Pull the pin and throw the grenade. And everybody would haul ass and get out. It would make a little pop sound. And we would laugh. You didn't see anybody jumpin' on them grenades.

One time in the field, though, I saw a white boy jump on a grenade. But I believe he was pushed. It ain't kill him. He lost both his legs.

The racial incidents didn't happen in the field. Just when we went to the back. It wasn't so much that they were against us. It was just that we felt that we were being taken advantage of, 'cause it seemed like more blacks in the field than in the rear.

In the rear we saw a bunch of rebel flags. They didn't mean nothing by the rebel flag. It was just saying we for the South. It didn't mean that they hated blacks. But after you in the field, you took the flags very personally.

One time we saw these flags in Nha Trang on the MP barracks. They was playing hillbilly music. Had their shoes off dancing. Had nice, pretty bunks. Mosquito nets over top the bunks. And had the nerve to have this camouflaged covers. Air conditioning. Cement floors. We just came out the jungles. We dirty, we smelly, hadn't shaved. We just went off. Said, "Y'all the real enemy. We stayin' here." We turned the bunks over, started tearing up the stereo. They just ran out. Next morning, they shipped us back up.

<hr>

SOURCE 6:   *An Infantryman Refuses "To Go Back In"*
(1990)

Charley Trujillo was an infantryman in Vietnam in 1970. In a later oral history of Hispanic soldiers in Vietnam, Trujillo recalled events after a firefight with the Vietcong. What does he reveal about soldiers' attitudes regarding the war and their commanding officers?

SOURCE: Charley Trujillo, ed., *Soldados: Chicanos in Viet Nam* (San Jose: Chusma House Publications, 1990), pp. 157–158.

We finally arived at the edge of the village. We looked like those guys in the Sergeant Rock comic books, tattered and exhausted. As we walked into the village, the South Vietnamese popular forces were playing volleyball. I began to think and try to make some sense out of what was going on. The South Vietnamese were supposed to be on our side and helping to fight the Viet Cong and North Vietnamese, but instead they were playing volleyball. The North Vietnamese, on the other hand, were very fierce and were kicking our asses. Something was not right.

Things were really getting to me. I was feeling very angry, especially toward the officers. When we got back I had an encounter with this guy named Riley. He had been a highway patrolman back in the world. I asked him where he had been when Jones and them had gotten killed. He told me that he had gotten heat prostration. I thought he was faking it. "Hell," I told him, "don't you think the sun shines on me." Some of the *gringo* soldiers would at times get angry at me because they thought I was gung ho. I didn't feel I was gung ho, I just felt that I had to do my best. Just because I felt that way did not mean I should be cannon fodder.

Greenwood and a couple of the other black soldiers who had thrown their weapons and ran, were choppered to an LZ where they met with the batallion commander. They didn't get into any trouble for running. Or to use the cliché, "Advancing in the opposite direction." Some of the black soldiers were saying things like, "The war's at home." This made me think for awhile. Actually, it was Greenwood who ignited the mutiny.

We were told that we were going in again in the morning. I, along with some of the other soldiers, told them that we refused to go in again. There wasn't any sense in it. It was clear by that evening that the majority of the soldiers did not want to go back in. A new company commander was brought in. He seemed like a sincere man and gave us a real good pep talk, just like those charismatic football coaches do. However, that didn't convince me or many of the other soldiers. We argued among ourselves through the night, the majority being against going in. The more we argued the more I was convinced it was stupid to go back in. We didn't receive any sniper or mortars throughout the night. But, in the morning a few individuals moved out on line towards the enemy as they were told. When these individuals moved out, the rest of us were more or less morally obligated to move with them. I did not move out with the first soldiers. I had told them that I wasn't going to. One of the first ones to get shot was the new CO. He died in the Medivac helicopter. There were some other deaths and one guy was even left behind. I'm glad I didn't know him. It seems as though the North Vietnamese had known what was going on and knew what they had to do in order to stop us. Within a few hours our company was picked up by helicopter and sent out to the bush where we continued our guerrilla war.

And I kept walking the point until I was also wounded and medivaced.

QUESTIONS TO CONSIDER

1. What do the biographical essay and primary sources in this chapter reveal about why the United States fought in Vietnam? What do they reveal about why American forces fought as they did?

2. How would you characterize Robert McNamara's approach to the war in Vietnam? How did his training and background influence that approach? Were antiwar protesters correct to see him as a fitting symbol for that war and the way the United States fought it?

3. What were Jan Barry's and the VVAW's criticisms of the American involvement in Vietnam? To what extent did they reflect his experiences there?

4. What do the experiences of Jan Barry and other American personnel who served in Vietnam reveal about the problems involved in fighting there? What do they reveal about why the war turned out as it did?

5. What do the essay and sources in this chapter reveal about why the Vietnam war and antiwar movement were—and remain—so controversial?

FOR FURTHER READING

Christian G. Appy, *Working-Class War: American Combat Soldiers and Vietnam* (Chapel Hill: University of North Carolina Press, 1993), examines the experiences of working-class soldiers, who came to make up the majority of the American troops in Vietnam.

David Barrett, *Uncertain Warriors: Lyndon Johnson and His Vietnam Advisers* (Lawrence: University of Kansas Press, 1993), is a concise analysis of the Johnson administration's decision-making regarding Vietnam.

David Halberstam, *The Best and the Brightest* (New York: Random House, 1972), remains one of the most engaging treatments of McNamara and the other advisers around John Kennedy and Lyndon Johnson.

George Herring, *America's Longest War: The United States in Vietnam, 1950–1975*, rev. ed. (Boston: McGraw-Hill, Inc., 2002), offers a useful overview of the war and its impact.

Andrew E. Hunt, *The Turning: A History of Vietnam Veterans Against the War* (New York: New York University Press, 1999), provides a brief look at one of the most important antiwar groups.

Deborah Shapley, *Promise and Power: The Life and Times of Robert McNamara* (Boston: Little, Brown and Company, 1993), is a thorough and illuminating examination of McNamara and his role as secretary of defense.

From Mystique to Militance:
Betty Friedan and Gloria Steinem

When Betty Friedan strode into the packed New York hotel conference room, she needed no introduction. Friedan was a founder of the National Organization for Women and the author of *The Feminine Mystique,* the 1963 bestseller that analyzed the widespread discontent of American housewives. In fact, the waiting reporters had often called her the mother of the modern women's movement. All that, though, was in the past. On this day in July 1972, the press was interested only in what Friedan had to say about feminist Gloria Steinem, who had just published the first regular issue of *Ms.* magazine and spoken at the Democratic National Convention. For several years, Friedan had listened to Steinem's attacks on the family, on men, and on women who wanted to make husbands equal partners in marriage. Now she was fed up. Women were not "forever wronged by men," Friedan declared. Feminists like Steinem who insisted otherwise were "female chauvinist boors" who threatened to corrupt the women's movement and create a backlash against it.

As she looked out at the crush of reporters, Friedan knew how many of them would interpret this attack. The often-abrasive Friedan, they would say, was jealous because Steinem had grabbed the media spotlight from her. Young, chic, and glamorous, Steinem had once worked as a Playboy Bunny to write an exposé of the Playboy Club's treatment of female employees. In just the past year, her smiling face had appeared on the covers of *Newsweek* and *New Woman.* She had even pushed aside the movie stars and models who frequently graced *McCall's* cover. Steinem was "the most visible of the activists," the magazine had announced in early 1972 as it named her its "Woman of the Year." She looked, *McCall's* proclaimed, "like a life-size, counterculture Barbie Doll." Friedan knew she never could have landed a job as a Playboy Bunny. Yet she also knew that her most important differences with Steinem were ideological, not personal. Steinem and many younger feminists focused too much on fighting private injuries committed by men against women. Instead, Friedan believed, the women's movement had to focus on changing women's public lives in politics and the workplace. Its top priority had to be an end to legal gender discrimination. Women's personal lives would improve after the battle for legal equality

❖❖ *Betty Friedan*   ❖❖ *Gloria Steinem*

was won, and that would never happen if Steinem and other feminists focused on their personal grievances and alienated men with antimale rhetoric.

Friedan also knew that the soft-spoken Steinem would not respond to her accusations. Confrontation was not Steinem's style. Claiming to have laryngitis, Steinem merely issued a press release. "Having been falsely accused . . . of liking men too much," it declared, "I am now being falsely accused . . . of not liking them enough." Steinem could remain silent, but that was not Friedan's style. The women's movement, she believed, was at a crossroads. And she was not going to stand by quietly as Steinem and other feminists destroyed what she had worked so hard to build.

"The Problem That Has No Name"

Betty Friedan had never been without strong opinions or a willingness to express them. Born in 1921, the daughter of a Peoria, Illinois, jewelry store owner, Betty grew up in comfortable but challenging circumstances. Her father, Harry Goldstein, was a Jewish immigrant from Russia who made sure that family dinners were occupied with serious discussions. He also demanded that Betty respond thoughtfully to his questions. Meanwhile, Betty and her mother fought constantly. Pretty and proper, Miriam Goldstein saw her daughter as unattractive, and the two frequently clashed over her appearance and dress. As a child, Betty also witnessed her parents' bitter fights, often provoked by her mother's outbursts. The daughter of a prominent physician, Miriam was a college graduate who had written for a newspaper society page until her marriage. She also was used to a certain lifestyle. The Goldsteins lived in an eight-room house in an upper-middle-class area of Peoria. After Betty and her younger sister and brother were born, Miriam devoted her time to golf, bridge, and shopping. She continued to spend even as business turned down during the Depression. Looking back much later on her parents' stormy relationship, Friedan observed that her own feminism "began in my mother's discontent." After Miriam quit her job at her husband's insistence, Friedan concluded, she had too much power inside her home and too little outside it. Her mother had "a typical female disorder"—that is, "impotent rage," which was often directed at her husband.

Isolation compounded Betty's unhappiness at home. In high school, her grade school friends joined sororities that excluded blacks and Jews. Feeling alone, Goldstein immersed herself in books. In fact, she read so much that her parents worried that there was something wrong and took her to a therapist. "It doesn't look nice for a girl to be so bookish," her father told her. Schoolwork, however, was her escape. She vowed that if her fellow students did not like her, they would at least respect her. The precocious child became a star student, skipped one grade, and wound up as one of the class valedictorians.

Betty Goldstein found college liberating. In 1938, she entered Smith, a women's college in Massachusetts. Many of Smith's professors were women. At a time when most women were expected to become housewives and mothers, they encouraged their female students' professional and intellectual ambitions. At Smith, Goldstein grew more interested in social and political issues. She also excelled academically. She became editor of the *Smith College Monthly* and the campus newspaper. Her first love, however, was psychology, and she was known on campus as "the psychology brain." Her last year, she submitted a thesis that one Smith administrator said "could stand for a Ph.D."

Her future seemed certain. After graduating summa cum laude in 1942, Goldstein headed to the University of California at Berkeley for graduate study in psychology. She won a scholarship that would have supported her until she finished her doctorate, but she turned it down. Later, in *The Feminine Mystique,* Friedan revealed that she had fallen in love with a jealous physics graduate student who told her she had to choose between the scholarship and him. As she related, she was in the grip of the "feminine mystique"—the widespread belief that women could find happiness only as wives and mothers. Her decision to leave graduate school may have been more complicated, however. As a senior at Smith, Goldstein had already said that a career as an academic no longer interested her. Furthermore, when she left Berkeley, she left academia *and* her boyfriend.

Soon, however, Goldstein was following the well-trod postwar path into marriage, motherhood, and suburban life. Fleeing Berkeley for New York City, she went to work for a radical labor newspaper. In 1946, she met Carl Friedan, who had only recently returned from the war in Europe. They were married within a year, and two years after that, their first child was born. Betty continued to work, writing for another labor publication. When she got pregnant again several years later, she was fired—not an uncommon experience for women at the time. By then, she had already found a new career as a housewife. The Friedans moved into an apartment in Queens and then to Rockland County, north of New York City. There Betty busied herself restoring the couple's old Victorian house on the Hudson River. Like millions of other postwar mothers, she diligently read *Baby and Child Care,* Dr. Benjamin Spock's guide to child rearing, which advised mothers of small children not to work outside the home. She even took classes at a local maternity center and at a cooking school.

Still, Betty Friedan never fell completely under the spell of the "feminine mystique" or the middle-class, suburban conformity that she later described in her book. For one thing, her reporting on workers' struggles stood in stark contrast to the flood of articles in postwar popular magazines promoting the joys of motherhood. And although the Friedans were part of the massive postwar migration of new parents to the suburbs, in many ways their experience was not typical. In Rockland County, they lived in a village of less than four hundred residents, many of whom were artists and writers. Betty pursued a successful freelance career writing for popular publications such as *Cosmopolitan, Harper's Magazine,* and *Mademoiselle,* which helped teach the legions of mostly white, middle-class, suburban women how to live. To millions of women who had taken wartime jobs, these magazines preached that they could find happiness as wives, mothers, and consumers in the home. In *The Feminine Mystique,* Friedan wrote that her articles had helped create an "almost childlike" picture of the modern housewife who was "gaily content in a world of bedroom and kitchen, sex, babies and home." Often, however, Friedan's pieces challenged conformity to domestic ideals or profiled independent women who had succeeded in careers.

Friedan's own marriage fell far short of the images of domestic contentment projected by the mass media. In fact, her union was just as stormy as her parents' had been. Betty was dissatisfied with the inadequate income of Carl's one-man advertising and public relations firm and felt that he did not support her career aspirations, an intellectually stimulating life, or equality in their marriage. According to friends, Carl complained that when he came home from work, Betty had been too busy writing to prepare dinner.

Friedan discovered the connection between her life and the lives of other women when she returned to Smith College for her fifteenth reunion in 1957. She realized that she was going back not as a successful psychologist but as a housewife. "It rankled me," she confessed, "because I hadn't lived up to my brilliant possibilities." Smith had already asked Friedan to put together a questionnaire about her classmates' lives and attitudes for the reunion. In their responses, she found a consistent theme: Her classmates had frequently written of a strange sense of emptiness and uncertainty about who they were. She later labeled this "The Problem That Has No Name." On the basis of the questionnaire results, Friedan wrote an article for *McCall's* criticizing women's role as homemakers and the monotony of housekeeping. When the magazine rejected the article, she submitted it to the *Ladies' Home Journal.* The editors there rewrote it to emphasize how education made women maladjusted as wives and mothers. Refusing the magazine permission to publish the article, she turned to *Redbook.* "Only the most neurotic housewife could agree with this," the editor informed Friedan's agent. Shortly after that, Friedan contacted a book editor. Six years later, *The Feminine Mystique* was published.

Friedan's book presented a picture of conformity to a "mystique" that trapped millions of middle-class housewives. They had accepted the message of advertisers, psychologists, and educators that happiness was to be found only as homemakers. Left with unfulfilled lives, she argued, they could find emancipation only outside the home. Friedan, of course, ignored the fact that most working women had not returned to domesticity after World War II and that millions of American women had to work to make ends meet. By focusing on the white middle class, *The Feminine Mystique* overlooked the experiences of white working-class and minority women. Nor did she offer any concrete solutions to the problem, besides insisting that women had to take responsibility for their lives. **[See Source 1.]**

Even with these shortcomings, Friedan's book had a tremendous impact. As sales climbed, letters poured in from female readers. They expressed gratitude to Friedan for having put into words their feelings that the promise of domestic bliss had proved empty. Meanwhile, Friedan began speaking around the country, preaching that women needed the same opportunities as men for meaningful work outside the home. The timing was right. Many women had found that the postwar domestic ideal poorly reflected their own experiences as wives and mothers. In addition, the millions of women who did enter the work force in the 1950s often found limited opportunities and pervasive discrimination. Between 1940 and 1960, the proportion of women who worked outside the home doubled from 15 to 30 percent. At the same time, the proportion of married working mothers jumped 400 percent. Yet in 1960, nearly two-thirds of all female workers still labored in occupations categorized as "women's work." In fact, newspaper help-wanted advertisements routinely specified whether jobs were for men or women. As a result, most women never had the same opportunities available to men. Few women served in professions such as medicine and law, and fewer still were corporate executives. Only a handful sat in Congress or on the bench. None sat on the Supreme Court. Even when women performed the same work as men, they received far less pay. In 1960, women were paid only 61 percent as much as male workers, a *drop* of 3 percent since 1955. Other issues plagued working women as well. Organized childcare was practically nonexistent. Many women also were subject to various forms of sexual harassment at a time when the term itself did not even exist, much less have legal standing. At the same time, a chorus of social scientists, psychologists, doctors, and other "experts" broadcast the message that working women were unfulfilled, unhappy, and even un-American.

When *The Feminine Mystique* was published, women were already stirring to action. In 1961, President John Kennedy had appointed the President's Commission on the Status of Women. Chaired by Eleanor Roosevelt, it had documented the inequalities women confronted in the workplace and had recommended the establishment of federal and state commissions to help women overcome them. About the same time, the civil rights movement was encouraging many women to confront their own inequality. Just as many nineteenth-century women's rights advocates had had their roots in the abolitionist movement, some modern women had participated in the fight for civil rights. Televised images of black protests against discrimination presented many other women with a powerful example of a movement for social change. Nowhere was the connection between the civil rights and women's movements more evident than in the Civil Rights Act of 1964. As a result of pressure from a handful of female activists, Title VII of the act made it illegal for employers to discriminate on the basis of sex as well as race.

As Friedan spoke to women around the country, she heard of more and more examples of gender discrimination. And as women began to flood the Equal Employment Opportunity Commission* with complaints, she came to realize that the federal government had no serious interest in enforcing Title VII. To get the civil rights law enforced, she concluded, women had to create a pressure group similar to the National Association for the Advancement of Colored People. In a Washington, D.C., hotel in 1966, Friedan and a handful of other women attending a conference of state women's commissions met to do just that. Writing on a napkin, Friedan defined the purpose of the new organization: "to take the actions needed to bring women into the mainstream of American society." She also scribbled a name for the organization: National Organization for Women (NOW). Then the women anted up and elected a president. When they were finished, NOW had $135 in its treasury and Betty Friedan as its leader. [See Source 2.]

"She Didn't Have To"

The Beach Book hit the bookstores the same year as *The Feminine Mystique*. As the title suggests, it was very light summer reading. In fact, it contained little more than excerpts from other books about beaches and author Gloria Steinem's sunbathing fantasies. "What a tan will do is make you look good," Steinem wrote, "and that justifies everything." In 1963, the twenty-nine-year-old magazine writer knew all about looking good—and having a great time. After all, Steinem was one of New York's "beautiful people," the young professionals in the early 1960s who turned their backs on suburban domesticity for a glamorous—and single—life in the big city. It was a life far removed from Betty Friedan's world of barbecues, station wagons, and Parent Teacher Association meetings.

It was also a long way from the life Steinem had known as a child. The daughter of a ne'er-do-well father and a mentally ill mother, Steinem grew up in a rat-infested house in Toledo, Ohio. Her father, Leo, was the son of a Jewish immigrant who had made a tidy fortune in real estate. Leo's mother was an early Ohio suffragette. Leo had inherited neither his father's business acumen nor his mother's concern for women's rights. Instead, the amiable college dropout took jobs and chased moneymaking schemes that never worked out. Gloria's mother, the daughter of a locomotive engineer, had come from far more modest circumstances. Like Betty Friedan's mother, Ruth Steinem was a newspaper society-page reporter who was forced to give up her job after her marriage. Unlike Miriam Goldstein, however, Ruth had a great fear of financial insecurity. In 1930, five years after the birth of the Steinems' first daughter, she suffered a nervous breakdown. By the time Gloria was born four years later, the Steinems had moved to Michigan, where Leo was developing a resort. As Leo pursued his latest dream, Ruth slipped into mental illness.

Gloria Steinem's childhood was defined by her father's declining financial circumstances and her mother's deteriorating mental state. When she was a girl,

---

*Equal Employment Opportunity Commission: The federal body established to enforce Title VII of the Civil Rights Act of 1964.

the family lived at the Michigan resort during the summer and traveled to California or Florida during the rest of the year, while Leo plied his second trade as an itinerant antiques dealer. Wartime rationing eventually sank Leo's resort, and conflicts about money between Leo and Ruth finally led to their divorce in 1945. By then, Gloria's sister, Susanne, had gone off to Smith College, and eleven-year-old Gloria was left to care for her mother. After they moved into a rundown house that Ruth's family owned in Toledo, Gloria grew up fast. While other girls were playing, she kept house and prepared meals. The experience left her independent and detached. Escape finally came in 1951, when Gloria spent her senior year in high school in Washington, D.C., where Susanne now worked. At her sister's urging, Gloria also applied to Smith and was accepted. The next fall, a decade after Betty Friedan had graduated, Gloria Steinem entered Smith's ivy-covered walls. With the help of money that her mother had managed to save for her college education, she thrived in her new environment. Making the dean's list three years in a row, she graduated in 1956 magna cum laude.

"Socially precocious," as one classmate put it, Steinem also had little difficulty attracting men. In her senior year, she fell in love with one and accepted his proposal of marriage. Then suddenly, she changed her mind. Having taken care of her mother for so long, she saw marriage as a loss of freedom and control. Unlike many of her college friends who sought security in marriage, she was terrified at the prospect. After graduation, while in London awaiting a visa to study in India, Steinem discovered that she was pregnant as the result of a final fling with her former fiancé. Overcome with panic, she even contemplated suicide. After finding a doctor who would perform an abortion, a procedure that was illegal in the United States, she felt a sense of responsibility for having taken control of her life.

After a year and a half abroad, Steinem returned to the United States, determined to land a job as a reporter in New York City. Gradually, she began to find writing assignments. In 1963, she spent three weeks working as a Playboy Bunny at the Playboy Club to gather information for an article for the entertainment magazine *Show*. The result, "A Bunny's Tale," caused a sensation. It also opened doors. Gradually, Steinem began to write celebrity profiles and articles on fashion for publications such as the *Ladies' Home Journal, Glamour,* and the *New York Times Magazine*. Steinem made her mark, however, with pieces that offered advice for single women.

Her timing was excellent. By the early 1960s, increasing numbers of young people, growing affluence, more leisure time, and the invention of the birth control pill had conspired to spark a "sexual revolution." Many young professionals had been attracted to the single life in New York and other large cities. Some of them had no doubt been inspired by Helen Gurley Brown's bestseller *Sex and the Single Girl,* which touted a single and sexually active life as an alternative to marriage. The chic Steinem epitomized this "swinging singles" lifestyle. She was an attractive, well-educated, professional, unattached woman. In the vanguard of the sexual revolution, Steinem was well positioned to offer advice to young women who had rejected the "feminine mystique" but were unsure about the sexual revolution's new rules. By 1965, she commanded three thousand dollars per article and made thirty thousand dollars a year—more than five times the median income for men. She also had become something of a celebrity.

In 1965, with only seven years' experience as a freelance writer, she was profiled in *Newsweek*.

Soon Steinem's involvement in numerous causes made her even more visible. She was active in the antiwar movement, organized peace demonstrations in New York, and worked on the unsuccessful presidential campaigns of Democratic candidates Eugene McCarthy and George McGovern. She helped raise funds in New York for the United Farm Workers, organized in 1966 by César Chávez to unionize migrant farm workers. She even marched in California with Chávez in support of the union's boycott of table grapes. To some observers, she personified "radical chic," a term coined by writer Tom Wolfe to describe the desire of affluent liberals to associate with causes such as Black Power and the unionization of farm workers. Steinem countered that label by saying that she identified with "out" groups because she belonged to one.

Compared to many other feminist leaders, Steinem had come relatively late to the women's movement. She had read *The Feminine Mystique* but thought it pertained mostly to white, middle-class, suburban women, with whom she had little interest in associating. She had not joined the rapidly growing NOW because she did not want to identify with women who were asking men for things. Thus she refused to join Friedan and other NOW members in 1969 when they attempted to change the policy of an exclusive restaurant in New York that barred women at lunchtime. Shortly after that, however, she attended a meeting on abortion held by a feminist organization called Redstockings. There she experienced a feminist awakening, just as Friedan had at her college reunion.

Formed by writers Shulamith Firestone and Ellen Willis, Redstockings was one of a growing number of radical feminist organizations. The members of these groups had often encountered widespread sexual exploitation in civil rights and antiwar organizations. For them, the comment by Student Nonviolent Coordinating Committee leader Stokely Carmichael that the "position of women in SNCC is prone," summed up their problem. These activists rejected as far too limited NOW's primary goal of gaining equal access for women. They attributed women's problems to class oppression rather than discrimination and believed that women needed not rights but liberation from a male-dominated society. At the Redstockings meeting, Steinem listened to the tales of women who had had illegal abortions or had tried unsuccessfully to get abortions. She began to realize that these women's experiences, like her own years before, were a reflection of women's subordinate position in society. No one at the meeting used the phrase "the personal is political," but that idea, soon popular with many feminists, was beginning to dawn on Steinem.

Steinem's awakening led her to a different view of women's struggle for equality than Friedan's. While Friedan and NOW worked to end gender discrimination, Steinem called for a fundamental restructuring of institutions to do away with the nuclear family and what she called "patriarchal society." Securing laws ending discrimination against women was not enough, she said. Instead, women needed to concentrate on sexual issues and a broad range of relationships between men and women. A growing number of younger women shared these views by the early 1970s. In fact, thousands of these women were coming together in numerous small groups that made up a grass-roots "women's liberation" movement. Many of these women rejected more than the makeup and feminine clothing worn by older women's rights advocates. They also spurned NOW as too stuffy, respectable, and conservative. They concentrated on creating numerous alternative institutions and services, from support groups to rape crisis centers to women's shelters. They also focused on the "hidden injuries" suffered by women as a class. In "consciousness-raising" sessions, small groups of women gathered to discuss their concerns regarding work, health, sex, family, and marriage. Attacking the everyday practices that seemed to degrade women, these feminists concluded that problems in their personal relationships reflected the organization of society. In thousands of protests, marches, and rallies, they called for sweeping changes in everything from college courses to childcare.

Steinem's career reflected these broader concerns. As a journalist, she focused on women's "capitulation to the small humiliations." In 1971, she founded *Ms.,* the first feminist mass-circulation magazine. By targeting housewives and other women who never read feminist publications or alternative newspapers, Steinem sought to bring the concerns surrounding "women's liberation" to a wider audience. *Ms.* concentrated on traditional women's rights issues such as the Equal Rights Amendment* and job discrimination, but it also took up the more "radical" issues of abortion rights, lesbianism, sexuality, pornography, women's health, and gender roles. **[See Source 3.]** Later issues of *Ms.* contained a "No Comment" page to which readers could submit advertisements that debased women. Steinem also emphasized the need for "sisterhood." **[See Source 4.]** *Ms.* began to receive a flood of letters from readers who for the first time felt that they were not alone. Within a year, the magazine had a circulation of 350,000 and an estimated readership of 1.4 million.

Once again, Steinem's timing was perfect. When the national media finally discovered the women's movement in the early 1970s, they thrust Steinem into the spotlight. To many journalists, Steinem had little competition: She was photogenic and quick-witted, and she made good copy. She also refuted the widespread assumption that feminists were either lesbians or, as *Newsweek* put it, "losers who couldn't play the game according to conventional rules." The newsmagazine observed, "What gets nearly everyone about Steinem as Liberationist is that she Didn't Have To."

"Thank God for Gloria Steinem"

After NOW's founding in 1966, Betty Friedan spent countless hours laboring in the fields, planting seeds of local NOW chapters all over the country. For Friedan, divorced in 1969, the struggle on behalf of women's equality involved endless picketing, petitioning, writing, speaking, and marching. Slowly, though, all that work began to pay off. By 1973, NOW claimed more than twenty thousand members. The growing women's movement also started to see concrete gains in the workplace and the law. NOW successfully challenged gender discrimination

---

Equal Rights Amendment: First proposed in 1923, the amendment called for equal rights for women under the law. It was taken up by NOW in the late 1960s and generally embraced by the women's movement in the early 1970s.

in newspaper help-wanted ads and secured gender as a category in affirmative action guidelines. Its efforts ended the widespread airline policy of dismissing flight attendants when they married or turned thirty-five. It also filed a successful complaint against thirteen hundred corporations, forcing them to give underpaid female workers back pay.

Friedan now believed that the biggest threat to further progress lay within the movement's own ranks. And in her mind, Gloria Steinem was the most obvious symbol of that growing threat. True, the lines separating Friedan and Steinem were often blurred. Friedan had come out shortly after NOW's founding in support of abortion rights, driving some women from the organization. Likewise, both Steinem and Friedan supported the passage of the Equal Rights Amendment and lobbied Congress to secure its passage. In addition, Steinem was hardly the most radical of feminists. Kate Millett, the author of *Sexual Politics* (1970) and Shulamith Firestone, the socialist author of *The Dialectics of Sex* (1970), and cofounder of Redstockings, were only two of the many visible and far more radical feminists. Firestone, for example, argued that gender was the root of women's oppression and that they needed to be freed as soon as possible from the obligatory tasks of bearing and rearing children. In fact, after *Ms.* began publication, radical feminists often attacked it for accepting advertisements that frequently depicted women as thin and rich. Still, Friedan did not appreciate the telegenic Steinem's increasing visibility in the movement and the media. A lot of unglamorous effort had gone into building NOW, and it was galling to watch Steinem steal the spotlight.

Friedan's growing bitterness toward Steinem was about more than jealousy, however. The NOW founder was convinced that sexual matters were private. The more antimale, antimarriage feminists discussed them, the more middle-class people would be alienated from the women's movement. Few feminists seemed more antimarriage than Steinem, who remained single and once declared that "a woman without a husband is like a fish without a bicycle." Younger feminists like Steinem, Friedan insisted in 1969, had to understand that the "gut issues" of this revolution were employment and education, not "sexual fantasy." Later, she said, "I didn't think . . . it mattered who was in the missionary position—if unequal power positions in real life weren't changed."

Friedan was especially worried about the potentially divisive and alienating issue of lesbianism. Opposed to shows of solidarity with lesbians in the movement, she characterized the lesbian issue as a "lavender menace." She also had little use for feminist consciousness-raising sessions, which often involved frank discussions of sex. Friedan and many older women's rights advocates were repulsed by what they considered a self-indulgent activity. Politics, she believed, involved hard work and discipline, not self-absorbed talk. Thus transforming one's personal life—or one's consciousness—was not a political act. As she put it, the women's movement could not "afford the mental masturbation" that such sessions represented.

In 1970, Friedan announced that NOW's primary "thrust" would be "political." Unlike some other feminists, Steinem actually agreed with Friedan about the importance of taking the feminist cause into the political arena. In 1971, several hundred women, including Friedan, Steinem, and Fannie Lou Hamer (see Chapter 11), formed the National Women's Political Caucus (NWPC). The idea was Friedan's. The NWPC's goal was to get more women elected to office. At the time, women held only 1.6 percent of the top jobs in government, including only one U.S. Senate seat and twelve seats in the House of Representatives. They held no governorships and no seats on the Supreme Court. Friedan and Steinem split immediately over the NWPC's membership. Friedan envisioned a mainstream organization in which even conservative Republican women were welcome. Allied with New York congresswoman Bella Abzug, Steinem wanted to open membership only to women who agreed on important issues. In her view, the NWPC's membership should be limited to those who wanted "to humanize society." In the end, Steinem and Abzug were able to define the guidelines by which female candidates would be evaluated. They included support for withdrawal from the Vietnam War, the Equal Rights Amendment, and the repeal of abortion and contraception laws. The division surfaced at the Democratic National Convention in 1972 when Steinem, not Friedan, was chosen as the NWPC's spokeswoman at the convention. After watching the takeover of the NWPC by Steinem and Abzug, Friedan had had enough. At a press conference called by *McCall's* magazine shortly after the convention, Friedan revealed why she was blasting Steinem and her approach to the women's movement in the magazine's next issue. "If we make men the enemy they will surely lash back at us," she observed. **[See Source 5.]**

Friedan's press conference generated much attention. The fight between Friendan and Steinem seemed to symbolize the split in the women's movement between "moderates," who fought primarily for equality under the law, and "radicals," who believed in the abolition of gender roles. Only later was it clear that the press conference actually marked Friedan's declining influence in an increasingly fragmented women's movement. As the movement spread, the women involved in it were splintering into thousands of organizations and groups. Meanwhile, Friedan had no organizational base from which to operate. No longer the head of NOW and eclipsed in the media by Steinem as the symbol of feminism, her visibility rapidly began to fade. When nearly five thousand women attended the National Women's Conference* in 1977, Friedan had no official position and her presence drew little fanfare.

By then, however, the movement that Friedan had helped spark had triumphed in many ways. Women's issues had become largely institutionalized in American society. Under assault by administrative, legislative, and court decisions, many barriers blocking women's access to institutions and equal treatment were finally falling. Beginning in 1971, Congress passed a flood of gender equity laws. They ranged from penalties for unequal funding of male and female school sports programs to a ban on discrimination in lending based on gender or marital status. Meanwhile, the courts began to overturn gender-labeled jobs and upheld the principle of equal pay for equal work. And in 1973, the Supreme Court upheld a woman's right to have an abortion in *Roe v. Wade.*

National Women's Conference: A conference held in Houston, Texas, in 1977. Originally proposed in 1975 during the United Nations' International Women's Year, it was funded by Congress to promote "equality between men and women."

The impact of these triumphs would be particularly evident in education and employment. By the mid-1970s, schools had begun to eliminate gender-segregated classes, all-male colleges had opened their doors to women, and publishers were working to rid textbooks of sexist stereotypes. In the 1970s, the number of female college students rose by more than 60 percent. By the decade's end, more women than men were enrolled in college. At the same time, the ranks of women workers continued to swell. Aided by numerous class-action suits and sex discrimination charges, millions of them worked in jobs that had once been classified as men's work. Meanwhile, Americans' attitudes about women and gender also were changing. In 1971, a minority of women in one poll approved of "efforts to strengthen and change women's status in society." Four years later, 63 percent approved of such efforts. As attitudes changed, so did sexist language—a major target of feminists. *Ms.*, for instance, came to replace *Miss* or *Mrs.* as a common form of address for women—a change that Steinem's magazine helped bring about.

Another measure of the movement's success by the mid-1970s was the growing assault on it. The antifeminist backlash was ignited by the landmark *Roe v. Wade* ruling on abortion. It was stoked further by the fight over the Equal Rights Amendment (ERA). Prohibiting discrimination based on gender, the ERA was passed by Congress and submitted to the states for ratification in 1972. Conservative antifeminists such as Phyllis Schlafly, however, argued that the ERA would erase differences between men and women and undermine the family. Schlafly, the founder of Stop ERA, asserted that feminism was a movement led by a "cosmopolitan elite" out of touch with the values of "traditional" families. In the late 1970s, as many Americans grew more conservative in a stagnate economy, Schlafly and other antifeminists found a larger audience. At the same time, many younger women began to reject the label "feminist" even though they actually accepted the movement's goals. Increasingly unaware of the struggles waged by women since the early 1960s, many of them simply took the gains of the women's movement for granted. By the time Ronald Reagan was elected president in 1980, the increasingly fragmented women's movement had lost its momentum and the ERA was a dead issue. The deadline for its adoption passed in 1982 without its ratification.

Even as the women's movement dissipated in the wake of its successes, Friedan and Steinem carried on their personal fight. Concerned about the growing conservative attack on the women's movement, Friedan continued her long struggle to disassociate it from "radical" feminists. In the mid-1970s, she blamed the ERA's defeat by various state legislatures on "extremist groups" such as *Ms.* magazine. Later, in *The Second Stage* (1981), she argued that they were responsible for the rise of antifeminism and called for a new stage in the women's movement in which women would move beyond the desire to "do it all." Women were no longer oppressed by a feminine mystique, Friedan concluded, but by a "feminist mystique." Feminists had to stop "wallowing in the victim state" and accept the importance of families. Meanwhile, under Steinem's guidance, *Ms.* simply wrote Friedan and NOW out of women's history and rarely mentioned them at all. Steinem remained convinced that the "first stage" of feminism—battling the pervasive sexism in American society—was not over, despite the movement's impressive legal victories. As a speaker, a writer, and *Ms.* editor, she continued to call for changes in the everyday lives of women.

By the 1980s, Steinem and her magazine no longer commanded the attention they once had. Steinem's goal in founding *Ms.* had been to bring the women's movement into the mainstream of American society. Despite the conservative backlash against feminism, the magazine had helped the movement do just that. As the *New York Times* put it in 1984, "'Women's Issues' have become everyone's." To many Americans, there now seemed little need for a mainstream feminist magazine. In 1987, Steinem stepped down as editor of *Ms.* when an Australian publisher purchased it, but she remained fixed in the public's mind as the symbol of the women's movement. Thus, when Sally Ride blasted off in 1983 as the first American woman in space, Ride's mother paid tribute not to Friedan but to her longtime rival. "Thank God," Joyce Ride exclaimed, "for Gloria Steinem."

PRIMARY SOURCES

Source 1:   Betty Friedan, *The Feminine Mystique*   (1963)

In 1963, Betty Friedan attacked the postwar domestic ideal in her best-selling book, The Feminine Mystique. *How does Friedan define the problem confronting middle-class housewives? What is her solution to it?*

The problem lay buried, unspoken, for many years in the minds of American women. It was a strange stirring, a sense of dissatisfaction, a yearning that women suffered in the middle of the twentieth century in the United States. Each suburban wife struggled with it alone. As she made the beds, shopped for groceries, matched slipcover material, ate peanut butter sandwiches with her children, chauffeured Cub Scouts and Brownies, lay beside her husband at night—she was afraid to ask even of herself the silent question—"Is this all?". . .

The suburban housewife—she was the dream image of the young American women and the envy, it was said, of women all over the world. The American housewife—freed by science and labor-saving appliances from the drudgery, the dangers of childbirth and the illnesses of her grandmother. She was healthy, beautiful, educated, concerned only about her husband, her children, her home. She had found true feminine fulfillment. As a housewife and mother, she was respected as a full and equal partner to man in his world. She was free to choose automobiles, clothes, appliances, supermarkets; she had everything that women ever dreamed of.

In the fifteen years after World War II, this mystique of feminine fulfillment became the cherished and self-perpetuating core of contemporary American culture. Millions of women lived their lives in the image of those pretty pictures of the American suburban housewife, kissing their husbands goodbye in front

Source: Betty Friedan, *The Feminine Mystique* (New York: W. W. Norton & Company, 1963), pp. 15, 18, 342, 344. Copyright © 1983, 1974, 1973, 1963 by Betty Friedan. Used by permission of W. W. Norton & Company, Inc.

of the picture window, depositing their station-wagonsful of children at school, and smiling as they ran the new electric waxer over the spotless kitchen floor. . . .

It would be quite wrong for me to offer any woman easy how-to answers to this problem. There are no easy answers, in America today; it is difficult, painful, and takes perhaps a long time for each woman to find her own answer. First, she must unequivocally say "no" to the housewife image. This does not mean, of course, that she must divorce her husband, abandon her children, give up her home. She does not have to choose between marriage and career; that was the mistaken choice of the feminine mystique. In actual fact, it is not as difficult as the feminine mystique implies, to combine marriage and motherhood and even the kind of lifelong personal purpose that once was called "career." It merely takes a new life plan—in terms of one's whole life as a woman.

The first step in that plan is to see housework for what it is—not a career, but something that must be done as quickly and efficiently as possible. . . .

The second step . . . is to see marriage as it really is, brushing aside the veil of over-glorification imposed by the feminine mystique. Many women I talked to felt strangely discontented with their husbands, continually irritated with their children, when they saw marriage and motherhood as the final fulfillment of their lives. But when they began to use their various abilities with a purpose of their own in society, they not only spoke of a new feeling of "aliveness" or "completeness" in themselves, but of a new, though hard to define, difference in the way they felt about their husbands and children. . . .

The only way for a woman, as for a man, to find herself, to know herself as a person, is by creative work of her own. There is no other way. But a job, any job, is not the answer—in fact, it can be part of the trap. Women who do not look for jobs equal to their actual capacity, who do not let themselves develop the lifetime interests and goals which require serious education and training, who take a job at twenty or forty to "help out at home" or just to kill extra time, are walking, almost as surely as the ones who stay inside the housewife trap, to a nonexistent future.

Source 2:   *NOW's Statement of Purpose*   (1966)

The National Organization for Women proclaimed its premises and goals after its formation in 1966. How do NOW's goals reflect Friedan's analysis of the problems facing women? Do its proposals to achieve equality pertain to problems confronting women in the "public" or "private" sphere of life?

Source: From NOW's Statement of Purpose (1966). Excerpt reprinted by permission of National Organization for Women. This is a historical document which does not reflect the current language or priorities of the organization. Reprinted in Betty Friedan, *It Changed My Life* (New York: W. W. Norton & Company, 1976), pp. 87–88, 90–91.

The purpose of NOW is to take action to bring women into full participation in the mainstream of American society now, exercising all the privileges and responsibilities thereof in truly equal partnership with men. . . .

NOW is dedicated to the proposition that women first and foremost are human beings, who, like all other people in our society, must have the chance to develop their fullest human potential. We believe that women can achieve such equality only by accepting to the full the challenges and responsibilities they share with all other people in our society, as part of the decision-making mainstream of American political, economic and social life.

We organize to initiate or support action, nationally or in any part of this nation, by individuals or organizations, to break through the silken curtain of prejudice and discrimination against women in government, industry, the professions, the churches, the political parties, the judiciary, the labor unions, in education, science, medicine, law, religion and every other field of importance in American society. . . .

There is no civil rights movement to speak for women, as there has been for Negroes and other victims of discrimination. The National Organization for Women must therefore begin to speak.

WE BELIEVE that the power of American law, and the protection guaranteed by the U.S. Constitution to the civil rights of all individuals, must be effectively applied and enforced to isolate and remove patterns of sex discrimination, to ensure equality of opportunity in employment and education, and equality of civil and political rights and responsibilities on behalf of women, as well as for Negroes and other deprived groups. . . .

WE REJECT the current assumptions that a man must carry the sole burden of supporting himself, his wife, his family, and that a woman is automatically entitled to lifelong support by a man upon her marriage, or that marriage, home and family are primarily woman's world and responsibility—hers, to dominate, his to support. We believe that a true partnership between the sexes demands a different concept of marriage, an equitable sharing of the responsibilities of home and children and of the economic burdens of their support. We believe that proper recognition should be given to the economic and social value of home-making and child care. To these ends, we will seek to open a reexamination of laws and mores governing marriage and divorce, for we believe that the current state of "half-equality" between the sexes discriminates against both men and woman, and is the cause of much unnecessary hostility between the sexes.

Source 3:   *"Wonder Woman for President"*   (1972)

Started in 1971 as a one-shot insert in New York *magazine, Ms. claimed to be a magazine for "female human beings." Early issues included articles such as "Raising Your Kids Without Sex Roles," "Women Tell the Truth About Their Abortions," and "Why I Want a Wife" (which detailed how wives created a lot of options for their husbands that wives themselves did not have). What does this cover from the first regular issue of Ms. in July 1972 reveal about its approach to the women's movement? How did its approach differ from that of the members of the National Organization for Women?*

Source: *Ms.,* July 1972.

Source 4: Gloria Steinem, *"Sisterhood"* (1972)

In this column from the preview issue of Ms. *magazine, Gloria Steinem discusses her feminist awakening. How does her analysis of this experience differ from Betty Friedan's in* The Feminine Mystique?

At first my discoveries seemed personal. In fact, they were the same ones so many millions of women have made and are continuing to make. Greatly simplified, they go like this: Women are human beings first, with minor differences from men that apply largely to the single act of reproduction. We share the dreams, capabilities, and weaknesses of all human beings, but our occasional pregnancies and other visible differences have been used—even more pervasively, if less brutally, than racial differences have been used—to create an "inferior" group and an elaborate division of labor. The division is continued for a clear if often unconscious reason: the economic and social profit of males as a group.

Once this feminist realization dawned, I reacted in what turned out to be predictable ways. First, I was amazed at the simplicity and obviousness of a realization that made sense, at last, of my life experience. I couldn't figure out why I hadn't seen it before. Second, I realized how far that new vision of life was from the system around us, and how tough it would be to explain this feminist realization at all, much less to get people (especially, though not only, men) to accept so drastic a change. . . .

Occasionally, these efforts at explaining actually succeed. More often, I get the feeling that most women are speaking Urdu and most men are speaking Pali.*

Whether joyful or painful, both kinds of reaction to our discovery have a great reward. They give birth to sisterhood.

First, we share the exhilaration of growth and self-discovery, the sensation of having the scales fall from our eyes. Whether we are giving other women this new knowledge or receiving it from them, the pleasure for all concerned is enormous. And very moving.

In the second stage, when we're exhausted from dredging up facts and arguments for the men whom we had previously thought advanced and intelligent, we make another simple discovery: women understand. We may share experiences, make jokes, paint pictures, and describe humiliations that mean little to men, but *women understand.* . . .

[Lack of self-esteem] is the most tragic punishment that society inflicts on any second-class group. Ultimately the brainwashing works, and we ourselves come to believe our group is inferior. Even if we achieve a little success in the world and think of ourselves as "different," we don't want to associate with our group. We want to identify up, not down (clearly my problem in not wanting to join women's groups). We want to be the only woman in the office, or the only black family on the block, or the only Jew in the club.

Source: Gloria Steinem, "Sisterhood," in *Outrageous Acts and Everyday Rebellions* (New York: Holt, Rinehart and Winston, 1983), pp. 113, 114, 116–117; © Gloria Steinem; originally from *Ms.,* December 1971 (1972).

Urdu and Pali: Two languages spoken on the Indian subcontinent.

The pain of looking back at wasted, imitative years is enormous. Trying to write like men. Valuing myself and other women according to the degree of our acceptance by men—socially, in politics, and in our professions. It's as painful as it is now to hear two grown-up female human beings competing with each other on the basis of their husband's status, like servants whose identity rests on the wealth or accomplishments of their employers.

And this lack of esteem that makes us put each other down is still the major enemy of sisterhood. Women who are conforming to society's expectations view the nonconformists with justifiable alarm. *Those noisy, unfeminine women,* they say to themselves. *They will only make trouble for us all.* Women who are quietly nonconforming, hoping nobody will notice, are even more alarmed because they have more to lose. And that makes sense, too.

The status quo protects itself by punishing all challengers, especially women whose rebellion strikes at the most fundamental social organization: the sex roles that convince half the population that its identity depends on being first in work or in war, and the other half that it must serve as docile, unpaid, or underpaid labor.

In fact, there seems to be no punishment inside the white male club that quite equals the ridicule and personal viciousness reserved for women who rebel. Attractive or young women who act forcefully are assumed to be either unnatural or male-controlled. If they succeed, it could only have been sexually, through men. Old women or women considered unattractive by male standards are accused of acting out of bitterness, because they could not get a man. Any woman who chooses to behave like a full human being should be warned that the armies of the status quo will treat her as something of a dirty joke. That's their natural and first weapon. She will *need* sisterhood.

SOURCE 5:   Betty Friedan, *"Beyond Women's Liberation"* (1972)

In this column for McCall's *magazine, Betty Friedan blasts Gloria Steinem and other feminists who think like Steinem. What is the basis of Friedan's disagreement with them?*

On a recent evening, over coffee in a sparsely furnished New York apartment, the forty-five-year-old male recipient of an act of female banishment talks of Gloria Steinem's proclamation of Sisterhood in the magazine *Ms.* In a tone of cold, measured outrage I find positively startling (previously he has identified completely with the women's movement), he says: "I think we have had just about enough of this." I reread the article, to find out why it makes him so murderous. Is it a certain tone implying that women are special and pure, forever wronged by men? "I get the feeling that we are speaking Urdu and the men are speaking

SOURCE: Betty Friedan, "Beyond Women's Liberation," *McCall's,* August 1972, pp. 82, 83, 134. Copyright 1972 by Betty Friedan. First published in *McCall's.* Reprinted by permission of Curtis Brown, Ltd.

Pali . . ." the article says. "Women understand. We may share experiences, make jokes, paint pictures, and describe humiliations that mean nothing to men, but *women understand*. . . . Any woman who chooses to behave like a full human being should be warned that the armies of the *status quo* will treat her as something of a dirty joke. . . . She will *need* sisterhood." . . .

If I were a man, I would object strenuously to the assumption that women have any moral or spiritual superiority as a *class* or that men share some brute insensitivity as a *class*. This is male chauvinism in reverse; it is female sexism. It is, in fact, female chauvinism, and those who preach or practice it seem to me to be corrupting our movement for equality and inviting a backlash that endangers the very real gains we have won these past few years. . . .

Female chauvinism denies us full humanity as women in another way, too, one that threatens backlash among women even more than men. Those who would make an *abstract ideology* out of sex, aping the old-fashioned rhetoric of class warfare or the separatist extremists of race warfare, paradoxically deny the concrete reality of women's sexuality, mundane or glorious, burden or pleasure, exaggerated or repressed, as it has been in the past. When Gloria Steinem dismisses marriage as "prostitution," in a speech to the League of Women Voters, the assumption is that no woman would ever want to go to bed with a man if she didn't need to sell her body for bread or a mink coat. Does this mean that any woman who admits tenderness or passion for her husband, or any man, has sold out to the enemy? . . .

I have always objected to rhetoric that treats the women's movement as class warfare against men—women oppressed, as a class, by men, the oppressors. I do not believe that the conditions we are trying to change are caused by a conspiracy for "the economic and social profit of men as a group," as Gloria Steinem sees it. The causes are more complex, and burden men as well as benefit them. My definition of feminism is simply that women are people, in the fullest sense of the word, who must be free to move in society with all the privileges and opportunities and responsibilities that are their human and American right. This does not mean class warfare against men, which denies our sexual and human bonds with them, nor does it mean the elimination of children, which denies our human future.

It seems to me that all the women's movement ever was, or needs to be, is a stage in the whole human rights movement, bringing another group—a majority this time, into the mainstream of human society, with all the perils and promises and personal risks this involves.

QUESTIONS TO CONSIDER

1. Citing specific primary sources, compare Betty Friedan's and Gloria Steinem's views about feminism's tactics and goals. Was the conflict between them primarily one of style or substance?

2. How did Friedan's and Steinem's backgrounds and experiences influence their views about the women's movement? Do you think their disagreements were influenced more by the life experiences that were unique to each woman, the different times in which they matured, or other factors?

3. Based on the essay and primary sources in this chapter, how would you respond to the argument of one historian that Friedan left unchallenged the dividing line between public and private issues in seeking equality for women, whereas "radical" feminists wished to make "personal life itself into a political issue"? Did Steinem make the personal political?

4. What are the similarities and differences between the rise of the women's movement in the late 1960s and the rise of the earlier civil rights movement? What are the similarities and differences between the issues that divided Friedan and Steinem and those separating Roy Wilkins and Fannie Lou Hamer (see Chapter 11)?

5. Did Friedan or Steinem have a bigger impact on changing the status of women in American society in the 1960s and 1970s? Why do you think Steinem frequently received more public acclaim than Friedan?

For Further Reading

William H. Chafe, *The Paradox of Change: American Women in the 20th Century* (New York: Oxford University Press, 1991), is a brief overview of the modern women's movement and the struggle for women's rights in the twentieth century.

Sara Evans, *Personal Politics: The Roots of Women's Liberation in the Civil Rights Movement and the New Left* (New York: Vintage Books, 1980), discusses the impact of the civil rights and student movements on the struggle for women's liberation.

Betty Friedan, *It Changed My Life: Writings on the Women's Movement* (New York: Random House, 1976), presents Friedan's views during the early stages of the movement.

Carolyn Heilbron, *The Education of a Woman: The Life of Gloria Steinem* (New York: Dial Press, 1995), offers a positive account of Steinem's life and contributions to feminism.

Daniel Horowitz, *Betty Friedan and the Making of the Feminine Mystique: The American Left, the Cold War, and Modern Feminism* (Amherst: University of Massachusetts Press, 1998), is a thorough examination of Friedan's life up to the publication of *The Feminine Mystique* that emphasizes the way she reinvented her life in the book.

Ruth Rosen, *The World Split Open: How the Modern Women's Movement Changed America* (New York: Viking Press, 2000), provides an engaging analysis of the women's movement and its impact on society.

Miriam Schneir, ed., *Feminism in Our Time: The Essential Writings, World War II to the Present* (New York: Vintage Books, 1994), includes selections from numerous women involved in the twentieth-century women's movement.

Individualism and the Environment in the 1980s: Edward Abbey and James Watt

The new bridge was a massive symbol of civilization's conquest of nature. Built on the Utah-Arizona border right next to the Glen Canyon Dam, it arched 700 feet over the Colorado River. As the governors of Utah and Arizona cut the ceremonial ribbons to mark the magnificent structure's opening, the assembled guests cheered. Then the fireworks began. The frightened spectators thought the pyrotechnics were part of the celebration, but they were wrong. The fireworks had been set off to clear the 400-foot-long bridge of people. As the last person ran off the structure, a huge explosion ripped it in two. Within seconds, the bridge sat in the sandstone canyon below, the victim of the Monkey Wrench Gang. The gang's next target was the dam itself. Behind its 792,000 tons of concrete and steel lay Lake Powell, a reservoir that had inundated some of the most spectacular desert land on earth. To these ecoterrorists, the dam was a sacrilege— the ultimate symbol of humankind's rape of the wilderness.

The bombing of the bridge at Glen Canyon, of course, never happened. It is the opening scene in Edward Abbey's novel *The Monkey Wrench Gang*, published in 1975. A park ranger turned writer, Abbey was a self-proclaimed "voice crying in the wilderness." Introduced to the deserts of the American Southwest as a young man, he saw them as both beautiful and sacred. He also believed that they were under an "immoral" assault by corporate interests and government bureaucrats. For Abbey, however, the destruction of the deserts was more than a crime against nature. Rather, it threatened Americans' very freedom, which depended on the existence of open, unspoiled land. With his fictional band, Abbey hoped to stir people to take actions that he was too "cowardly" to perform himself. He did. In the 1980s, ecoterrorists claimed credit for acts of sabotage against developers, ski resorts, power and timber companies, and other private interests doing business on public lands. They were inspired, they said, by Abbey's writings.

Whether real or fictional, environmental saboteurs appeared frightening and dangerous to many people. James Watt, for one, had nothing but contempt for them. The secretary of the interior under Ronald Reagan, Watt shared Abbey's belief that freedom was associated with access to the vast areas of the American West. And like the creator of the Monkey Wrench Gang, he considered himself

❖ *Edward Abbey*   ❖ *James Watt*

an individualist with a strong distrust of government. But unlike Abbey, Watt believed that the land was to be used for the economic benefit of the people who lived on it. Guided by flawed assumptions about people's proper relationship to nature, environmentalists had succeeded in setting aside far too many areas as wilderness. The time had come to restore the right to earn a living from the land. In the early 1980s, Watt stepped forward to lead that fight.

"Keep It Like It Was!"

Although Edward Abbey's roots were far removed from the desert, they were close to nature. Born in 1927, the first of Paul and Mildred Abbey's five children, Edward grew up on a small, rundown farm in the backwoods of Appalachia. For the Abbeys, contact with the natural environment was an integral part of their existence. The family's food and livelihood came directly from the land. When not tending crops, Paul Abbey took his sons hunting and trapping in the woods and meadows. The family gathered nuts from the land and tapped the numerous maple trees on the farm for syrup. While Mildred Abbey cultivated wildflowers for sale, Edward and his brothers and sister often explored a large tract of uncut forest near the farm.

The greatest influence on Edward was not the outdoors, however, but his father. Although Mildred was a churchgoing Presbyterian, Paul Revere Abbey was a radical who frequently railed against capitalism and religion. While Mildred played the family piano and taught the children good manners and proper English, Paul exposed them to unconventional ideas. At family gatherings, Paul often held forth on the virtues of socialism. He also liked to recite passages from the work of the nineteenth-century poet Walt Whitman. One of his favorites, from the preface to *Leaves of Grass*, would stay with Edward his entire life. "This is what you shall do," Whitman wrote: "Love the earth and sun and the animals, despise riches, give alms to everyone that asks, stand up for the stupid and crazy, devote your income and labor to others, hate tyrants . . . have patience and indulgence toward the people, take off your hat to nothing known or unknown."

Years later, Edward Abbey wrote that his father was "cantankerous, ornery, short-tempered, and contentious. . . . He had strong opinions on everything and a neighborly view on almost nothing." The other Abbey children claimed that Edward bore a remarkable resemblance to their father. Indeed, Edward demonstrated a rebellious streak from a young age. At ten, he stormed out of Sunday school when the teacher told him that everything in the Bible was true. A couple of years later, Edward and his brother Howard were crossing the street when a car pulled into the crosswalk. Howard walked around the front of the car, but Edward went straight up over its hood, leaving a large dent in it.

Abbey admitted much later that he enjoyed "provoking people." At the same time, however, he had a thoughtful side. Finding farm chores disagreeable, he preferred to spend time reading and writing stories. Fascinated by his father's stories about his travels in the American West, Edward realized that there was "something else out there." A year before he graduated from high school, the seventeen-year-old got his first opportunity to travel west. He went by himself. When Howard asked Edward why he did not want him to go along, Edward answered, "Because frankly you bore me." As Edward left, his father told him that things would go better on the trip if he were not so arrogant.

Arrogant or not, things went well enough for Edward. He was thrown in jail only once—in Flagstaff, Arizona, for vagrancy. Hitchhiking and riding the rails, he traveled to Seattle, down the Pacific coast to California, and back across Arizona and New Mexico to the East. Although he saw the verdant Northwest, Yosemite National Park, and California's fragrant orange groves, it was the deserts of the Southwest that stole his heart. "It was love at first sight," he said later. When he got home, he was determined to return.

After high school and a two-year stint in the U.S. Army, which left him even more distrustful of regulations, Abbey enrolled at the University of New Mexico, where he studied on and off for the next decade. In college, he developed an interest in philosophy, anarchy, and exploring the desert in an old Chevrolet. He realized that anarchy was not about bombs but about opposition to coercion, especially by government. He also came to believe that anarchy was associated with open space. The West, he concluded, offered a place where free individuals could live without the constraints imposed by organizations. Unfortunately, the possibilities for freedom there were rapidly disappearing. The place was being "foreclosed, outmoded, fenced out, smothered under progress," he observed.

After earning a B.A. in 1951, Abbey studied in Scotland on a Fulbright scholarship and then enrolled in a master's program in philosophy at the University of New Mexico. Completed in 1956, his master's thesis was titled "Anarchy and the Morality of Violence," themes that figured prominently in all his writing. Starting with *Jonathan Troy*, a novel about a young anarchist published in 1954, Abbey began to explore the clash between civilization and freedom. With its appraisal of modern technology's destruction of nature, the book foreshadowed Abbey's later work. Two years later, he published *The Brave Cowboy*, a novel about another anarchist, named Jack Burns, who loses his freedom as barbed wire intrudes on the open range. Burns protests the invasion of powerful ranchers on public lands by cutting the barbed wire. As he flees the authorities, he is hit by a truck loaded with plumbing products. In the end, he lies bleeding by the side of the road on a Navajo rug. A remnant of the Old West, Abbey's hero does not fit into the New West.

Abbey's early novels brought him only modest success. *The Brave Cowboy* was made into the movie *Lonely Are the Brave* in 1962, starring Kirk Douglas, but Abbey was paid only seventy-five hundred dollars for the screen rights. The same year, he published *Fire on the Mountain*, a novel about a proud, independent rancher who loses his land. Meanwhile, Abbey faced the problem of making a living. He had been briefly married to a fellow student before he graduated from college. Then in 1952, he had married a fine artist named Rita Deanin. Unable to support himself by writing, he had taken a series of jobs with the U.S. Forest Service and the National Park Service, including stints in remote fire lookout towers on the North Rim of the Grand Canyon, at Glacier National Park, and at Organ Pipe Cactus National Monument. Abbey had quickly come to dislike the Department of the Interior's bureaucracy and regulations. The work and a series of affairs also ended his second marriage in 1965. Nonetheless, these jobs suited his temperament and gave him plenty of time to write. His first assignment for the Park Service took him to remote and seldom visited Arches National Monument in Utah. There he kept a journal, which became the basis for *Desert Solitaire*, a semiautobiographical series of essays about his time at Arches.

Published in 1968, *Desert Solitaire* came out amid growing environmental activism. By the mid-1960s, increasing concern about pollution and ecological destruction had contributed to rising ecological awareness and transformed an older *conservation* movement into a broader *environmental* movement. Conservationists in the first half of the twentieth century were chiefly concerned about the efficient use of resources. Environmentalists in the second half were primarily concerned about the health of the entire ecosystem. In 1949, Aldo Leopold published *A Sand County Almanac*, a call for a new ecological consciousness. Trained as a forester and wildlife manager, Leopold argued that an "ecological conscience" would change the role of "*Homo sapiens* from conqueror of the land-community to plain member and citizen of it." Thirteen years later, a former researcher for the U.S. Fish and Wildlife Service named Rachel Carson published *Silent Spring*, which awoke many Americans to the threat of chemical pollution. *Desert Solitaire* reflected this new ecological consciousness. It argued that a human-centered view of nature had to give way to a biocentric view in which all species had an equal standing. At the same time, it decried the way "industrial tourism" centered on the automobile threatened to destroy the national parks.

Desert Solitaire quickly became an underground environmental classic. Within four years, it had sold 500,000 copies and its author was an environmental cult figure. Thus Abbey already commanded a large audience as he responded to the signal event in his life as a wilderness defender: the building of the Glen Canyon Dam sixty miles north of Grand Canyon National Park. The dam created Lake Powell—the second-largest reservoir in the United States. Abbey and the few thousand other people who trekked into the sandstone wonderland eventually inundated by the lake found it to be of incomparable beauty. The Bureau of Reclamation, however, viewed the dam as a "cash cow." Completed in 1962, it would generate cheap electric power for the burgeoning cities of the Southwest. Sales of this power in turn provided funds for the bureau to finance other reclamation projects designed to provide low-cost water primarily to western farmers and ranchers. To Abbey, these water users were nothing more than "welfare parasites" who mouthed antigovernment rhetoric while relying on government assistance.

The decision to build the Glen Canyon Dam was part of a larger battle over the use of public lands that extended back to the beginning of the conservation movement. At the turn of the twentieth century, Sierra Club founder John Muir and other preservationists had argued that nature should be preserved for its own sake. At the same time, Gifford Pinchot, head of the U.S. Forest Service under Theodore Roosevelt, had insisted that natural resources should be used for the economic benefit of many. In the first decade of the twentieth century, Muir and Pinchot went head-to-head in a battle over a proposal to dam the Tuolumne River near Yosemite National Park in California. The dam would provide badly needed water for San Francisco, but it would also flood the magnificent Hetch Hetchy Valley that rivaled nearby Yosemite Valley. Arguing that preservation was an act "of worship," Muir fought to include the valley in the national park. Insisting that preservation should not override the "economic and moral aspects of the case," Pinchot fought for flooding the valley. In the end, Roosevelt sided with Pinchot. Like Glen Canyon half a century later, Hetch Hetchy was destroyed.

By the time the environmental movement emerged in the 1960s, Glen Canyon was already doomed. Even after the dam was finished, relatively few people cared about the canyon's destruction. For Edward Abbey, however, its loss symbolized the threat that modern, technological society posed to nature—and to the freedom that he associated with it. Like Muir, Abbey elevated his love of nature to a religion, and also like Muir, he was stirred to action by a dam's destruction of nature. The result was his best-known work of fiction, *The Monkey Wrench Gang*. Published thirteen years after the completion of the dam, the novel centered on a gang of ecoterrorists who do battle with the forces invading and exploiting the red rock canyons and plateaus of the Southwest. Their rallying cry is "Keep it like it was!" **[See Source 1.]** The novel and its sequel, *Hayduke Lives!* (published posthumously in 1990), turned Abbey into an internationally recognized writer. According to *Newsweek*, he had "invented a new fictional genre, the ecological caper." Many readers, however, were not amused. One Tucson newspaper reviewer, for instance, called *The Monkey Wrench Gang* "eco-pornography." In the *New York Times*, another reviewer expressed amazement that such a violent novel could be published with no consequences.

The Monkey Wrench Gang would no doubt have sparked an even larger controversy were it not for the growing acceptance of the ecological perspective. Environmental disasters such as the Santa Barbara oil spill in 1969 had already provoked widespread fears about the destruction of nature. The blowout of an offshore oil well platform had sent 235,000 gallons of crude oil into the ocean and blackened beaches for thirty-five miles. The next year, Americans celebrated the first Earth Day, an indication of a growing ecological consciousness. As environmental awareness grew, so did the desire to preserve wilderness areas. The bitter three-year battle over a trans-Alaska oil pipeline, finally approved by Congress in 1973, only fed the sense of urgency regarding preservation. At the same time, the rise of a youth counterculture provided a further boost to wilderness appreciation. By the early 1970s, many young people were attempting to live on the land or seeking wilderness experiences as an escape from society.

Americans' growing concern for the environment was reflected in the scores of environmental groups that vied for the public's support. Like the civil rights and women's movements, environmentalism was split into numerous organizations representing a diverse array of views and tactics. The Natural Resources Defense Council, for instance, emphasized litigation in the courts. The Sierra Club, the Wilderness Society, and other groups often concentrated on political activity and had considerable experience lobbying in the halls of power. It was actually longtime Sierra Club leader David Brower, for instance, who had cut the political deal dooming Glen Canyon. Later, the Wilderness Society's Howard Zahniser would receive most of the credit for shepherding the Wilderness Act of 1964 through Congress. That act set aside large tracts of federal land as wilderness areas, where any economic activities and even motorized vehicles were barred. Meanwhile, groups such as Greenpeace, founded in 1971, and Earth First! turned to the direct-action approach of the earlier civil rights and antiwar demonstrators. The most radical group, Earth First! was founded in 1979, four years after the publication of *The Monkey Wrench Gang*. A relatively small group, Earth First! was organized by Dave Foreman and several other former Wilderness Society employees. Much like Fannie Lou Hamer and the Black Power advocates of the late 1960s (see Chapter 11), they had grown disgusted with the willingness of moderate organizations to compromise. Such an approach, Foreman believed, was doomed to fail.

Ironically, by 1979, mainstream environmental organizations could take credit for a growing body of environmental legislation. In 1969, the National Environmental Policy Act had ordered all federal agencies to develop environmental impact statements to assess "potential damage to the environment from any government action." Four years later, the Endangered Species Act had forced federal land managers to survey public lands and to prohibit uses that would endanger threatened wildlife. In 1974, Congress had created the Environmental Protection Agency, the first independent federal agency to assume responsibility for environmental regulation. And in 1976, the Federal Land Policy and Management Act and the National Forest Management Act had called for "scientific land-use planning"—that is, the development of long-range plans for federal lands based on ecological principles rather than economic use. By the end of the 1970s, roughly two-thirds of all public lands were still open for multiple uses, including mining, grazing, timber cutting, and motorized recreation. Nonetheless, ecological awareness and the desire to preserve wilderness were increasingly reflected in federal policy.

For many people, however, the environmental movement's success was precisely the problem. To many westerners, who traditionally had access to public lands and resources, it appeared that environmental "radicals" had succeeded in closing off access to anyone not wearing a backpack. When Ronald Reagan won the presidency in 1980 with the promise to "get the federal government off the backs of the people," James Watt believed the time had come to end the "privileged position of the select few" (that is, environmentalists) on public lands. Abbey and other environmentalists, of course, had a very different view of things. Yet that did not entirely explain their angry response to news of Watt's appointment as Reagan's secretary of the interior. As one environmental writer put it, the "real source of their objections [to Watt] springs from who he is."

"Trample the Wilderness in Expensive Hiking Boots"

James Watt traced his roots to the frontier West. Traveling from St. Louis in a covered wagon, one of Watt's grandparents had homesteaded in Sheridan County in north-central Wyoming. James was born in 1938, the second of William and Lois Watt's three children. Home for them was Lusk, Wyoming, a small ranching town where William practiced law. While growing up, James spent summers on the family ranch, performing chores such as mending fences and pumping water for the cattle. It was that experience, he later claimed, that gave him a love of the West "in the special way of those who have to grapple with its sometimes hostile environment."

Early on, James also developed a love of politics. When he was a child in Lusk, Lois organized the family into a club to play games and teach the children parliamentary rules. She recalled that James "liked to make speeches" at the club's meetings. In junior high school, he became interested in reading about current events. Later, he was active in a variety of high school clubs and varsity sports. He also was the natural choice as the local American Legion post's delegate to Boys State, where he was elected "governor" of Wyoming. By then, the family had moved to Wheatland, the county seat of Platte County in southeastern Wyoming. There William, a conservative Republican, continued to practice law and became active in local Republican Party politics. "Franklin Roosevelt was a cuss word in our house," recalled James, who eagerly absorbed his father's views.

After graduating from high school as valedictorian, Watt headed off to the University of Wyoming in Laramie. Sociable but serious, he won a number of honors. Naturally, he was involved in student government, winning election as student body business and finance manager. In his sophomore year, he married his high school sweetheart, Leilani Bomgardner, who had entered the university with him. A diligent student, he graduated with honors in 1960. By then, he also had completed his first year of law school. When he graduated two years later, after having served as editor of the *Wyoming Law Journal,* he was admitted to the Wyoming State Bar. Only twenty-four, Watt was already the father of a son and daughter. With the help of connections, he quickly found work.

In 1962, Watt worked as a volunteer in Wyoming Republican Milward Simpson's campaign for the U.S. Senate. Simpson happened to be a longtime Watt family acquaintance and the father of Watt's college friend and future U.S. senator Alan Simpson. Milward Simpson won the Senate seat, and after the election, Watt moved east to work as Simpson's legislative assistant and counsel. He did not realize it, but Washington would be his home for a long time to come. His love of politics had led him in the opposite direction from Abbey—away from his beloved West. Ironically, it also had landed him in the federal bureaucracy so despised by the Watt family.

Despite his political views, Watt's attraction to Washington was in many ways fitting. For much of their history, Americans have held a romantic view of the West as a place of limitless freedom for "rugged individualists." In the West, however, myth and reality have often been at odds. In fact, the federal government has long played a dominant role in the region's development, from the construction of the transcontinental railroads in the nineteenth century to the building of massive water projects in the twentieth. Even as Watt packed his bags for the nation's capital, the federal government continued to play a crucial role in the region's economy, pumping billions of dollars into water development, military bases, and roads. It also owned and administered most of the land in the West. **[See Source 2.]** In short, the region's well-being was tied to the federal government. Whatever their views about the government, therefore, westerners could not afford to ignore it. That was especially true of those whose livelihoods were tied directly to the land. Naturally, they were interested in making sure that federal agencies operated in a friendly manner—especially the Department of the Interior, charged with overseeing vast public rangelands, controlling numerous dams and water development projects, and administering the national parks and monuments.

In his new job, Watt was perfectly positioned to learn all about the Interior Department. Milward Simpson sat on the Senate Committee on Interior and Insular Affairs, which had control over public land policy and oversight over the Interior Department. As Congress passed a host of important environmental bills in the mid-1960s, the young staffer sat in on the committee's meetings, and he began to learn about land use issues. About the same time, Watt had another experience that would influence his views about such issues. Shortly after moving to Washington, he had a religious awakening. After attending a gospel meeting for businessmen, he joined the fundamentalist* Assembly of God Church. As a born-again Christian fundamentalist, Watt took literally the declaration in the Book of Genesis that man had dominion over the earth and all its creatures. That reading of the Old Testament conformed perfectly to his belief that people in the West should have the freedom to use the land for their own economic benefit. Now Watt would fight for his land use views with a religious zeal.

Simpson retired four years after his election because of poor health, but Watt's work on the Committee on Interior and Insular Affairs had attracted the attention of the U.S. Chamber of Commerce, a pro-development organization that lobbied for the interests of businesses. Hired as a lobbyist, Watt was on the losing end of some major battles as Congress passed a wave of environmental bills in the late 1960s. His work as a probusiness lobbyist, however, caught the attention of the Nixon administration. Starting in 1969, he was named to a series of Interior Department posts and soon became the principal spokesman for the administration on recreation and conservation issues. In 1975, Nixon's successor, Gerald Ford, named Watt to the Federal Power Commission, the agency responsible for the development and oversight of federal energy projects such as hydroelectric dams.

The election of Democrat Jimmy Carter in 1976 halted Watt's steady rise as a federal administrator, but he would soon have another opportunity to fight

---

Fundamentalist: Related to the twentieth-century Protestant movement based on the literal interpretation of everything in the Bible and on the belief that such a reading of the Scriptures is fundamental to faith and morals.

for his views. After the conservative Colorado brewing heir Joseph Coors established the Denver-based Mountain States Legal Foundation (MSLF) to fight environmental legislation, Watt landed the job as the organization's first president. In his new role, he took on the Environmental Protection Agency, the Sierra Club, and even his old employer, the Interior Department. In his words, he was out to fight "those bureaucrats and no-growth advocates who challenge individual liberties and economic freedoms." With Watt at the helm, the MSLF filed nearly fifty legal cases reflecting its free-enterprise agenda. Frequently, the cases involved disputes over the use of public lands, such as the defense of ranchers' permits to graze their livestock on rangeland controlled by the Interior Department. By 1980, Watt had drawn the ire of environmentalists, but he also had gained the attention of the leaders of a resurgent conservative movement centered on the presidential campaign of Republican Ronald Reagan.

By the late 1970s, rising energy prices had sparked high inflation, an economic recession, and widespread fear about the erosion of America's power. At the same time, the Sagebrush Rebellion, led by disgruntled ranchers and other users of public lands, had erupted in many western states. Rebels called for the transfer of federal lands to the states and an end to policies that "protect endangered species to the detriment of human beings." By 1980, a number of western politicians had endorsed the Sagebrush Rebellion, including Reagan, who said that a handful of "environmental extremists" had succeeded in locking up the nation's public lands. Fulfilling the nation's energy needs, he asserted, could not be "thwarted by a tiny minority opposed to economic growth." By that time, many Americans were receptive to the argument that America's natural resources, especially energy resources on public lands, needed to be tapped more aggressively. Holding out the hope that the country would be able to solve its energy and economic crises with little sacrifice, Reagan won a landslide victory over Carter.

Shortly after his election, Reagan named Watt secretary of the interior. Because of the Interior Department's large role in western affairs, it has traditionally been headed by someone from that region. Watt was the logical choice for that and other reasons. He believed that Reagan's election was an "opportunity to make [a] massive change" in the nation's environmental policies. He assumed that such a change was crucial to realizing the new president's vision of economic growth, abundant energy, and national security. Thus, he declared, his goal was to make more land available for "multiple uses" rather than just wilderness or recreation. Watt also appealed to Christian conservatives who supported Reagan. "My responsibility," he said, "is to follow the Scriptures, which call upon us to occupy the land until Jesus returns." And, as he announced after his appointment, he did not know "how many future generations we can count on before the Lord returns."

News of Watt's appointment elicited a wave of criticism from environmental organizations such as the Wilderness Society, whose director called Watt "a joke" and his appointment "disastrous." Nonetheless, he was easily confirmed by the Senate and took office in early 1981, moving quickly to carry out his program. [See Source 3.] In his first year in office, the new interior secretary opened nearly half of the offshore continental shelf surrounding the United States to oil drilling, a move that brought back memories of the Santa Barbara oil spill. He also ordered a halt to further federal land purchases and ended three major national park purchase programs. The next year, he announced plans to sell thirty-five million acres of wilderness to reduce the federal debt. He also called for a relaxation of "regulatory burdens" on coal exploration on federal lands and an easing of environmental rules. Ordering a rewrite of department man-agement regulations, Watt was determined to make federal resources available even if existing laws prohibited the development of public lands. Meanwhile, in the national parks, Watt instituted a policy of road, campground, and latrine construction to provide "easy access" and "safe shelter" to park visitors. The "vast majority of Americans," the secretary observed, are not "rugged young backpackers." In frequent speeches around the country, Watt linked his depart-ment's resource policy to a "war" to protect "liberty and freedom." Environ-mentalism, he said in 1982, was "bad for the economy, bad for the environment, bad for freedom." At the same time, he continued to lash out at "radical envi-ronmentalists." These "elitists," he told a group in Reno, Nevada, wanted "to lock away the land so that it [could not] be used—except by those with the time, money and good health to trample the wilderness in expensive hiking boots."

"The Ideology of a Cancer Cell"

Long dismayed by what he called "our contemporary techno-industrial greed-and-power culture," Edward Abbey was not surprised by Watt's appointment. In fact, Reagan's secretary of the interior only confirmed his worst fears for the Southwest. Nonetheless, Abbey found outrageous Watt's assertion that envi-ronmentalists were "elitists." A journey into the wilderness, he countered, was "the freest, cheapest, most non-privileged of pleasures." All it took was two legs and a pair of $17.95 army surplus boots. In public appearances and rallies in op-position to Reagan administration policies, Abbey urged concerned citizens to become activists, admonishing one audience in 1983 not to be a "tick on a dog, ornamental but useless."

By 1982, Watt's policies had elicited widespread media and popular scrutiny. *Time* magazine's coverage was typical. Its August 23 cover story featured a pic-ture of the secretary and the headline, "GOING, GOING . . . ! Land Sale of the Century"—a reference to Watt's proposal to sell millions of acres of federal land. In the early 1980s, membership in environmental groups increased dramatically. For instance, between 1981 and 1983, membership in the Sierra Club and the Wilderness Society roughly doubled. The growth of environmental organiza-tions was particularly impressive because it came during a period of economic recession. It reflected many Americans' rejection of Watt's premise that eco-nomic growth had to come at the expense of the environment. Even hunters and sportfishing enthusiasts were worried about the impact of Watt's policies on their ability to use public lands. Millions of Americans now considered them-selves "environmentalists" even if they did not belong to an organized group.

The uproar over Watt's policies alarmed some conservatives. Watt, they now believed, alienated too many voters and threatened to strengthen the envi-ronmental movement. By playing right into his opponents' hands, he could jeopardize the entire "Reagan Revolution." Conservative columnist George Will, for instance, observed in 1982 that Watt was stimulating Edward Abbey's brand of environmental radicalism. As Will put it, Watt had only made more popular the type of environmentalism that wanted to put "sand in the gears of industrialism."

Under pressure from fellow Republicans, Watt began to take on a more conciliatory tone. In 1983, he announced that there would "not be a massive land sell-off," and in an effort to help the "eastern press corps" better understand him, he projected a less confrontational style in interviews. **[See Source 4.]** Yet Watt could not avoid bad publicity. After he insisted on auctioning off Interior Department coal leases, an eight-month investigation concluded that the leases had been disposed of at "fire sale" prices. He also continued to make remarks that environmentalists found outrageous. In a *Business Week* interview, for instance, he compared environmentalists to Nazis, declaring that each sought "centralized planning." Speaking to a meeting of U.S. Chamber of Commerce lobbyists in the fall of 1983, Watt made what *Newsweek* called his "last gaffe" when he described the members of a coal-lease commission as "a black . . . a woman, two Jews and a cripple." This "latest misfiring of his infamous mouth," as *Newsweek* put it, immediately brought calls for his resignation. Facing reelection the next year, Reagan and many Republicans realized that Watt was a political liability. Three weeks after his Chamber of Commerce speech, he resigned.

By the time Watt settled down to a law practice and relative obscurity, many mainstream environmentalists had developed remarkably similar concerns about Edward Abbey. As with Watt, many people who sympathized with Abbey's views came to believe that his extremism only played into the hands of their opponents. His endorsement of ecoterrorism as "illegal but ethically imperative" was especially troubling. The Sierra Club and other politically active environmental organizations had been working for years to broaden their movement and bring it into the mainstream of American life. To them, Abbey was an embarrassment and counterproductive to the cause.

Just as embarrassing were Abbey's views about numerous social issues, from gun control to the women's movement and immigration. No feminist, Abbey developed a reputation for treating women as little more than sexual objects. Frequently bored with his wives and lovers, he was married five times in all. His antifemale reputation was reinforced by the shallow treatment of women in his published works and by the run-ins he had with feminist leaders such as Gloria Steinem (see Chapter 13). Feminists, he believed, were fighting a "trivial" battle. Why would women "wish to fulfill their human potential in offices, boutiques, boardrooms, army tanks, or coal mines," he asked in a scathing review of Steinem's book *Outrageous Acts and Everyday Rebellions* (1983). Calling himself "Cactus Ed," he wrote a letter to *Ms.* magazine that began "Dear Sirs." "Out here a womin's place is in the kitchen, the barnyard and the bedroom in exactly that order," he wrote, "and we don't need no changes." Even if Abbey was just poking fun, many people did not appreciate his humor. Nor did they approve of his membership in the National Rifle Association or his opposition to gun control. Equally embarrassing were his attacks on immigration from Mexico. Open borders, he argued in a 1988 essay, were bringing an influx of "millions of hungry, ignorant, unskilled, and culturally-morally-generically impoverished people." **[See Source 5.]**

Aside from an ability to alienate their own allies, however, Abbey and Watt had something else in common. By associating individual freedom with the western landscape, both reflected the romantic assumption that the West was the last domain of the unrestrained individual. Both also saw the land, and thus freedom, under assault. For Watt, defending the American faith meant doing battle with powerful outside forces that had the West in their grip. Abbey, too, feared such forces. In his mind, they threatened the liberty that he associated with access to the land. "Oppose the destruction of our homeland by those alien forces from Houston, Tokyo, Manhattan, D.C. and the Pentagon," he once urged at an Earth First! rally.

What Watt and Abbey disagreed on, of course, was the exact nature of the threat. Watt associated economic growth with personal freedom. For him, federal bureaucrats in league with "elitist" environmentalists were the danger. Because neither bureaucrats nor urban environmentalists had to wrest a living from the land, they did not understand the importance of individuals' freedom to use the resources of the West to their own advantage. By contrast, Abbey perceived the danger as emanating from those exercising such unfettered freedom: ranchers, farmers, miners, and corporations in league with their powerful allies in the government. Worse, all these "individualists" were riding an uncontrolled technological wave. Engaged in a lifelong battle against unthinking growth, Abbey, unlike Watt, rejected the dominant American faith in technology and progress. The twenty books that Abbey wrote before his death in 1989 stand as an eloquent cry against this often unquestioned faith. Growth for growth's sake, he maintained, was "the ideology of a cancer cell." It threatened to rob individuals of a more important kind of freedom: from the very constraints of civilization. In the end, what separated these two environmental "extremists" was not their differing views of the land but the meaning that they assigned to freedom itself.

PRIMARY SOURCES

SOURCE 1:   Edward Abbey, *The Monkey Wrench Gang* (1975)

The Monkey Wrench Gang remains Edward Abbey's best-selling novel. Based on certain real people, the little gang of ecoterrorists is led by Doc Sarvis, an Albuquerque physician. Other members are George Washington Hayduke, a mentally unstable former Green Beret; Bonnie Abbzug, a refugee from the Bronx; and Seldom Seen Smith, a polygamous Mormon river guide. Do you think Abbey's purpose was only to entertain his readers or also to challenge them? What is Doc Sarvis's message in this excerpt?

SOURCE: Edward Abbey, *The Monkey Wrench Gang* (Philadelphia: J. B. Lippincott, 1975), pp. 109, 110, 134, 148–149, 153–154. Copyright © 1975 by Edward Abbey. Reprinted by permission of HarperCollins Publishers, Inc.

During the early morning, Hayduke and Bonnie had "borrowed" the front license plates from tourist automobiles from three different states and attached them (temporarily) to their own vehicles. Assuming, naturally, that the loss would not be noticed for hundreds of miles.

Bonnie driving, they went up the road to the rim of Black Mesa. From a vantage point near the road, armed with binoculars, they examined the layout of the coal transmission system.

To the east, beyond the rolling ridges on the mesa's surface, lay the ever-growing strip mines of the Peabody Coal Company. Four thousand acres, prime grazing land for sheep and cattle, had been eviscerated already; another forty thousand was under lease. (The lessor was the Navajo Nation, as represented by the Bureau of Indian Affairs under the jurisdiction of the U.S. Government.) The coal was being excavated by gigantic power shovels and dragline machines, the largest equipped with 3600-cubic-foot buckets. The coal was trucked a short distance to a processing depot, where it was sorted, washed and stored, some of it loaded into a slurry line for a power plant near Lake Mohave, Nevada, the rest onto a conveyor belt for transportation to storage towers at the railhead of the BM & LP railway, which in turn hauled the coal eighty miles to the Navajo Power Plant near the town of Page.

Smith and Hayduke, Abbzug and Sarvis were especially interested in the conveyor belt, which seemed to be the weakest link in the system. It ran for nineteen miles from mine to railhead. For most of this distance the conveyor was vulnerable, running close to the ground, half concealed by juniper and pinyon pine, unguarded. At the rim of the mesa it descended to the level of the highway, where it rose again, over the highway and into the top of the four storage silos. The belt ran on rollers, the entire apparatus powered electrically.

They sat and watched this mighty engine in motion, conveying coal at the rate of 50,000 tons per day across the mesa and down to the plain and up into the towers. Fifty thousand tons. Every day. For thirty–forty–fifty years. All to feed the power plant at Page.

"I think," said Doc, "these people are serious."

"It ain't people," said Smith. "It's a mechanical animal."

"Now you've got it," Doc agreed. "We're not dealing with human beings. We're up against the megamachine. A megalomaniacal megamachine."

"No sweat," Hayduke said. "It's all rigged up for us. We'll use that fucking conveyor to blow up the loading towers. Nothing could be prettier. Look—it's so goddamned simple it makes me nervous. We take our shit out in the woods there, close to the belt. We throw it on the belt, light the fuse, cover it up with a little coal, let it ride up over the road and into the tower. *Ka-blam!*". . .

The doctor was thinking: All this fantastic effort—giant machines, road networks, strip mines, conveyor belt, pipelines, slurry lines, loading towers, railway and electric train, hundred-million-dollar coal-burning power plant; ten thousand miles of high-tension towers and high-voltage power lines; the devastation of the landscape, the destruction of Indian homes and Indian grazing lands, Indian shrines and Indian burial grounds; the poisoning of the last big clean-air reservoir in the forty-eight contiguous United States, the exhaustion of precious water supplies—all that ball-breaking labor and all that backbreaking expense and a heartbreaking insult to land and sky and human heart, for what?

All that for what? Why, to light the lamps of Phoenix suburbs not yet built, to run the air conditioners of San Diego and Los Angeles, to illuminate shopping-center parking lots at two in the morning, to power aluminum plants, magnesium plants, vinyl-chloride factories and copper smelters, to charge the neon tubing that makes the meaning (all the meaning there is) of Las Vegas, Albuquerque, Tucson, Salt Lake City, the amalgamated *metropoli* of southern California, to keep alive that phosphorescent putrefying glory (all the glory there is left) called Down Town, Night Time, Wonderville, U.S.A.

Source 2: *Map of Federal Lands* (1978)

In 1978, just three years before James Watt's appointment as secretary of the interior, the federal government controlled approximately 900 million acres of land, of which 516 million were controlled by the Department of the Interior. What does this map reveal about the likely response to Watt's message by many people in the West?

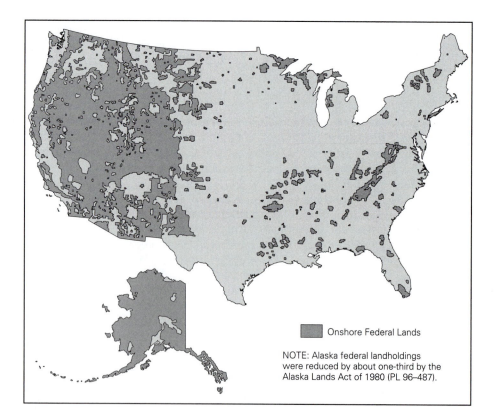

Onshore Federal Lands

NOTE: Alaska federal landholdings were reduced by about one-third by the Alaska Lands Act of 1980 (PL 96–487).

Source: *Congressional Quarterly,* June 3, 1981, p. 1903.

Source 3:   *James Watt Outlines His Program*   (1981)

In this interview with U.S. News and World Report, *conducted shortly after his appointment as secretary of the interior, James Watt discusses his plans for opening public lands to greater development. How does he intend to accomplish this?*

Q: Mr. Secretary, people are afraid that you are going to push for greater development of natural resources at the expense of the environment. How do you respond?

A: With our technology, we can protect the environment and still bring on the development that is necessary for improving the quality of life and bolstering national defense. Environmental sensitivity requires a balance of economic development and environmental preservation.

In the last 10 years, we have not had proper energy and mineral development in America. If a crisis comes because of shortages and the political scene dictates a crash development program, I fear that it will be done without regard to the ecology. That's what we must avoid. . . .

Q: Why do we need more development of federal lands?

A: Because America needs more energy, more timber, more agricultural grazing. We have not had an oil-and-gas lease issued onshore Alaska since the mid-1960s. We have not had a major coal lease issued since the early 1970s. Applications have been pending for oil-and-gas leases in the overthrust belts of Wyoming, Montana and Idaho for 10 years. Our mining industry is in very bad shape. Yet we ask why there's an energy crisis. . . .

Q: Why do you favor a moratorium on the creation of new national parks when so many are overcrowded?

A: There has been deterioration and degradation in almost every park because we have not been good stewards of what we have.

The emphasis in recent years has been on acquiring more and more lands while at the same time refusing to take care of the park lands we have.

We will reverse that. We have put a moratorium on the acquisition of additional lands until the economic situation changes. In the meantime, we have shifted substantial money to the National Park Service for restoration and improvement of these fragile lands.

Q: How can you make the most popular parks accessible to more people if you don't expand the parks?

A: We need to provide proper access and development of facilities to handle people in the areas where they want to be. For example, they want to see Old Faithful. It doesn't help people to see that geyser if we buy another 100,000 acres outside the present boundaries of that park. So we're clearing up transportation bottlenecks and improving accommodations near popular attractions.

For our major parks—the "crown jewels"—people will be better served if we improve management techniques and give direction to the concessionaires to build the environmentally compatible facilities that allow people to enjoy the parks.

Q: Are more restrictions needed on park use?

A: In recent years, there's been a movement in the National Park Service to make parks available only to the select few. Attention needs to be given to all Americans—backpackers and people who go rafting on the rivers—as well as those who roll up to the park on a bus tour. We want parks to be attractive and accessible to people of all economic levels and not just to people who have lots of time and money.

A graphic illustration of this is the Colorado River in the Grand Canyon National Park. The purist wants that stretch of river to be available only to oar-powered rafts. But how many people can afford to get to Page, Ariz., and then commit lots of money and eight to 12 days to go down that river? People with less time available should also be allowed to use the river in motor-powered rafts. The only limitation should be to protect the resource base.

Source 4:   James Watt, *"It's the People's Land"*   (1983)

Increasingly under fire by 1983, James Watt tried to be more conciliatory in dealing with the media. How does his message in this interview differ from his message in Source 3?

On proper use of public lands: You enjoy these lands in many ways . . . by picnicking, by looking at them and by grazing on them, by taking the trees from them to build cheaper houses, by using their energy, coal, oil, gas, uranium, etc. But you do that in a way that retains the value of those lands, so that when we—this generation—pass them on to the next generation, they will be in as good as or better condition than when we inherited them. . . .

There will not be a massive land sell-off, there was never intended to be a massive land sell-off. Last year we sold 1,312 acres. This year we've offered [approximately] 5,500 acres for sale . . . and sold 3,500 acres. People don't even want some of the land. . . . It's totally a political, partisan issue. How can a governor complain from Idaho when he sells about 18,000 acres in one year, and we sell, across the country, 1,312?

On the national parks: We need to acquire more parkland, and I'm hopeful that within the next year or so . . . we'll be able to aggressively increase the amount of acreage required for national parks and refuges and wetlands. But right now we don't have economic strength in this country, and so we have to make the decision, where do you want your priorities? Do you want to take care of what you have, or do you want to acquire? The Carter administration . . . made the same decisions we made that at this time of economic distress, America could not afford to continue purchasing land at, say, $300 or $400 million a

Source: Mary Hager, "It's the People's Land," *Newsweek*, July 25, 1983, p. 25. © 1983 Newsweek, Inc. All rights reserved. Reprinted by permission.

year. I would like to, and I would hope that yet in my tenure we will be spending $300, $400, $500 million a year to acquire the needed parklands.

On wilderness areas: We're continuing to recommend more additions to the wilderness system. . . . How much is enough? I don't know. I can't put a figure on it. . . . We can't afford to lock it *all* up, but we do have sufficient numbers of real wilderness areas, and I mean it in the literal sense here, that we can afford to set aside millions of acres for just pure wilderness value.

SOURCE 5: Edward Abbey, *"Immigration and Liberal Taboos"* (1988)

Edward Abbey was widely criticized for this essay on immigration. What is the connection between Abbey's fears regarding immigration and his environmental views? Were mainstream environmentalists' criticisms of Abbey as counterproductive to their cause justified?

In the American Southwest, where I happen to live, only sixty miles north of the Mexican border, the subject of illegal aliens is a touchy one—almost untouchable. Even the terminology is dangerous: the old word *wetback* is now considered a racist insult by all good liberals; and the perfectly correct terms *illegal alien* and *illegal immigrant* can set off charges of xenophobia, elitism, fascism, and the ever-popular genocide against anyone careless enough to use them. The only acceptable euphemism, it now appears, is something called *undocumented worker*. Thus the pregnant Mexican woman who appears, in the final stages of labor, at the doors of the emergency ward of an El Paso or San Diego hospital, demanding care for herself and the child she's about to deliver, becomes an "undocumented worker." The child becomes an automatic American citizen by virtue of its place of birth, eligible at once for all of the usual public welfare benefits. And with the child comes not only the mother but the child's family. And the mother's family. And the father's family. Can't break up families, can we? They come to stay and they stay to multiply.

What of it? say the documented liberals; ours is a rich and generous nation, we have room for all, let them come. And let them stay, say the conservatives; a large, cheap, frightened, docile, surplus labor force is exactly what the economy needs. Put some fear into the unions: tighten discipline, spur productivity, whip up the competition for jobs. The conservatives love their cheap labor; the liberals love their cheap cause. . . .

Meanwhile, here at home in the land of endless plenty, we seem still unable to solve our traditional and nagging difficulties. After forty years of the most fantastic economic growth in the history of mankind, the United States remains burdened with mass unemployment, permanent poverty, an overloaded welfare

SOURCE: "Immigration and Liberal Taboos" from Edward Abbey, *One Life at a Time, Please* (New York: Henry Holt and Company, 1988), pp. 41–42. © 1988 by Edward Abbey. Reprinted by permission of Henry Holt and Company, LLC.

system, violent crime, clogged courts, jam-packed prisons, commercial ("white-collar") crime, rotting cities and a poisoned environment, eroding farmlands and the disappearing family farm, all of the usual forms of racial, ethnic, and sexual conflict (which immigration further intensifies), plus the ongoing destruction of what remains of our forests, fields, mountains, lakes, rivers, and seashores, accompanied by the extermination of whole species of plants and animals. To name but a few of our little nagging difficulties.

This being so, it occurs to some of us that perhaps ever-continuing industrial and population growth is *not* the true road to human happiness, that simple gross quantitative increase of this kind creates only more pain, dislocation, confusion, and misery. In which case it might be wise for us as American citizens to consider calling a halt to the mass influx of even more millions of hungry, ignorant, unskilled, and culturally-morally-generically impoverished people. At least until we have brought our own affairs into order.

QUESTIONS TO CONSIDER

1. According to the essay, both Edward Abbey and James Watt feared that powerful external forces were assaulting the West and undermining individual freedom. Abbey and Watt, however, ended up on opposite sides of the environmental debate. Citing specific primary sources, compare Abbey's and Watt's views about the environment and the threat that these external forces posed to the West and to individual freedom. What did each see as the connection between the land and liberty?

2. What were the most important factors in Abbey's and Watt's backgrounds in determining their views about the environment? What were the most important developments by the 1980s working to make their views popular?

3. What does the battle over the environment in the early 1980s reveal about the extent to which an "ecological ethic" prevailed among Americans? What do the receptions given to Watt's program and Abbey's ideas reveal about the appeal of environmental radicalism in the late twentieth century?

4. One critic said that Abbey's views were "childish"—and typically American—because they reflected a desire to "have everything," to revolt against authority, and to escape from the responsibilities of civilization. Do you agree? Do you think that the same criticism could be leveled against Watt?

FOR FURTHER READING

Edward Abbey, ed., *The Best of Edward Abbey* (San Francisco: Sierra Club Books, 1988), is a useful introduction to Abbey's work, including selections from a number of his most popular books.

Ron Arnold, *At the Eye of the Storm: James Watt and the Environmentalists* (Chicago: Regnery Gateway, 1982), is a sympathetic discussion of Watt's life prior to his appointment as secretary of the interior and the controversy over his policies during his first two years in office.

James Bishop Jr., *Epitaph for a Desert Anarchist: The Life and Legacy of Edward Abbey* (New York: Atheneum, 1994), contains a brief treatment of Abbey's life and reviews of his major works.

Marc Reisner, *Cadillac Desert: The American West and Its Disappearing Water* (New York: Viking Penguin, 1986), details Americans' efforts to irrigate the arid West by damming its rivers and the consequences of doing so.

Hal K. Rothman, *Saving the Planet: The American Response to the Environment in the Twentieth Century* (Chicago: Ivan R. Dee, 2000), is a brief overview of the growth of environmental consciousness in the twentieth century.

CHAPTER

15

Conservatism and the Limits of Consumer Capitalism: Irving Kristol and Ralph Nader

The automobile company executives clinked their forks nervously on the luncheon china as Ralph Nader took the podium. In the fall of 2000, Nader needed no introduction. Visiting Detroit as the Green Party's candidate for president, Nader was well known to this crowd. Long the nation's leading consumer advocate, he routinely attacked business leaders as "corporate supremacists." The most serious political problem facing Americans, he repeatedly charged, was the strangulation of American democracy by big business. As he put it, the nation's government was "of the Exxons, by the General Motors and for the DuPonts."

For Nader, the Detroit luncheon had to be a moment of triumph. Thirty-five years earlier, he had taken on the auto industry with the publication of *Unsafe at Any Speed*, which argued that car manufacturers made huge profits from selling cars they knew were dangerous. Nader's exposé had led Congress to pass legislation in 1966 establishing federal safety standards for automobiles. It also had made Nader a household name. In the following years, he headed a growing consumer movement that reflected many Americans' discontent with corporate practices. The result was a battery of new regulations on industries ranging from airlines to insurance.

Shifting uncomfortably in their seats, the Detroit automotive industry brass no doubt would have preferred hearing from someone like Irving Kristol. Over the past thirty-five years, Kristol had been an activist of sorts, too. In that time, he had emerged as the leading intellectual light of the nation's conservative movement. A columnist for the *Wall Street Journal*, editor of the *Public Interest* magazine, and a prolific writer, Kristol had had a long career assaulting the regulations championed by Nader. In fact, he argued, modern capitalism had not failed consumers, but rather had satisfied their preferences all too well. It had created abundance and, in the process, an elite "new class" in society. The members of this class were well educated and worked outside of business. Thus they did not understand the way corporations functioned, the "heroic" work performed by those who ran them, or how government regulations stifled capitalism's potential. Worse, these people were waging—and winning—a war against capitalism. Capitalism was losing that war because the "new class" had more

<table>
<tr><td>❖   *Irving Kristol*</td><td>❖   *Ralph Nader*</td></tr>
</table>

influence in society than business leaders, Kristol said. And that was why, he might have told this Detroit audience, Ralph Nader now stood before them as the general of the opposition forces.

"The Anal Effusions of Society"

Ralph Nader has never been one to dwell on the influences that made him pursue consumer activism with such single-minded passion. Some of them, however, are hard to ignore. Born in 1934 in Winsted, Connecticut, the son of Lebanese immigrants, Nader learned about the importance of community and civic duty as a boy. His father, Nadra, taught him that democracy required active citizens who took responsibility for their government. For instance, after Congress voted itself a salary increase, Nadra organized a march in Winsted to protest it. Working in his father's restaurant, Ralph also participated in his father's debates with patrons about everything from working conditions in factories to human rights. Later, Ralph said that these discussions were his best education. Although Ralph loved baseball, his only extracurricular activity in high school was the drama club. Above all, he was a student. By age twelve, he was a regular reader of the *Congressional Record*. He also read the works of Progressive era muckrakers, including Upton Sinclair's *Jungle*, a novel about the gruesome conditions in Chicago's meatpacking plants at the turn of the twentieth century. (See Chapter 7.)

When Nader entered Princeton University in 1951, he thumbed his nose at Ivy League snobbery and quickly earned a reputation as a nonconformist. He rejected the classmates' tweed jackets and white shirts and once arrived for class in a bathrobe. He also chose to hitchhike wherever he went, claiming that it allowed him to meet interesting people. While most students attended parties and participated in other social activities, the studious Nader demonstrated a more serious bent. Walking across campus one morning, for instance, he noticed dozens of dead birds littering the ground along an elm-lined path. Startled, he inquired about it and discovered that the trees had been sprayed with the chemical DDT the night before. Horrified, Nader wrote a letter to the university newspaper, explaining what had happened, but the editors refused to print it. When he pressed the issue, they claimed that it was nothing to get excited about. Nader was convinced that DDT was dangerous. If it could kill birds, he reasoned, it could kill people. Nothing came of his protest, but ten years later, biologist Rachel Carson published her book *Silent Spring*, which showed the dangers of DDT to the entire ecosystem.

After graduating from Princeton in 1955, Nader enrolled at Harvard Law School. Although the future attorneys at Harvard were far more studious than his Princeton classmates, Nader concluded that they were incapable of criticizing what they read or seeing the faults in society. Nader found the environment at Harvard stifling. His agile mind allowed him to do well on the exams, but his attendance record was atrocious. He also came to detest the motives of most of the law students, who seemed interested only in fame and money. He hoped, by contrast, to devote himself to public service. In fact, after winning election as editor of the law school newspaper, he turned it into a muckraking journal with articles on topics such as the exploitation of migrant workers and the plight of Native Americans. After some of his stories were voted down by the paper's governing board as too controversial, Nader resigned in disgust.

About the same time, while hitchhiking between Harvard and Winsted, Nader witnessed a car accident that left a little girl decapitated by a glove compartment door. He never forgot that scene. It spurred his interest in automobile safety, especially after he read an article in the *Harvard Law Review* suggesting that car manufacturers might be liable for injuries suffered by passengers as a result of negligent design. He wanted to learn as much as he could about the impact of automobile accidents on the body and even enrolled in a medical-legal seminar at Harvard. His third-year paper summarized the results of his research. Shortly after graduation, he turned the paper into an article titled "The Safe Car You Can't Buy," which was published in the *Nation* magazine in 1959. In it, Nader called car design a "national health emergency" and blasted automobile manufacturers for being more concerned with style than with safety.

Nader had taken up the main cause of his early career. Yet his fame as an automobile safety advocate was still several years away. After graduating from law school, Nader joined the Army Reserves. Following six months of active duty, he returned to Connecticut and opened a law office in Hartford. He left the Army impressed with the way it got things done through organization, clear objectives, and discipline. He later claimed that the only purchases he made while in the service were four dozen pairs of socks and one dozen pairs of dress shoes, the last shoes and socks he ever bought. Though unlikely, the story illustrates something about Nader's Spartan existence. Already he had developed a preference for simple accommodations, unprocessed foods, and older technology. He did not even own an electric typewriter and refused to buy a car. Meanwhile, his law practice bored him, and in 1963 he hitchhiked with one suitcase in hand to Washington, D.C., where he worked as a freelance writer for various magazines and landed a job as a consultant to the Department of Labor.

By then, the topic of Nader's law school paper—automobile safety—was beginning to receive more notice by politicians and the press. The nation's automobile production had soared in the postwar years. As highway builders had laid down thousands of miles of highways across the country, the number of passenger miles driven by Americans had soared as well. So had the number of traffic deaths. By 1960, traffic accidents claimed the lives of roughly thirty-eight thousand Americans every year. In the face of the growing carnage on the nation's highways, the Kennedy administration launched an investigation of automobile safety in 1963. It was conducted by Assistant Secretary of Labor Daniel Patrick Moynihan, who also had written on the subject. As an assistant to the governor of New York, Moynihan had written an article that appeared in the *Reporter* magazine, which happened to be edited by a young man named Irving Kristol. Moynihan's article had come out within weeks of Nader's piece in the *Nation* and offered a preview of many of Nader's later arguments in his book *Unsafe at Any Speed*. Together, these two articles represented the opening shots in a growing battle about automobile safety. Now, as Moynihan's assistant, Nader drafted the Labor Department's report on highway safety that appeared in 1965, the same year he published *Unsafe at Any Speed: The Designed-In Dangers of the American Automobile*.

Nader's most famous book, *Unsafe at Any Speed* focused on General Motors (GM) and its design policies, particularly for the compact Corvair. Because of design flaws in its suspension system, the car had a tendency to skid going into curves. Yet it was the interior design of the Corvair and other cars that Nader found most troubling. He called attention to what he called the "second collision," which occurred after an automobile crashed into something. In the early 1960s, car manufacturers were not required by federal law to install seat belts. Thus the force of an impact often threw passengers around inside the car and caused a far deadlier collision than the one outside. For helpless passengers, stick shifts, glove compartment doors, mirrors, dashboards, and windows became lethal objects.

Nader argued that these design flaws were common to all the major manufacturers, but his main target was GM. The company fought back by hiring investigators to investigate Nader's private life. They were unable to dig up anything on the squeaky-clean Nader, but he responded by suing the company for invasion of privacy. He won a $425,000 settlement and a public apology, which GM delivered before a Senate committee. The company also admitted that it was guilty of wrongdoing in regard to safety. Overnight, Nader was transformed into a folk hero, and in 1966, with Nader at his side, President Lyndon Johnson signed the Traffic and Motor Vehicle Safety Act. The legislation, which passed Congress without a single opposing vote, took away from the car manufacturers the power to determine how safe their vehicles should be and gave that power to the federal government. In Nader's words, it "launched the nation on a great life-saving program." In the coming years, Nader would launch a far-reaching program of his own to protect American consumers.

Nader's efforts built on a long history of consumer activism in the United States. By the early twentieth century, many progressive reformers had already made consumer protection a high priority. Spurred into action by the publication of Sinclair's *Jungle,* they fought for passage of the federal Pure Food and Drug Act in 1906 to ensure the purity and safety of the nation's foods and drugs. A generation later, the emergence of a consumer-driven economy and the rapid expansion of the advertising industry had sparked growing concern about the inflated claims of Madison Avenue. In 1927, for instance, economist Stuart Chase had published *Your Money's Worth,* a scathing indictment of the advertising industry that called for the government to submit consumer products to standardized tests and publish the results. Although that did not happen, the popularity of *Your Money's Worth* had led to the founding of Consumers Union, which subjected consumer products to impartial testing and exposed the false claims of advertisers in its monthly magazine, *Consumer Reports.* During the Great Depression, advertising had come under sharper attack for promoting waste in the midst of scarcity. Indeed, by the end of the 1930s, nearly two dozen national organizations were lobbying for consumers, assisting them with brand selection, and scrutinizing advertising claims.

After World War II, a resurgent economy had led to an even stronger consumer movement. In the postwar years, an expanding middle class enjoyed growing incomes and a cornucopia of consumer goods. Corporations turned increasingly to a new consumer product—television—to sell them. It proved a powerful medium to stimulate sales but also provoked growing concern about advertisers' manipulation of consumers. In 1957, author Vance Packard's best-seller, *The Hidden Persuaders,* had created a furor by detailing Madison Avenue's sophisticated efforts to control consumer spending and "channel our unthinking habits." Barraged with advertisers' claims, many Americans were becoming ever more cynical about them. Not surprisingly, the circulation of *Consumer Reports* magazine, only eighty thousand before World War II, had soared to nearly a million by 1961.

In the 1960s, therefore, Nader had a large and receptive audience. What he had in mind, though, was more than consumer education, the traditional thrust of the twentieth-century consumer movement. Rather, he believed that entire industries needed to be restrained with regulations. Here, too, Nader's timing was right. Beginning in the late 1960s, many Americans were becoming more concerned about corporate accountability. A growing environmental movement was already targeting corporate responsibility for air and water pollution. The rise of an antiwar movement and the emergence of a counterculture in the late 1960s boosted suspicions about corporations even further. Protesters against the Vietnam War often perceived an unholy alliance between large corporations, and government, which they referred to as the "Establishment" and whose values and goals they rejected.

Always sporting a conservative suit and short hair, Nader was no "hippie." Yet his clean-cut style made his arguments even more effective. As he broadened his concerns beyond automobile safety in the late 1960s and 1970s, Nader effectively tapped the growing concerns of many middle-class Americans about corporate power. At the same time, Lyndon Johnson's Great Society was creating new federal programs and regulations in areas such as education, job training, and welfare. An extension of Franklin Roosevelt's New Deal, the Great Society reflected widespread optimism about the government's ability to solve problems. In this environment, Nader won the support of many Americans as he began to take on new targets. With his GM settlement money, Nader hired a group of young attorneys, known as Nader's Raiders, who pushed for new regulations on insurance companies, food producers, health care providers, corporate lobbyists, toy companies, and those who polluted the environment. Then, in 1971, Nader founded Public Citizen, a consumer rights umbrella group that would go on to spawn numerous watchdog organizations. Congress Watch oversaw the U.S. Congress on behalf of consumers and lobbied for health care, safety, and environmental issues. The Health Research Group concentrated on health care and food and drug safety. The Litigation Group specialized in filing lawsuits in the name of consumers. The Critical Mass Energy and Environment Project dealt with energy issues. And Global Trade Watch fought against international trade arrangements and the expansion of corporate power.

Nader's organizations were responsible, at least in part, for dozens of new laws and government regulatory agencies. They included the Safe Drinking Water Act, the Occupational Safety and Health Administration, the Environmental Protection Agency, and the Consumer Product Safety Commission. These and other government agencies brought new regulations to the economy and society in an attempt to clean up the environment and make the workplace and products safer. In time, these regulations would be responsible for the recall of millions of consumer products. Meanwhile, Nader also helped secure the amendments to the Freedom of Information Act in 1974 that provided more access to government records. That in turn made it easier for investigators to follow the paper trail of business deals and legislation, carefully establishing links between corporate power and the government. In addition, Nader created or influenced dozens of other organizations, such as the Clean Water Action Project, the Disability Rights Center, and the Public Interest Research Groups. As he once put it, he was concerned with "the anal effusions of society." Into the 1970s, many people shared that concern. At the head of a well-organized consumer movement, Nader and his organizations had emerged as a powerful force in American society.

The "New Class"

About the same time that Ralph Nader took up his fight for the consumer, Irving Kristol began his own battle. As one of the nation's leading conservative thinkers, Kristol would be engaged in a long struggle against what he might call "noxious cultural emissions." For Kristol, the central political issues of the late twentieth century had little to do with the distribution of wealth and power— or making sure that those with power did not abuse it. Rather, they involved values—or what he called the "cultural climate" within which capitalism operated in American society. "It is the culture of a society," he said in 1978, "its religion and its moral traditions . . . which legitimizes or illegitimizes its institutions." Kristol was convinced that American culture in the late twentieth century was destructive of the very prosperity that capitalism had created. For three decades starting in the late 1960s, he worked to demonstrate the link between America's "cultural climate" and its economic policies. Toward the close of the twentieth century, he claimed a share of the credit for making "values" and "cultural" concerns potent political issues for many Americans.

Kristol's upbringing no doubt had much to do with his concern about values and morality. Born in New York City in 1920, he was raised in a working-class Orthodox Jewish family. Although his father attended the synagogue only once a year and his mother never went, Irving's parents dutifully sent him off for religious training under the watchful eye of the rabbi. As a boy, he began to take pride in his Jewish heritage. After his mother died when he was sixteen, he turned to his religion for comfort, attending morning prayers at the synagogue every day for six months.

Still, it was only later as an adult that Kristol embraced religious faith as the indispensable core of his life. As a student at City College of New York, Kristol became a true believer of another sort. Like many college students in the 1930s, he was drawn to Marxism.* During the Great Depression, capitalism seemed to many students to be a failed economic system. At City College, Kristol was especially drawn to the ideology of Leon Trotsky, the Russian Bolshevik* who had called for a permanent revolution. Trotsky's desire to spread communism immediately had led to his break with Soviet dictator Joseph Stalin, who believed that communism needed to be firmly established in the Soviet Union before it could spread around the world. For some American college students who were disillusioned with capitalism but aware of the brutality of Stalin's regime, Trotsky's brand of communism was very appealing. Repelled by the authoritarian bent of the campus Stalinists, Kristol spent hours debating politics with other Marxists, many of whom went on to distinguished careers as professors, journalists, and activists. At one such meeting, Kristol met a woman named Gertrude Himmelfarb. "Bea," as everyone called her, was a history student and would go on to a distinguished career in academics. Kristol immediately fell in love with her, and a short time later they were married.

About the same time, Kristol and Himmelfarb ended their flirtation with Marxism. Many young Marxists who became staunch anticommunists during the cold war later pointed to the signing of the Nonaggression Pact between Germany and the Soviet Union in the summer of 1939 as the cause of their disillusionment. With that agreement, Stalin appeared to many American Marxists to have made a deal with the Devil. By the next year, Trotsky had been murdered in exile by Soviet agents and Kristol had come to the conclusion that the brutality of the Soviet regime was not an aberration, as Trotsky had argued. Rather, it could not be divorced from Marxist doctrine. In time, he would join many former Marxists in a bitter crusade against communism.

Kristol served in the armored infantry in Europe during World War II, then returned to the United States determined to become a writer. While Himmelfarb finished her graduate studies at the University of Chicago, he wrote several articles for *Commentary*, a new magazine of political and cultural criticism. When

*Marxism: The political and philosophical system of the nineteenth-century German-born philosopher Karl Marx. Marxism emphasized class conflict as a method for analyzing society and concluded that history was moving inevitably toward a revolution that would overthrow capitalism and establish a classless society without private property—that is, communism.

*Bolshevik: A member of the Russian communist party that seized power in the Russian Revolution of 1917 and established the world's first communist state.

Himmelfarb received a fellowship to study in England, Kristol joined her and continued writing articles and book reviews for various publications. Shortly after the couple returned to New York in 1947 "with no visible prospects," Kristol was offered a job as an editor for *Commentary*.

By the late 1940s, Kristol considered himself a liberal—that is, he supported the idea of an activist government that intervened in the economy, regulated business, and provided social programs to improve the lives of the poor. In the terminology of the day, he was a New Deal Democrat. As the onset of the cold war raised growing fears about communism at home, however, Kristol became alarmed at the stance of many liberals who were defending the civil liberties of communists. In Kristol's view, these liberals were far too complacent about communists and the threat they posed to the American system of government. He did not agree with some liberals that communists were simply fellow "progressives." Instead, he thought they were totalitarians whose ideology was anti-American and antidemocratic. Nor were they merely reformers hoping to make the world a better place. They were violent, dangerous revolutionaries out to destroy the civil liberties that Americans cherished. Writing in *Commentary* in 1952, Kristol described the communist-hunting Republican senator Joseph McCarthy as a "vulgar demagogue." Yet he also said that communists and their sympathizers were not worthy of certain civil liberties and that many liberals were worthy of their fellow Americans' suspicion.

Kristol's article created a storm and marked his debut as a political writer. Over the next decade, he would emerge as one of the best-known anticommunist liberals. In 1953, Kristol moved to London to edit the anticommunist *Encounter* magazine. Published by the American Congress for Cultural Freedom, *Encounter* was intended to offset the intellectual influence of communists, especially in Western Europe. It was also, Kristol would learn many years later, funded by the Central Intelligence Agency. In 1958, Kristol returned to the United States, and the following year he became editor of another anticommunist liberal publication, the *Reporter*. In 1959, he accepted and ran an article written by Daniel Patrick Moynihan on automobile safety. Kristol struck up a friendship with Moynihan, who later became a Democrat senator from New York. After Kristol had a falling-out with the *Reporter*'s publisher, he became executive vice president of Basic Books, a position he would hold from 1961 to 1969.

By the mid-1960s, Lyndon Johnson's Great Society had extended the welfare state with a host of new programs. Kristol found himself increasingly skeptical of the "liberal ideas behind it." He was especially appalled by one Great Society program, the War on Poverty. It was based, he believed, on "the sociological fantasy that if one gave political power to the poor, by sponsoring 'community action,' they would then lift themselves out of poverty at the expense of the rich and powerful." Becoming "politically militant," Kristol said later, "was no way for poor people to lift themselves out of poverty." It seemed to him all too reminiscent of the socialist idea of class struggle. Along with Daniel Bell, a sociologist at Columbia University and an old friend from his City College days, Kristol founded the *Public Interest* magazine to voice their skepticism of government programs. At that point, Kristol was still a Democrat who associated conservatism with Barry Goldwater, the Republican presidential candidate defeated by Johnson in 1964. Kristol considered Goldwater's views extreme, but the antiwar protests and rise of the counterculture in the late 1960s and early 1970s pushed him further to the political right.* He viewed the counterculture as self-indulgent and hedonistic. It was based, he believed, on the same "utopian" assumptions that underlay liberal social programs. At the same time, he was appalled by student radicals' assaults on institutions and their disregard for authority and traditional norms. He concluded that these upheavals were related to a permissiveness that he associated with liberals' flawed, romantic assumptions about the innate goodness of individuals. As he later put it, he discovered that he had been a "cultural conservative" all along.

By the early 1970s, Kristol had become one of the leading "neoconservatives," a term frequently applied by journalists and others to former leftists who had moved to the other end of the political spectrum. Along with Kristol and Bell, the neoconservatives included Moynihan, *Commentary* editor Norman Podhoretz, and sociologist Nathan Glazer. All of them had been staunch anticommunist liberals, but now, like Kristol, they were repelled by what they perceived as a degenerate licentiousness of the counterculture and by the left-wing student protests and their frequent anti-American rhetoric. As one of the first neoconservatives, Kristol was frequently referred to in the press as the "godfather" of the movement. If he was not the founder of the movement, he was certainly one of its most vocal champions. As the editor of *Public Interest*; professor at the New York University Graduate School of Business; fellow at the Washington, D.C.–based American Enterprise Institute, a conservative think tank; and columnist for the *Wall Street Journal,* he widely and effectively broadcast the neoconservative message. At the heart of that message was a defense of free-market capitalism and attacks on government regulations. **[See Source 1.]**

By the late 1970s, Kristol also had become a vocal champion of supply-side economics. Promoted by Arthur Laffer, an economist at the University of Southern California, and Jack Kemp, a congressman from New York, supply-side economics held that cutting taxes, especially on businesses and the wealthy, would increase production (the supply side of the economic equation). Greater production in turn would increase government revenues despite the reduced tax rates. Tax cuts, in other words, were the key to greater prosperity. Such thinking was not new. Secretary of the Treasury Andrew Mellon had promoted similar tax policies in the 1920s, as had President John F. Kennedy in the 1960s. By the late 1970s, after a decade of economic stagnation, supply-side economics seemed a powerful way for conservatives to become the champions of economic growth. Kristol also realized that it was a way for conservatism to become more popular.

Still, Kristol remained convinced that conservatives had to be concerned with more than economic policies. In fact, his primary focus in the coming years would be on what he called the moral or cultural climate of American society,

---

Political right: The part of the political spectrum occupied by conservatives—that is, those generally resisting an activist government and the creation of social welfare programs. The terms *left* and *right* date back to the French Revolution, when more radical delegates sat on the left side of the assembly and more conservative members sat on the right.

which he believed was just as important for economic health as government policies. According to Kristol, at the very heart of capitalism lay a dangerous paradox: Capitalism's material success spawned moral decadence. The moral decline in an affluent, capitalist nation such as the United States, he argued, was manifested in the rejection of "traditional" values—that is, a decline in respect for institutions, authority, and the values of hard work, sobriety, diligence, thrift, and delayed gratification. In the cultural climate fostered by an affluent capitalist society, hedonism and moral relativism replaced those traditional middle-class values. The result was the spread of pornography, the rise of out-of-wedlock births, and higher divorce rates. Ultimately, though, the triumph of such values was reflected in economic policies. And that Kristol blamed on the rise of a "new class" of professors, lawyers, social workers, and other educated— and often public-sector—employees. This class, he argued, was waging a cultural war against business by fostering unrestrained, hedonistic cultural freedom. It also supported policies designed to override the decisions of an efficient capitalist marketplace that simply gives the public what it wants. Through the government, this new class imposed on business and society "utopian" schemes for perfection that were rooted in an abstract notion of the "public interest." [**See Source 2.**]

During the 1970s, the call for "traditional" values began to resonate with many voters weary of protests by antiwar activists, feminists, and environmentalists. Meanwhile, years of high inflation combined with rising unemployment increased the appeal of cutting regulations on business. As corporations pointed to the rising costs of meeting new federal regulatory standards and responding to lawsuits, many people began to change their views about both regulation and business. The regulations championed by environmental and consumer activists now seemed to many Americans responsible for economic stagnation. By 1980, Kristol's moment had arrived. In the presidential election that year, Republican Ronald Reagan, another convert to supply-side theory, promised to "get the government off the backs of the people." Reagan's pledge proved appealing to many voters. After he defeated President Jimmy Carter in a landslide, Kristol was elated. The "godfather" of neoconservatism was even happier when Congress passed the Reagan administration's massive tax cuts and began to lift many environmental and other regulations on business. After fifteen years of proselytizing, Kristol had finally seen his ideas triumph.

"Our Fundamental, Unmanageable Problem"

Ralph Nader was not happy. The mood of the country had swung against him. Nader insisted that deregulation would only increase corporate power at the expense of consumers. Unrestrained by regulations, corporations would degrade the environment, exploit workers and the middle class, and rob taxpayers. Supply-side economics, he predicted, would only increase the federal debt, while government cutbacks would gut social programs and regulatory agencies. Meanwhile, "corporate welfare"—expenditures for the benefit of business—would go on. On issue after issue, however, Nader was defeated. As defense spending and budget deficits grew in the Reagan years, budget cuts hit regulatory agencies especially hard. The Occupational Safety and Health Administration was forced to fire many of its inspectors, the Consumer Product Safety Commission saw its budget chopped by a third, and the Environmental Protection Agency took big cuts. A disappointed Nader also watched as Congress deregulated the savings and loan industry. The move allowed savings and loan institutions to invest depositors' funds in risky assets such as "junk bonds"—securities with high yields and high risks. He was equally dismayed when Congress passed a $500 billion bailout plan for the industry in 1989 after many savings and loans went under.

Out of favor in the 1980s, Nader spent much of the decade out of the lime-light. In 1980, he resigned his position as director of Public Citizen, the organization that funded his numerous other consumer and public interest groups, and left Washington, D.C. He traveled extensively around the country working on building a grass-roots consumer movement. The way to fight the probusiness policies of the Reagan era, he believed, was getting laws passed at the local level that forced corporations to be more responsible. But he was gloomy. In 1986, exhausted from extensive travel, he contracted Bell's palsy, a nerve disease that affected his left eye and his speech. By the next year, he was at a low point. In an interview with *Rolling Stone* magazine, he called contemporary Americans a "throw-away generation" and said that they were "going to wreck this society." In 1988, he was back in the national spotlight, leading a successful campaign in California to lower automobile insurance rates. Reenergized by that fight, Nader gradually reemerged in the 1990s as perhaps the best-known foe of corporations.

By the early 1990s, Nader began to focus increasingly on the globalization of business. The "corporate imperialism" of multinational corporations, he charged, was leading to a dangerous concentration of economic and political power in the hands of an antidemocratic business elite. That trend was especially apparent, he said, in the approval of the North American Free Trade Agreement (NAFTA), which created a free-trade zone comprising the United States, Canada, and Mexico. With the support of the Clinton administration, a Republican Congress, and business, NAFTA was enacted in 1993. Nader feared that it would result in the loss of American jobs as businesses relocated south of the border, where environmental and labor laws were far less stringent. Similar concerns led to his vocal opposition to the General Agreement on Tariffs and Trade (GATT). Approved by Congress in 1994, GATT lowered trade barriers between industrialized and developing nations and established the World Trade Organization, a body with more than 144 member nations charged with overseeing international trade. Nader argued that GATT would gut protections for consumers, workers, and the environment by placing important economic and policy decisions in the hands of an international body dominated by large corporate interests. Indeed, he charged, GATT represented nothing less than an ongoing corporate assault on democracy.

Nader's growing concern about international trade reflected a new approach to politics. He rejoiced when the Clinton administration increased the power of the Environmental Protection Agency and other regulatory bodies. He also supported the administration's antitrust suit against Microsoft Corporation for its monopolistic control of the computer software industry. Yet the Clinton administration's support for NAFTA and GATT confirmed in Nader's mind that the

Democrats were as much the pawns of large corporations as the Republicans. Alarmed by the growing corporate domination of the political process, he decided to get involved in electoral politics himself. Consumer protection, workers' rights, and environmental protection, he argued, could not be won—or preserved—without addressing a broader issue: the growing danger that corporate power posed to democracy. The two major political parties, he said, were simply tools of the corporations, dependent on corporate dollars to win and maintain power. In 1992, therefore, he launched a write-in campaign for the U.S. presidency. Although it attracted little support, it did provide an opportunity for Nader to lay out an anticorporate platform that became the central focus of his growing political activism. **[See Sources 3 and 4.]**

As Nader grew ever more alarmed by the Clinton administration's promotion of free trade, Irving Kristol had many reasons to be happy. He continued to edit the *Public Interest* and write columns for the *Wall Street Journal*. Moreover, beginning with the election of 1980, much had changed. Under Ronald Reagan and his successor, George Bush, Republican administrations had been in power for twelve years. The growth of many federal programs had been slowed, and other programs had been eliminated altogether. In the early 1990s, the cold war ended, the Soviet Union fell, and Kristol proclaimed the triumph of capitalism. Nevertheless, he continued to worry. Whereas Nader charged that corporations had too much power in politics, Kristol feared that an antibusiness "intellectual" class had too much power in the culture. The result, he said, was the spread of anti–middle-class values, which were responsible for increased teen pregnancies, drug use, and violence. American culture, Kristol concluded, represented "our fundamental, unmanageable problem." **[See Source 5.]**

The battle lines drawn by Nader and Kristol continued to run across the political landscape at the end of the twentieth century. The so-called culture wars—political battles over contemporary American values—offer a case in point. By the 1990s, many Americans shared Kristol's fears about the glorification of sex and violence in the popular culture. Congress responded to their concerns with Nader-style regulations when it passed the Telecommunications Reform Act in 1996. The new law required television manufacturers to install a computer chip in new television sets to give parents the ability to block out unwanted programming. Yet nowhere were these battle lines more evident than in the 2000 presidential campaign. Four years earlier, Nader had won the Green Party nomination for president. With only five thousand dollars to spend, though, he had barely been able to get voters to notice his campaign. In 2000, again the Green Party's nominee, Nader had growing grass-roots support, especially among Democrats who had concluded that the Clinton administration had been too cozy with big business. In some ways, the Democratic candidate, Al Gore, echoed Nader by calling for more stringent controls on the environment. The Republican candidate, George W. Bush, ran as a "compassionate conservative." Many neoconservatives were delighted with this label, which sounded a lot like the moderate conservatism championed for decades by Kristol.

Nader blasted his opponents with harsh rhetoric. He charged that corporate donations filled his opponents' campaign coffers and that those donations would guarantee access to the new administration. "Americans," he said, faced "a plutocracy—rule by the rich and powerful." **[See Source 6.]** When voters cast their ballots, however, they overwhelmingly rejected his anticorporate message. Winning only 2.7 percent of the nationwide vote, Nader fell short of the 5 percent that would have qualified the Green Party for federal funds in the next presidential election. Nevertheless, he made an impact. In Florida, where the disputed outcome was ultimately resolved in favor of Bush by the U.S. Supreme Court, Nader won enough votes to deny Gore the White House. In the end, the main result of Nader's campaign against what he called the "corporatist grip" on American politics was not what he had intended, and it was certainly not what Irving Kristol most feared.

PRIMARY SOURCES

Source 1: Irving Kristol, *"The Hidden Costs of Regulation"* (1978)

Irving Kristol's most famous defense of capitalism came in his 1978 book, Two Cheers for Capitalism. *In this excerpt, he discusses the issue of government regulation. What does Kristol think is bad about regulation?*

In all of the recent discussion of our economic condition, there has been controversy over whether tax cuts are really necessary and, if so, what kind would be most beneficial. To the best of my knowledge, no one . . . has dreamed of proposing *a tax increase.* Yet that is what we keep on getting—specifically an increased tax on corporate income—only no one seems to notice.

It is not really as surprising as one might think that our economists, our accountants, even our business executives should be oblivious to the steady increase in corporate taxation that has been taking place. Habitual modes of perception and conventional modes of reckoning are likely to impose themselves on a changing reality rather than go through a painful process of adaptation. And the learned economist or alert executive can fail to observe an important feature of a situation simply because he wasn't looking for it.

Here is an example of what I mean. Corporation X, in order to meet water pollution standards set by the Environmental Protection Agency, has to install new filtering equipment that costs $2 million. How is this expenditure to be accounted for? Well, at present, it is counted as a "capital investment" and is carried on the books as an "asset" of the corporation. But does that make any sense?

After all, a "capital investment" is supposed to promise an increase in production or productivity, or both. An "asset," similarly, is supposed to represent earning power, actual or potential. But that new filtering equipment may do none of these things. Indeed, it may actually decrease productive capacity and pro-

Source: From *Two Cheers for Capitalism* by Irving Kristol. Copyright © 1978 Basic Books. Used by permission of the author and Writers Representatives, Inc. (New York: Basic Books, 1978), 50–51, 53, 54.

ductivity. In short, the $2 million ought properly to be counted as a government-imposed cost—in effect a surtax or effluent tax—and the company's stated after-tax income should be reduced accordingly.

Instead of imposing an actual tax and using the proceeds to purchase and install the equipment, the government mandates that the firm do so. The end result, however, is the same.

I am not saying that the new filtering equipment is just money down the drain. It does buy cleaner water, after all. But that cleaner water is a free "social good" and a "social asset" to the population in the neighborhood (and for the fish, too); it represents no economic gain to the corporation, which has only economic assets and knows nothing of "social assets." It also buys governmental "good will," but so do bribes to foreign officials, and I am not aware that anyone has yet thought to capitalize them. On the other hand, the new equipment is unquestionably an *economic cost* to the corporation and, of course, to the economy as a whole.

As things now stand, we render those economic costs invisible. That is both silly and undesirable. Silly, because they are real costs. Undesirable, because we shall never persuade the American people to take the problem of regulation seriously until they appreciate, in the clearest possible way, what it is costing them as stockholders, consumers, and employees.

The costs we are talking about are by no means small, and their impact by no means marginal. In fact, they are far, far larger and more serious than most people realize. Unfortunately, there are no comprehensive, precise estimates available. But one can get a sense of the magnitude of such costs from the following bits and pieces of information.

• In 1977 U.S. Steel signed a seven-year agreement with federal, state, and local environmental agencies that will require it to spend $600 million over that period to eliminate air pollution from its Clairton Coke Works in Pittsburgh.

• The steel industry as a whole will be spending well over $1 billion annually on pollution controls—and that is a conservative estimate. This expenditure amounts to over one quarter of the industry's total annual capital investment.

• Meeting EPA's 1983 waste pollution standards will cost all of American industry, over the next seven years, about $60 billion for capital equipment and another $12 billion annually in operating and maintenance costs.

• Meeting noise pollution standards, as mandated by Congress and enforced by the Occupational Safety and Health Administration (OSHA), will involve expenditures of over $15 billion in capital costs and $2 billion to $3 billion in operating costs in the years immediately ahead. If these noise standards are raised to the level recommended by the U.S. National Institute for Occupational Safety and Health—a recommendation endorsed by the EPA—the capital costs will climb over $30 billion.

• According to the *Wall Street Journal*, new health regulations in the cotton industry will, in the period from 1977 through 1983, cost some $3 billion. It has been estimated by Professor Murray Weidenbaum that American industry's cost[s] to meet OSHA safety standards in 1977 alone were over $4 billion. . . .

It may be argued that these economically unproductive expenditures do, after all, create jobs (temporarily) and do contribute to the Gross National Product. But so would the corporate construction of beautiful pyramids, at governmental behest. That would create jobs (temporarily), inflate the GNP, and provide us with a "social good" (a great spectacle). But it would be a cost to the economy, and if our conventional statistics are incapable of showing it as such, then those statistics need revision. . . .

The situation we have gotten ourselves into would be ridiculous if it were not so serious. We have been much exercised—and quite rightly—by the fact that the OPEC monopoly has cost this country well over $30 billion in increased oil prices since 1972. But in that time we have inflicted upon ourselves much larger economic costs through environmental and other regulations and will continue to do so, perhaps at an increasing rate.

Yes, these economic costs do buy real "social goods." But may the price not be too high? Is the resulting inflation of prices, constriction of productive capacity, and increase in unemployment worth it? Would it not be appropriate for us to ask ourselves this question openly, instead of going along with the environmentalists' pretense—so pleasing to our politicians—that our "social goods" cost us nothing at all? Isn't it time that business stopped bleating in a general way about those costs and showed us what they really mean, all the way down to the bottom line?

SOURCE 2:   Irving Kristol, *"Corporate Capitalism in America"*   (1975)

Beginning in the mid-1970s, Irving Kristol offered a sociological explanation for what he perceived to be antibusiness values in American society. He based it on the rise of what he called the "new class." Who, according to Kristol, makes up this class? What does he see as the consequences of its rise?

THE NEW CLASS

[The left in Europe] was regarded as an "un-American" thing, as indeed it was. True, the movement of "Progressive-reform" was "elitist" both in its social composition and its social aims: It, too, was distressed by the "anarchy" and "vulgarity" of capitalist civilization. But in the main it accepted as a fact the proposition that capitalism and liberalism were organically connected, and it proposed to itself the goal of "mitigating the evils of capitalism," rather than abolishing liberal capitalism and replacing it with "a new social order" in which a whole new set of human relationships would be established. It was an authentic reformist movement. It wanted to regulate the large corporations so that this concentration of private power could not develop into an oligarchical threat to democratic-liberal capitalism. It was ready to interfere with the free market so that the instabilities generated by capitalism—above all, instability of employment—

SOURCE: From "Corporate Capitalism in America" by Irving Kristol, *Public Interest*, Fall 1975, pp. 133–135. Reproduced in *Neoconservatism: The Autobiography of an Idea* by Irving Kristol, published by The Free Press. Originally published in *The Public Interest* (Fall, 1975). Copyright © 1975 Irving Kristol. Used by permission of the author and Writers Representatives, Inc.

would be less costly in human terms. It was even willing to tamper occasionally with the consumer's freedom of choice where there was a clear consensus that the micro-decisions of the marketplace added up to macro-consequences that were felt to be unacceptable. And it hoped to correct the "vulgarity" of capitalist civilization by educating the people so that their "preference schedules" (as economists would say) would be, in traditional terms, more elevated, more appreciative of "the finer things in life."

Ironically, it was the extraordinary increase in mass higher education after World War II that, perhaps more than anything else, infused the traditional movement for "Progressive-reform" with various impulses derived from the European Left. The earlier movement had been "elitist" in fact as well as in intention—i.e., it was sufficiently small so that, even while influential, it could hardly contemplate the possibility of actually exercising "power." Mass higher education has converted this movement into something like a mass movement proper. . . . The intentions remain "elitist " of course; but the movement, under the banner of "the New Politics," now encompasses some millions of people. These are the people whom liberal capitalism had sent to college in order to help manage its affluent, highly technological, mildly paternalistic, "post-industrial" society.

This "new class" consists of scientists, lawyers, city planners, social workers, educators, criminologists, sociologists, public health doctors, etc.—a substantial number of whom find their careers in the expanding public sector rather than the private. The public sector, indeed, is where they prefer to be. They are, as one says, "idealistic"—i.e., far less interested in individual financial rewards than in the corporate power of their class. Though they continue to speak the language of "Progressive-reform," in actuality they are acting upon a hidden agenda: to propel the nation from that modified version of capitalism we call "the welfare state" toward an economic system so stringently regulated in detail as to fulfill many of the traditional anti-capitalist aspirations of the Left.

The exact nature of what has been happening is obscured by the fact that this "new class" is not merely liberal but truly "libertarian" in its approach to all areas of life—except economics. It celebrates individual liberty of speech and expression and action to an unprecedented degree, so that at times it seems almost anarchistic in its conception of the good life. But this joyful individualism always stops short of the border where economics—i.e., capitalism—begins. The "new class" is surely sincere in such a contradictory commitment to a maximum of individual freedom in a society where economic life becomes less free with every passing year. . . .

Meanwhile, the transformation of American capitalism proceeds apace. Under the guise of coping with nasty "externalities"—air pollution, water pollution, noise pollution, traffic pollution, health pollution, or what have you— more and more of the basic economic decisions are being removed from the marketplace and transferred to the "public"—i.e., political—sector, where the "new class," by virtue of its expertise and skills, is so well represented. This movement is naturally applauded by the media, which are also for the most part populated by members of this "new class" who believe—as the Left has always believed—it is government's responsibility to cure all the ills of the human condition, and who ridicule those politicians who deny the possibility (and therefore the propriety) of government doing any such ambitious thing.

Source 3:   Ralph Nader, *"The Concord Principles"*   (1992)

In 1992, Ralph Nader ran for president of the United States as a write-in candidate. On the steps of the state capitol in Concord, New Hampshire, Nader unveiled the Concord Principles. In this excerpt, he refers to these principles as the "new democracy tool box" to protect "voters from having their voting powers diluted." What "tools" does he propose?

Whereas, a selfish oligarchy has produced economic decline, the debasement of politics, and the exclusion of citizens from the strengthening of democracy and political economy;

Whereas, this rule of the self-serving few over the Nation's business and politics has concentrated power, money, greed, and corruption far beyond the control or accountability of citizens;

Whereas, the political system, regardless of Party, has degenerated into a government of the power brokers, by the power brokers, and for the power brokers that is an arrogant and distant caricature of Jeffersonian democracy;

Whereas, Presidential campaigns have become narrow, shallow, redundant, and frantic parades and horseraces which candidates, their monetary backers, and their handlers control unilaterally, with the citizenry expected to be the bystanders and compliant voters;

Whereas, a pervading sense of powerlessness, denial, and revulsion is sweeping the Nation's citizens as they endure or suffer from growing inequities, injustice, and loss of control over their future and the future of their children; and

Whereas, we, the citizens of the United States, who are dedicated to the reassertion of fundamental democratic principles and their application to the practical, daily events in our Nation, are committed to begin the work of shaping the substance of Presidential campaigns and of engaging the candidates['] attention to our citizen agendas during this 1992 election year;

Now, therefore, we hereby present the ensuing *Concord Principles* to the Presidential candidates for the 1992 election and invite their written, consistent, and continual adherence to these principles during their entire campaign and in whatever public offices and responsibilities they hold or may hold upon cessation of their campaigns:

First, democracy is more than a bundle of rights on paper; democracy must also embrace usable facilities that empower all citizens

   a) to obtain timely, accurate information from their government;
   b) to communicate such information and their judgments to one another through modern technology; and
   c) to band together in civic associations as voters, taxpayers, consumers, workers, shareholders, students, and as whole human beings in pursuit of a prosperous, just and free society.

Second, the separation of *ownership* of major societal assets from their *control* permits the concentration of power over such assets in the hands of the few who control rather than in the hands of the many who own. The owners of the public lands, pension funds, savings accounts, and the public airwaves are the American people, who have essentially little or no control over their pooled assets or their commonwealth.

The American people should assume reasonable control over the assets they have legally owned for many years so that their use reflects citizen priorities for a prosperous America, mindful of the needs and rights of present *and* future generations of Americans to pursue happiness within benign environments.

Third, a growing and grave imbalance between the often converging power of Big Business, Big Government and the citizens of this country has seriously damaged our democracy and weakened our ability to correct this imbalance. We lack the mechanisms of civic power. We need a modern tool box for redeeming our democracy by strengthening our capacity for self-government and self-reliance both as individuals and as a community of citizens. Our 18th century democratic rights need re-tooling for the proper exercise of our responsibilities as citizens in the 21st century.

Fourth, the new democracy tool box contains measures for the purpose of protecting voters from having their voting powers diluted, over-run or nullified. These measures are:

　　a) a binding none-of-the-above option on the ballot;
　　b) term limitations—12 years and out;
　　c) public financing of campaigns through well-promoted voluntary taxpayer checkoffs on tax returns;
　　d) easier voter registration and ballot access rules;
　　e) state-level binding initiative, referendum, and recall authority, a non-binding national referendum procedure; and
　　f) a repeal of the runaway White House/Congressional Pay Raises back to 1988 levels—a necessary dose of humility to the politicians. . . .

Without this reconstruction of our democracy through such facilities for informed civic participation, as noted above, even the most well-intentioned politicians campaigning for your vote cannot deliver, if elected. Nor can your worries about poverty, discrimination, joblessness, the troubled condition of education, environment, street and suite crime, budget deficits, costly and inadequate health care, and energy boondoggles, to list a few, be addressed constructively and enduringly. Developing these democratic tools to strengthen citizens in their distinct roles as voters, taxpayers, consumers, workers, shareholders, and students should be very high on the list of any candidate's commitments to you. Unless, that is, they just want your vote, but would rather not have you looking over their shoulder from a position of knowledge, strength and wisdom.

SOURCE 4:   Ralph Nader, *"It's Time to End Corporate Welfare as We Know It"*   (1996)

As Ralph Nader became more involved in electoral politics in the 1990s, he made the issue of "corporate welfare" one of his central campaign issues. In this excerpt, what does Nader charge is the result of this government assistance to business? How would you compare his argument here to Irving Kristol's in Source 1?

If I utter the following words, what images come to mind: crime, violence, welfare and addictors? What comes to mind is street crime; people lining up to get their welfare checks; violence in the streets; and drug dealers—the addictors.

And yet, by any yardstick, there is far more crime, and far more violence, and far more welfare disbursement (and there are far more addictors) in the corporate world than in the impoverished street arena. The federal government's corporate welfare programs number over 120. They are so varied and embedded that we actually grow up thinking that the government interferes with the free enterprise system, rather than subsidizing it.

It's hard to find a major industry today whose principal investments were not first made by the government—in aerospace, telecommunications, biotechnology and agribusiness. Government research and development money funds the drug and pharmaceutical industry. Government research and development funds are given freely to corporations, but they don't announce it in ads the next day.

Corporate welfare has never been viewed as debilitating. Nobody talks about imposing workfare requirements on corporate welfare recipients or putting them on a program of "two years and you're out." Nobody talks about aid to dependent corporations. It's all talked about in terms of "incentives."

At the local community level, in cities that can't even refurbish their crumbling schools—where children are without enough desks or books—local governments are anteing up three, four, five hundred million dollars to lure very profitable baseball, football and basketball sports moguls who don't want to share the profits. Corporate sports are being subsidized by cities.

Corporations have perfected socializing their losses while they capitalize on their profits. There was the savings-and-loan debacle—and you'll be paying for that until the year 2020. In terms of principal and interest, it was a half-trillion-dollar bailout of 1,000 savings-and-loans banks. Their executives looted, speculated and defrauded people of their savings—and then turned to Washington for a bailout. . . .

One professor studying corporate crime believes that it costs the country $200 billion a year. And yet you don't see many congressional hearings on corporate crime. You see very few newspapers focusing on corporate crime. Yet 50,000 lives a year are lost due to air pollution, 100,000 are lost due to toxics and trauma in the workplace, and 420,000 lives are lost due to tobacco smoking. The

SOURCE: Reprinted in Ralph Nader, *The Ralph Nader Reader* (New York: Seven Stories Press, 2000), pp. 154–155, 156, 158; copyright © 2000 Seven Stories Press. Used by permission; originally from *Earth Island Journal,* Fall 1996.

corporate addictor has an important role here, since it has been shown in recent months that the tobacco companies try to hook youngsters into a lifetime of smoking from age 10 to 15.

When you grow up corporate, you don't learn about the reality of corporate welfare. The programs that shovel huge amounts of taxpayer dollars to corporations through inflated government contracts via the Pentagon, or through subsidies, loan guarantees, giveaways and a variety of clever transfers of taxpayer assets get very little attention. . . .

Among the five roles that we play, one is voter-citizen, another is taxpayer, another is worker, another is consumer and another is shareholder through worker pension trusts. These are critical roles in our political economy. Yet they have become weaker and weaker as the concentration of corporate power over our political and cultural and economic institutions has increased year by year.

We're supposed to have a government of, by and for the people. Instead we have a government of the Exxons, by the General Motors and for the DuPonts. We have a government that recognizes the rights and liabilities and privileges of corporations, which are artificial entities created by state charters, against the rights and privileges of ordinary people.

Jefferson warned us that the purpose of representative government is to counteract "the excesses of the monied interests"—then the merchant class; now the corporations. Beware of the government that doesn't do that.

Source 5: Irving Kristol, *"The Cultural Revolution and the Capitalist Future"* (1992)

During the 1990s, Irving Kristol continued to warn about the dangers that popular values posed to business. He also continued to blame intellectuals in particular for promoting anticapitalist values. In this source, do you think his analysis is valid, or do corporations also play an important role in promoting the values that Kristol laments?

John Adams once wrote that he and other members of his generation were compelled by circumstance to devote their lives to war and politics so that their descendants could devote their lives to the study of philosophy and the arts. In our modern democracy, a significant percentage of these descendants, having tasted the fruits of affluence, and having enjoyed the benefits of a superior education, have nevertheless developed a passionate interest in politics—indeed, have come to believe that they are more fit to govern than others less privileged. They have developed a keen and irrepressible desire for political power, firm in the conviction that they are uniquely qualified to exercise this power in the "public interest." These activists are practitioners of what has been called "supply-side politics," in which entrepreneurship creates a market for their programs. . . .

The politics generated by this approach is what we call "contemporary liberalism." Because the intrusion of government involves large numbers of accomplices—sometimes whole professions or institutions—it creates a substantial political base for itself. The consequence is that in all Western democracies with a two-party system, one of those parties has only an expediential, as distinct from principled, commitment to a free-market economy, much preferring an economy in which all businesses and corporations function, or try to function, as regulated public utilities. . . .

It is not, then, the economics of capitalism that is our fundamental, unmanageable problem. That problem today is located in the culture of our society, which is in the process of outflanking our relatively successful economy. While the society is bourgeois, the culture is increasingly, and belligerently, not.

In a bourgeois society, certain virtues are accepted as a matter of course by the majority of the people. These virtues—today we defensively call them "values"—include a willingness to work hard to improve one's condition, a respect for law, an appreciation of the merits of deferred gratification, a deference toward traditional religions, a concern for family and community, and so on. It is a commitment to such beliefs that creates a middle class, which then sustains a market economy.

Today, the old-fashioned animus against a market economy is evolving into an aggressive animus against the bourgeois society that is organically associated with our market economy. If you delegitimate this bourgeois society, the market economy—almost incidentally—is also delegitimated. . . .

This is not a challenge that the defenders of a bourgeois society and its market economy are finding easy to cope with. Bourgeois society is so vulnerable because it is primarily a society oriented toward satisfying the ambitions of ordinary men and women. These are modest ambitions—in the eyes of some, lowly ambitions. They are, in most cases, what earlier eras would have called "domestic" ambitions: bettering the economic conditions of one's family, moving from a "rough" neighborhood to a "nice" neighborhood, and above all, offering one's children the possibility of moving still further ahead in economic and social status. Because bourgeois capitalism has, however irregularly, managed to satisfy these ambitions, it has engendered popular loyalty and kept radical dissatisfaction from achieving a popular base.

But the world is not inhabited by ordinary people alone. From the very beginnings, persons have emerged who found this new order boring and vulgar since it emphasized self-interest as the engine of economic growth and improvement of the common lot as its goal.

These people—we call them intellectuals and artists, and some have indeed been entitled to that label—do not like the marketplace and find the notion of their own participation in it repugnant. They cannot imagine themselves producing commodities for sale or exchange, even if they welcome the profits from such a sale. And whatever they may say about equality, they do not believe that they are merely equal to other people; they believe that their talents and sensibilities make them superior.

SOURCE 6:   *Ralph Nader Announces His Candidacy for the Green Party's Nomination*   (2000)

In 2000, Ralph Nader was the Green Party's candidate for president of the United States. In this excerpt announcing his candidacy for the party's nomination, Nader expresses his major concerns about corporate influence in politics. What does he see as the results of that influence? What does he propose to do about it?

This campaign will challenge all Americans who are concerned with systemic imbalances of power and the undermining of our democracy, whether they consider themselves progressives, liberals, conservatives, or others. Presidential elections should be a time for deep discussions among the citizenry regarding the down-to-earth problems and injustices that are not addressed because of the gross power mismatch between the narrow vested interests and the public or common good.

The unconstrained behavior of big business is subordinating our democracy to the control of a corporate plutocracy that knows few self-imposed limits to the spread of its power to all sectors of our society. Moving on all fronts to advance narrow profit motives at the expense of civic values, large corporate lobbies and their law firms have produced a commanding, multi-faceted and powerful juggernaut. They flood public elections with cash, and they use their media conglomerates to exclude, divert, or propagandize. They brandish their willingness to close factories here and open them abroad if workers do not bend to their demands. By their control in Congress, they keep the federal cops off the corporate crime, fraud, and abuse beats. They imperiously demand and get a wide array of privileges and immunities: tax escapes, enormous corporate welfare subsidies, federal giveaways, and bailouts. They weaken the common law of torts in order to avoid their responsibility for injurious wrongdoing to innocent children, women and men. . . .

In the sixties and seventies, . . . when the civil rights, consumer, environmental, and women's rights movements were in their ascendancy, there finally was a constructive responsiveness by government. Corporations, such as auto manufacturers, had to share more decision making with affected constituencies, both directly and through their public representatives and civil servants. Overall, our country has come out better, more tolerant, safer, and with greater opportunities. The earlier nineteenth century democratic struggles by abolitionists against slavery, by farmers against large oppressive railroads and banks, and later by new trade unionists against the brutal workplace conditions of the early industrial and mining era helped mightily to make America and its middle class what it is today. They demanded that economic power subside or be shared.

SOURCE: Ralph Nader, *The Ralph Nader Reader* (New York: Seven Stories Press, 2000), pp. 4, 5. Copyright © 2000 Seven Stories Press. Used by permission.

Democracy works, and a stronger democracy works better for reputable, competitive markets, equal opportunity and higher standards of living and justice. Generally, it brings out the best performances from people and from businesses.

A plutocracy—rule by the rich and powerful—on the other hand, obscures our historical quests for justice. Harnessing political power to corporate greed leaves us with a country that has far more problems than it deserves, while blocking ready solutions or improvements from being applied.

Questions to Consider

1. Citing specific sources, how would you compare Ralph Nader's and Irving Kristol's views about the regulation of business? Why were Nader's views more popular in the 1960s and Kristol's more popular in the 1980s? Whose views are more popular today?

2. In the last decades of the twentieth century, Nader argued that corporations had too much power in politics. At the same time, Kristol contended that business had too little influence on American culture. On what grounds did each come to his conclusion? Did Nader overlook evidence of the constraints on corporations? Did Kristol ignore evidence regarding the ability of big business to control its own environment?

3. Both Kristol and Nader believe that the policies advocated by the other pose a fundamental threat to American society. What do the primary sources reveal about the major threats that each sees in the other's policies?

4. What contemporary issue do you think best reflects Nader's and Kristol's differing views about American society and politics? Given your understanding of their analyses, what do you think Nader and Kristol would say about that issue? Whose case do you think you would find more compelling? Why?

For Further Reading

Teresa Celsi, *Ralph Nader: The Consumer Revolution* (Brookfield, Conn.: Millbrook Press, 1991), is a brief but insightful biography of the consumer advocate.

Lee Edwards, *The Conservative Revolution: The Movement That Remade America* (New York: Free Press, 1999), provides an overview of the rise of conservatism in the second half of the twentieth century.

Irving Kristol, *Neoconservatism: The Autobiography of an Idea* (New York: Free Press, 1995), includes an autobiographical memoir and many articles written from the neoconservative perspective.

Robert N. Mayer, *The Consumer Movement: Guardians of the Marketplace* (Boston: Twayne Publishers, 1989), offers a brief overview of the modern consumer movement.

Photo Credits

p. 184 Originally from *History Teacher's Magazine*, September 1917; p. 99 Reprinted in Stephan Vaughn, *Holding Fast the Inner Lines: Democracy, Nationalism, and the Committee on Public Information* (Chapel Hill: University of North Carolina Press, 1980), p. 87; originally from Records of the Committee on Public Information, National Archives (photo 5.4); p. 100 Reprinted in Stephan Vaughn, *Holding Fast the Inner Lines: Democracy, Nationalism, and the Committee on Public Information* (Chapel Hill: University of North Carolina Press, 1980), p. 165; originally from Records of the Committee on Public Information, National Archives; p. 107 Hulton Archives/Getty Images; p. 130 (left) Courtesy Lilly Library, Indiana University, Bloomington, Indiana, (right) © Bettmann/CORBIS; p. 141, © Bettmann/CORBIS; p. 144 Reprinted in Greg Mitchell, *The Campaign of the Century: Upton Sinclair's Race for Governor of California and the Birth of Media Politics* (New York: Random House, 1992), between pp. 332 and 333; p. 145 University of South Carolina Newsfilm Library Archive; p. 146 Department of Special Collections, University of California Library, Davis, California. Reprinted in Upton Sinclair, *I, Candidate for Governor: And How I Got Licked* (1934; reprint, Berkeley: University of California Press, 1994), p. 171; p. 149 (left) Center for Oral and Public History, California State University, Fullerton, California, (right) National Archives; p. 168 (left) © Bettmann/CORBIS, (right) © Bettmann/CORBIS; p. 189 (left) Time and Life Pictures/Getty Images, (right) Time and Life Pictures/Getty Images; p. 212 (left) LBJ Library photo by Yoichi Okamoto, (right) AP/Wide World Photos; p. 232 (left) AP/World Wide Photos, (right) Photo copyright © Sheldon H. Ramsdell, courtesy the Estate of Sheldon H. Ramsdell; p. 254 (left) AP/Wide World Photos, (right) © Bettmann/CORBIS; p. 268 Ms. Magazine, July 1972; p. 274 (left) Jack Dykinga Photography, (right) © Bettmann/ CORBIS; p. 293 (left) © Bettmann/CORBIS, (right) © Bettmann/CORBIS.